Beyond the New Pa

V

Beyond the New Paternalism

Basic Security as Equality

———————◆———————

GUY STANDING

V
VERSO
London • New York

First published by Verso 2002
© International Labour Organization 2002
All rights reserved

2 4 6 8 10 9 7 5 3 1

Verso
UK: 6 Meard Street, London W1F 0EG
USA: 180 Varick Street, New York, NY 10014–4606

Verso is the imprint of New Left Books
www.versobooks.com

ISBN 1–85984–635–1
ISBN 1–85984–345–X (pbk)

British Library Cataloguing in Publication Data
A catalogue record for this book is available from the British Library

Library of Congress Cataloging-in-Publication Data
A catalog record for this book is avilable from the Library of Congress

Typeset by Exe Valley Dataset Ltd, Exeter, Devon, England
Printed by Biddles Ltd, Guildford and King's Lynn
www.biddles.co.uk

Contents

List of Tables and Figures

Tables

Figures

Preface

In the mid 1990s, a well-known British newspaper printed an arresting cartoon showing two tramps sitting slumped in the gutter, clearly having used newspapers for more than giving them warmth, since they had read and picked up the rhetoric of the politicians and pundits. One tramp says, "We must think the unthinkable", to which the other responds, "Speak the unspeakable", to which the first retorts, "Do the undoable", to which the second mutters, "Smell the unsmellable". At the top left-hand corner, there is a caption, "Welfare reform latest".

The message was clear. It was supposed to be an era of experimentation, an era of fresh thinking. But those on the edge of society were being lectured and being told they must find ways of reintegrating themselves into society. They must stand on their own feet and not be dependent. However, without the caption there is another way of looking at the cartoon. It points to the wretchedness associated with a society of winner-takes-all, loser-loses-all. It mocks the idea that unbridled individualism can be expected to result in everybody functioning successfully.

For many years during which the policies addressed in this book were being developed, applied and legitimised, there was a woeful lack of constructive response, and for much of the time there was a lack of anger. The young – sometimes called "freedom's children" – were encouraged to seek out their individual fortune and to consume goods and gadgets with a passion. AIDS may have cowed the libido; unemployment and economic insecurity may have curbed the romantic zeal in all spheres of life. One recalls the Brazilian saying, "It is hard to be a hero in bed if one is a victim in the streets". Being a hero intellectually is hard too when the only vision on offer is bland materialism and the sterile abstractions of what purports to be modern economics. It was no wonder that students had been shunning economics and going directly to business courses. Understanding and changing society seemed less important than making loads of money out of it.

There is no justification for weary disengagement though. New thinking is young thinking. Another adage comes to mind, "If only youth knew, if only age could". Those who have left their youth behind can patter to the ballot box, or stay at home and grumble about the corruption of politicians, or write letters to newspapers. Not so the young. Whatever the constraints, youth should have something special. They should be angry – angry about the mess they see that their elders have created around them. They should be angry about the poverty and insecurity they see amidst the affluence and conspicuous consumption and wealth. They should be angry about the fact that so few people in positions of authority or influence care enough to do much about it. They should be angry about the fact that history is being ignored. They should be angry that their political leaders and their youthful bevy of advisers seem intent on telling them to behave in certain ways that they deem are correct, and only then can they earn entitlement to social support.

They should be angry . . . and they should be optimistic – optimistic that change is possible, optimistic that they can do something to help, and optimistic that the future will be brighter and better, and more equal. This book is about that optimism. What was exciting at the turn of the new millennium was that there were signs that anger was reviving. It was a messy, incoherent, degenerate sort of anger; most of us, this writer included, could not identify with much of what has been happening, and have been riled by some of the excesses. Yet the anger bodes well. It means that there is a discontent about injustice *per se*. There is a growing recognition that we should not accept the conventional wisdom that "there is no alternative". Globalisation, flexibility, employability, privatisation and much else are not necessarily fixed prescriptions or desirable in the forms made explicit or implied by politicians and commentators over the past few years.

Yes, we are perhaps in a new era when anger will generate fresh thinking and a more progressive vision of a "Good Society". After the dismal failures of the main twentieth-century visions, there is an understandable reluctance to look beyond the present. I recall a two-day meeting of mostly young political and economic advisers to an assortment of national political leaders from a wide range of industrialised countries, held in a hotel in Maryland in the United States in the mid 1990s. One man, who has since moved into a high office in his country, stood up and declared with conviction that "we must think small". It was the voice of the tamed shrew, habituated to an era of defeat and concession.

The pragmatism that goes for realism at the beginning of the twenty-first century may give way sooner than we expect. History teaches us that this is how it has usually been. However, only if the anger surges into the "politics of paradise", as Michael Foot called his wonderful book on Byron, will the march towards real freedom and social progress resume. We will start moving forward more successfully when we accept that there is no going back to some mythical Golden Age or some idealised version of "the welfare state".

This brings us to a peculiar feature of the era. Children in many parts of the world – and almost all British children – learn early the immortal quip of Humpty Dumpty, "When *I* use a word it means just what I choose it to mean". Mostly they like the idea, because it seems to give them an excuse for using long words that they do not quite understand. But modern social scientists have perfected the art of using words as codes, to secure agreement or to seek condemnation of some idea. Their political charges use them as stock-in-trade "sound bites".

There is nothing new in this, of course. Francis Bacon warned his contemporaries in the sixteenth century about the "idols of the marketplace". However, the breathlessness of what passes for political and intellectual debate has produced a cacophony of competing sound bites. The babble of euphemisms and the heavy use of metaphor as analysis threaten to stifle critical thinking. The market is a noisy place, but it is not where values are formed; it is where they are "distorted".

This babble of euphemisms is particularly relevant for the subjects covered in this book, and consequently an effort has been made to highlight the euphemisms that have shaped many aspects of the analytical and political debates. To those who are irked by them, apologies; for those who see the amusing side, keep smiling . . . but reserve some anger for those who seek to mislead by them.

Sadly, the fact is that part of the challenge is to recapture the language for more progressive agendas. In mid 2000, a well-meaning man, prominent in the international community of civil society organisations, said to me: "You must avoid the word 'redistribution'. It implies taking away income that has been earned." The politically minded might nod sagely, the radical thinker would probably grit her teeth. Both would be right. The man who made the remark was not someone who favoured the sort of gross inequality that had spread around the world in the latter part of the twentieth century. He was responding to the loss of intellectual legitimacy of words and ideas that he and I, and perhaps you, grew up to respect.

That loss of legitimacy must be rectified, perhaps with new "key words", perhaps by a recovery of nerve, certainly by a renewed sense of social energy. In the 1980s and 1990s, those who like to think, intellectuals, like so many others, found that fear had changed sides. They hid from their bolder selves, muttering rather than shouting about the injustices. Historically, periods such as this have never lasted very long.

This book, and the empirically more detailed one that was published in 1999, is an attempt to rethink the place of work in society and to propose a coherent strategy for strengthening basic economic security and a sense of occupational security. For this endeavour, it is essential to distinguish between work and labour, between labour and employment, and between jobs and occupation. This set of distinctions is made in detail in the final chapter. For the earlier parts, it suffices to state that the main policies and institutions of the twentieth century were oriented to the promotion of labour, not work, and were based on labour in determining individual entitlements and statuses.

In the twenty-first century, there should be a greater emphasis on strengthening occupation, in which creative, multi-competence work is combined with a greater appreciation of the value of contemplation. We may view work as the vital activity of human existence, more than can be captured by the sheer instrumentality of earning a living. However, there are good reasons for reserving primacy to reflection or contemplation as the most human of activity, as Hannah Arendt so persuasively argued in *The Human Condition*.

In the rush of high-tech existence, we neglect this need for reflective stillness at our peril. Yet contemplation is part of great work, implicit in the idea of creativity. As Cato put it all those centuries ago, in describing man in action, "Never is he more active than when he does nothing". Contemplation gives a balance to the functions of work, strengthening and developing human personality, as well as fulfilling more immediate needs. The drive to tie social entitlements to labour is a distortion of this powerful verity. The distortion is also linked to the paternalistic twitch of benevolent elites everywhere. It must be defeated, and it will be.

Acknowledgments

Acknowledging contributions, or thanking people for their help or inspiration, is never easy, because over the years so many friends, colleagues and relations contribute to one's thinking, often inadvertently and often in ways that sink into the memory. This book is closely related to one published in 1999, *Global Labour Flexibility: Seeking Distributive Justice*. Consequently, those thanked there deserve equal gratitude now.

In particular, Laci Zsoldos deserves thanks for his brilliant assistance. For their friendship, inspiration and encouragement, I would also like to thank Richard Anker, Robert Boyer, Sam Bowles, Bob Deacon, Zsusza Ferge, Ian Gough, Renana Jhabvala, Katherine McFate, Claus Offe, Philippe van Parijs, Ajit Singh, and John Weeks, inter alia. I also thank Robin Blackburn for pushing me to write this book, which was intended initially to be a more accessible version of the earlier book. Chapter 6, on unemployment benefits, was presented as part of a public debate in the Geneva Social Summit with Robert Holzmann, head of the social protection division of the World Bank; the debate was enjoyable, and highlighted some rather fundamental differences and interesting challenges in assessing new approaches to social protection.

As this book was written while directing the ILO's programme on "socio-economic security", gratitude is due to all my colleagues in our team, for their support and for the work they have been doing, particularly on the Enterprise Labour Flexibility and Security Surveys and on the People's Security Surveys, which are means for examining some of the themes and trends covered in this book. Of course, none of the conclusions in this book should be attributed to the ILO or to them. Above all, thanks go to Frances, Peter, Andre, Melissa, and Graeme for their tolerance, love and much more.

Prologue: Security versus Control

The desire for security is a basic emotion, a common feeling that is individually definable. Not everyone wants the same amount of security, and being secure does not necessarily provide happiness. Ask a woman or man in the street whether she or he wants to be secure, and you are likely to be regarded with scorn. Ask them if they do feel secure, and you will probably hear a torrent of complaints, minor or major as their mood or experience moves them. Ask them if they worry about their insecurity and you will receive a range of views that will have more to do with personality differences than with differences in their situations.

Security can be defined as a sense of well-being, of being in control over one's development and activities, and of feeling a sense of sustainable self-respect. It can be measured in terms of assurance, that is, in terms of an acceptable or tolerable range of variability of outcomes, or in terms of perceived needs satisfaction. Simply listing these desirable aspects of the idea shows its haziness. Indeed, the word has been used in a pejorative sense, as a culpable absence of anxiety, or a carelessness. However, in general it has positive connotations. Literally, the main meanings are (i) freedom from anxiety, (ii) a condition of being protected from, or not exposed to, danger, (iii) freedom from doubt, a sense of confidence and assurance, and (iv) a condition of being securely fixed, a stability.

You can have too much security. Complete assurance of whatever we want is conducive to passivity, irresponsibility, indolence, moral collapse and opportunism – the super rich tend to produce supine offspring. The same is true of lack of variation in life circumstances. If all our perceived needs are satisfied, *ennui* will follow very quickly, perhaps along with a reckless risk-taking. An extreme position is the one mouthed by Hecate in Shakespeare's *Macbeth*:

> And you all know security
> Is mortals' chiefest enemy

This conveys the dangers of being lulled into passivity and lack of preparedness. They are real enough. A modicum of insecurity is part of the glue holding society together. It is a margin to induce self-control. But at the other end of the spectrum, chronic insecurity would mean having no assurance of anything, extreme variability in opportunities and outcomes, and arbitrary controls exercised over our behaviour. Too little security can induce anomie, moral collapse, retributive action against the privileged and those around us, and a wretched short life. One of the more intriguing aphorisms of Confucius captures this view: "Insecurity is worse than poverty." Presumably he had in mind chronic insecurity rather than essential insecurity or mild anxiety.

What is required, one may surmise, is basic security, without which creative, risk-taking behaviour is likely to be beyond the imagination. We try to define what this could entail in the latter part of this book. Intriguingly, philosophers have been hesitant about the place of security in theorising about distributive justice and about procedural justice, and have left it at the margins of their discourse on equality.

It is useful to make several further distinctions. One may envisage essential insecurity, such as the anxiety that most parents feel for their children, and existential insecurity, that due to external events and pressures. Security also has objective and subjective dimensions. One may feel secure, but the objective circumstances may not justify it, and vice versa. In their thinking on this, psychologists have used what is called – somewhat puzzlingly for a layman – the expectancy value model.[1] This looks at the perceived threat to a valued situation according to the strength of the threat and the powerlessness to overcome it. Meanwhile, economists and others have focused on the nature of risk, often treating this as synonymous with security.

One should also distinguish between individual security and several forms of collective security – societal, community, class, occupational group or some organisational entity such as an enterprise. Collective security reflects a human need to identify with (and belong to) a social group, often to exert control over the behaviour of others or to limit their control. One should not narrow it to identification with any one group, for rich security comes from multiple forms of identity. But take away any form of group-based identity and one is likely to lose a base on which to rely.

For much of this book the focus is on individual security with respect to work and labour, and particularly with respect to the idea of occupation. In particular, it concentrates on socio-economic security, or economic security for short, which is a reflection of material circumstances and prospects and of a state of mind, mostly derived from real circumstances. As such, we may say that economic insecurity is a sense of relative deprivation, relative to one's perceived needs, the income of one's social peer group, and so on. It is also linked to a sense of opportunity, particularly good opportunity to act in ways that seem likely to improve individual and collective well-being. And it is linked to a sense of balanced reciprocity, a belief that if one follows certain rules of conduct one can expect certain entitlements that provide economic security.

Above all, security is based on self-control – being in control of what we do, what we are and what we try to become. Reasonable security in this sense is a necessary condition for real freedom and autonomy. Security is the base of real freedom. By contrast, we may say that economic insecurity is both a source of injustice and a form of it. The distribution of economic security is thus an ethical issue, just as much as the distribution of income or wealth.

The implications of this claim are explored later, along with a strategy based on it.

The main sources of economic insecurity include the following:

- absence or reduction of self-control over aspects of work;
- absence or reduced probability of upward mobility in status or income;
- necessity of increasing effort to obtain any given income;
- increased risk of an adverse outcome from a given activity;
- increased uncertainty about outcomes;
- fear that one could not do anything to rectify an adverse outcome.

As defined and discussed in the course of this book, possible *effects* of economic insecurity include the following:

- a sense of oppression or exploitation;
- demoralisation or anomie;
- demotivation, non-co-operation;
- stress, ill-health, "burn out";
- absenteeism from work, or alternatively "presenteeism";
- quitting work, high labour turnover;
- sabotage or pilfering.

These lists are by no means exhaustive, and should be seen as merely making the notions less abstract. Consider a few examples. Suppose an individual, or group of workers, found that their labour was intensified, so that the "pores of the working day were closed" or that the working day seemed to go on longer. The intensification could undermine the sense of balanced reciprocity on which the labour relationship was based, the sense that effort and application of "skill" were balanced by the rewards and promise of support. The intensification could erode the worker's commitment and loyalty, which depend in part on a perception that the former work relationship was non-exploitative and 'just'. Similarly, if an individual lost control over aspects of the work process, subjective or perceived security could diminish. If one feared one's skills were becoming obsolescent, their perceived value would decline, so intensifying feelings of insecurity. If the probability of a future of rising income or status declined, a person could be demoralised, leading to non-application of effort and skill. If one had a full-time job and written assurance of three months' notice in case of employment termination, that would provide employment security. But it would be reduced if there were no prospect of redress if the promise were abrogated.

Numerous examples could be given of how insecurity is intensified by changes in relationships or experience. But what further complicates analysis is that insecurity may reveal itself in ways that do not appear to support it. For example, in a society in which employment is made pivotal to social status, fear of loss of employment typically induces stress, which may induce absenteeism, premature retirement or high labour turnover. Leaving one's employment "voluntarily" may seem a strange response to fear of employment loss, yet the reaction may be a rational emotional adaptation to insecurity. Similarly, and perversely, income insecurity might induce someone to hold on to a disliked job, giving the impression that employment security had increased.

The predominant attitude to the desirability or otherwise of social and economic security for ordinary people has fluctuated throughout human history. Given its persistent and growing influence, it is significant that economics, or political economy, has evolved through eras in which economic security has been perceived as either desirable or undesirable – at least for "the common man". In the eighteenth century, Adam Smith was on the side of the security optimists. He and some of the leading lights of the French Revolution, such as Condorcet, advocated high wages and security for workers as the means of raising the wealth of nations. Thomas Malthus, a religious man, represented the opposing doctrine of insecurity and fear as the necessary conditions for inducing productive (rather than reproductive) activity.

The conflicting attitudes to security have continued ever since. In the 1920s, which was the last time before the 1980s when insecurity and low wages were seen as appropriate, Alfred Pigou and the Chicago economists represented the market regulationists. In the 1930s, Keynes, the Fabians, the New Deal, Beveridge and their followers successfully launched an era of social and economic security, one based firmly on labour. This was matched in continental Europe by the Swedish and other social democratic economists, most notably in the work of the principal architects of the Swedish model, Gosta Rehn, Rudolph Miedner and Gunnar Myrdal. And the state socialism model that took root to the east gave labour security a very high profile.

Almost everywhere, the 1950s and 1960s were decades in which the conventional wisdom was that labour security, individual and collective, was a social right. It was seen as fully compatible with economic growth, and it was presumed that if a policy did not enhance security it was unjustifiable. These were the high-water-mark years of labour security.

The 1970s saw a resurgence of the ethics of insecurity and inequality, initially tentative and defensive in tone, then increasingly strident. In the 1980s, under the cloak of libertarianism, those favouring the cold bath approach were back in ascendancy with a vengeance, and it is no coincidence that in the latest era of insecurity no less than eight Nobel Prizes have been awarded to economists from the University of Chicago, where what is often called the Chicago school of law and economics depicted protective regulations as impediments to growth. From Chile to the UK to Russia, taking in much of Africa, Asia and Latin America, the supply-siders were prancing like peacocks. In the 1980s and 1990s, economic security was derided as the source of "rigidity" and "dependency", while protective regulations were attacked and regarded as supportable if and only if they demonstrably fostered economic growth.

Epitomising this mood, social policy debate in the USA came to be dominated by writers such as Lawrence Mead and Charles Murray, who represented the latest in a long line of advocates of insecurity as the stick of necessity. There and across most of the world, libertarians and supply-side economics set the agenda and tone, came up with the best phrases, images and euphemisms, and dominated international discussion. For most of the last quarter of the twentieth century the libertarian views that gave credibility to policies intensifying insecurity were in the ascendancy. Moralising about family values and social responsibility neatly combined with the market ethics of individualism and efficiency.

However, in the late 1990s, as economic insecurity intensified and became more widespread, and as the adverse repercussions became more visible, the tide of debate began to turn, and by the beginning of the new century it was possible to anticipate a move in the direction of policies to promote greater social and economic security. The evidence suggests a new crisis of insecurity. The big questions are: What forms of security are desirable and feasible? What policies and institutions would best provide such security? And what place should security be given in the Good Society of the twenty-first century?

Consideration of the place of security should be linked to the assessment of mechanisms of control exercised over people. We all know that throughout history some distinctive groups have controlled the activities of others, usually for the advantage of the controllers. But somehow in the mainstream of social and economic analysis, there has been a failure to conceptualise what this means.

Control is complicated not just because it takes so many forms and degrees of intensity, but because there has always been an ambivalence about whether or not we as individuals want some control over our lives. There is the Hobbesian thesis that people opted for a despotic paternalism to give them security. The patron–client model, which has been seen as the essence of feudal society and paternalistic capitalism, is based on a system of structured reciprocities involving a loss of freedom. But against the wilder notions that people do not want real freedom, we may assert that the normal man or woman wants collective environmental security in which to exercise responsible self-control, or autonomy. We want to be able to make choices rationally, with limited "downside risk" and broadly known parameters of the probability of success.

Controls over people obviously cover every aspect of living. In the sphere of our work it is crucial. Questions of control cover all the elements of work – over the person's simple freedom, over the use of time, over the development and use of competencies (skills), over access to materials and means of production, over access to the output of the person's work, and over the income or proceeds from the work. And there are several means of resistance to each type of control. It is a mistake to focus on one element without considering the whole context of control.

The twentieth century saw an ebbing and flowing in the use and legitimacy of forms of labour control. At the outset of the twenty-first century, the world is still struggling to overcome the worst forms – bonded labour, slavery, debt peonage and the like. Say what it is that you dislike about those situations and then consider the more sophisticated forms that evolved through the

twentieth century – "scientific management", contrived "worker participation" schemes, "human resources" (and that irksome acronym, HRD),
corporate paternalism with its elaborate apparatus to create an "enterprise-
as-family" atmosphere – until you arrive at the most subtle forms of "social
engineering" and the paternalism of the modern welfare reformers who treat
the poor and the disadvantaged as in need of social integration.

One need not dwell on the motives of those who espouse such prescriptions – although the paternalistic personality must be a rich source of inspiration for psychologists. The point is that they offer a vision of security
that stems from their morality, and usually they make that quite clear and
explicit. The question for us is fundamental: Is what they offer the security of
the free?

The tension between security and control lies at the heart of the following
analysis. Analogously, the protracted debates over "labour market flexibility"
have been about the tension between a desire by representatives of capital for
subordinated flexibility – workers must be more adaptable and there should
be fewer constraints on employers – and a desire among ordinary people for
liberating flexibility – working patterns should allow greater opportunity for
diverse lifestyles. By the end of the twentieth century, that tension had
certainly not been resolved.

Under other terms, the tension between controls, security and flexibility
have always been at the heart of the social struggle. With that in mind,
we may draw inspiration from what one can call a Polanyian framework.
Capitalism has evolved through eras of upheaval and eras of stability. In the
latter, there is advancing security for a large proportion of the population, at
least in terms of forms of security perceived as critical to their lifestyles. Over
time, rigidities and tensions arise until, for whatever reasons, there is an era
of upheaval in which the economy is dis-embedded from society.

Each era of stability is characterised by a main system of regulation, a
main system of social protection, and a main system of distribution. Combined, these mechanisms achieve some redistribution, creating or reinforcing
a sense of legitimacy as well as economic dynamism. By contrast, in an era of
upheaval these three systems – regulation, social protection, redistribution –
break down, becoming ineffectual, dysfunctional or even having effects contrary to their original effects. In breaking down, they contribute to a growth
of social and economic insecurity in the face of a host of inequalities. But
that cannot go on for long. Sooner or later, if the economic growth process
is to continue, the state takes steps to re-embed the economy in society, with
new forms of regulation, protection and redistribution. This is the point
reached at the outset of the new century.

We should be looking for the new forms of regulation, protection and
redistribution. Until we do find them and see them implemented, the
turmoil of the unhappy citizen and the anarchic crowd will persist, alongside
the bestial violence of criminality that has been encouraged by the ethics
of greed that is the basis of a market society. They will be found, even if we
cannot quite foresee how they will appear.

1

Recalling the Century of Labouring Man

1 Introduction

The year 2000 marked the end of the century of labouring man. In the early years of the new century, youth face a profoundly different worldview compared with the one most of their predecessors perceived just twenty-five years earlier. And they enter higher education – if they do so – with a strange reversal of what was on offer one hundred years earlier. Think back. At the turn of the last century, the youth of the time were joining their elders in shouting for the rights of labour.

For some wild spirits, these were all to do with the freedom from labour – the freedom to tell "bosses" to go to hell and the freedom to say "Drop dead" to those who treated them as labour, to be cajoled and coerced to work. Across Europe, the USA and elsewhere, there were small groups with even wilder fancies. There were the anarchists futilely rejecting the labourist regimes being strengthened around them, and there were the Bolsheviks and others like them, who wanted to see the end of labour altogether. Or at least some of them did, even though they sentimentally idealised labour in art, poetry and prose, depicting the strong young, fresh-faced labourer, not the sweat-stained, crooked figures that have always been the reality of labour.

However, there was another train of thought, whose adherents were more cerebral and sober in their earnest moderation. Those attached to it – including social democrats, Fabians and others like them – were also radical at the time. But they were not revolutionary in their outlook or actions. They thought in terms of improving the conditions of labour – freedom in labour – without actually challenging the labour relationship *per se*. Young workers should have bosses, but they should receive more than their elders had received and be treated decently. These decent labourists were not liked by ruling elites, but they were tolerable – they did not challenge the system or the continued legitimacy of the ruling elites. In much of the world, uneasy alliances developed between them and middle-class groups, and they coalesced to oppose the radicals who wished to see the end of labour.

Part of the world went to a crazed labour model, which was based on the premise that "he who does not labour shall not eat", as the Soviet Constitution put it, and which denied the freedom that comes with work by hingeing everything on labour. Typically, twentieth-century commentators focused on military matters and the lack of "freedom" and "democracy" in their critique of the communist or state socialist model, understandably so. But perhaps one of its most terrible features was its unwithering drive to turn labourism into a godless religion. One cannot defeat the human spirit for long. The Soviet worship of the proletariat and material labour trapped adherents and critics alike. But it was against the grain.

What happened in state socialism is for another occasion. For our purposes, looking to the future, this is less interesting than what happened in the rest of the world while that model was crumbling into its paralysis and virtual demise. In the "west", by the middle of the century, following the Great Depression and the Second World War, youth was seduced by the call for the right to labour, seeing this as the right to have and to retain a job, for wages, for decent family wages. This was epitomised by what should be a candidate for slogan of the twentieth century, a slogan that would have seemed strange to the youth of the end of the nineteenth century – Full Employment. Most of them then would have asked what was so wonderful about having all the young in employment.

In 1945, that slogan was a tonic for the soldiers, sailors and airmen returning from the warfront. The post-war governments of western Europe and north America were determined not to repeat the mistakes of their predecessors in the years after the Great War of 1914–18. The 1920s had seen a dis-embedding of the economy from society, opening up inequalities and strengthening the position of asset holders, employers and financiers, until their frenzied profiteering collapsed in the hubris of the Great Depression. The post-1945 era demanded a re-embedding of the economy. This was achieved by a mix of Keynesian economics and the welfare state, in its various guises.

What resulted is what we may call the era of statutory regulation, because of its heavy reliance on laws and legal regulations, as well as formal public planning. It gave a secondary role to a particular form of voice regulation, through the incorporation of workers' and employers' representatives in the centralised governance of social and economic policy. A key feature of the era was that it hinged on the activity and values of labour, and above all on the ethics of labouring man. Although it was part of it, this was more than can be conveyed by the euphemism of "the bread-winner model". It made labour the primary objective – being in labour, having labour to do, and achieving circumstances in which there was a high aggregate demand for labour. Being without labour was a source of shame, a reflection of in-adequacy or of being a misfit. All working-class men were expected to be in full-time labour from the time they left school or college until the time they retired. Women were expected to be wives, only intermittently in labour, perversely when they were not anticipating or recovering from the other form of "labour".

Adding to the perversity of the time, in both communist and welfare states, there was a concerted – and for a while successful – attempt to make labour less like a commodity. Indeed, in a strange one-line paragraph in the International Labour Organisation's triumphant call for a new world of labour in its Philadelphia Declaration of 1944, approved by all its member countries, the world's political democracies joined the Soviet bloc in asserting confidently, "Labour is not a commodity".[1] Although this was deeply ambiguous, the message would have been supported by Lenin in the early years of the twentieth century and was vigilantly supported by his successors, just as it was by the Labour Parties and social democrats who surged into power in various parts of the world after 1945. In most democracies, even their opponents felt obliged to adopt their language and commit themselves to the right to labour, through a commitment to so-called Full Employment.

The forward march of labour was in full flood, and the euphemisms of the time, the key words as Raymond Williams described them, all came from that camp. Who could be against Full Employment, or welfare (not warfare), or progressive taxation? New social rights were identified, defined, and strengthened, and soon exported to where new democracies were supposed to flourish. The labourist model of social security was presented as the logical extension of a labour-based society.

There should be no misinterpretation. Labourism, epitomised by the right to labour, was indeed a triumphant advance compared with nineteenth-century industrial capitalism, with its grotesque disregard for its labourers and their communities. It was also an advance on the welfare capitalism of the early twentieth-century, in which corporate paternalism briefly flourished, most notably in the USA. But welfare state capitalism was always in danger of creating what Hannah Arendt, with remarkable prescience in the late 1950s, called the jobholder society. It took the 1960s to show that the norms of the post-1945 era were also in danger of crushing the human march by encouraging and rewarding conformity. The more educated youth of the time were less enamoured by the call to labour. Liberal education liberated, and stimulated a desire for lifestyle diversity.

It was not this liberation that undid the post-1945 labourist model. But in the 1970s, the right to labour almost collapsed, with the return of mass unemployment and radical changes in economic orthodoxy and political philosophy, which are the subjects of the next part of this book. It is the irony of this that should be highlighted here – that by the end of the twentieth century a remarkable chorus of politicians and commentators from across the political spectrum were preaching that everyone had a duty to labour. People had to be responsible and to contribute, and unless they took jobs or took training to prepare for jobs, they were undeserving of state support.

So, in short, during the course of the century the balance of rhetoric shifted from exulting over the rights of labour through demanding the right to labour and then ending up emphasising the duty to labour. What a strange transformation.

2 The Era of Statutory Regulation

Much of the twentieth century was dominated by competition for global supremacy between two models of development, both based on the values of labour. There is no need to go into them in any great detail here. But it may be useful for later reflection to recall some of their features, notably those they had in common. The first model is *welfare state capitalism* (not "welfare capitalism", which is a term better used for the corporate paternalism that flourished in the USA in the early decades of the twentieth century). The second model is state socialism.

Both development models initially had some success on their own terms, and both were exported vigorously – if not always ethically, to put it mildly – to so-called developing countries. Both were held out as the development path to follow, even if some of those on the left debated on whether capitalism was needed before socialism, generating a large literature that seems sadly lost in the new century.

Although similarities of the two models can be exaggerated, the commonalities were greater than most critiques of one or the other would care to admit. In essence, they promoted seven forms of labour security, and formally at least both relied heavily on statutory regulations, or state rules and procedures.

In the forms pursued under welfare state capitalism, the seven forms of labour security can be listed as follows:

- *Labour market security* – Adequate employment opportunities, through state-guaranteed full employment;
- *Employment security* – Protection against arbitrary dismissal, regulations on hiring and firing, imposition of costs on employers, etc.;
- *Job security* – A niche designated as an occupation or "career", plus tolerance of demarcation practices, barriers to skill dilution, craft boundaries, formally defined job qualifications, restrictive practices, craft unions, etc.;
- *Work security* – Protection against accidents and illness at work, through safety and health regulations, and limits on working time, unsociable hours, night work for women, etc.;
- *Skill reproduction security* – Widespread opportunities to gain and retain skills, through apprenticeships, employment training, etc.;
- *Income security* – Protection of income through minimum wage machinery, wage indexation, comprehensive social security, progressive taxation, etc.;
- *Representation security* – Protection of collective voice in the labour market, through independent trade unions and employer associations incorporated economically and politically into the state, with the right to strike, etc.

Although all these forms of security were pursued in the post-1945 era, it is crucial for subsequent analysis to appreciate that primacy was reserved for labour market security and that all forms were made dependent on the performance of labour, or at least the willingness to perform it. It is also important to recognise that employment security differs from job security, although in much of the literature the terms have been used interchangeably. Many workers may have had assurances that they would be protected against loss of employment, or compensation for loss of it. But many of those had little choice if they were told they had to change the work tasks they were required to perform within that secure employment.

One should also distinguish between job security and what might be called occupational security. In practice, job security was interpreted narrowly or in ways that actually reduced the sense of occupation in a wide range of "jobs". Implicit in its absence from the table above, one is tempted to make the strong statement: Occupational security was given no priority in the era when labour security in general was promoted most strongly (that is, between about 1945 and about 1975).

Both labourist models had distinctive modes of redistribution, regulation and social protection, which is how the economy was embedded in society. Of course, within the general model of welfare state capitalism, there were important inter-country variations, which have been elucidated by a host of social scientists following Richard Titmuss' early attempt to differentiate welfare state types. Nevertheless, it is not to belittle the differences to suggest that there were some common features of the leading welfare state capitalism countries. It is worth recalling the main features.

They generally relied on Keynesian economics, with one of several modifications being the Rehn-Meidner, or Swedish, model, which operated macro-economic policy to achieve less than "Full Employment", so as to limit inflationary pressure.[2] The crucial point is that Keynesianism meant targeting macro-economic policy on the maintenance of "Full Employment" and micro-economic policy on inflationary pressures. In other words, fiscal and monetary policy was used to manipulate aggregate demand to secure a high and stable level of employment. The use of inverted commas round the term Full Employment is appropriate, because there was never full employment in the proper sense of the word, since women were regarded as a "secondary labour force", typically having a low and cyclically fluctuating labour force participation rate, while special schemes were often used to take surplus workers out of the measured labour force.

Another feature of the era was "the mixed economy", in which the state sector was expected to expand steadily in relative and absolute terms. Although many foresaw a future in which there was full nationalisation, for socialists, the mixed economy was an article of faith – with nationalisation and state ownership of the "commanding heights" of the economy being coupled with a desire to see public social services expand and the government to be "employer of last resort" to ensure that open unemployment did not rise above some politically accepted level. Even for their opponents, there was little questioning of the mixed economy – although for them the state sector was expected to grow more slowly than the private sector, and was expected to account mainly for social services and non-tradable production.

There were several key premises of this model and its variants. Looking back, insufficient attention was given to one in particular, the fact that while ownership changes between nominally private and nominally public were the focus of political tension, the managerial right to manage was widely accepted. This was a historical loss of nerve. The management right to control the where, when and why of production could be said to represent the surrender of job and occupational security by workers and their social-democratic political parties. The right to manage was epitomised by tacit acceptance of Taylorist and related work organisation techniques and hierarchical control relations in labour. It is worth dwelling on this, if only to emphasise a few implications and to speculate on what might have been the outcome if this surrender of job security had not occurred and if it were to be reversed in the early decades of the twenty-first century.

The right to manage, taken to its extreme form in Tayloristic "scientific management", meant that jobs were splintered as the detailed division of labour was accentuated in occupation after occupation, industry after industry. In the second half of the century, labour process theorists, building in particular on the influential analysis of Braverman, succeeded in showing many of the devices used to advance the detailed and social divisions of labour – or forms of social stratification. We will come back to this in later chapters. There was never total acceptance of this by workers. But, for the most part, unions did accept management's right to manage in return for improvement in money wages and social security. In some cases, unions tried to strengthen their position by insisting on job demarcation, arresting change but scarcely ever setting an agenda for work reorganisation (except to some extent in Scandinavia). Often the opposition by unionists was merely atavistic. Often it reflected pressure from the ageing members of trade unions who stood to lose if their particular "skills" were diluted. Printing was the most visible example. But it was not alone.

An implication was that while the technological and social division of labour proceeded, purely atavistic opposition was brushed aside, often after social struggles that entailed great cost to both capital and the labouring groups directly involved. Passive resistance was ultimately untenable, because it offered no vision of social or distributive justice. There was no assertion of a just claim for the human right to occupation, merely a cry for the retention of privilege from entrenched interest groups. Even those who rallied to their side mostly felt a twinge of unease in doing so. Atavism has never been a winning route for progressive action.

By contrast with employment security, job security was never a strong feature of social democratic labour movements, because by contrast with the nineteenth century the vanguard of public and electoral pressure was manual labour, and then public social services, in which the craft ethic was weak. We will come back to the implications of this, and to the need to change priorities.

Another premise of welfare state capitalism was the presumption that modern economies rested on a stable production structure, or one that changed only slowly, so that labour adjustments at the margin could be made without much dislocation, as new cohorts entered the labour force. It was a time of relatively slow technological change, in which process innovation predominated over product innovation. Terms such as "technological stale-mate" emerged, alongside Marxisant notions of "late capitalism", and interest in Kondratief long waves. Corresponding to the sense of stable production structure was the expectation that the norm was full-time industrial wage labour, and the expectation in developing countries was that this would become the norm.

Although one could cite studies stating the contrary, there was also a common presumption that the international division of labour was almost static, even though industrialisation was expected to occur in developing countries. There was what amounted to a closed economy model of development, in which trade in competitive goods took place between countries with similar labour rights and costs (wages and other costs offset by productivity differentials), while trade in complementary goods took place between industrialised and "underdeveloped" countries based on unequal exchange and long-term paternalistic arrangements. Franklin Roosevelt and his colleagues towards the end of the Second World War had wished to take labour rights and standards out of the realm of international trade. For about a quarter of a century, this was largely what happened. It is symbolic that the ILO, the international body entrusted with setting up labour standards in its numerous Conventions and Recommendations, was awarded the Nobel Peace Prize in 1969 – perhaps the time of the peak of the labourist approach.

Few economists at the time recognised how the welfare state was dependent on the closed economy system. Gunnar Myrdal was one who saw the welfare state as essentially protectionist. As long as trade was mainly with countries with similar labour costs and rights, the pattern of social protection was feasible.

In spirit, the post-1945 era was an egalitarian age. It was conventional wisdom that a reduction in inequality of income and wealth was both desirable and feasible. The core of political discussion was about the extent of reduction and the pace of change, rather than the direction of it. Of course, of the many forms of inequality, some were given more attention than others. But the dominant ethos in public discourse and intellectually was that inequalities should be diminished and were diminishing. Income redistribution was expected to come primarily from attaining a high and stable level of male full-time employment, in which men were paid a "family wage", enough to support a standard two-adult, two-children household. This was to be backed up by progressive direct taxation and substantial consumer subsidies.

Social protection, while never powerfully redistributive, was mostly universalistic in principle, linked firmly and unequivocally to the performance of labour and Beveridge's dictum that social security was for "temporary interruptions of earning power", whether in childhood, sickness, unemployment or old age. Social security was based firmly on the image of an industrial society in which the working class was expected to remain or become the overwhelming majority of the population and the norm for social behaviour.

The regulatory system implied by welfare state capitalism was historically distinctive. The term governance only came into vogue in the 1990s, but the prevailing system of governance in the 1950s and 1960s combined heavy reliance on statutory regulations with a particular type of voice regulation. The laws and decrees that comprised the statutory regulation were predominantly protective of workers and pro-collective, in that they facilitated and presumed collective bargaining and the entrenchment of collective groups in the network of institutions that made up the state.

The features are fairly easy to recall, even though it passed its peak more than a third of a century ago. Tripartism, or "neo-corporatism" (not quite the same, although closely linked) involved ostentatiously public negotiations and posturing by organisations representing big and middle-sized business as employers and big blocs of workers represented by the major trade unions. They were orchestrated by governments, which typically contained members from their ranks, in what amounted to a historically distinctive revolving-door process, in which leading members of governments swapped roles with leaders of union and employer bodies. Between them, they often forged increasingly comprehensive incomes policies, in some countries by statutory means, in others by messy rounds of negotiations.

Tripartism was a peculiar feature of the mid-twentieth century. It worked reasonably well when society consisted largely of bureaucratic industrial enterprises and a situation in which a majority of workers were in stable full-time industrial wage labour, whose respective interests were fairly clearly defined. Structural changes on both sides – some induced by their own achievements – were to undermine all that, since the increasing hetero-geneity of social and economic interests chipped away at its feasibility, functionality, legitimacy and equity.

3 Social Income: Post-1945 "Decommodification"?

An aspect of the middle years of the twentieth century was the drive to labour decommodification, both in state socialism and welfare state capital-ism. What decommodification meant was that the wage would become a dwindling and small part of total income. In state socialism, this was made an explicit objective; Lenin himself had envisaged the withering away of the money wage in the transition to communism. In welfare state capitalism, there was to be a gradual shift of total income towards state benefits, occupational welfare and publicly provided social services. This was com-patible with the labourist orientation, since a guiding principle of the social system was that there should be "redistribution with growth", based on a popular notion of Full Employment.

Perhaps the best way of describing the labour decommodification of the time is that average social income rose faster than wages. It was a peculiar form of decommodification, and it largely concerned men. Social income may be defined as the flow of resources acquired by any individual, reflecting the underlying social relations of production and distribution and the networks of social support. A way of depicting this – and a way of presenting later developments associated with globalisation – is to consider the total income (social income) of any individual in any society as consisting of five components, some of which may be negligible or non-existent. This can be defined as an identity:

$$SI=W+CB+EB+SB+PB$$

where *SI* is the individual's total social income, *W* is the money wage or income received in work, *CB* is the value of benefits or support provided by the family, kin or the local community, *EB* is the amount of benefits provided by the enterprise in which the person might be working, *SB* is the value of state benefits provided, in terms of insurance benefits or other transfers, including *subsidies* paid to workers or through firms to them, and *PB* is private income benefits, gained through investment, including private social protection.

We can disaggregate the elements as follows:

$$SI=(W_b+W_f)+(FT+LT)+(NWB+IB)+(C+IS+D)+PB$$

where W_b is the base or fixed wage, W_f is the flexible part of the wage (bonuses, etc.), *FT* are family transfers (in money or in kind), *LT* are local community transfers, including any income from charity, non-governmental organisations, etc., *NWB* are non-wage benefits provided by firms to their workers, *IB* are contingency, insurance-type benefits provided by firms to their workers, *C* are universal state benefits (citizenship rights), *IS* are insurance-based income transfers from the state in case of contingency needs, and *D* are discretionary, means-tested transfers from the state.[3]

We do not have data on the distribution of social income, or of the weights of the several components. However, based on anecdotal and scattered data, we can guesstimate the modal patterns in the major regions of the world during the era of statutory regulation. In a stylised way, we can guess that, relative to other regions and as a proportion of total personal income, in the post-1945 era the average values of the components of the social income, as expressed in the first identity, were as follows:

Table 1.1. Structures of social income in era of statutory regulation, by region

	W	EB	SB	PB	CB
Africa	Medium	Low	Low	Low	High
Western Europe	Medium	Medium	High	Medium	Low
Eastern Europe	Low	High	Low	Low	Low
North America	Medium	Medium	Low	High	Low
Latin America	Medium	Medium	Low	Low	Medium
South Asia	Low	Medium	Low	Low	Medium
South-East Asia	Low	Medium	Low	Low	High

For example, in western Europe, for the median average person the share of total social income accounted for by the money wage was about average for the world, whereas the share coming from state benefits was high by world standards and the share coming in the form of informal transfers from the local community was low. In eastern Europe, the money wage was a relatively small part of social income, while enterprise benefits comprised a very high share. In east Asia, money wages were not only low in absolute terms but were a small share of social income, while community transfers comprised a high share – in effect, wage workers were subsidised by their predominantly rural kinship communities.

The significance of the global pattern of social income will be considered later. The point here is that when commentators said that "labour is not a commodity", and when later commentators referred to "decommodification" that took place in the middle decades of the twentieth century, they meant in part that a growing proportion of social income was coming from non-wage, non-monetary elements – from the state and/or from their enterprises. But this was not all.

An aspect of decommodification rarely taken into account is that the labour securities promoted so assiduously in much of the twentieth century, being valuable for those possessing them, constituted part of the social income. How much they were worth to any individual is impossible to say, and the value would have varied according to the state of the economy, social position of the individual, and so on.

All we are sure about is that some groups have had much greater labour security than others, and that the possession of strong employment security, for instance, is worth some income. What proportion of one's money income would one be prepared to surrender for the assurance that one could not lose employment arbitrarily? Similarly, to have institutional mechanisms that lower the probability of work accidents or illnesses, and that assure compensation or redress if rules are broken, is worth income. These forms of security cannot be converted easily into insurable risks. If they are taken away, workers and their community are likely to feel the loss, and it will be a real erosion of social income. They were certainly part of social progress. The ethos of the era was that the ordinary man and woman should have risks removed, as long as they showed commitment to labour.

4 Crumbling of the Era

The labourist era of statutory regulation has been called many names, some of them silly, such as the "Golden Age" of capitalism. It was a period in history when there was progress in distributive justice, particularly in a few industrialised countries, but also in some developing countries. Criticism should be tempered by that acknowledgement. It was a period when the economy was embedded in society, in the way that Karl Polanyi meant by the term.[4] Those who hark back to the era as a Golden Age lose a sense of history in doing so. It did not seem to be a Golden Age for many people at the time, and with good reason.

It was an era in which the privileged part of the world advanced more than the rest of it. It was an era in which wage labour was regarded as defining the world of work, in which male full-time employment was made the fulcrum of social policy, and in which the mechanisms of social protection and redistribution were based mainly on direct taxation, with progressive income tax and corporation tax alongside confidently installed systems of social insurance based on contributions paid by employers. The economy was embedded in society in a particular way that depended on a particular set of circumstances.

No such embeddedness lasts once the economic system changes, along with the dominant forms of technology and the underlying relations of production. It all came unstuck in the 1980s. But long before then the cracks were visible; they could be traced to the period when the triumph of the labourist welfare system seemed most successful, and specifically to when youth started to bridle at the nature of society into which they were expected to integrate. The 1960s were a rude awakening. It *was* a remarkable decade. Among the many reasons were the "winds of change" in developing countries and the fact that it was a time when youth in industrialised countries grew sufficiently frustrated and angry with conforming to the labouring ideals, and with the norms and control systems that had been built up in the late 1940s and 1950s, that they wanted to overhaul them. Decent labour was resented, as dulling the senses, shrinking the horizons and offering at best one of those jobs that "keep the aspidistra flying", as George Orwell memorably called one of his novels about the struggle to retain drab decency in the 1930s.

Mirroring this disillusion was the first hints of a fragmentation of the class structure of society in what became a "globalising" economy. The presumption for most of the twentieth century was that the working class was going to become and remain the largest and most powerful group. Its demands were respected by political parties and the welfare state was built in the interest of it and the middle class. But by the 1970s it was realised in many parts of the world that the working class was *not* growing in relative terms and indeed was shrinking in terms of bargaining strength and numbers. Fear changed sides. Since then concessions have been numerous, and inequality and worker insecurities have spread. But as the voice of labour has faded and become more conciliatory, so the voices of citizenship, community and work have been trying to be heard.

Many factors contributed to the erosion of welfare state capitalism, both in countries where it was strongly established and as a model for others to emulate. It would be wrong and unnecessary to try to identify a single cause. It was a systemic failure, or a reflection of incapacity to respond to economic and technological changes. The emergence of a few developing countries as semi-industrialised and the spread of multinational corporations played a part, marking a changing international division of labour.

The oil crises of the 1970s, in which market power was used by people and countries not meant to use it, merely confirmed the inflationary pressures under which economies were operating. The resultant deflationary policies, and the use of statutory and centrally negotiated incomes policies to roll back labourist advances, slowed economic growth, hitting some groups in society much harder than others, and put any rough social consensus about the pace and direction of income redistribution under such strain that it cracked. Industrial strife came at the same time as rising unemployment. It was the end of an era.

2

The Era of Market Regulation

1 Introduction

Recalling the changes of the 1970s and 1980s, one feels a bit like the woman in Oscar Wilde's *The Importance of Being Earnest*, who counselled her niece to study a particular book with the words: "The chapter on the Fall of the Rupee you may omit; it is somewhat too sensational."

The last quarter of the twentieth century was a period of extraordinary social and economic upheaval, when the certainties of the 1960s became the apparent folly of the past. Although the symbolism of 1968 lingers, we need not discuss its relevance here. Nor need we try to pinpoint an exact time when major social, economic and political change started. Suffice it to assert that the last quarter of the twentieth century was one of those historical eras when not just the extent of change is enormous, but also the pace of it. For our purposes, we need only recall the factors that eroded the old era and the contours of the economic and political orthodoxy that arose from the ashes. One can easily quibble with the story, but surely only on details.

In reviewing what happened rather impressionistically, it should be kept in mind that the purpose is to build a case for a new system by which the emerging economy can be embedded in society, based on feasible and attractive mechanisms and institutions of social protection and distribution. Just as there is no need to pinpoint years of dramatic change in direction, so it is not particularly useful to look for a "smoking gun"— a single factor that undid the era in which welfare state capitalism attained its greatest attraction.

2 Economic Liberalisation

A remark attributed to John Maynard Keynes is that every economist is either a little inflationist or a little deflationist. In the post-1945 era, economic policy was dominated by little inflationists. Deflation was associated vividly with the Depression, and the memory of mass unemployment created an atmosphere when any rise in measured unemployment was regarded as a signal for political change. But as Milton Friedman and others were to argue in the late 1960s and early 1970s, people learn to adapt their behaviour. Inflationary pressures built up because employers, workers, consumers, savers and anybody in a position to be a price-setter either hoisted prices or acceded to higher prices because they felt governments would inflate aggregate demand to prevent a rise in unemployment. The "oil crisis" of 1973 changed policy psychology definitively. Middle-eastern oil producers, suddenly realising their (temporary) monopoly power, set prices on a much higher plane, and for several years inflationary pressure threatened to drift out of control.

At the same time, economic growth slowed in much of the world, in part precisely because governments had to act to damp down the inflationary pressure by curtailing aggregate demand. Governments initially felt obliged to take up the labour slack by expanding their role as employer of last resort, or by expanding public services, or as in the Swedish model by absorbing larger proportions of the labour force in so-called active labour market policies. It was about this time that the notion of "active" labour market policy changed from its original sense of counter-cyclical policy to that of preparing workers for jobs and, later, to achieving "social integration".

Public expenditure rose as a share of GDP, and public sector deficits became a greater source of disquiet in political and economic circles. Meanwhile, with rising inflation, slower economic growth and the slowdown in the expansion of full-time, well-paid jobs, the distributional consensus of the post-war era cracked. Taxation as an instrument for redistribution seemed to be "saturated", with high marginal rates deemed to depress saving and investment. Social security became perceived as less redistributive than many had believed it was or hoped it would be. The losers became more discontented, or frustrated in wanting more of the progress that had come with the post-war economic growth. The winners in society became more resentful about sharing their gains, thinking that they and their peers would have little need for help, so weakening their perceived need for "social insurance".

The sense of social solidarity in the advanced industrialised countries began to fray. It was a time of tension. There are times in history when social protests by "the crowd" seem progressive and in tune with the spirit of the time; and there are times when they seem less legitimate and more atavistic, resisting desirable or almost inevitable change. This was one of those latter periods. Almost everything "the people" did to protest at new or old injustices seemed to rebound in their faces.

Meanwhile, unemployment in its various guises was rising around the world, and there were signs that poverty and inequality were worsening. In industrialised countries, the changes can be summed up in one phenomenon: Fear changed sides. In the 1950s and 1960s, the distributional concessions were made mainly by employers, managers and their representatives. From the 1970s onwards, it was the workers, their unions and their political representatives who made most of the concessions. Trade unions, once the valiant spokesmen of workers and society, became perceived as fussy old men, often speaking only for themselves and for a privileged body of mostly male workers, a source of "rigidity", blocking progress, and so on. It may have been grossly unfair, but the social mood changed. There were plenty of people with a grudge or an ideological perspective and set of interests keen to promote this image. The mass media, being privately owned and in the hands of wealthy elites, did all this vividly and effectively. Unprepared and slow to react, the unions in most places lurched to the margins of institutional relevance with remarkable rapidity.

Of course, this did not happen to the same extent everywhere, but even where tripartism persisted it did so in a climate of concession bargaining – the unions seeming to hope that others would see their moderation as reason enough to keep the show on the road – the cliché seems apt. But in the main there was no disguising the loss of momentum and legitimacy.

While fear changed sides, an intellectual paradigm shift was taking place. In economics, Milton Friedman's monetarism and Robert Lucas' path-breaking papers ushered in supply-side economics and rational expectations theory. The key points of direct relevance are that the old macro-economic policy and statutory regulation policy was depicted as the source of rigidities and conducive to adaptive behaviour that prevented the self-regulating market economy from functioning. The outcome was that the policy targeting of Keynesianism was reversed. Macro-economic policy, essentially monetary policy, was to be targeted on controlling inflation, while micro-economic policy was to influence employment by reforming institutions and regulations in order to lower the "non-accelerating inflation rate of unemployment" (the NAIRU) and the "natural rate" of unemployment.

An outcome of the former policy, which crystallised later, was the view that central banks, such as the Bank of England, should be independent of political government, so that the credibility of monetary policy would be enhanced. Although there were exceptions, this became the norm around the world in the latter part of the twentieth century. An irony was that the IMF and the World Bank, the institutions that were set up as the global macro-economic stabilisers following the Second World War, greatly expanded their role by advocating and working for the rejection of macro-economic stabilisation *per se*. If they believed what they preached in the 1980s and 1990s, they should have closed their macro-economic stabilisation and adjustment programmes.

An outcome of the revised role for micro-economic policy was an ideo-logically motivated onslaught on "regulations" and institutions of social protection and redistribution in favour of workers and their most immediate interests. The euphemism of "deregulation" emerged. It is not being cynical to recall that there was much less emphasis on the need to erode regulations that protected the interests of asset-holders and the winners in society. That aside, the new orthodoxy – sometimes known as the Chicago school of law and economics – ruled that regulations were desirable and justifiable if and only if they promoted economic growth. This quickly led to the view that statutory regulations were generally not helpful or desirable.

A less noticed but ultimately even more significant aspect of the new orthodoxy was that the reversal of Keynesian policy targeting meant that henceforth governments gave up the pursuit of Full Employment by economic means. The neo-Walrasian basis of the new economics meant that the levels of employment and unemployment were supposedly ground out by the institutional and regulatory structures of society. It was these that determined the NAIRU. If there was high unemployment, it was because institutions and regulations were inappropriate.

Actually, unemployment was made the responsibility of individual workers and individual firms. The old terms structural unemployment and voluntary unemployment returned. Pure monetarists attributed no blame to workers and unions for unemployment, presuming rational behaviour would adapt to monetary conditions and that therefore unemployment was a monetary phenomenon and a reflection of the structure of regulations and institutions. But gradually the image of behavioural responsibility took precedence.[1] The new orthodox position was that it was no use artificially boosting public expenditure and the size of the public sector to absorb the unemployed. Workers and employers should work it out for themselves, and behave accordingly.

So emerged the view that the public sector should shrink and not be the employer of last resort. Of course, there were also other reasons for this view. The public sector was perceived as a primary source of slow economic growth, and as "crowding out" private investment and employment. Although privatisation always had a powerful ideological underpinning, it drew on an unverified rationale that the private sector was more efficient than the public, conveniently bypassing the messy reality that any such dualism was an over-simplification.

While the new economic orthodoxy was taking shape, philosophical and political thinking was being profoundly influenced by the rise of libertarianism and related schools of thought. The seminal work was Robert Nozick's book *Anarchy, State and Utopia*, published in 1974. Libertarianism gave an intellectual respectability to those wanting to disassociate themselves from the post-1945 consensus that social and economic policy, and the institutions and regulations that it promoted and defended, should reduce economic and social inequality. Libertarianism stated that only procedural justice was required. As long as fair procedures were established and followed, any economic transaction was valid and just. The outcomes were deemed equitable and legitimate. Greater inequality of outcomes was not only regarded as acceptable but was demonstrative of freedom and a dynamic market economy.

The radical changes in policies and institutions, along with the language of political and economic discourse, reflected a combination of the Chicago school of law and economics, libertarianism and its offspring, and the fact that fear changed sides. Everywhere, workers and their social democratic representatives were on the defensive, floundering in a morass of populism and atavism. As the new orthodoxy spread into the sphere of development strategy, there were a few gurgles of alternative thinking. For a few years, liberal development economists pinned their hopes on a basic needs approach, calling for an international effort to provide the poor with the essentials of life. It went with the equally populist set of thoughts around the theme that "small is beautiful" and a romanticising of some ill-defined and elastic "informal sector". In various guises, this stream of thought continued as an undercurrent for the remainder of the century, so that a vision of the future evolved consisting of flexible specialisation and industrial districts (which could be summed up as stating that small is beautiful as long as units of production are grouped together to gain economies of scope and scale).

However, the proponents of the new orthodoxy, and the interests they represented, went on remorselessly, crystallising in what has been called the Washington Consensus, a term that came into being in about 1984, and that is usually attributed to John Williamson. Before dealing with that, one should mention three powerful developments that pre-dated it.

By the 1970s, Japan had emerged as a major economic power, leading to all sorts of pathological and economic scares in other industrialised countries, and bringing in its wake a small group of newly industrialising countries quickly labelled NICs. Together they began to alter the international division of labour. For some economists, it remained a comforting sentiment that the share of world exports accounted for by the NICs and other developing countries remained quite small during the latter decades of the century. But the effect of their emergence cannot be measured by such simple figures. They heralded a shift in thinking about development. There was a shift from import-substitution development to export-led industrialisation, from acceptance of semi-closed economies to pressure on developing countries to become open economies. Several analyses have since questioned whether the NICs were open, in the sense that was becoming part of the new orthodoxy. But the fact is that proponents were able to convince enough influential people that having open export-led economies was essential.

In any case, as Japan and the NICs became part of the international trading system in being exporters of competitive manufactured goods, and later other tradables such as modern services, so labour costs became more important, even though in many sectors direct labour costs may have been a dwindling proportion of total costs. In response to the increased relevance of relative labour costs, a crucial pillar of the welfare state capitalism model was chipped away. To a large extent, social benefits were paid from "non-wage labour costs" – contributions that were equivalent to a tax wedge that raised labour costs. These were not a major problem when countries selling competitive goods to one another had roughly the same set of labour cost structures. But the changing international division of labour altered that.

We will come back to this when considering the restructuring of social income. For the moment we need only note that this accelerated a process by which policymakers in industrialised countries gradually stopped thinking in terms of extending their welfare state and thought increasingly in terms of creating or strengthening the *competitive state*. The notion of competitiveness became a fetish in the 1990s, a euphemism used to justify or rationalise numerous changes that would have been anathema in the previous era.

The second powerful force was the spread of multinational enterprises and the associated acceleration of the internationalisation of financial capital markets. Some analysts have claimed that the developments were merely returning to the world order of the several decades before 1914. Yet the world economy was profoundly different in the last few years of the twentieth century. Many more countries were sucked into the global economy, the number of multinational firms and their size were much greater, their backward and forward linkages were so extensive that decisions in board-rooms in the USA, Japan or western Europe could trigger waves of reper-cussions all over the world. And the role of government and public expend-iture was vastly greater than it had been a century earlier.

The other powerful force was the technological revolution that began in the 1970s. One way of interpreting it is that it established a new "heartland" technological base, just as the steam engine, electricity or the motor car had done. In this spirit, the arrival of micro-electronics marked an upturn phase of a fifth Kondratief long wave, the thesis being that in the development of capitalism there have been sharp breaks in which a major technologic breakthrough has established a new surge in potential economic growth for a prolonged period. To the extent that one accepts the idea of historical long-waves driven by technological upheavals every sixty years or so, it is apparent that each such revolution has brought a new geographical locus of production in the world. For instance, the eighteenth century upturn marked out the UK as the new global leader of industrial dynamism. In the mid nineteenth century, Germany and the USA emerged, and in the early twentieth century the centre shifted decisively to the USA. The late twentieth century seemed initially to shift economic dynamism to south-east Asia or "the Pacific basin". However, it seems more correct to see this as the first truly global technological revolution, in which potentially production can be located and moved across most of the world almost at will, to wherever the basic infrastructure, laws and regulatory frameworks exist and are regarded as stable.

An image that captures the essence of the upheavals is Jagdash Bhagwati's vision of "kaleidoscopic comparative advantage", reflecting more footloose firms, higher labour turnover and greater mobility of "highly skilled" workers.[2] It is this almost limitless and selective mobility that is so distinctive about the latest technological revolution. It makes almost all aspects of production and distribution mobile, and in the process greatly strengthens the economic and political power of the controllers of production and distribution, over both non-controllers – workers – and governments – as regulators, tax collectors, social security designers and as dispensers of justice. This has far-reaching implications that will preoccupy us in later chapters.

The emergence of NICs, coupled with the spread of multinational enterprises, and the technological revolution, contributed to the adoption of a new euphemism that swept into fashion in the 1990s – globalisation. This seemingly awesome word has come to provide a powerful set of images and a capacity to induce the most extreme emotional and intellectual reactions. Essentially, it means that national economies have become more open, even where little or no legislative or regulatory reform has been introduced. The notion of "openness" is not an easy one. For our purposes, it means that the ease with which goods, capital and labour can be moved is greater, that potential mobility is greater still, and that the costs of doing so have been cut. Exports and imports have tended to become a rising share of GDP, and a growing share of national production has consisted of so-called "tradables".

Some observers have been inclined to dismiss globalisation as nothing new, or have asserted that it is essentially returning the world to the situation that prevailed before 1914. This is not tenable. The share of international trade in global GDP is much greater, as is the share of foreign direct investment (FDI).[3] And there has been a shift of FDI to low-income, low-wage countries. There has also been a sharp increase in the concentration of economic power. Indicative of that, between 1983 and 1999, the combined sales of the top 200 corporations in the world grew from 25 per cent to 27.5 per cent of global GDP.[4]

Not only is the speed of reaction and the magnitude of economic change so much greater, but in the era of globalisation, capital and technology have become more mobile than labour, in particular compared with the movement of people without technical qualifications and status. In the period from about 1870 to 1914 the movement of people, as labour, was probably greater than the mobility of capital. By contrast, during the twentieth century, many countries introduced or extended immigration controls, putting up regulatory walls.

If globalisation is characterised by greater relative mobility of capital and technology, it is also distinguished by the impact on fiscal policy. Because taxation and public expenditure have been so much greater than in previous eras, the mobility of both direct and portfolio capital has increased under the influence of tax competition and other fiscal mechanisms.

The global rules and regulations enable multinational corporations to have greater control over where products and made and exported or imported, notably through such WTO mechanisms as TRIPS (Trade-related Intellectual Property Rights), which grants patents to firms that have often incurred little or none of the research expenditure, and the activities of patent organisations such as WIPO (World Intellectual Property Organisation). In previous centuries, ideas were mostly free. Now, the benefits go to those who can register ownership.

Much of the research and development that leads to new products and technological breakthroughs is funded by governments, who raise the funds from ordinary taxpayers. Often the benefits of the research are turned over to private corporations that market the products, and they, through patenting the innovations, are enabled to obtain monopoly rents. This is part of the winner-takes-all character of globalisation in the era of market regulation. Since the USA is able to account for nearly half of all research and development expenditure, it is not surprising that this gives the country a competitive advantage. The high incomes gained by particular firms and individuals do not necessarily reflect outstanding merit on their part. They benefit from the system of regulation.

With production at the margin being adjustable by decisions in distant boardrooms, with technology being transferable through little more than patented possession of knowledge, and with enhanced capacity to make and declare profits where the producers see fit, globalisation is fundamentally about the transfer of power. In that lies a key to the future, if globalisation is to be checked. For the growth of new forms of power has always generated social forces attempting to limit, regulate and redirect it.[5] Although one should not be deterministic about asserting that change is inevitable, it is unlikely that the greater concentration of power and wealth that has been associated with globalisation and its correlates is sustainable, or that the growing inequality and insecurities should be accepted as "inevitable".

3 The Washington Consensus

Before globalisation emerged as the euphemism of the era, a set of policy prescriptions had crystallised as the new orthodoxy and had become instrumental in accelerating economic globalisation. This is the ubiquitous Washington Consensus. The approach offered a model consisting of twelve main elements, with more being added as its "success" spread. Briefly, the elements are:

- trade liberalisation,
- financial market liberalisation,
- privatisation of production,
- "deregulation",
- foreign capital liberalisation (elimination of barriers to FDI),
- secure property rights,
- unified and competitive exchange rates,
- diminished public spending (fiscal discipline),
- public expenditure switching (to health, schooling and infrastructure),
- tax reform (broadening the tax base, cutting marginal tax rates, less progressive tax),
- a "social safety net" (selective state transfers for the needy), and
- flexible labour markets.

This last element has been expressed in numerous World Bank, IMF and OECD reports, and has generally meant policies designed to decentralise labour relations and cut protective and pro-collective regulations. To some it has meant little more than lower and more flexible wages coupled with less employment protection.

Note that while property rights have been stressed as essential for the overall framework, there has been no place for equivalent worker rights. And so it is perhaps not coincidence that in regional economic agreements, such as MERCOSUR, there has been a guaranteed right to free capital mobility, but no such right for workers. Finally, note the language. The term "deregulation" is put in quotation marks because in many respects it is a misnomer, just as the term "social safety net" is a euphemism suggesting broad support for those who fall off the globalising economy whereas it means a narrow, targeting approach.

An aspect of the set of prescriptions comprising the Washington Consensus is that for first time in history all countries were being encouraged to follow similar policies. This is relevant to the notion of globalisation. Thus, "shock therapy" was the form proposed for countries supposedly in "transition" from state socialism to capitalism. This was matched by "structural adjustment" advocated for developing countries, and by "supply-side economics" in industrialised countries. All had a similar rich array of common euphemisms, such as deregulation, social safety nets, employability, and active labour market policy. And it has been a feature of the approach that so much analysis and policy discussion has been conducted in terms of metaphors and catchy sound-bites.

A key part of the Washington Consensus and its progeny of shock therapy and structural adjustment is the sequencing of structural reforms. It is this which highlights the political objective. Countries being eased into the global economy have been expected to begin by liberalising prices and markets. This has tended to ignite inflationary pressures, threatening to lead to hyper-inflation. So, the next phase in the sequencing is macro-economic stabilisation, that is, a sharp deflation, cutting public expenditure and raising interest rates, pushing up unemployment and lowering the incomes of the poorer groups in society. Particularly in the ex-state-socialism countries, part of the process of cutting public expenditure has been a switch from universal schemes of income support to more selective, lower-cost schemes. There and in developing countries, with the higher poverty and unemployment resulting from the cut in public spending and stabilisation, the next phase has been introduction of a social safety net – a minimal support scheme to ease the burden on the poor. This has been seen as making the reform process sustainable.

The next phase in the sequencing is rapid privatisation, of economic activities and of social policies, in the spheres of education, health and social services. Only at the end of the sequencing has come restructuring of firms and institutions. This has meant that the state has been shrunk at the outset, so that making the reforms effective and equitable has been practically impossible. The desire for privatisation has been the dominant motive.

The Washington Consensus has been a set of policies that facilitated what has become known as globalisation. The midwife that eased the global economy into the era of globalisation was what has since been labelled "the international financial architecture", consisting of the international financial agencies (IFAs), mainly orchestrated from Washington DC, by the US Government, through the IMF and World Bank, and trickled down through regional development banks and linked to major national and regional monetary authorities such as the US Federal Reserve and latterly the European Central Bank. The GATT and then the World Trade Organisation have been instruments, but as the events in Seattle in late 1999 demonstrated, these have not been independent centres of powerful decision-making; they have been the mechanisms for putting strategic decisions into practice. The failure to achieve anything at Seattle was the result of a failure of governments and their representatives to agree on a common programme, not a reflection of a lack of power. It may not have been a coincidence that it coincided with the aftermath of the Asian financial and economic crisis, which threw the IFAs into confusion, and with a lack of clarity on the respective roles of the major IFAs.

The fact is that the era of market regulation has seen a substantial growth in the role and power of multilateral financial institutions, notably in establishing and enforcing an "international credit regime". Ostensibly financial bodies, their stretching tentacles have spread to practically everything to do with legal, institutional, political and social policy. They are accountable to a small elite and are dominated by a small circle of people with particular values. They have imposed structural adjustment and shock therapy strategies on numerous countries, often paying little heed to national cultural and institutional structures. It is significant that the teams of well-paid economists sent to prescribe policies and institutional change in various countries are described as on "mission".

In doing so, they have resorted to increasingly extensive conditionality in the provision of financial assistance to countries that are faced by an economic crisis (ironically often due to their becoming "open" when their economies were too fragile to sustain it). The conditionality must be unravelled, because it is steering political and social policy choice, and constraining consideration of alternative options. It affects everyone. In a globalising economy, imposing policies in one part of the world can influence the options and perspectives in other parts. Economists (and other social scientists) who shrink from this topic often do so in self-interest – they want a contract from one or other of those international financial agencies, and they want the kudos that go with invitations to those conferences, "missions" and seminars. This is not a cynical statement or merely a matter of polemics, since self-censorship on the part of social scientists is a vivid reality in the era of globalisation, and has contributed to its hegemony.

Conditionality has spread from financial commitments to broader economic goals and targets to the design of social protection policy, including commitments on the extent and pace of privatisation, and legal and political institutions and processes ("governance"). The motives may be well-intentioned benevolence. So are the dangers of paternalism. The missions and those responsible for them preach democracy, transparency and accountability, but only by stretching the meaning of the term could they be described as acting democratically in imposing the conditions on client governments. And conditionality is invidious, because it also allows certain policymakers to escape responsibility for their actions, since they can attribute an unpopular policy to the fact that the IMF, World Bank or other agency requires it to take them.

Conditionality has been one of the major instruments by which a single model of economic and social policy has been engineered. Talk of "best practices" and "sound policy" has its appeal in a context of democratic accountability. But linking aid to "best practices" as defined by some powerful interest group, or by the governments of a small number of rich countries, is at best merely paternalistic; it is ultimately corrosive of social responsibility and freedom.

At the end of the twentieth century, there was the mildly ludicrous spectacle of leading figures in international financial agencies stating that the World Bank should become "the knowledge bank" for the world. The thought of a sprawling bureaucracy – with its thousands of "staffers" allied with its thousands of "consultants", its conditionally financed "think tanks" and client central bankers and ministers of finance keen to retain its good will and support – should be enough to convince the liberal-minded that social policy should be prised away from these benevolent paternalists. They may have a role to play in global governance, but it should not be as producer or director of knowledge.

4 Fiscal Policy as Tax Competition

For many of the early years in the new era, changes in fiscal policy received less attention than they deserved. This may have reflected the arid and complex nature of fiscal policy, and the difficulty of making sense of the sparse and questionable data available. Of course, there was some attention paid to the claims that high and progressive taxes were deterring incentives to invest, save and labour and encouraging tax avoidance and evasion. But in general the increasingly regressive character of tax changes was allowed to continue with little critical evaluation. Perhaps the reason was that those best placed to understand the changes were among those who gained most from them. In any case, globalisation and the thrust of economic liberalisation have made fiscal policy more inegalitarian.

As has been well documented, there has been a shift of tax incidence from capital to labour, commonly rationalised on the grounds that for tax-raising efficiency purposes it makes sense to tax relatively immobile factors of production and reduce tax on factors that are relatively mobile. Even though governments have been cutting tax rates on capital and profits, and raising them on wages through higher payroll taxes, the total tax share from capital could rise because the functional income distribution has shifted in favour of capital.

As capital has become more mobile, the argument goes, it should be taxed less because otherwise it will flee the country. The effect has been that, even though the pre-tax share of GDP going to capital has increased (reflecting widening functional income inequality), the share of total tax revenue derived from capital has declined in industrialised countries, and in many others. There has been a sharp increase in the share of tax revenue coming from payroll taxes (commonly called "social security", although this is a misnomer, along with its implicit core concept of "social insurance"). In the European Union, the effective tax on labour rose to 40 per cent of the wage bill by the end of the century. And there has been a rise coming from consumption (mainly VAT). So, while payroll taxes rose from 18 per cent of total tax revenue in 1965 to 25 per cent in 1995, consumption taxes rose from 12 per cent to 18 per cent. These trends must be seen in the context of a rise in the tax share of GDP in that period and a fall in capital taxation.

While these regressive trends were gathering pace, a powerful and rein-forcing trend towards international tax competition has emerged, which has had considerable implications for resource allocation and for income distribution. It has been argued, with empirical support, that changes in tax systems have made the effective tax on capital practically zero. A major cause of this was the US government's abolition in 1984 of withholding tax on interest paid to foreigners, since when no major capital-importing country has been able to impose such a tax for fear of capital flight. This means that people can earn investment income free of host-country taxation in any of the world's major economies.[6] As for foreign direct investment, over 100 countries were offering generous "tax holidays" (nice euphemism) for foreign corporations, while several have established themselves as "production tax havens" (including Ireland and Belgium), so that corporations can establish their nominal headquarters there without being taxable. A further sign of the times was the report that seven of the top US corporations, including the world's biggest corporation, General Motors, actually paid less than zero in federal income taxes, because of rebates.[7]

Economic liberalisation has tended to make tax competition more per-vasive. For instance, the progressive removal of tariff barriers as part of the GATT-WTO process has meant that there is much less pressure on firms to make direct investment in countries where they have a substantial market, or where they want to have one. They can thus choose where to set up or to expand depending on fiscal enticements. This might explain why capital mobility seems to have become more sensitive to fiscal policy in recent years.

The tendency of globalisation to proceed via the strengthening of regional blocs has led to rationalised cuts in levels of taxation to make their zones more competitive and more integrated. Thus, the countries in the Eurozone agreed in 1999 to reduce taxes, limit government spending and cut public deficits. Politicians gladly adopted the language of the need to cut "the tax burden", a delightfully appropriate euphemism. Literally, it means the ratio of tax receipts to GDP. It is ideological to describe this ratio as a burden, just as it would be to describe it as the opposite of burden, whatever that is. The tax ratio reflects a society's way of paying for its hospitals, schools, roads, railways, sewage works and environmental protection. These are not some-thing one necessarily wants to cut. The words "tax burden" are loaded because they convey an ideological hostility to public goods and services. Who could possibly want a "burden"? So, in their zeal – and manifestly limited imagination – governments are cutting income taxes, corporate taxes and other taxes. If they then want to cut "public deficits", they will either have to borrow more (as the USA has done through capital inflows) or cut back on hospitals, roads, and so on. Who bears the burden of that?

Because fiscal policy has become part of the response to globalisation, the perception has also grown among politicians and commentators that there is an upper limit on the level of social protection and extent of redistributive policy. It is a matter of speculation why the subject of fiscal policy as an arm of national competitiveness has not crept up the policy agenda among those who profess concern for poverty, inequality and social solidarity. It should do so.

5 Social and Labour Policies of the Era

In the 1980s, as part of the emerging debate on economic liberalisation and supply-side economics, profound changes took place in the norms of social protection policy, labour regulations and labour market policy. The main motives for the main changes were a desire to cut rising unemployment – due partly to the abandonment of Keynesianism and the operation of deflationary macro-economic policy that led to a structurally low level of aggregate demand – and the desire to make national economies more "competitive". The latter was not a powerful notion in the post-1945 era, but became remarkably influential in the last two decades of the century.

Competitiveness has become a classic euphemism, for acceptance of the Washington consensus represented a shift in thinking encapsulated by that seductive word. It is a macho notion, separating the political realists from the naïve, the men from the boys. Who could be against being more competitive? We all have to be more competitive "if we want to survive". The "more" refers both to our past and present situation and to the levels or capacities of others, be they other firms and other workers or other countries and regions of the world. The need to be more competitive has been used to justify numerous reforms and a reordering of priorities.

Ironically, the labour securities that were held out as the primary objectives of the post-war era became perceived or presented as obstacles to economic growth and national competitiveness, derided as "non-wage labour costs" to be reduced. The colourful image of Eurosclerosis came to life in the 1980s, seized upon by the political right. It was used to suggest an elderly arthritic man, suffering from a stiffening of the sinews and an inability to summon up the blood. In the 1990s, social democrats embraced its central message. It went with a new-found desire to celebrate the entrepreneurs and to be "pro-business", because "they produce the wealth" and give a country its competitiveness.

A wholesale re-regulation process was launched around the world based on the appeal of deregulation, as a mechanism for removing "rigidities" that were allegedly impeding competitiveness. The misuse of words was mischievous. There is no such thing as a deregulated labour market. What happened was that there was a shift from pro-collective regulations to pro-individualistic regulations, and from systems based strongly on protective statutory regulations to the increasing use of fiscal measures to regulate behaviour, and limit the freedom of workers.

In this, what happened in Chile in the 1970s and 1980s was immensely influential. The Pinochet regime was remarkable for being an archetypal test case of the Washington Consensus, being orchestrated by US economists and their Latin American students. The Pinochet regime did not deregulate. It first emaciated the strong rights of freedom of association, banning trade unions by laws, and then once the radical strength had been crushed allowed carefully curtailed rights through the legislated enforcement of decentralised company-level unions.

In most parts of the world, such draconian measures were not required. But the strategy was always one of restructuring regulations, rather than anything like deregulation. The US and UK Governments of the 1980s did not deregulate; they introduced reforms, as did governments in other countries, to curtail the strength of collective representation and limit the protective rights of workers, sometimes weakening employment protection, sometimes limiting the right to strike. In all of this, there was a strong international trend to curtail the rights of collective labour, and to introduce regulations to facilitate and promote individual risk-taking behaviour.

This is why it is appropriate to call the latter part of the twentieth century the era of market regulation. Statutory reforms curtailed labour rights while strengthening market mechanisms, by the use of fiscal and directive measures – using taxes, subsidies and transfers to steer workers' and citizens' behaviour, either to perform more labour or to withdraw from the labour market altogether.

The slow shift in social protection policy was also profound, and is reviewed later. Essentially, it became part of regulation policy. The most important trends were (i) piecemeal partial privatisation of social protection, a process that was also given a boost by Chile, through its famous pension privatisation, (ii) a shift from universalistic systems to more selective schemes, mainly from insurance to assistance-type benefits, and (iii) a shift from income support given as a citizenship right, with moderate conditions, to schemes that applied more and tighter conditions, limiting entitlements.

The language of social policy became heavily loaded.[8] Words such as "targeting" became popular, so that "targeting on the poor" became a euphemism for means-tested assistance schemes that ostensibly reached the poor and only the poor. Schemes with moderate conditions came to be called "passive", while schemes to impose obligations and direct behaviour were called "active". The art has been to say "passive policy" with tight lips or a slight sneer, and say "active" with a lift of the eyebrows, a stretch of the neck and a lift in the tone of voice. Who could be in favour of passive when you could be active? The macho virility of the term is enough to convince many commentators of its appropriateness and to inhibit potential sceptics. Image matters, just like size. Never mind that the evidence to justify the faith in the success of "active labour market policy" is hard to find, and that numerous costly empirical studies have shown very large deadweight and substitution effects, meaning that the costs of jobs supposedly created by such schemes have been very high. Extending active policies is showing that something is being done.

The scornful tone is deliberate, because the youth of the world who have been the main targets of the active policies deserve better than the presumption that they are scarcely employable, unprepared and often unwilling to work. Often the supporters of active policy are well-meaning and only reluctantly accept "compulsion". But behind active labour market policies has been a middle-class presumption that a significant minority of people, most of them young and unlike themselves, are in need of integration into a labouring society. We will return to this in chapter 7.

6 Global Labour Flexibility[9]

In the 1980s and 1990s, there were developments in production and labour markets that had not been remotely anticipated in the preceding era – labour flexibility and economic informalisation. For our purposes, there are three outcomes to be kept in mind.

First, there has been the emergence of global managerialism. Technological changes, economic reforms and structural changes have allowed many more managerial options, in terms of organisational structures, relations of production, locational choices and speeds of relocation. If one desired option is not available or possible in one place, firms can shift quite easily and without great cost, at the margin or completely. This has sharply altered bargaining powers in favour of managers and in favour of controlling shareholders, and has accelerated globalisation.

Second, and related to the first trend, there has been what can be called a growth of global flexibility in production systems and labour arrangements. The growth has been pervasive in all parts of the world. One can identify seven forms of flexibility, which give a context for assessing mechanisms of social protection and economic security:

- *organisational flexibility* – more turnover of firms, more use of subcontracting and production "chains", and a tendency to contract out the employment function;
- *numerical flexibility* – more use of external labour, such as contract workers, outworkers, homeworkers, agency labour, temporary workers, and teleworkers;
- *functional flexibility* – more changes in work tasks, job rotation, and skill for individual workers;
- *job structure flexibility* – more changes in the structure of jobs, associated with changes in job titles, number of them, etc.;
- *working time flexibility* – more continuous working, flexible hours, etc.;
- *wage system flexibility* – a shift from fixed to flexible wages, monetisation of remuneration, greater use of bonuses, etc.;
- *labour force flexibility* – less attachment to sectors, companies or occupational groups, erosion of "collective labour", and greater tendency for workers to move in and out of the labour market and labour force.

Flexibility has become one of those powerful words that shape policy and public perceptions. As the term gained in power, politicians, economists and commentators first attributed their country's economic ills to a lack of flexibility, and then took care to claim that their country had more flexibility

than others, stating this as a means of justifying claims that foreign investment should come to their country. The reality is that across the world, even
in developing countries where they have always been flexible, labour markets
and labour forces have become more flexible in all respects. Yet nobody
seems to have asked the obvious question: Could there be too much flexibility? Like Dickens' Oliver, all economists have asked for is "more". Basic
school physics teach us that a highly flexible system is also a highly unstable
one. To read most economists, politicians and commentators, you would
suppose that this does not apply to labour markets.

The third major trend has been what might be called global informalisation.
Those economists who were taught development economics in the post-1945
era were imbued with the models of Ricardo, Arthur Lewis and others, in
which development meant a steady transfer of surplus "informal" labour to
"formal" wage labour. By the early 1970s, there were worries about the slow
pace of the process. The misleading notion of the "informal sector" emerged,
first associated with survival activity and then as a source of economic
growth, leading to a romanticised image of untapped dynamic potential. In
the 1980s, partly because of the effect of structural adjustment strategies and
partly because of changes in the structure of production, the informal sector
became perceived as the main source of employment in developing countries
and an increasing source almost everywhere. By the end of the century, in
developing countries there was no longer an expectation that a majority of
workers would transfer into regular, regulated, unionised jobs. Extensive and
growing informalisation was a reality. This was also the case in industrialised
countries, and in so-called transition countries, where the huge old state
enterprises were dissolving and where petty survival activities and small-scale
firms were hastening to fill the gap.

The world seemed to be facing the prospect of spreading informalisation,
more flexible labour systems and more unstable labour markets. The sirens
of flexibility were in danger of luring humanity onto the rocks of insecurity.
There is no need for despair, but there is a need to understand the character
of the challenge that these changes represent, which is the objective of the
next chapter. There is also one aspect of the developments that deserves
special emphasis.

This is what is elsewhere described as feminisation.[10] The term may jar,
but is intended to convey the double meaning of what has been happening.
Although women have continued to face discrimination and disadvantage
across the world, they have been drawn into labour force activities alongside
men. In many countries the female labour force participation rate has risen
steadily, while the male equivalent has fallen, and the female open unemployment rate has fallen relative to the male. This is one aspect of
feminisation. At the same time, and partly explaining the gender changes in
labour markets, the type of jobs traditionally pushed onto women has been
spreading relative to the type taken by men. Jobs are being feminised, in that
a growing proportion are precarious, low paying and low status. This
feminisation is a primary feature of the global flexibility and informalisation.
It is in turn shaping policy dilemmas and institutional options.

7 Social Dumping

In the 1980s, and more sharply in the 1990s, economic liberalisation produced a predictable phenomenon sometimes given the colourful name of
social dumping. In order to attract FDI, to curb import penetration, to
increase the country's share of international trade and to raise economic
growth, governments increasingly resorted to policies to lower labour
standards, to cut levels of social protection, and to alter labour regulations to
make them more attractive to national and foreign firms relative to those
found in potentially competitive countries.

The extent to which social dumping has occurred is controversial. But it is
what one would expect in an internationally open economic system,
particularly at a time when workers' bargaining strength has been weakening.
Empirically, it is hard to assess the extent of social dumping, because so
much of the changes will have been pre-emptive, meaning that the fear of
being made "less competitive" would induce changes that would be copied
elsewhere, leaving relatively little effect on investment and trade but leaving
a lower level of protection in general. As a result, one can predict that social
dumping will lead to a convergence on types and levels of labour regulation,
social protection and fiscal policy.[11] This is what seems to have been
occurring, with implications considered in the next two chapters.

8 Conclusions

Globalisation has created intellectual confusion. Many commentators assert
with confidence that it opens up more freedom and choice for more people
than at any time in history. Yet it is also claimed that it puts unprecedented
constraints on what choices governments, firms and individuals can make. In
particular, it is suggested that governments cannot maintain or introduce
policies that diverge from something close to an international norm. The
words that come from politicians and their bureaucrats are harmonisation,
convergence and standardisation. These are not the words that spring to
mind when considering freedom and choice.

The euphemism of a social safety net has been a key to the process of
globalisation. Developing countries finding themselves destabilised by global
economic forces have had to turn to the IMF, and by one means or another
have been obliged to accept a set of prescribed reforms and a particular
sequencing of such reforms. These have brought hardships for many, usually
presented as a short-term pain for longer-term gain. To counter that,
advocates of the international strategy have emphasised the need for short-
term social safety net measures to alleviate the increased poverty, usually
involving some means-tested minimum income scheme, or a social fund or
workfare scheme. Such schemes are typically just short-term palliatives, often
expensive, rarely effective and commonly inequitable.

Meanwhile, industrialised countries have also been put under pressure to
adopt policies and institutions deemed to be the norms desired by inter-

national financial centres and by major multinational corporations, and by the rich men linked to them. They too have been urged to opt for a safety-net approach to social protection, and to opt for labour market regulations that promote economic growth rather than labour security. It is hard to imagine that anything other than greater social and economic insecurity would be the outcome of such changes. And this is what has happened.

3

The Spread of Labour Insecurity

1 Introduction

By contrast with the preceding era of statutory regulation, the era of globalisation, flexible labour markets and advancing informalisation ushered in one of those historical periods of spreading social and economic insecurity. The adverse trends are unsustainable in the longer term, but unless addressed satisfactorily are tragically unsettling and will unnecessarily ruin the lives of millions of people in the shorter term. This chapter summarises the main trends. In doing so, some of the nuances of inter-country variation will be overlooked, but this may be acceptable if the narrative tells the essential or modal tendencies.

Chapter 1 suggested that the key to understanding the two labourist models of development pursued during the middle decades of the twentieth century was the pursuit of seven forms of labour-based security, with primacy given to labour market security. A basic thesis stemming from the era of market regulation outlined in chapter 2 is that globalisation, flexible labour markets, and economic informalisation – and the policies and institutional changes that have gone with those trends – have ushered in an era of intensified human insecurity. No strategy should have much appeal unless it manages to address that pattern of insecurity, and in order to develop a strategy it is essential to recognise the nature of the challenge.

The primary claim made in this chapter is that in the late twentieth century trends in all seven forms of labour security went into reverse, and in many respects differences between groups in their subjective and objective security became substantially greater. We will briefly review the stylised facts in each case.

2 Labour Market Insecurity

The story is familiar. The commitment to Full Employment – always a sexist notion – was turned into a hollow gesture in the 1970s and 1980s, or dropped altogether. The reversal of Keynesian targeting meant that levels of employment and unemployment were made the responsibility of the *behaviour* of workers and firms and the structure of regulations and institutions. Even where Finance Ministers spoke the talk, they walked away from adjusting monetary and fiscal policy to try to produce or maintain anything like Full Employment. This changed in the late 1990s.

Let us begin by recalling the stylised facts. Open unemployment rates rose in most parts of the world, and although they subsequently fell back in the USA and then eventually in the UK, even there the much refined figures still meant that about one in every twenty-five workers was unemployed, or one in every twenty if account were taken of discouraged potential labour force participants. In most industrialised countries in the 1980s, unemployment rates rose to levels that for many years after 1945 had been regarded as no more than nightmarish recollections of the 1930s. By the end of the century, some countries had managed to alter their statutory, labour market and social protection structures so as to massage their unemployment rates down. But in most countries the levels were still much higher than they had been forty years earlier.

In countries undergoing a "transition" from state socialism to a market economy, unemployment rose to levels that were unimaginable a few years earlier, and the levels were substantially under-recorded. In industrialising countries, urban unemployment rates rose in most parts of the world, and rural unemployment tended to rise as more people were loosened from the land. In the world's most populous country, China, a huge number of unemployed were quietly recognised, but all informed observers knew that many millions more were only kept out of unemployment by being retained in enterprises as surplus labour, in virtual unemployment.

As the situation in China and major eastern European countries such as Russia and Ukraine testify, the open unemployment figure can be seriously misleading as a measure of labour slack. In economies based on full-time industrial employment, the unemployment rate is a reasonable proxy for labour surplus and labour market security. But in both developing countries and those in which flexible labour relations predominate, it is quite unreasonable. This has not stopped policymakers, commentators and social theorists from continuing to focus on unemployment. But it is about time to think of better indexes of labour market insecurity. No ideal proxy has been proposed.

Here is not the place to propose an alternative index for all types of economy. But an alternative suitable for industrialised countries is worth presenting, since it points to the changes in labour market insecurity that have occurred in recent years. For this, it is essential to adjust both the unemployment and employment measures.

In the case of the unemployed, one should treat those who are looking only for part-time jobs as half in the labour force and half out of it. The unemployed should also include those who want or need employment but who have given up looking, or have not started, because of discouragement. In the case of employment, those who are employed part-time who want full-time employment but cannot obtain it for economic (demand) reasons should be counted as half in employment and half in unemployment. And those who are on layoff from employment should not be counted as employed but as unemployed. Those working short-time for economic reasons should also be called partially employed, partially unemployed. Those working part-time voluntarily should be counted as half in employment and half outside the labour force.

Taking account of these different patterns of labour force participation, one can calculate a labour slack rate. Although this need not be the case, it turns out that for European Union countries this gives higher levels of labour market insecurity than the conventional unemployment rate, which seems realistic. And in the countries that have supposedly had "good" employment performances, most notably the Netherlands, the difference between the two proxy indexes of such insecurity has tended to grow. In most EU countries, unemployment and labour slack levels both tended to fall in the late 1990s, but they remained much higher than in the 1960s and 1970s. Figure 3.1 portrays the changes in unemployment rates and labour slack rate in some EU member countries since the 1980s.

It is also apparent that the growth in employment, hardly impressive, has been less than implied by the standard statistics, since a growing proportion of the total has consisted of part-time jobs. It is reasonable to suggest that a part-time job is the equivalent of half a full-time one (and part-time jobs are therefore expressed in ful-time equivalent numbers). If that is accepted, then one can see that the job machine across western Europe has been unimpressive by its own standards, as the graphs in figure 3.2 show.

These are what might be called "objective" indices. There are also subjective measures to take into account. For some reason, according to opinion polls, ordinary people who do not know much about the statistics often think that the actual level of unemployment is much higher than the official statistics suggest. One may speculate on the reasons for this. But it does suggest that subjective labour market insecurity may be even higher than is implied by those objective indices.

One factor is that, because orthodox economic analysis has attributed unemployment to the rigid and slow-learning behaviour of workers and firms, it has been relatively easy for commentators to describe the outcome as "voluntary" unemployment. This increases the stigmatisation of unemployment, because it implies it is a reflection of inadequate or incorrect behaviour. If governments and commentators then attribute unemployment to "generosity of unemployment benefits", they are further accentuating the social threat of unemployment, by suggesting that the experience of it will be financially hard to bear.

In central and eastern Europe, developments have been spectacularly worse than in western Europe. Few commentators outside seem to have noticed. In most countries, the decade following the fall of the Berlin Wall was marked by a huge rise in open unemployment. In some, including Russia and Ukraine, the two biggest countries, the rise was artificially disguised by poor statistics. But the situation was much worse than could be explained by those. The main reason was that most of the labour surplus took the forms of long-term unpaid leave – or lay-offs – and non-payment of wages and fringe benefits. In 1999, for example, four out of every five factories had not paid the wages of workers for an average of five months.[1] In central Europe, open unemployment was much more common, and widespread.

Figure 3.1. Indicators of labour market insecurity (unemployment and labour slack), European Community, 1983–99

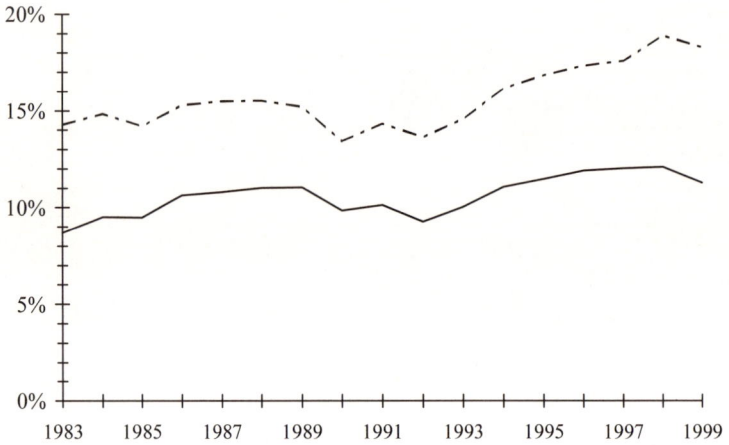

Italy

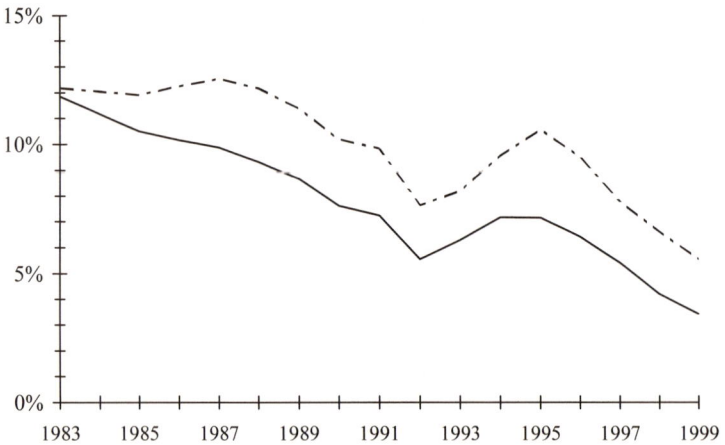

Netherlands

Source: Eurostat LFS data

Figure 3.1. (*continued*)

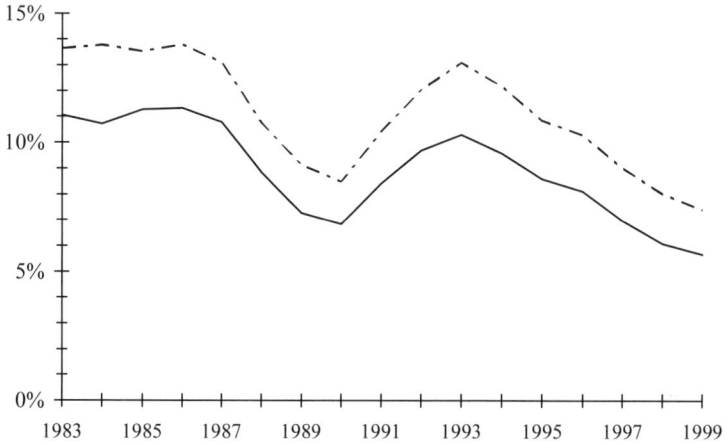

UK

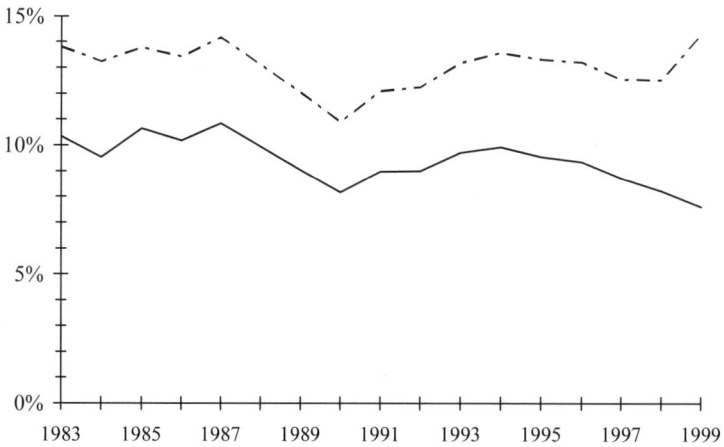

Total, all EC countries

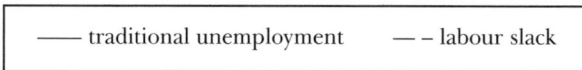

——— traditional unemployment   — — labour slack

Source: Eurostat LFS data

Figure 3.2. Total employment and its full-time equivalent, European Union countries, 1983–99

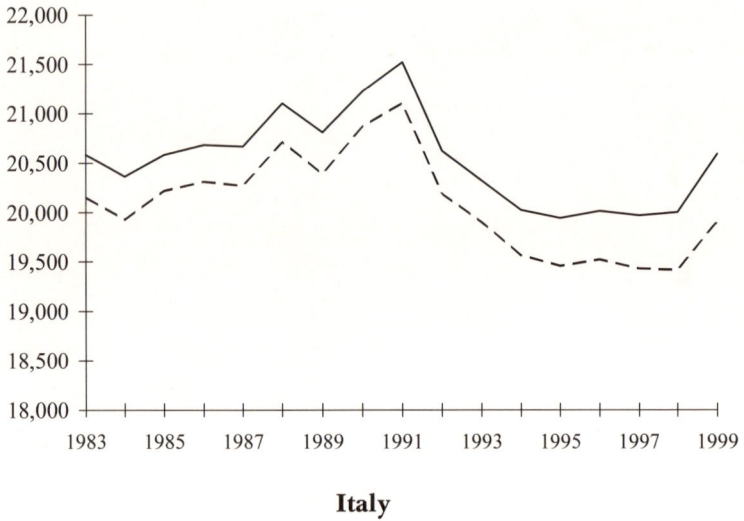

Italy

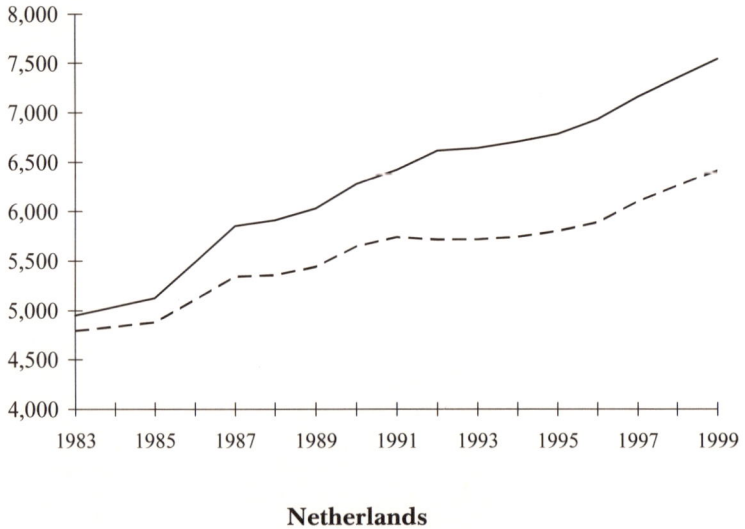

Netherlands

————— employment   — — employment full-time equivalent

Source: Eurostat LFS data

Figure 3.2. (continued)

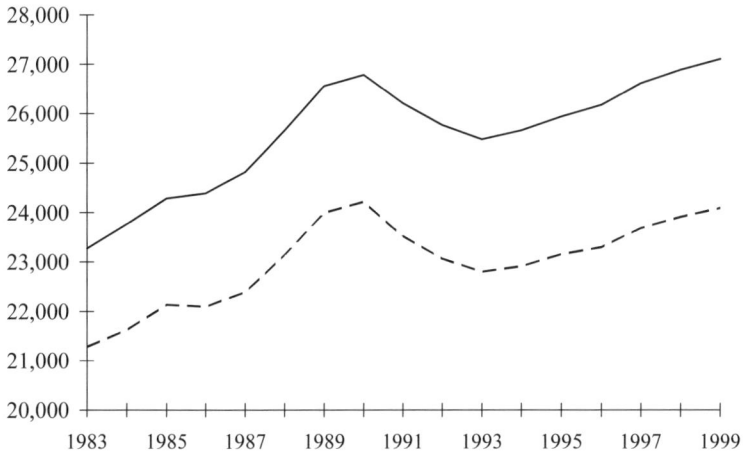

UK

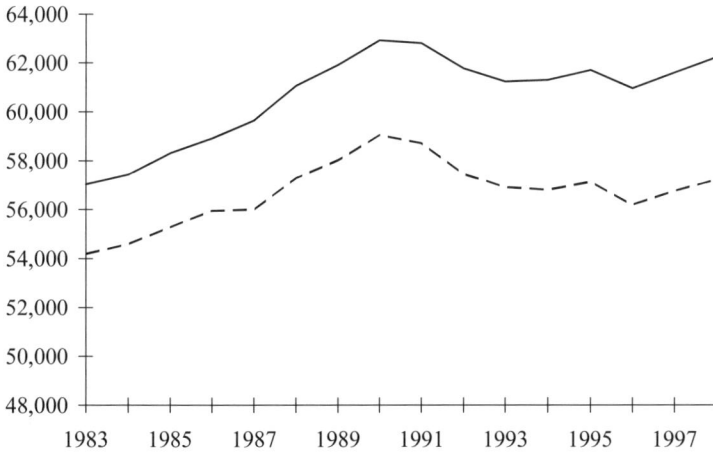

Total

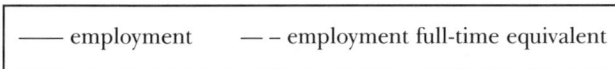

Source: Eurostat LFS data

In developing countries, the pattern was more mixed. In most regions, the 1980s and 1990s were marked by rises in unemployment, to the extent that we can be reasonably confident on the basis of available statistics. The exceptions included most countries of eastern Asia. In China, the situation was much worse than official statistics suggested, for reasons that were similar to those in eastern Europe. Surplus labour in the massive enterprises was a phenomenon waiting to explode into the open. Elsewhere, numerous workers made redundant drifted into the informal economy or back to their villages. Meanwhile, in most of Latin America and the Caribbean open unemployment rates rose, as they did in much of Africa and the Middle East.

In short, globally, there were many millions of people unemployed at the end of the century, more than at any time in human history. Many millions more were in various forms of "underemployment". Labour market insecurity had become the global norm. Governments in some parts of the world could point to a decline in open unemployment in the last few years of the twentieth century. But besides the special US case, sustained by a substantial expansionary fiscal policy (underpinned by the earned-income tax credit) and a balance of payments deficit that no other country could contemplate, there are awkward aspects of this improvement, to the extent that it is an improvement. There should be a concern that it represents a new trade-off in which other forms of security are eroded.

Altering the dynamics between unemployment and wages, by such measures as decentralisation of wage bargaining, tightening of eligibility to state benefits, and cuts in tax rates and social security contributions, may indeed lower unemployment.[2] But we need to know the trade-offs in order to decide whether growth in other forms of insecurity is worth the small gains in labour market security. This issue has been given little attention by commentators or economists.

In 2000, two "think tanks" – one set up by the British Government, the other by the French – issued a report claiming that "full employment is achievable". The Policy Network and the Conseil d'Analyse Economique (actually, Geoff Mulgan, Richard Layard and Jean Pisani-Fery) asserted that it could be obtained by removing labour market rigidities, compelling the unemployed to take jobs and giving them "more active help" in finding jobs. They also advocated improving "fiscal competitiveness" and, in order to raise labour force participation rates, ending early retirement incentives. This supply-side perspective was a far cry from the social democratic strategy of the era of statutory regulation. If the market does not clear, let us clear the market. The underlying paternalism of this response to labour market insecurity should prompt us to ask: Is the question the right one? Full employment is always achievable. But the technocrats should be asked to indicate the point at which its achievement would be acceptable. Middle-class, middle-aged men have always been eager to prescribe a dose of compulsion for "the poor", for their own good, of course.

3 Employment Insecurity

In spite of the explicit commitment to employment security in many societies, not even in highly industrialised countries was there ever a period in which most workers had strong employment security, in which they had strong protection against dismissal or sudden loss of employment for some other reason. But there was long an image or expectation that employment security was possible, that a growing number of workers would have secure well-paid employment, and that acquisition of middle-class salaried status would ensure that security. No more. The trend has been reversed, so that – possibly even more than has actually been the case – there is now the expectation that in the future there will be less employment security than twentieth century "salary man" had taken as the anchor of his life.

In many countries, there has been explicit erosion of employment security through legislative reforms weakening employment protection, openly encouraged by international financial agencies and numerous well-protected commentators. The explicit erosion has also been the result of extensive concession bargaining by unions and workers, in some cases giving up employment security in return for money wages. And there has been implicit erosion of protection through a drift from the type of jobs that had seemed protected, by statutory regulation and by collective agreement, to those forms of labour that had little or no such protection. And there has also been a less noticed drift from labour contracts, which have characterised traditional employment relationships, to commercial contracts, individual agreements between firms or intermediaries and individuals for the provision of services, leading to consideration of new enforcement mechanisms that have made employment more contingent on performance and the individual matching of obligations to performance.

The simple fact is that employment security has never been the experience, or expectation, of the vast majority of workers in most parts of the world. For a time, it was not too fanciful to depict a distant future in which a majority would have such security. But by the end of the century commentators and policymakers no longer expected it to become the norm for the majority. Even in highly industrialised countries, only a minority of adults had stable, regular, full-time jobs. This does not mean that in those countries a majority are now living in chronic economic insecurity. It does mean that more people are deriving whatever security they achieve from something other than employment security. It also means that more are dependent on other sources of support, whether successfully or not.

For a time, employment security was a feature of being middle class, but there is ample evidence that it has been declining, even though in 2000 several reports suggested that the tight labour market had slowed the trend in the USA. There are reasons to expect that erosion to continue. And, as suggested later, the reality of employment security may be undesirable.

4 Job Insecurity

Never strong for the majority of people anywhere, early in the twentieth century, job security was conceded or drastically weakened by Taylorism and variants of so-called scientific management. This sought to extend the technical and social divisions of labour, so that workers did with their hands what managers did in their heads.[3] Specialists and the specialised evolved together. And then trade unions tended to defend the existing division of labour through demarcation rules and a patchwork of collective agreements at national, sectoral and local levels. The resulting job security was artificial and rigid, and brittle.

In the last few decades of the twentieth century, defensive rules and agreements were chipped away. They have been further eroded by outsourcing and other forms of external labour flexibility and by the spread of functional flexibility, with the expectation that more workers will be moved between jobs and will have to change the range of tasks on the job in a whirl of adaptation.

"Make yourself adaptable" has been the exhortation to the young and the old. There has been no equivalent public exhortation to firms to make jobs more adaptable to the needs and aspirations of people. By the end of the century this had evolved into a new euphemism – employability – to which we will return.

Job insecurity represents the loss of a sense of occupation, or vocation. It means the absence of identity, or a loss of identity, as a worker defined in terms of an occupation. The hesitancy with which people describe themselves may be a rough guide to this absence or loss of identity. The acquisition of such an identity is the main topic of the final part of this book.

5 Skill Reproduction Insecurity

The sense of skill is a sensitive barometer of the nature of work in society. It is a peculiar feature of statistics and modern thinking that, although there is an extraordinary amount of noise about the need for more skills, there is no country in the world with comprehensive statistics on the level or distribution of skills in the population. Statistically, we simply do not know about the skills people possess. At best, all we have is rough information on the structure of jobs and employment, and some usually incomplete information on the level of formal schooling completed by the population. This has not stopped politicians, social scientists and commentators from repeating the persistent reference to "skill shortages" and "structural unemployment".

Despite the lack of aggregative statistics, there are strong grounds for believing that modern, flexible economies have turned the notion of skill more into a narrow functionalism. The ancient sense of "craft" or vocation has been eroded, symbolised in part by the virtual collapse of apprenticeship as a system of training. The mysteries of a craft are often derided, or let to fade; the technical expertise to perform and to execute a job is elevated, with what some call social skills displacing technical capacities. For many workers, vocational training has been absent, while there has been a shift to job training and its surrogate, labour market training, carried out by or on behalf of state authorities, often heavily subsidised by public funds.

To compound the challenge, information technology appears to have been accelerating the rate at which skills become obsolescent. It seems that, as a result, skill development and reproduction are less embedded in occupational competencies. The notion of modular training is symptomatic of that, as is the pressure to create more and more jobs. It surely has not helped the development or maintenance of a culture of skill formation and respect for the discipline of occupation that many countries have introduced "special schemes" called labour market training measures ("active") that have been little more than thinly disguised attempts to reduce the unemployment count. Cynical policies may have wondrous effects, but securing youthful adherence to a culture of learning is not one of them.

More flexible labour markets seem more easily to marginalise those with low levels of skill in the technical sense of the term. The apparently growing incidence of churning of firms, bubbling into existence and then disappearing shortly afterwards, and the spread of smaller units within enterprises, have tended to curb the extent of enterprise-based vocational training, partly because there is the expectation of a shorter period in which to recover the economic returns to training, partly because of a fear of poaching of trainees, partly because high unemployment suggests that skilled labour is easily available if needed, and partly because technological change makes today's skills tomorrow's embarrassments.

Schooling seems increasingly to have been displacing education. Schools and even universities seem almost frantically designed as the means of preparing young people for jobs, to produce "human capital".[4] Schooling aptly has a double meaning in the English language, meaning both to learn and be tamed, as in "schooling a horse". The dictates of efficiency and rates of return to school have little respect for contemplation and "idle curiosity". In the individualised societies of the early twenty-first century, the young thinking about their education are expected to look at the costs and their burdening debts from the loans on which they have to depend. As a consequence, market mechanisms will ensure that the young will gravitate to subjects and courses that hold out the prospect of the highest rate of private economic return. One wonders what this is doing for the culture of work.

6 Work Insecurity

Occupational health and safety is another one of those areas where available statistics conceal as much as they reveal. Statistics on accident rates and occupational injuries and diseases do exist, and on the surface these provide some grounds for encouragement about recent trends in many countries, which show declines in accident rates. In recent years, the number injured in work-related accidents per 100,000 insured or employed has declined in EU countries, and also in central Europe.[5]

In part, this reflects industrial restructuring and the decline of heavy manual jobs; these have been major factors in central and eastern Europe since 1990 or thereabouts. But more flexible labour markets have also been associated with an erosion of institutional safeguards – voice mechanisms that can prevent the imposition of onerous working conditions and dangerous work schedules, that can keep the issues under scrutiny, and that can prevent workers from taking unnecessary or excessive risks or working excessively long because they need or desire more money income.

In some countries, there has been explicit erosion of work security because of cuts in statutory regulation. Perhaps more influential has been implicit erosion, due to the spread of forms of labour traditionally less protected or less easily protected. Establishing adequate procedures in small firms is hard, and ensuring that contract workers and other outworkers have adequate safety and access to mechanisms to limit work insecurity is harder than for those in regular wage labour.

With more flexible production, with numerous smaller firms, with lower levels of trade unionism and with an ethos regarding statutory regulations as labour costs, the pressures on firms to provide work security has been reduced. Most worrying has been the virtual collapse of safety and health committees in many factories in countries of the former Soviet Union, as we observed in several enterprise surveys.

In general, with more labour market insecurity and non-regular labour, there is a greater threat to occupational safety and health because safeguards do not cover some categories and because their weak bargaining position induces them to accept more onerous or risky labour. Thus, a report by the World Health Organisation concluded that as a result of flexibilisation of labour contracts there had been a substantial increase in work-related accidents, most notably among the self-employed in the construction industry.

Shadow work, or undeclared employment, definitionally blocks entitlement to health or disability insurance, and has also been associated with more exposure to toxic substances and related dangers. In the USA and elsewhere, part-time workers are also less likely to be covered by health insurance than full-time workers.[6] Teleworking also brings work security risks. Among these are onerous conditions imposed in offshore information processing in developing countries, where jobs have involved long unsocial hours, health hazards and low wages.[7]

A popular term in the 1990s was self-regulation, the idea that individual workers should be encouraged to learn and apply their own safety practices, and that this should be in place of complex rules and procedures developed under the umbrella of statutory regulation. There is no reason to accept that this erosion of formal protection is beneficial for work security, although it is consistent with a reduction in the costs and in transferring to workers much of the cost of attaining work security and compensating for the consequences of work insecurity. In effect, there has been a privatisation of the costs of providing work security, helping to lower those non-wage labour costs that are supposed to undermine "competitiveness".

The statistics may also be misleading us and may further be leading us to look at the wrong symptoms. The data needed are what have been called "elusive statistics". Studies have indicated that injuries and illnesses associated with labour are more systematically under-reported for those working in flexible and informal labour statuses than in the so-called standard forms of employment. They are more under-reported for women than for men, and for ethnic minorities, migrants and non-unionised workers. All of these groups have grown proportionately in most workforces, which implies that the recorded rate of occupational illness and injury will be an increasingly inaccurate proxy for the actual rate, and that those most at risk may not be shown as such in conventional statistics. It is also easier in flexible labour markets for firms to ease out workers deemed to be high-risk, or simply to avoid employing them.

Besides these failings, much more attention should be given to other aspects of work insecurity linked to the intensification of labour. There is ample anecdotal evidence that those in flexible labour statuses are relatively prone to suffer from stress, and, particularly in the case of so-called "teleworkers" and other outworkers, from the corrosive effects of social isolation.[8] Those finding themselves in these positions can be expected to be exploited in various ways, notably by elaborate and contrived piece-rate payment systems and high-tech controls. They can also expect to suffer from creeping self-exploitation, losing touch with social reality as they struggle against some unknown but deeply imagined norm of effort and performance. This is particularly likely to become acute for anyone living alone, or who have children to support or who have little or no social life.

It is all very well for commentators to claim or to presume that flexi-workers have a choice. Without protective voice, in the form of an organis-ation representing their interests in bargaining over wages, benefits and working conditions, and without basic economic security, the choice is likely to be a pitifully narrow one.

Indeed, work insecurity could also be expected to accompany erosion of representation security. In the UK, the TUC has reported that injury rates are twice as high in firms where there is no union–employer safety com-mittee as where there is one.[9] In the USA, work-related fatalities have been much higher in "right-to-work" states, where unions have been prevented from pressing collective safety demands as effectively as in other states.[10] The problem extends to the basic right to go to the toilet, which many workers do not have, and which can cause illness and penalties. A toilet break is not a general right under Federal law or under the law of most States. Firms often argue that giving such a right would encourage shirking and loss of managerial control. In recent years, over 40 per cent of collective agreements have not included a right to a rest period, and in non-union plants the pattern has been worse.[11]

Then there is what might be called labourholism – were it not such an ugly and unmelodic word. The pressure to work needs to be tempered, for otherwise the "incentives" and inducements can become overwhelming. We may feel that we have to work long hours in our job and to put in "overtime" in order to retain "employability". The long-hours culture is a peculiar aspect of globalisation, even though there have always been men and women who have ploughed through their lives like drone bees. The culture is new in its global connectedness (*sic*) – linking up numerous individuals in a noise of emails, e-commerce, websites and networks.

Explicit erosion of work security may have been increased by reforms to make working time more flexible and to weaken protective regulations over working time. This has meant that firms have been able to adjust work time to suit their needs, rather than the workers' desire for a stable or predictable schedule. More workers are obliged to work long shifts or "unsocial hours", surely causing physical and medical problems.

One indicator of overwork is the proportion of workers with long work-weeks. The average can be misleading. In several industrialised countries, there has been some polarisation, with a growth of part-time working coupled with a growth in the number working long hours. In the UK, according to the government's publication *Social Trends*, full-time workers had longer average workweeks in 1996 than in 1986, and men's average workweek in 1996 was 45.8 hours compared with 44.5 in April 1978. On average, women in full-time jobs had experienced an increase from 37.5 to 40.6 hours. High-status, high-income groups experienced the greatest increase. In 1996, the longest average workweeks were those of full-time managers and adminis-trators (48.4 hours), the lowest clerical and secretarial workers (41.8 hours). The share of workers working long weeks has risen, just as the share of those doing part-time jobs (figure 3.3).

In 1995, in the UK 61 per cent of workers said they worked at least some time on Saturdays and 41 per cent did so on Sundays. That is not unusual. In western Europe, working in jobs on Saturdays and Sundays and at night became more common in the 1990s. The EUROSTAT data summarised in tables 3.1 and 3.2 suggest slightly lower figures for the UK than implied by the Social Trends study, but still one is impressed how many people were doing income-earning work outside the timeframe of the normal working week. And the EUROSTAT data for earlier years indicate that the trend has been upward.

Work insecurity may have grown for "white-collar" employees, who seem increasingly expected to work long workweeks and in many cases *must* do so to keep up with competitor workers, and to remain attractive enough to retain their "employability" with their employers, merely to maintain adequate knowledge. A US survey found that nine out of every ten top managers worked more than ten hours a day, 18 per cent worked twelve or more hours, and over nine in every ten did some work at the week-end as well.[12] Non-managerial "white collar" employees in the 1990s were working the equivalent of four weeks a year more than their equivalents in 1970, reflecting what Juliet Schor called "a shrinkage of leisure".[13] Ironically, increased labour intensity had coincided with high unemployment and a spread of part-time jobs. The incidence merely spread as the economy tightened.

Figure 3.3. Distribution of usual weekly hours of work in employment, United Kingdom, 1983–99

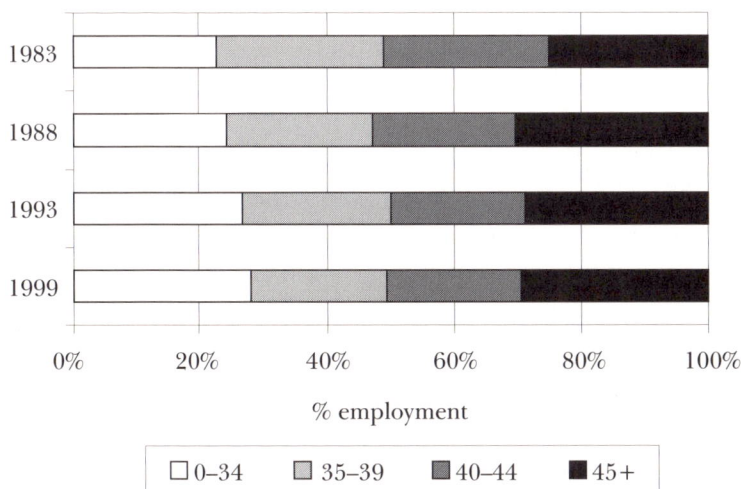

Stress-related illnesses have increased. There is ample evidence that much of it is real, but part of the reason is that more conditions have been recognised and legitimated as illnesses, with more being covered by medical insurance, or recognised by healthcare providers, firms, and insurance companies and by workers themselves. Some of these conditions have become sources of profits for insurance companies, and to some extent have become sources of moral hazard, inducing people to classify themselves as sufferers.

In the USA, a survey in July 1997 found that 73 per cent of workers said they experienced more stress at work than they had twenty or thirty years earlier, and 59% said that they had to work harder.[14] In the UK, a survey by the Institute of Management found that 77 per cent of managers considered the amount of time they had to devote to their job was stressful and were worried about the impact on their family. The Industrial Society identified stress as the fastest-growing workplace health hazard, according to its survey of employers.[15] Yet very few were doing anything about it, in spite of its cost to their firms. It has been estimated that stress-related illness and absenteeism cost about 10 per cent of GDP in the UK, 2.5 per cent in Denmark and 10 per cent in Norway; and that about half of the working days lost to absenteeism in the USA are stress-related.[16] Based on a survey by the Massachusetts Institute of Technology, it was calculated that labour-related depression cost the US economy $47 billion a year.

Among occupational psychologists there is a consensus that the primary cause of stress in work is lack of control over one's situation. An atmosphere of insecurity induces stress that not only feeds back into labour costs, but blocks any rational pursuit of occupation. Although this extends to many other groups of workers, it mostly relates to salaried people in clerical

Table 3.1. Atypical economic activity, European Community, 1999 (percentage of employment)

	Shift				Evening				Night			
	Usually	Sometimes	Never	N/A	Usually	Sometimes	Never	N/A	Usually	Sometimes	Never	N/A
Austria	13.9	2.6	69.8	13.7	14.8	17.5	67.7	0.0	9.5	9.7	80.8	0.0
Belgium	7.3	0.0	75.5	17.3	5.1	28.6	66.2	0.0	2.7	12.4	84.9	0.0
Denmark	0.0	0.0	0.0	100.0	0.0	0.0	0.0	100.0	0.0	0.0	0.0	100.0
Finland	19.9	0.0	66.2	13.8	24.2	25.5	50.2	0.1	8.7	9.2	82.0	0.1
France	8.3	0.0	79.6	12.2	8.5	26.1	65.3	0.1	3.9	12.1	83.9	0.0
Germany	6.5	1.0	82.8	9.6	20.8	18.7	59.9	0.6	7.9	6.8	84.5	0.8
Ireland	0.0	0.0	0.0	100.0	0.0	0.0	0.0	100.0	0.0	0.0	0.0	100.0
Italy	13.6	3.0	55.2	28.3	13.0	16.2	70.8	0.1	5.2	7.7	86.9	0.1
Luxembourg	0.0	0.0	0.0	100.0	0.0	0.0	0.0	100.0	0.0	0.0	0.0	100.0
Netherlands	7.5	0.7	80.3	11.5	17.0	10.6	72.4	0.0	2.3	8.5	89.1	0.1
Portugal	5.7	0.0	66.7	27.5	0.0	0.0	100.0	0.0	8.9	0.0	91.1	0.0
Spain	0.0	0.0	0.0	100.0	0.0	0.0	0.0	100.0	0.0	0.0	0.0	100.0
Sweden	20.9	1.5	61.3	16.3	21.1	19.5	53.3	6.1	7.1	5.8	81.0	6.1
UK	8.6	1.3	66.5	23.6	30.8	21.2	42.3	5.7	11.9	9.8	72.6	5.7

Table 3.2. Weekend economic activity, European Community, 1999 (percentage of employment)

	Saturday				Sunday				Home			
	Usually	*Sometimes*	*Never*	*N/A*	*Usually*	*Sometimes*	*Never*	*N/A*	*Usually*	*Sometimes*	*Never*	*N/A*
Austria	26.5	23.5	50.0	0.0	15.2	14.3	70.5	0.0	11.5	6.2	82.3	0.0
Belgium	9.6	27.3	63.1	0.0	4.7	18.2	77.1	0.0	6.2	8.0	85.8	0.0
Denmark	24.2	19.9	55.2	0.7	18.7	16.5	63.9	0.8	10.7	5.5	83.8	0.1
Finland	25.1	13.1	61.6	0.1	17.8	10.2	71.9	0.1	10.3	5.8	83.5	0.3
France	24.0	29.1	46.8	0.0	8.5	21.0	70.5	0.0	4.4	2.5	93.1	0.0
Germany	0.0	0.0	0.0	100.0	0.0	0.0	0.0	100.0	4.1	7.7	87.7	0.5
Ireland	0.0	0.0	0.0	100.0	0.0	0.0	0.0	100.0	0.0	0.0	0.0	100.0
Italy	38.5	21.5	39.9	0.1	8.3	14.1	77.5	0.1	4.0	2.6	93.3	0.1
Luxembourg	0.0	0.0	0.0	100.0	0.0	0.0	0.0	100.0	8.9	8.5	82.6	0.0
Netherlands	27.1	15.3	57.5	0.0	15.2	10.7	74.1	0.0	6.2	0.0	93.8	0.0
Portugal	29.4	0.0	70.6	0.0	12.0	0.0	88.0	0.0	2.6	4.2	93.2	0.0
Spain	0.0	0.0	0.0	100.0	0.0	0.0	0.0	100.0	0.8	1.2	97.9	0.0
Sweden	18.6	20.2	55.1	6.1	16.9	18.2	58.9	6.1	8.3	4.5	81.0	6.1
UK	25.1	28.3	35.4	11.2	12.9	23.0	52.9	11.2	2.4	21.6	70.1	6.0

Source: Eurostat, LFS.

and "professional" jobs. Most firms still seem to see long workweeks as an indicator of employee commitment, and there have been reports that in some countries at least the practice of requiring workers to "clock in" has spread up the employee scale – to people whose commitment to the firm previously would have been taken for granted, a reflection of their status.

The pressures may be unhingeing. At its extreme, it has fatal consequences. The Japanese have a word for it – *karoshi* – to capture the phenomenon of death from overwork. Statistics show that in Japan this spread gruesomely during the 1980s and 1990s. It somehow symbolises the ultimate absurdity of the great competitiveness rush.

More generally and less visibly is the uncharted territory of presenteeism, which has typically received rather less attention than absenteeism. This is a tendency to work regularly and display over-the-norm intensity of effort even when the person could take paid leave or paid sick leave. It is a sickness mocking the jobholder society. Apparently, according to insurance companies, doctors and others, many people fearful of losing their job or their "employability" or their "promotability" (or simply their niche in the pecking order of perks), remain doggedly labouring, even when they have the contractual entitlement to take paid leave. Then when eventually they have to take leave the illness or injury is much worse, or the fatigue more debilitating, so that they have to stay out of employment for longer, or simply cannot resume at all.

The tendencies are as old as labour. But the pressures on people to show flexibility and the culture of competitiveness make such tendencies much stronger. Little research has been done on this, which reflects a bias of the age. But in Switzerland, according to health insurance companies, it has been associated with a decline in the number of spells of absenteeism, and an increase in the average duration of sick leave.[17]

Then there is the vague but sinister burn out syndrome, an inability of those working with great intensity to sustain the pace after a few years. The spectre of whizz kids wired up, working for huge salaries, private perks and mind-softening shares has been captured in films and the media. One can see them cockily flitting through airports and business lounges, portable computers slung over shoulders. Then, the hum of personal and business relationships is stilled and at age $32\frac{1}{2}$ they lose the plot, take to drugs or alcohol, or become so greedy that they overstep the legal limits once too often.

Their frenetic pace is not just unhealthy for themselves and for those directly in their lives. In too many cases, it also results in a spiral of decisions that have drastic consequences for workers and communities affected by their financial or technical activities. These aspects are too glibly ignored by those who preach that it is "a free world".

Work insecurity may also be linked other forms of labour insecurity. For instance, if workers feel "overskilled" for their jobs, or frustrated by the controls exercised over them, they may feel a sense of inequity and react with disruptive performance or show psychological distress and lower tolerance of other stressors. Generalised labour insecurity can also induce work insecurity among those not immediately affected. Surveys have suggested that bursts of job-cutting in "downsizing" leave a sort of survivor syndrome among those who remain. According to research in Finland, for instance, those who survive mass redundancies are twice as likely as workers not affected by such experiences to take sick leave in the period afterwards.

Paradoxically, although it is often presumed that employment security is beneficial for mental calm, workers of all types may suffer from what has been called "golden handcuffs" due to employment security, in which fear of changing jobs results in a self-imposed limitation on pursuit of a "career" or occupation, creating years of stress. By contrast, flexiworkers may suffer from career stress simply because they cannot obtain a niche for long enough to gain control over their own career development.

Work itself may be a source of personal security through the network of support mechanisms that may be associated with the resultant interactions with fellow workers. However, the two modern forms of labour relations, "human resource management" and external flexibility, can threaten that space. Psychologists have suggested that in a paternalistic firm or organis-ation, social support and guidance from supervisors may actually be a source of insecurity. Yet in the modern context of outsourcing, downsizing and other forms of external flexibility, there is an increasing incidence of situations in which workers are isolated from networks that could offer potential support.

Work insecurity overlaps with income insecurity. For example, according to a report funded by US business, a declining proportion of US workers has been covered by employer health plans.[18] Losing a job in such circumstances becomes disastrous, for the person and his or her family, especially if falling ill while in a job results in a rundown of savings or an accumulation of debt incurred to meet medical bills. In the UK, firms apparently have responded to pressure to cut non-wage labour costs by selecting for redundancy workers with poor sick records.[19]

A survey of civil service workers in London, known as the Whitehall Study, found that those in low-grade positions with little control over responsibilities had a 50 per cent higher probability of developing symptoms of heart disease than those in higher-level jobs with greater autonomy.[20] The conclusion was that boring and repetitive jobs induced heart disease. This prompts questions about the advisability of pursuing labour market security through a prolifer-ation of low-level jobs. It also suggests that greater personal control, and worker-determined flexibility, rather than job-determined flexibility, would improve workers' health status, and that the unequal situation of people in terms of jobs contributes to broader forms of social injustice.

Although there is no need for this to be the case, so powerful is the labouring ethic that loss of employment can become psychologically unbear-able. Every recession induces a sharp rise in suicides, usually concentrated among those with relatively high incomes, wealth and status. In Japan during the recession of 1997 suicides rose by 16 per cent. The link between job stress and suicides was taken to extremes in the former Soviet Union, where suicides among young men almost doubled in the 1990s, largely attributable to the stress of adjusting to new forms of employment.[21]

Stress, labourholism, presenteeism, burn-out and the ultimate human sacrifice of *karoshi* are the new indicators of work insecurity. They have not displaced the more traditional hazards of labour – maiming accidents, diseases from exposure to chemicals, pollutants and toxic waste, and the less specific effects of years of exposure to eye-damaging, ear-damaging or body-impairing working conditions. They have merely added to them.

In modern industrialised economies, it is almost as if the labouring ethic has imprisoned or drugged people. The job becomes a commitment, while home is a distraction to be avoided as much as possible, a place where "chores" (work) must be done as quickly as possible.[22] Work at home has become perceived as constraining labour in the job, rather than part of leisure. The result is that families try to "outsource" family work, such as childcare, housework and gardening. Parenthood-outsourcing is a reflection of labour market flexibility.

Work insecurity has profoundly inegalitarian consequences, with Darwinian overtones. Within any social spectrum, the winners can emerge as exemplary. Those who suffer illnesses or failure, which results in their intensification of self-exploitation until they implode psychologically, may drift into catastrophic circumstances. Those who win can gloat from the bank, like those frogs that make it to the bank in Tawney's famous image. But the winners also move into the sphere of cumulative advantage. This is a reality of global capitalism. It is a frogspawn economy. And the pattern of work security plays a cruel role in fawning to the winners and mocking the losers.

Stress and self-destruction are consequences of giving labour excessive priority, coupled with the market regulation that removes vital checks on self-exploitation. So, while some forms of work security may be improving, in some parts of the world, the spread of "modern" forms of work insecurity may be a haunting reflection on the century of the labouring man that could precipitate a civilising response. Quite simply, humanity will have to reduce the pressure.

7 Representation Insecurity

It is no coincidence that while other forms of labour security have been declining, labour representation security has been weakening almost everywhere. The fall in membership of trade unions has even been called "the counter revolution of our time".[23] One might prefer to call it the primary symptom of the crisis of labourism.

Representation security comes from the existence of organisations able to defend the interests of those in vulnerable positions, giving those subject to controls a collective voice to bargain with controllers. There is no reason for that to depend on trade unions, but during the twentieth century it was presumed that unions could "voice regulate" labour relations. Unions have always had a dualistic character, being a means of resistance to control – improving the security of their members – and a means of managing labour.

In the historical development of capitalism, the predominant forms of representation have changed. In the nineteenth century, craft unions evolved from guilds, reflecting the separation of owners and workers. This represented proletarianisation and a decline of artisanal security, with craft unions being defensive associations of working men intent on preserving control over their skill, work organisation, wage rates and social status. In many places, they operated to limit labour supply.

The early years of the twentieth century saw a shift to industrial unions and sectoral (or centralised) collective bargaining. This reflected loss of worker control over occupations. Industrial unions evolved within mass production and Tayloristic work organisation, which was a concerted managerial effort to turn working-class occupations into jobs. Although institutions and processes varied from country to country, the character of representation shifted to the labourist priorities, of raising the social wage, and giving members improved labour security, through protection of working conditions. Mostly, unions went along with Tayloristic job structures and often became defenders of them through demarcation agreements and the like.

For most of the century unions, and the union movement, were in the vanguard of social progress, an instrument for the pursuit of distributive justice in terms of advancing the interests of the labouring man. In the postwar era, unions were integrated into the state in distinctive ways in the two development models, and this shaped the evolution of representation security in the market regulation era. It might be useful to trace the main trends in each type of economy and society.

(i) From State Socialism[24]

Representation security in state socialism was more formal than substantive, in that extremely high unionisation was offset by the fact that the unions were little more than organs of the Communist Party and agents of management, mainly concerned with labour discipline and the dispensation of enterprise benefits and services to workers and their families.

The collapse of state socialism in eastern Europe induced rapid de-unionisation, coupled with fragmentation of unions, new and old. Unions and employer organisations often had unclear organisational boundaries, and demarcation lines between policy concerns were hazy. They had to struggle to maintain morale and credibility in the context of declining (and often passive) membership and unsettled bargaining routines. Among the worst aspects for development of voice regulation were cleavages between local, regional and national bodies, and hazy lines of organisation on sectoral or occupational lines.

At national level, through nominally tripartite bodies, voice regulation was promoted in many countries, an exception being the Czech Republic. Much of that amounted to ineffectual formalism as well, since the representative character of employer and union associations on tripartite bodies was often dubious, while information at their disposal was often scanty and unreliable, and the capacity to make and implement decisions often minimal. Typically, decisions were taken by officials from several government ministries and pushed through the tripartite bodies or introduced without reference to them.

Representation insecurity has become pervasive, reflected in the declining unionisation. If one puts aside the few countries where the old union structure has been preserved because the character of the state has hardly changed, then with fragmentation and a reformed old union structure retaining a central role, de-unionisation has reflected the following:

- real decline caused by anti-union stance of enterprises;
- real decline due to the emergence of new, private firms in which union representation has not been possible because of size or employer resistance;
- real decline caused by the withdrawal from unions of "passive" members;
- real decline caused by withdrawal of working members due to the unpopularity of unions because of past associations;
- real decline due to the growth of categories of workers with a low propensity to join unions, such as higher-status, higher-income workers and migrants;
- real decline caused by the erosion of enterprise benefits, for which unions had been responsible and which gave workers an incentive to join unions;
- real decline due to the rising cost of union dues, both absolutely and relative to the income needs of workers;
- real decline caused by workers feeling less inclined to join unions because employers bypass them in decisions on wages, working conditions and other matters;
- real decline caused by the existence of alternative structures, such as company unions or their equivalent, or enterprise boards that seem to offer a workers' voice in enterprise affairs;
- real decline caused by the much higher levels of unemployment;
- real decline because of inter-union rivalry, sometimes fomented by outside critics of "old" unions;
- real decline because unions were seen to represent losers in a time of stagflation;
- artificial decline, caused by more realistic estimates of union membership and by more monitoring of membership numbers.

It would be hard to estimate which factors have been most important, although privatisation surely played a prominent part. In Russia, unionisation in privatised firms is much lower.[25] This is also true in Ukraine and Bulgaria. Given their role in supervising enterprise benefits, unions have suffered from the decline in the range and value of those benefits, being resented by workers as possibly responsible for the decline and being less attractive because the declining function of allocating benefits has eliminated the main appeal of membership.

Unions have also failed to attract younger workers, which is why a high and rising proportion of union members have been old, with many more being economically inactive.[26] This erodes the strength of unions as bargainers. In the longer-term, the failure to attract the young is symbolic of the atavistic appeal of trade unions in general.

Although the tale of de-unionisation in former state socialism countries is worrying for those who believe that unions are required for representation security, several positive points should be noted. Very high unionisation was artificial, and undermined the legitimacy of unions, which is a prerequisite for strong voice. The erosion has created pressure on those who recognise the need for collective voice to seek alternative institutions more appropriate for the emerging flexible labour markets. For the meantime though, there is no representation security in these countries, and little prospect that the vacuum will be filled in the near future.

(ii) From Welfare State Capitalism

In welfare state capitalism, representation security was seen as requiring independent unions, with high unionisation and the state-guaranteed right to strike as a means of limiting the control of capital and of ensuring income security. This was coupled with existence of employer associations representing mainstream capital, able to negotiate on its behalf, to make concessions and negotiate compromises. Unions and employer bodies were incorporated economically and politically into the state.

These assumptions and requirements began to fade in the 1960s and 1970s. In industrialised countries, the forward march of labour coincided with a fattening of the working-class stomach and more socio-economic mobility. While attesting to the success of the extension of labour security, these eroded collective working-class strength. It was always too fanciful to speak of the end of the working class, as Andre Gorz put it, but surely not wrong to depict a dwindling of its size, power and cohesion, as well as a process of class fragmentation that eroded representation security.[27] Whether the view was correct, unions and their political allies seemed to become atavistic, and looking back to the 1970s and 1980s, that must be the biggest "failure" for those who value distributive justice.

Whether or not those social forces could have done anything to arrest the erosion of security is moot, since one may guess that the game was up, and that those bulwarks of the conservative working class were institutionally incapable of responding positively to the currents that were sweeping them aside. This is merely recognition that all institutions belong to historical eras. In any case, by the 1990s it was too late to arrest the trends.

De-unionisation has been extensive in all parts of the world, except in southern Africa (Figures 3.4 and 3.5). Even where high rates of unionisation have persisted, the strength and effectiveness of union activity has often been reduced. Although it was always quite low, could anyone in the post-war era have predicted that less than 10 per cent of the French labour force would belong to trade unions by the 1990s?

In the USA, private sector unionisation declined to about 11 per cent. In the UK, by 1997 union membership as a percentage of the labour force (31 per cent) was the lowest for over sixty years. There were 7.2 million

Figure 3.4. Trade union density by sector, 1985–95 (unweighted average of union membership percentages of individual countries, years 1985 and 1995 or closest)

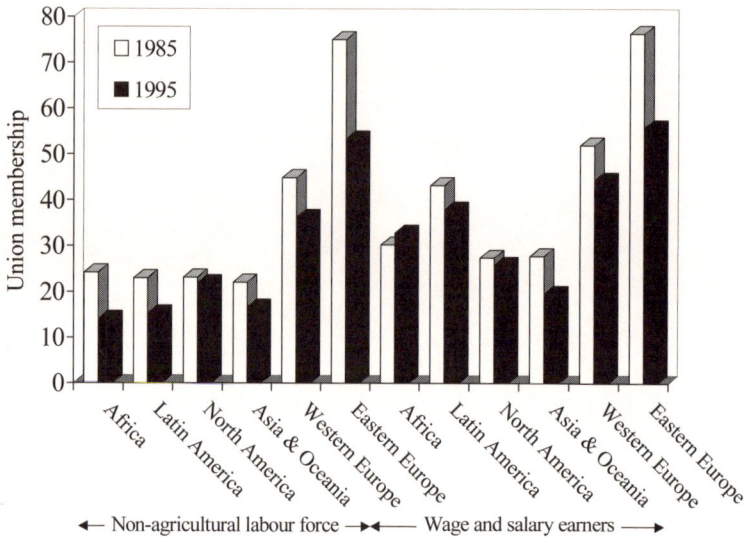

Source: ILO

Figure 3.5. Change in trade union density by sector, 1985–95 (unweighted average of change in union membership in percentage points of individual countries, period 1985 to 1995 or closest)

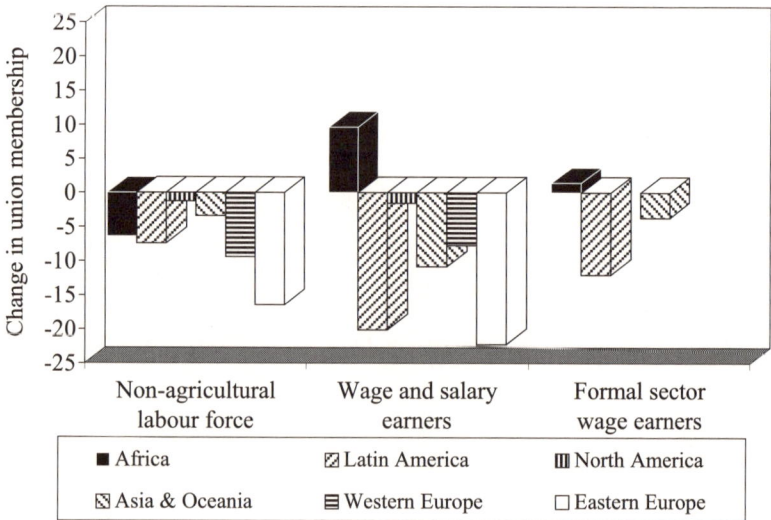

Source: *World Labour Report, 1997–98*, pp. 239–40

members, compared with nearly 9 million in 1989. Supporters took comfort from the fact that the rate of decline had fallen from 3 per cent a year in the 1980s to 1 per cent in 1996. In 1998 and 1999 there was a small net gain, but the figure remained historically low. In many other countries union-isation has fallen, in some cases by much more than the recorded decline, since an increasing proportion of the membership has consisted of retired workers, as in Italy, or were non-employed for other reasons.[28] So, actual bargaining strength in the workplace is overstated by unionisation statistics.

The main reasons for the global decline in unionisation are the following, again in no implied order of significance:

- Labour market insecurity has eroded membership, directly, through fewer workers being employed, and indirectly, through making it easier for firms to resist or de-recognise unions and through making it harder for workers to organise or have the confidence to do so.
- External flexibility has made many jobs less unionisable. Temporary, part-time and other non-regular workers are less likely to be in unions. Unions have found it hard to organise flexiworkers, notably teleworkers, other home workers, and temporary and casual labour, as well as those having an intermediary labour status, regarding themselves as "self-employed" even if hiring themselves out from job to job as consultants or contract workers. Reasons include the difficulty of reaching and retaining such workers, their tendency not to identify with unions, the difficulty of inte-grating flexiworkers into union structures, and the ambiguity over the legal position of contingent workers, which inhibit them from joining unions. This has caused friction in the USA. As an AFL-CIO report concluded, "Working people not classified as 'employees' in the labour law are subject to open reprisal for seeking to join a union and have no legal right of recourse."[29]
- Just as most of these forms of labour are costly to organise, most in such jobs seem ambivalent about the advantage of unionisation. Union involve-ment may have a substantial cost, through increasing the probability of being dismissed and of not being rehired. This has been a barrier to unionisation in developing countries.[30] One countervailing tendency might be that as insecurity spreads up the "skill" spectrum, such workers may find more appeal in unions. To some extent this has been happening in the USA, as agency labour has extended to technically skilled groups; other regular workers threatened by displacement have joined unions, even including scientists.

External flexibility has eroded the propensity to unionise, not just in the organisational sense that it is hard for unions to reach outworkers and flexiworkers but in the sense of collective consciousness. The "collective worker" has been the basis of trade unionism, so that the modern equiv-alent of the putting-out system weakens the collective worker sentiment by individualising the workforce. The "labour movement" is the appropriate description for the agency giving voice to collective labour. But just as the "flexible firm" can expect loyalty without commitment, so the best that labour unions can expect from individualised workers is loyalty without commitment, because the appeal to commitment depends on the organisational memory – unions are what defend the rights of labour.

- The changing composition of the labour force and greater labour force flexibility have tended to lower unionisation, since intermittent and marginal labour force participants are less inclined to join or stay in unions. Even though women have become less marginal, their unionisation has remained lower than for men. Thus, in the USA although women's unionisation has not fallen by as much as men's, their level has remained much lower.

- In many countries, an increasing proportion of jobs have been in small-scale firms with a short life. These are less unionisable. Decentralisation, through splintering of firms and sub-contracting, makes organisation and retention harder. And decentralised structures makes pattern-setting bargaining harder, with different terms and conditions between units and with non-union plants weakening the bargaining power in organised plants.

- Governments have taken advantage of union weakness to tighten regulations over their activities, making any benefits of unionisation more unpredictable, recognition harder, de-recognition easier, and the right to strike more limited. Anti-union legislation, such as that passed in Britain, may have played a smaller role than commentators suggest, reflecting unions' weakness and their poor public image as much as being a cause of the decline.[31] However, it surely has been a factor. In many countries, legislation has chipped away at the strength of freedom of association in the conventional sense envisaged in trade unions. Only a few countries openly ban unions, such as Saudi Arabia. But others prevent them in selected sectors, as in export-processing zones. Others preclude independent industrial unions, as in Chile since the Pinochet reforms. In many countries, the right to strike, the right to picket and the right to bargain have been curtailed. And the right to representation itself has been eroded, little by little. Governments have been encouraged to go in this direction by the homilies of globalisation, along the lines that unless reforms of this type are made, foreign portfolio and direct capital will go elsewhere, along with their own firms and private investors.

- Statutory regulation has helped maintain higher unionisation in some countries, notably where unions have retained a role in providing social protection. In Germany, representation security has been retained to some extent because under co-determination worker representatives are on supervisory boards of large and medium-sized firms, and in the coal and steel industry workers nominate personnel directors. According to Germany's largest employer federation, the Gesamtmetall, some personnel directors need union backing to keep their jobs, and unions insist that they be union members as a precondition for a collective agreement.

- A historical image of unions has impeded their appeal to those groups that have been accounting for a growing share of the labour force, including more educated, more individualistic workers, women and minorities, even though there is evidence that unions often actually benefit some of those more than male manual workers. There is concern over the representative character of unions, which is not necessarily fair or due to the intentions or values of unionists themselves. In most countries, women and immigrants remain under-represented, as in the Netherlands, for example. This means there has been a growing divergence between the image of unions and the composition of the labour force. Unions have been criticised for protecting "insiders" at the expense of "outsiders", such as women, young labour-force entrants, migrants, and ethnic minorities. The criticism may be unfair, since their "sword of justice" effect in this regard has been widely documented. Nevertheless, the impression that unions represent the values and aspirations of labouring man is ingrained in the public mind.

- Employer and managerial attitudes to unions have changed. In the period of industrialisation, employers commonly created communities or estates on which the bulk of the workforce lived. This paternalism produced a controlled workforce, but also created a sense of identity and solidarity. More flexible production systems, and mass transport, have encouraged large-scale firms to dispense with this tactic. A classic case was the UK mining industry. In the 1980s, as part of a managerial onslaught, British Coal did not build new estates to accompany new pits, but dispersed miners over surrounding villages. This weakened the mineworkers' solidarity and representation.

- Many firms have been emboldened by the weakness of their institutional adversaries to restrict the capacity of union bargaining or to bypass unions altogether. This has been encouraged by the tendency to move away from group contracts to individual employment contracts.

- As unions have evolved from craft to industrial to general unions, they have become more distanced from the interests and self-image of potential members. Increasingly workers do not identify with a particular "sector", industry or even recognised craft. Sectoralism as a principle of industrial relations and representation has been eroded, even though in a few countries there have been attempts to strengthen it, as in Canada, South Africa and Zimbabwe.

- Independent unions have been threatened by the efforts of firms and governments to set up company-based alternatives. These have long been regarded as "pet" unions easily co-opted by management, part of the managerial control system. Enterprise unionism has been pushed by some governments, and has spread because of the influence of Japanese labour practices, particularly to industrialising economies such as the Republic of Korea, Malaysia and Chile. Where long regarded with hostility by traditional unions, they have spread because of union weakness, and because managements have seen them as useful as part of the labour control system and as conducive to work process flexibility.

- Unions are less capable of exerting pressure through traditional mechanisms. Strikes are less successful in globally integrated production systems. If the union prevails, the local firm's perceived competitiveness is weakened, leading to job losses or job transfers within a geographically diversified enterprise, or to bankruptcy. In many countries, unions have suffered from whipsaw bargaining, by which firms have put pressure on local unions to settle tamely under threat of relocation of production and employment to another country. Concession bargaining has spread, and in some countries has left unions looking as if they are part of management rather than the independent voice of workers' interests. It has scarcely enhanced their image as the main means of ensuring collective or individual economic security.

- Unions have lost credibility and legitimacy, as a result of the incessant ideological attack on them. One labour historian has predicted that private-sector unionised plants would become a rarity in the UK, confined to the north of the country, because workers did not identify with them. In the USA, a poll conducted when unionisation was at its lowest for generations found that 40 per cent of the public believed unions had too much power while only 22 per cent thought they did not have enough; 50 per cent believed that private-sector workers should not have the right to strike without the risk of losing their job. The negative consciousness has eroded worker representation. Most worrying about a survey of worker opinions carried out for the Dunlop Commission in 1994 was that, faced with a hypothetical choice between a strong organisation that would face managerial opposition and a weak one that would cooperate easily with management, workers chose the latter by three to one.

- While more corporations are internationally mobile, with greater capacity to relocate production, unions have been unable to develop equivalent capacity. International unionism has been financially weak. For instance, the ICFTU receives 1 per cent of the income of member organisations willing and able to pay, whereas by contrast Amnesty International receives 30 per cent of the income of their national affiliates. With limited financial strength, the ICFTU is limited.

- Globalisation has altered institutional rights. Regional integration agreements have given formal rights to capital (backed by the WTO and others) but not corresponding rights to labour – giving, for example, guaranteed freedom of movement of capital but not the guaranteed right to strike. This and other instances have been noted for the NAFTA and MERCOSUR arrangements for Latin America.[32]

- There has been an international trend to decentralisation of collective bargaining, to plant or company level (figure 3.6), and this has made it easier for firms to erode and bypass unions and move to individualised contracts.

In sum, unionism is in deep trouble. It might be that other forms of representation have been taking the place of more traditional forms of trade union. Works councils are one mechanism, which are compatible with unions or could exist without them. They have been well established in continental western Europe, and workers elect representatives to works councils in Belgium, Denmark, France, Germany, the Netherlands and Spain. However,

Figure 3.6. Trends to company/plant-level collective bargaining from mid-1980s to mid-1990s, by region of the world

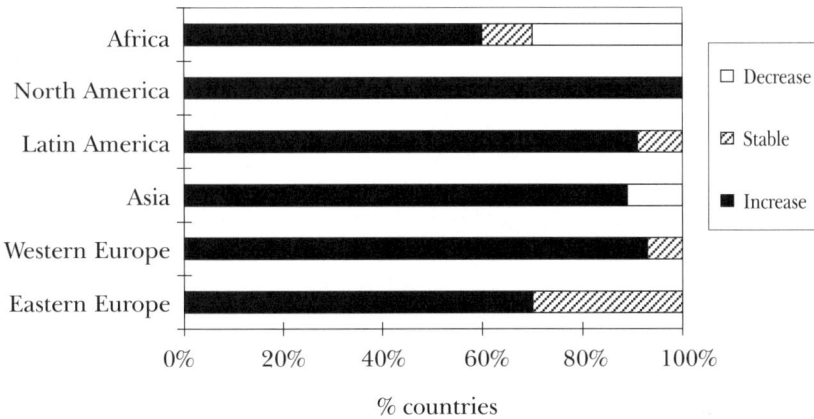

Source: ILO

they may not be a force for co-determination. They benefit insiders over others. As they are mainly in larger companies, voice regulation is stronger in those, and as they are more common in firms with predominantly male workers, it gives men stronger voice potential than women. In the Netherlands, 83 per cent of all works council members were men.[33] So, voice regulation may not be egalitarian in effect. And workers not in regular employment have no participation rights, since in countries such as the Netherlands short-term, part-time and trainee workers do not have voting rights. And there is often little contact between works councils and unions, while managements often bypass works councils, with impunity. In the UK, only a fifth of workers have access to a works council or similar structure, and most believe that they have little or no influence.[34]

Works councils may also have strengthened workplace segmentation, the representatives being more concerned to defend the interests of core insiders than other groups. Works councils seem better tuned to stable industrial structures based on mass production than to flexible labour markets in which small firms and flexible forms of employment relation are growing. They do not promise a community voice.

Representation security in terms of consultation and negotiation with workers is not extensive even in western Europe. A survey in 1996 found that 48 per cent of UK firms gave no worker representation in decision-making and in the Netherlands the figure was even higher (57 per cent). Only 16 per cent of French firms involved workers in negotiations or decisions on work organisation, and only 18 per cent of UK firms did so. Paradoxically, firms that did consult workers were more likely to report cost reductions and had better performance in terms of output, quality and absenteeism, and were more likely to have cut employment.[35]

As representation security is derived from a sense of community among workers, in a globalising labour market, with fragmented groups with dissimilar interests and patterns of labour force participation, traditional unions cannot offer a sense of community. Special interest groups have proliferated, but competition between them has probably undermined their collective strength.

Many commentators have welcomed the erosion of representation security as a reflection of individualisation and flexibility. However, without strong voice regulation, other forms of security will be fragile. Besides more income insecurity for many groups, even potentially advantageous changes in work organisation can be undermined. In the USA, for instance, workers in "high performance" work settings reported much greater job-related stress than other workers.[36] Absence of strong independent collective voice means there is no check on excessive labour. Without voice, participatory labour schemes, "teamworking", so-called self-directed teams, delegation of responsibility and so on may merely increase labour insecurity.

More invidiously, social allegiance to trade unionism has been eroded. A loss of craft identity has contributed to this. Workers are less likely to have allegiance to a specific union if they expect to change types of work several times during their working lives. And they are even less likely to feel allegiance to an industrial union if they expect to change sectors or cannot feel a historical or cultural identity with the sector. And it is harder still for workers to identify with what perhaps has become the most common form of union, the general union. At best, it will be an instrumental allegiance, which is far from loyalty or commitment. Remove the political, and you remove the bond.

Beyond this corrosive tendency, structural changes have made what is on offer less representative and less effective. The character of unions has been changing, so that most tailor their rhetoric to appear moderate and responsible, keen to co-operate with employers and government. Around the world, company unions have been growing, often at the expense of more independent unions. This means that a given level of unionisation represents a lower level of independent worker voice, if one accepts the view that unions set up or subsidised by management, are less likely to express the voice of workers effectively, and are more likely to control or moderate it.

As unions have become more defensive and cautious, they have made concessions that have further eroded their appeal. In some countries they have remained part of the governance structure, whether in a form of tripartism or in long-term agreements with employer organisations. This was once a way in which labour unions could advance workers' interests. But increasingly unions make concessions in order to prevent the structure from collapsing. For example, in 2000, the French trade unions were prepared to accept reforms to unemployment benefits advocated by the national employers' organisation, MEDEF, because of the employers' threat to withdraw from the joint union-employer-management of the French social security system if they did not agree. It was reported that the unions feared losing large numbers of members employed by the state and parastatal bodies of the social security system. This is no basis for progressive voice representation, and anybody who wants to go in that direction must recognise that, in their cups or out of them.

Unions have always faced a conflict between their desire to provide effective resistance against employers and capital, and their desire for public legitimacy. Their current desire to attract and retain members is a source of weakness, since they find themselves in the business of marketing as a service provider and as a force for consensus. Instruments of consensus rarely lead to passionate commitment.

8 Concluding Points

With its emphasis on the need for flexibility, economic liberalisation has intensified labour market, work and skill insecurities. But in the growth or spread of labour insecurity, there has also been a squeeze on time. This is a global issue, although it has attracted particular attention in highly industrialised countries. Yet in economies in which scrambling for survival is the preoccupation of most people, the squeeze on time can be the major source of social and economic insecurity, or at least one of the major sources of it.

Recently, while carrying out exploratory research in Gujarat in India, we sat in a back street and interviewed a group of women outworkers about their lives and work. I asked them about their use of time. It turned out that they spent about six hours a day every day doing their income-earning labour, rolling incense sticks, or making *bidis* – those little Indian cigarettes – or sewing garments delivered to them by a middleman. They spent, on average, about four hours a day waiting for the orders or for raw materials; they spent about three hours a day in travel for work purposes, three hours a day on shopping and travel for that purpose, and three hours for housework and cooking. This left less than five hours a day for the simple act of sleep. Most of us can pass a day or two with only five hours of sleep. But to have to do this day after day, week after week, year after year is to induce a profound inability to function rationally or optimally.

In a high-technology, global economy, time takes on unusual significance. According to Richard Sennett, "Time is the only resource freely available to those at the bottom of society."[37] In one sense that may be trivially true. But it depends which society one is contemplating and what we mean by freely available. The example of the street vendors and outworkers in Ahmadabad shows how many restrictions on time the poor can face, leaving them to drop into bed after midnight every night and obliging them to rise at 5 a.m., to renew the struggle in which the sheer act of waiting for labour consumes a large amount of nominally free time.

Further up the scale, all over the world the time freely available for the unemployed usually hangs heavy. The impoverished unemployed person has plenty of time, but it is not what we might call vocational time, that is, time in which creativity can flourish. Even with energy, he or she does not know where any activity leads. For such a person, time is not a "resource"; it is something to be endured, to be filled. It is not freely available because it is undirected time. It may even be the most unfree time of all – chipping away at the capacity to use time constructively or reflectively, or inducing a person to labour with greater discipline, out of desperation.

Time control has always been a feature of capitalism, as E.P. Thompson so memorably demonstrated. Modern technologies give potential controllers the most powerful set of instruments for achieving this. The internet and the PC allow it to be done remotely and discretely. But it also intensifies a form of desperate insecurity, which threatens to block the pursuit of occupation. It isolates while putting people in constant touch with each other. It controls time while allowing people to have the feeling of having greater control over their time, through the day and night. The internet allows firms to reduce the appearance of bureaucratic, hierarchical controls – seemingly a liberating trend – but only because it provides a new source of control.

Insecurity may induce a greater culture of compliance, as some observers have described it, and as some interests may want it to do. But insecurity as a means of control induces a low-effort bargain, a mentality that means trying to do as little as possible. Fear of demotion or dismissal might induce more effort in the job, but it is unlikely to induce commitment, loyalty or that spark of creativity. That may not matter, and it would be wrong to think that more management training is what is required. Management consultants idealise the notion of teamwork. Yet the ethos of teamwork sits uneasily with the idea of individual creativity. Collaborative compliance is usually wanted from workers more than individual creativity. It would be a mistake to presume that even modern dot.com companies want all their colleagues to leapfrog with their software wizardry. It may go down well for management professors to use the glib language of empowerment as necessary for commitment, and commitment as necessary for creativity, and creativity as necessary for innovation, and innovation as necessary for competitive advantage and growth. Back in the reality of the labour market, objectives and behaviour are rather more mundane.

"McGrad" jobs represent the ultimate loss of the sense of occupation. This does not just affect the poor or those without "education". In several affluent economies, there is anecdotal evidence that many graduates from university, apparently a majority of whom are men, drift into an existence of a series of casual jobs that do not engage their competencies or education. Many stay with their parents or share "digs" rather than marry. This pattern may reflect the changing nature of the labour market and jobs. If there are few highly paid career jobs and a gulf between such vocational options and the mass of lower-level opportunities, there will be what sociologists and psychologists call a cognitive dissonance, or a sense of relative deprivation, creating a "losers' barrier" to work in the available jobs, preventing young labour-force entrants from making a commitment to such jobs. This can only foster an instrumentality ethic.

Such a syndrome would be missed by those who extol the virtues of "jobs, jobs, jobs" as their vision, and a policy of raising "employability" as the primary tool for strengthening the labour market. Labour thrives on insecurity, but human development does not.

Individualism as a creed has been a powerful aspect of globalisation, with its emphasis on eroding collective and protective regulations, privatisation with its subtle message that individuals must look after themselves and look up to those brave entrepreneurial spirits, admiration for risk-takers, incentives for individual aggrandisement, and so on. But the consequence of economic individualism has been a malaise of social isolationism. This has been epitomised by a spate of books and articles highlighting the growth of such phenomena as "singleton" living, of "bowling alone" (the title of a book by Robert Putnam), and a trend away from social activities to do-it-by-yourself activities, including a reduction in participation in team sports alongside a shift to activities such as jogging and going to the gym.

One may surmise that this has something to do with the time squeeze, which stems from the relentless pressure to be competitive, efficient and "moving ahead", and from the intense pressure on workers to be more pro-ductive and employable. Labour intensification, associated with work insecurity and strange forms of morbidity, is linked to the isolationism that has been scaring so many commentators.

4

The Crunch of Income Insecurity

1 Introduction

In a market economy most people crave income security, or at least the
assurance that they will have enough to subsist adequately and with reasonable assurance that this will continue. The limited decommodification of
labour in the post-1945 era gave income security to increasing numbers
of people based on the interests of labouring man, through guaranteed
minimum wages, labour-based social security, employment security, and
enterprise welfare that gave benefits as the incentive to show loyalty to a firm
or organisation. In state socialism, cradle-to-grave benefits were organised
through the labouring collective.

At an abstract level, income security is a matter of adequacy of income for
perceived needs, assurance that income adequacy will continue, and a sense
of relative income, a perception that one's income is adequate and fair
relative to others' income. So, it is linked to income inequality. Most people
seem to measure their security by a sense of relative deprivation. They may
relate their income to a previous level, to some notion of what is fair
or feasible for someone in their circumstances, to those higher up in the
income spectrum, or to a combination of these.

In the latter part of the twentieth century, income insecurity increased in
several ways. Numerous reports attested to the growth of the incidence of
poverty in most parts of the world, using several definitions and many
sources of data. Even in the booming USA of the 1990s, the official poverty
rate remained above the level achieved in the 1970s. And even if benefits
such as the Earned Income Tax Credit were taken into account, about one in
ten Americans were in poverty, while a much higher proportion of children
were. In the EU, by the mid-1990s over 50 million people were in poverty,
according to EUROSTAT data. Personal income inequality also grew in many
countries, as was shown by Gini coefficients for income distribution, collated
by the United Nations, World Bank and others. Inequality increased in twenty
of the twenty-one industrialised countries for which data were available.[1]
World income inequality also seems to have increased, in that it has
increased in a large majority of all countries.[2]

In the USA, whereas economic growth was linked to reductions in
inequality in the 1950s and 1960s, it was associated with widening inequality

in the 1980s and early 1990s. It apparently stabilised in the 1990s, but this in itself is remarkable, because the economy was experiencing the tightest peace-time labour market conditions of the century. In the UK, inequality grew so remorselessly through the 1980s and 1990s that it reversed all the modest redistribution achieved during the twentieth century. Tony Atkinson and others have suggested that it has stabilized since then. Even so, there are reasons to believe that the income data used to monitor these trends actually underestimate the growth of inequality of social income, because of what has happened to the level and incidence of state, enterprise and private benefits and services.

Less well known than the trends in personal income distribution is the fact that functional income distribution has become more unequal, notably in European countries, in some of which the labour share has shrunk by more than 10 percentage points, but less noticed, even more so in low-income developing countries. Across the world, the share of national income going to wage earners has declined, the share going to capital owners has grown. The rate of return to capital, or to financial investment, has sharply risen, as those with shares will tell you with smug satisfaction, while the return to labour has stagnated, so that even in industrialised countries many more people are finding that they do not receive enough from their labour to provide a decent income. The phenomenon of the new poor is certainly not new, but even in European Union countries the numbers who are working without obtaining an adequate income from their job have grown, and these new poor include many in full-time jobs as well as many in the growing number of part-time jobs. While unemployment is associated with poverty, the possession of a job does not necessarily prevent it.

To make matters more unequal, taxes on high incomes and on capital have generally declined. For instance, in the USA the top marginal tax rate declined from 70 per cent in 1980 to 39.6 per cent in 2000. Perversely, the rich have been paying more of the total tax, simply because the incomes of the wealthy have risen much more than those of other groups. But while high-income earners have been able to avoid or evade taxation, by contrast, taxes on standard forms of labour have tended to rise, compounded by a tendency to shift social insurance contributions from firms to workers. As shown later, changes in social transfers have also intensified the income insecurity of the unemployed and those on the margins of the economy and labour markets.

Globally, income insecurity has also increased because of the changing character of production relations. By itself, labour informalisation, through greater concentration of employment in small-scale firms, casual labour, flexi-working and so on, leaves more people in a precarious situation. And the spread of that type of arrangement must affect others not in one of those statuses, imparting a concern that they or their children or parents will soon be in them too.

In developing countries, the long-expected trend by which more workers would enter the formal economy, covered by protective regulations, social protection and labour security, went into reverse, and by the end of the century there was no expectation that most adults would soon enter the sectors and statuses giving relatively reasonable income security. In industrialised countries, including most of western Europe and the whole of central and eastern Europe, the "new poor" phenomenon became accepted reality – encouraging governments to consider tax credits as the means of bringing up their incomes to a level of survival.

Other sources of income have also been under pressure. In developing countries, urbanisation, partial industrialisation and the commercialisation of agriculture eroded culturally specific community networks of support, so that when there was an economic or social crisis, as in east Asia in 1998, many found that they could not rely on those traditional sources of support. In most of eastern Europe and the former Soviet Union, the income insecurity of the 1990s was made much worse because all community networks had been systematically destroyed in the previous decades of state socialism. The collapse of the state socialism pillars of social protection pushed millions of people into life-threatening situations with a weak or non-existent network of social support.

To compound this, income security has also become more differentiated because state benefits have become more selective, harder to obtain and often worth less. Meanwhile, income from capital (private benefits, in the sense defined in the idea of social income) has jumped for those with high incomes, while workers and those on the margins of the labour market have been obliged to rely more on the support of relatives, their local community, voluntary organisations and charity. These trends have produced, and have been accentuated by, the main understated story of the era – the new stratification of globalisation that will surplant the standard class imagery that shaped analysis during most of the nineteenth and twentieth centuries.

2 The "New" Global Stratification

Alongside the various forms of organisational and labour market flexibility, the era of globalisation has accentuated a socio-economic fragmentation of societies, and made the social structure more global in character. Any analysis should consider this, because ultimately this will shape the feasible politics of the next era, and the principles on which a new socially just structure could emerge.

For several decades, class was an over-used word, a token of one's faith and ideology. Then in the 1990s, reflecting the loss of confidence in any progressive agenda, it was pushed into the intellectual shadows. It should not be lost. As a result of globalisation, the technological revolution that is sweeping everybody into new ways of living and interacting with others, more flexible labour relations and the global process of economic informalisation, class structures have become more fragmented. This does not mean that class *per se* has become redundant or disappeared. On the contrary, the fragmentation of class interests has created new tensions and new interests that are pervasive. But a peculiar feature of global capitalism is that all groups in society are marginalised in some sense, and all groups suffer from anxiety and insecurity of one type or another.

There are several ways of approaching this, none of them ideal. However, we are in the realm of images and anecdotal ways of representing reality, which in time should yield firmer concepts and statistical profiles that satisfy mainstream social thinkers, economists and policymakers. Conventional labour statistics are not helpful. For instance, there are no peasants in international statistics, and no landlords. And we have no information on classifications based on the range of income sources and controls by which patterns of economic security are reproduced or undermined.[3]

For our purposes, we might find it useful to consider the following image of social fragmentation taking place internationally. The point of the exercise is to identify groups that have distinctive sets of entitlements and patterns of social protection and security, and that are likely to have a particular attitude to political reforms and various forms of social protection.

Perhaps the most intriguing aspect of the socio-economic fragmentation that has been taking place in the era of market regulation and globalisation is that growing numbers of people are either detaching themselves from or being detached from mainstream national regulatory and protective systems. There seem to be seven major groups that have emerged, which are presented in descending order based on average social income.

The Elite

At the zenith of the globalising economy is an elite, consisting of a tiny minority of absurdly rich and high-earning people, whose impact on policy and economic activity is out of all proportion to their number. Some of these individuals have long since reached the stage of seeing their incomes rising almost exponentially. They are global citizens. Although he took losses in early 2000 (losses that to ordinary mortals were absurdly and obscenely large), Bill Gates still had wealth greater than the national income of a majority of countries, and despite that blip it had been rising faster than any of them. In a few years the world's richest 200 individuals apparently doubled their net worth to over $1,000 billion, giving them a total wealth greater than the combined income of the world's poorest 2.5 billion people. In 1999, according to the World Wealth Report 2000, the number of people with liquid financial assets of more than $30 million rose by 18 per cent – to 55,400 individuals.

Moving comfortably in their league, chief executives of major companies have been receiving huge salaries, and more importantly have been given fancy "share options", exaggerated signing-on bonuses and shameless pay-offs when they have their contracts curtailed due to failure, with "golden handshakes" on arrival matched by "golden good-byes" when they depart. For instance, the newly appointed head of Conseco, the US insurance group, was paid $45 million (£30 million) in cash for starting his job, with a guarantee of $31 million in shares and a bonus of $8 million if he stayed for at least two years.[4] He was not alone. The boss of Computer Associates received merely $4.6 million in salary and bonus in 1999; he also received over $650 million in what was described as performance-based compensation. The USA has been a world leader in this process, given that numerous non-salary payments have enabled their executives to receive much more than US workers and relatively much more than managers in any other country of the world. A survey of Standard and Poor's 500 leading companies found that in 1999 chief executives took home 475 times more than the average worker in manufacturing. The nearest comparison was Venezuela, where the bosses took 50 times as much. The UK led the western European league, but there it was only 23 times as much; in Switzerland, it was just 11 times. All these figures seem higher than in the past, but if the US is the "leader", we must watch other countries spawning an executive elite in the very near future.

Table 4.1 adds to the picture of an elite in the USA, showing how the number of dollar billionaires multiplied in the 1980s and 1990s. No doubt, the figures are systematically underestimated. Interestingly, it shows too that the ratio of billionaires to million workers was last comparable at the turn of the last century, when economic liberalisation was also favoured. Even so, the number and ratio were both substantially larger in the 1990s. *Forbes Magazine* counted 267 billionaires in the USA in 1999, compared with thirteen they had found in 1982.

Considering dollar millionaires around the world, it has been estimated by Merrill Lynch (one of those wealth-making organisations that look after the interests of the elite) that their number increased by one million in 1999 alone, raising the total to seven million – 2.5 million in the USA, 2.2 million in Europe, 1.7 million in Asia and the remainder scattered across the rest of the world. It was forecast that the super-rich, those with more than $30 million in liquid financial assets, would see their collected wealth rise from $25,000 billion in 1999 to $44,000 billion in 2004, largely because they could benefit from their wealth by being able to invest in the highest-yielding "investment products", such as hedge funds.

Besides having such assets to play with, the modern elite benefited from a peculiar feature of the latter part of the twentieth century, which was that social norms seem to have accepted much greater income differentials than

Table 4.1. Billionaires in the USA, 1900–96 (expressed in GDP-adjusted terms)

Year	Number of billionaires	Billionaires per million workers
1900	22	0.8
1918	30	0.7
1925	32	0.7
1957	16	0.2
1968	13	0.2
1982	23	0.2
1996	132	1.0

Source: B. DeLong, *Robber Barons* (Berkeley, California, University of California Press, 1998)

in the middle years of the century. Tony Atkinson and Ajit Singh have both cited this as the explanation of changes at the top end of the income distribution.[5] The trouble with this is that it leaves unexplained what changed the social norms. Is there a suggestion that globalisation, techno-logical change and economic openness require much greater inequality? There is no evidence that this is the case, and neither Atkinson nor Singh would subscribe to this. It would be a remarkable rationalisation for a pragmatic acceptance of the elite. Of course, it also leaves open the tantalising prospect that social norms could be amenable to the opposite trend.

Whether or not one should expand the stratum down to multi-millionaires, the most relevant point about the elite is that those belonging to it are detached from national regulatory and social security systems, neither need-ing nor contributing to them, either psychologically – not feeling committed to their maintenance or improvement – or politically. The elite has very strong income security indeed, and whatever they need of other forms of security. They scarcely look to the state to protect their interests. Indeed, they gather wealth through their wealth.

Their biggest dangers are hubris and being caught in criminality. Mafioso capitalism is not a fiction of student campuses and Hollywood films, nor is narco-capitalism. This is not to suggest that most of the elite are criminals. Some do have strange habits, such as a tendency to fall off their boats in the Atlantic or indulging in a spell in an open prison for fraud. Most seem to have a pathological desire for money. They have their critics. They also have their dedicated fans. Some economists laud their "animal spirits", as if they galvanise the global economy. Yet there is no evidence that their income and wealth are necessary or even functional. Some politicians salute their entre-preneurial flair, being careful to hold out their hands for supportive contributions. They are feared by many who depend on their good will, which include some prime ministers and presidents. Their number may be tiny, but their influence is out of all proportion to that. The pandering to their whims by politicians should be more worrying than it appears to be.

Recent analyses have tried to describe the lifestyle of the new "super rich", but it is best not to put all the wealthy in this elite category. One analysis has lumped all the wealthy in a single group, which the authors call cosmocrats.[6] They concoct a figure of 20 million people in the world as belonging to this category. This is misleading, because it lumps the merely very affluent with those whose wealth could not possibly be attributed to their "productivity". In any case, they are not a ruling class. They may be symbolic of a hege-monic morality, the creed of libertarianism taken to its extreme. But they do not rule.

The justification for leaving the elite to enjoy their extraordinary wealth and income would seem to be something like the following: Unequal out-comes are not unjust; justice lies in legal acquisition, and if nobody can prove that you have acquired the wealth illegally, it is just; if you become very rich, it is because you merit it, and we live in a world of equal opportunity for meritocracy. This is the line. But the elite make money while they sleep, as

François Mitterand once lamented. Actually, merit does not seem to play much part in it, once they move into the elite.

It is disingenuous to argue that globalisation and economic growth depend on the existence of such an elite, implying that if anything were done to reduce their wealth the global economy would grind to a halt or become more unstable. This is pure dogma, dressed up in the garb of "liberalism" and freedom. It is hard to imagine that the global problem of economic insecurity for the majority can be rectified unless the wealth and security of the elite are checked.

Proficians

Below the elite in terms of income is a stratum that we could label proficians. This is a heterogeneous group, which has attracted considerable journalistic attention. As the name implies, they are a mix of professional and technician, mostly working as consultants or in short-term employment contracts. They may be professional in lifestyle or aspiration, but are technician in having a mix of technical skills and "on-the-job" experience that they seek to turn into a definable niche. There is no set pattern. Some are working as individuals, giving themselves "business cards" defining themselves as small companies. Some mix contract work with a salaried job that they can do from time to time. Some have moved into a more secure existence in which they have a contract of employment with a firm but only work for it when there is work to do in it or when they have no other more lucrative activity from their consultancy network. This group may be a harbinger of the more secure "portfolio" workers that some authors have lauded. They are likely to work on the basis of commercial contracts rather than with labour or employment contracts.

Among the proficians are the new craftsmen of the global flexible economy. However, most seem to focus on making money and being prodigious consumers.[7] A term that has the potential for congealing into a concept is "bobos", which one observer has called "the new information elite", defined as "highly educated folk who have one foot in the bohemian world of creativity another foot in the bourgeois realm of ambition and worldly success".[8] This gives them an unjustified gloss. The bohemian element is weak, although some who fit into this stratum of global society do have a creative aura. But it is the bourgeois motivation that seems to drive their existence. They measure their success in consumerism and material terms.

Commonly there is a peculiar combination of smugness and insecurity, which to some extent reflects the long-term shift of formal education to schooling, in which the development of the capacity to question and criticise existing structures has given way to the dictates of technical "human capital". Brooks is happy to celebrate what he sees as the reconciliation of the bourgeois and the bohemian. But the groups he describes have more to do with a commodification of creativity; it is only beautiful if it is commercially valuable. Eric Hobsbawm captured similar nineteenth century tendencies in his book *The Age of Capital*. But that variant was narrow and limited by comparison with the early twenty-first century global blend of commerce and creativity. For these reasons, the term "bobo" is unsatisfactory, because it suggests a balance that is absent.

In general, proficians operate in a climate of insecurity, but are well compensated for this. Besides their lack of employment security, which they accept as the price to pay for high incomes and the sense of freedom that they enjoy, perhaps their main form of insecurity is work insecurity, epitomised by the frenzied pace of their erratic work schedules and evident stress under which they live and work. Their mobile phones and bleepers control their time as electronic leashes. They are often able to evade or avoid taxation, and are at least partially detached from state-based social protection systems. Among them are what a report by Price Waterhouse Coopers called the "nomadic networker", the person who is on call to work almost anywhere in the world on a short-term contract.

Proficians belong to a milieu of respectability, an alliance of the privileged. Ironically, they have a dependency relationship with politicians and with corporate giants. If they can capture the right language and tone, they are on the path to fame and fortune. If they get it wrong they disappear into suburbia and the life of *American Beauty*. In a strange way, they are marginalised, by their dependency on transient networks and relationships, opportunistic peers and a rapidly changing discourse of euphemisms. They are often very rich, but on the edge it is the affluence of the whore, always hingeing on the reflection in the mirror. Who has the power? None of them and all of them.

Reflect on the marginalised existence of the proficians. They have a frenetic lifestyle, conducive to "burn-out", scary opportunism and economic irrationality. You will see them scurrying around airports, in business lounges, laptops on the alert, mobile phones incessantly tapped and lifted. Time is money. Money is the corrosion of time. Because you are affluent, because you could be more affluent if you take advantage of your advantage, you must fill every moment of the day, and of the night if possible. The character type has become a cliché. They embrace what Micklewait and Wooldridge called the Sabbatical Man – the academic who is rarely in his ivory tower or teaching students – and the Agency Man – the international bureaucrat who pushes paper and emails to others and slips between airports and other bureau-cracies. These types are on the edge of the profician group, helping to give the stratum its parasitic character.

The proficians are the closest to being a new or emerging ruling class. They hover around political leaders, write their speeches, and invent their buzz words, their euphemisms and their "sound bites". But they listen to the interests they need to placate. What is that they will want to give them economic security? The answer to this question is a key to the future of political, economic and social policy strategy, to which we will return in the final chapters.

The elite does not rule; it influences, it seduces and it threatens those who adopt a ruling pose or those who might disturb their way of life. It disburses large amounts of money, with discretion, paternalistically. But increasingly those who shape policy are from one rung below the elite. It is a chosen few from among the proficians, who are in their way marginalised, even when linked to "think tanks" and respectable civil society organisations (CSOs). They may be nomadic or philosophically rootless, but understanding policy changes and policy options requires an understanding of their rationality and insecurities.

The Salariat

Alongside the proficians are those still wedded to regular employment as salaried employees, including those working in civil services, large corporations, parastatals and other bureaucracies. They have a high degree of labour security overall, but probably suffer from some job and skill reproduction insecurity, because they may be moved around at the whim of their superiors and/or gain promotion in their enterprises only by leaving technical skills behind them – de-skilled by promotion. Because of their reasonably high incomes and a tendency to identify with managements and employers, and often nurture a quiet aspiration to join the elite and profician strata, members of the salariat typically feel detached from the state social protection system, seeing their future and income security in terms mainly of private insurance benefits and earnings from judicious investment.

The salariat suffer from a fear of loss of status. For several decades they were the fortunate and the envied, with the best fringe benefits and relatively relaxed work styles. But in recent years those in the public sector have operated against the backdrop of a fear of privatisation, while those in large corporations have experienced the threat of displacement, and the loss of respect for the "stable employee", seen as risk-averse and non-entrepreneurial. In many countries they are no longer the most respected citizens guiding social development. Commentators and policymakers have depicted those in the public sector as unproductive and a drag on the public purse. A politician is judged on the macho stance *vis-à-vis* the public sector, and corporate management has tended to wish to show that it could downsize while raising output. The news that Xerox was cutting its workforce by 10 per cent resulted in the company's share value rising sharply. There seems to be a culture of uncertainty extended even to well-paid salaried employees.

The conflicting tendencies have produced a wide range of reactions. There are plenty of anecdotes of middle-aged salaried people pining for an opportunity to join the proficians "next year" or "when the kids are out of school" or "when the mortgage is paid". This aspiration encourages them to feel detached from the state system of benefits. But it is the salariat that seems to have experienced the greatest stress, resorting to extraordinarily long workweeks, to *presenteeism*, and in Japan to *karoshi* – death from overwork. They also suffer from some strange forms of job and skill insecurity, including de-skilling that results from promotion into posts in which they cannot use or develop their occupational competencies.

In most countries, their employment security has undoubtedly deteriorated in recent years. In the case of those in the public sector, this is in part because of the fear of privatisation and the contracting out of public services, and in part it reflects the political rhetoric about cutting the public sector. They have also lost some of their social status, and are no longer quite the respected citizens guiding society's development that they once were or were expected to be. There have been some attempts to restore their status, claiming that they are the basis of sustained company performance.[9] But in the public and corporate spheres, they have been shrinking, losing status, numbers and security.

Core Workers

Coming below the proficians and salariat in terms of average income and status are what can be called the core of the workforce, with a slight sense of irony. These are the bulwark of what those of us with long memories used to call the working class. Welfare states were created to serve the needs of such core workers, those people, mostly men, in full-time, regular, typically unionised jobs, usually with manual skills. During the era of statutory regulation, it was implicitly presumed that these workers represented the norm and that a majority of workers in all countries would eventually belong to this stratum. The larger the proportion of people belonging to it, the more people would be in a position to support, contribute to and benefit from the mainstream, insurance-based social protection system and the mainstream regulatory system.

Surely, this is the group that has not been marginalised. Not so. The trouble is that, although the legitimacy of a redistributive welfare state depended on core workers, they never comprised a majority of the economically active in most countries and since the 1970s have been shrinking. This is not just a reflection of "de-industrialisation" in industrialised countries, or the dispersion of manufacturing wage labour around the world. It is also due to various forms of labour market flexibility. Core workers traditionally benefited from most forms of labour security, but with wage system flexibility a growing proportion of their income has come in insecure forms. They also suffer increasingly from job insecurity and employment insecurity, while their unions have been weakened almost everywhere. The institutions on which they have relied have lost their power and they have lost their capacity to draw others into their sphere. Above all, with core workers dwindling in numbers and not expected to grow, their agenda has ceased to have a presumed legitimacy.

Flexiworkers

These comprise a disparate group of people in non-regular work statuses, including casual workers, outworkers, sub-contracted and contract labour, agency workers and domestic workers. Their common characteristic is labour insecurity in almost all respects. In the era of statutory regulation and welfare state capitalism, it was presumed that these "informal" forms of employment would decline as economies developed.

In recent years, they have appeared to be the future for the majority of people without higher-level qualifications, and for many with them as well. In the European Union, it has been estimated that 42 million people are on flexible contracts, a growing number working for employment agencies. It is generally recognised that the official statistics are serious under-estimates. But the bigger number still consists of those working with no contract at all, most in developing countries. Not only have the number of people trapped in petty activities in rural and peri-urban areas grown, but increasingly flexible labour processes have boosted many other forms. Among the associated trends, growing proportions of labour forces have lacked entitlement to mainstream statutory protection and have been disentitled to state transfers and occupational welfare provided by enter-prises for which they work. They generally lack income security, and most forms of labour security.

The Unemployed

These deserve to be regarded as a social category because so many of them spend long periods in this state. Almost everywhere – although in some countries they do not appear in the statistics – the number of people in a status close to the conventional image of unemployment has risen in the era of market regulation. They suffer from labour market insecurity, given higher unemployment, and from greater income insecurity than in the past, because, as indicated later, benefits have been cut, duration of entitlement has been shortened, and conditions for entitlement have been tightened. They have also suffered from a change in public attitude, from being depicted as predominantly victims and "involuntarily" unemployed to being seen as "scroungers" or presumed to be "voluntarily" not working.

The Detached

This is a growing minority in many countries, a lumpenised group of people cut off from mainstream state or enterprise benefits, lingering in poverty, anomic and threatening those above them in the income spectrum, not so much by their violent agitation but simply because others fear falling into their ranks. In recent years, politicians have been inclined to treat these, many of whom are victims of economic liberalisation, as in need of "reintegration". They linger in the streets, in bus and train stations, in city parks. They make those above them in the social order feel uncomfortable or smug, depending on where they fit. The detached represent fear. And it is fear of joining them that induces concessions from the near poor – fear being the ultimate tool of inequality. At the edges of the detached are those who become the trans-gressing poor, who end up incarcerated in prisons. The USA has certainly led the way in dealing with its detached in this manner. Although reported crime levels declined steadily in the 1990s, the number in prison rose equally steadily, reaching 1.8 million in 1998, or one in every 150 Americans.

Whether imprisoned, in some government scheme, or wretchedly in the streets, the detached have attracted more than their fair share of colourful epithets, including the underclass. How their number is reduced tells us as much about a society as their number itself. What the late twentieth century seemed to forget is that their number tends to be correlated with the size and affluence of the groups at the top of the income spectrum.

In sum, we may depict the evolving globalisation economic structure in terms of seven social strata. Depicting society in these terms does not cover everybody. There are the "retired", who depend on a pension, savings or support from their community. They could be incorporated into the seven strata if one stretched the definitions, just as children and students could be treated separately or as part of the various groups according to their parents' status. And there would be those who would wish for a more "gendered" approach. No typology is ideal for all purposes. Our primary objective is to examine the dynamics of work and economic security.

With the stratification as background, in order to understand the growth of income insecurity, it should be useful to try to picture modal trends in the structure of incomes. For this, we need to consider the stylised facts on trends in wages and wage systems and the components of social income, starting with trends for those in employment.

3 Income Security of the Employed

Income security in both state socialism and welfare state capitalism was made to depend on the performance of labour or the willingness to labour. In welfare state capitalism, it was expected that a growing majority of the adult population would be in stable, full-time employment underpinned by a minimum wage and protected through a tiered system of collective bargaining, at plant, sectoral and national levels, in which protective coverage was extended beyond the bargaining unit, formally as in western Germany or informally, because even non-unionised firms moved wages in line with negotiated wages, for ease of administration and to forestall unionisation.

In the era of statutory regulation, there was an international trend towards centralised bargaining and to statutory incomes policy. This strengthened income security directly and by offering the prospect of compressing wage differentials, as was made explicit in the Swedish solidaristic wage policy, or implicit through moral suasion and competitive pressure elsewhere. Low wage differentials translated into modest income differentiation as a result of progressive income tax, plus consumption subsidies that accounted for a large share of the income of the low-income workers.

In the 1980s and 1990s, all these trends went into reverse, so that institutional pressures to reduce wage differentials and strengthen income security at the bottom of the labour market were eroded. The nature of the labour market was reshaped, not de-regulated.

The Minimum Wage

Throughout the twentieth century, the statutory minimum wage was regarded as the primary weapon for providing basic income security in the labour market. But in recent years, in the name of flexibility and employment promotion, in most parts of the world minimum wages have been eroded, with declines in their real value and in their value relative to average incomes, and with diminishing coverage. The erosion of coverage has happened explicitly – in that fewer categories of worker have been covered – and implicitly – in that more people have drifted into statuses precluding them from coverage. The erosion was accelerated by hostile critiques of a statutory minimum wage from many sources, including the OECD, World Bank, IMF and what one might call "neo-liberal" governments.

In 1998, after many years in which minimum wage protection had been cut, the UK became one of the few countries to try to buck the global trend, when a national minimum wage was introduced as part of its Third Way strategy. But it was quite modest. Elsewhere, declines have been substantial. In the USA, the upgrading of its minimum wage in 1996 merely returned the level to what it had been many years earlier and still left it a low percentage of the average wage by international standards. In western Europe, cuts took place in several countries, such as the Netherlands and Portugal, and there has been a trend towards multiple-tier minimum wages, with lower rates for youths, or for some regions and sectors, as in Japan.

In eastern Europe, minimum wages fell to farcically low levels in the 1990s, mostly falling to tiny fractions of officially determined subsistence incomes.[10] In developing countries, often influenced by pressure from international financial agencies and by papers written for them by economists critical of minimum wages as a source of labour market rigidities, they have been eroded considerably, as ILO studies have shown.

In sum, the minimum wage has ceased to be an instrument for social solidarity or for providing a floor of income security. In more flexible and informal labour markets, it is also less likely to protect low-paid workers. It remains potentially useful, but largely as a means of setting a standard of decency and a signal for wage bargaining, rather than as an effective means of ensuring basic income security.

Bargained Wages

In the 1980s and 1990s, there was an onslaught on centralised wage bargaining all over the world. This had an ideological cutting edge, since it was unashamedly intended to weaken the bargaining strength of workers and unions. Often this was the intention of governments, as in the Netherlands, the UK and Chile, and it was for this reason that it was also promoted by international financial agencies. Whatever the effects on flexibility and inflation, decentralisation of bargaining and individualisation of wage determination tend to widen wage differentials and contribute to the income insecurity of many more workers.

Statutory incomes policy also lost its appeal, so removing a force for wage compression and predictable real wages, and was only resurrected in a few places where it took the form of organised concession bargaining, scarcely providing workers with the prospect of enhanced income security.

Flexible Wages

In most parts of the world, the sustained pressure to achieve greater wage flexibility has resulted in wage systems giving a lower weight to the fixed wage and a growing weight to flexible supplements. The more secure part of any wage is that established by statute or collective bargains, so the trend to other forms is increasing income insecurity for many groups of workers.

The decentralisation and individualisation of wage determination create more insecurity. They raise the scope for non-payment of contracted wages, since they weaken monitoring mechanisms, and increase the risk for any aggrieved worker contemplating action, given the lack of collective or statutory support. Privatisation of public services also leads to greater wage flexibility and insecurity. It also spreads the use of "performance-related pay", definitionally increasing insecurity because wages are rarely known in advance.

Multiple-tier wage systems have spread, representing a further form of decentralisation. It is now more common for young workers to be paid lower wages simply because of their age, and in some countries lower wages are paid for longer probation periods. Temporaries and casual labour are usually paid lower wages and more flexibly determined wages than regular workers, which means that employers have more discretion in taking advantage of their insecurity. And outworkers, typically paid on a piece-rate basis, are not provided with enterprise benefits or entitlements to state-based social protection. Wage insecurity has also been increased by the reality and fear of concession bargaining.

Flexibility has resulted in looser wage systems, meaning that workers are more likely to experience a fluctuation in their incomes or a drop in real wages at short notice. This has become common for those changing jobs, but has also increased for those who do not change jobs.[11] Flexible pay systems simply mean greater income insecurity for all workers, whether they change jobs or not.

Wage Differentials

Meanwhile, although some forms of wage inequality have declined a little (notably between men and women in some countries, albeit by not enough for gender equity), wage differentials have tended to widen. One reason is precisely that wage systems have become more flexible, with an international trend towards decentralization of collective and individual wage determination.

In the 1980s and 1990s, wage differentials widened in most countries for which data are available. In the UK, they widened to the point where it was estimated that the gaps between the top decile of wages and the median wage and those earning low wages returned to what they had been in the late nineteenth century.[12] Widening differentials have been attributed in part to the growth of performance-related pay, and to other forms of flexible pay. Similar trends have been found in the USA and Canada. In developing countries, wage inequality widened quite sharply.

Many economists believe that in industrialised countries such as the USA "skill"-based differentials are being widened by globalisation, partly as a result of actual or potential trade with developing countries.[13] With a regionalised or global labour market, this must be true to some extent, even though the effect could be moderated by controls over labour mobility and by productivity differentials. Other economists have attributed the major role to new technology, reducing the demand for "unskilled" labour, while others have concluded that it is hard to separate the various aspects of globalisation. An interesting view is that because economic liberalisation weakened the capacity of unions to defend wages, the low-skilled have suffered most because the greatest achievement of unions had been to narrow wage differentials by raising the wages of the low-skilled.

Whatever the full explanation, wider differentials are a reality and intensify the income insecurity of those on low wages, especially if there is little prospect of upward mobility. But whatever has happened to wages, it is only a small part of a story of socio-economic stratification. The growth of inequality is due mainly to what has happened at the top end of the income spectrum, which has little to do with wage differentials.

Non-wage Enterprise Benefits

Although reliable aggregative data are scarce, there are enough anecdotal and survey data to conclude that in the era of globalisation, enterprise benefits have become a major source of greater inequality. Whereas they have grown in number and value for privileged groups, they have shrunk for core workers and flexiworkers. There has been a remarkable spread of the US practice of paying the salariat and proficians in the form of share options and other longer-term "incentives". This has tended to widen income inequality within the workforce quite dramatically. They can also be a source of income insecurity, because usually they allow for discretionary treatment of individuals and groups. The fact that they are often operated "confidentially" allows for undeclared incomes rather more easily.

Employment flexibility has been associated with both erosion and more differentiated access to enterprise benefits. Thus, for instance, in Canada those in temporary jobs or working part-time, or working in small firms, or in non-union firms all have a below average probability of access to such benefits. In the USA, a similar pattern has been found. Those in long-established firms are more likely to receive family-friendly benefits, such as health insurance, pensions, life insurance, paid vacations, sick leave, parental and maternity leave, childcare benefits, parenting workshops or counselling, and even company picnics.[14] Between 1982 and 1996, according to research by the Economic Policy Institute and the Women's Research and Education Institute, high-income earners on average gained in enterprise benefits, while the low-paid lost them. While all groups tended to lose enterprise-provided health insurance, the loss was much greater for low-wage workers.

Firms may have been differentiating their workforces more by differential entitlement to such benefits than from changes in their wages, even though wage and salary differentials have widened as well. To compound the resultant inequality and insecurity, it is the lower-paid who tend to have the greater need for such benefits, as in the case of health cover, given their greater tendency to suffer from on-the-job injuries and sickness.

In eastern Europe, the greatest source of the severe income insecurity in the 1990s was the virtual collapse of enterprise welfare. Decommodification in the Soviet era meant that a large part of social income had come from enterprise benefits and services. These simply dried up. Although money wages appeared to rise in parts of the region, in many this was a delusion. Loss of those benefits was worth more than any gain in money wages.

Elsewhere in the world, enterprise benefits are playing a greater differ-entiating role than used to be the case. Those with secure employment, particularly higher-income employees, have found that a growing proportion of their income has come from these, with hefty bonuses and share options coming to the forefront. Others have been less privileged, being in labour statuses blocking them from access to them.

The weakening of representation security has also contributed to the erosion and increasingly selective provision of enterprise benefits and services. Unionised firms in both industrialised and industrialising economies have tended to provide workers with a wider array of benefits than otherwise similar non-unionised firms, and firms with independent unions are more likely to provide them than those with company unions.[15] One senses that the weakening of unions actually contributed more to the general erosion of enterprise benefits, even in firms that remained unionised.

Cost of Employment Loss

In the era of statutory regulation, in most industrialised countries the cost of employment loss was not much greater for low-income workers than for salaried "white-collar" employees. Both could expect a redundancy payment, or both had a similar probability of receiving one. And both could expect to find another job relatively easily, paying a similar wage to the one they had lost.

In recent years, for most workers the cost of employment loss has tended to rise, largely because benefits outside employment have been less assured, have had lower value or are expected to have lower value, duration of entitlement has tended to fall, conditionality for entitlement has been tightened, "in-work" benefits have been extended, and the probability of returning to a job paying a similar wage to the one that has been lost has fallen. A study in the USA, for instance, found that whereas in the 1970s most of those losing jobs found another paying as well, in 1996 only a minority did so. Ironically, given that it had long advocated policies that created the outcome, the OECD estimated that in industrialised countries income loss from employment separation increased during the 1990s.[16] This reflected greater employment insecurity and labour market insecurity.

Alan Greenspan, US Federal Reserve Chairman, has given a series of speeches in which he attributed low US unemployment to a lack of inflationary pressure, due largely to workers' fear of losing their job and "the signific-antly higher capacity for job dismissal" than in other countries. But those countries may have moved to what is euphemistically called "a soft conver-gence", so that a price for lower unemployment will be greater income insecurity.

In sum, changes in payment systems have tended to make income from labour more unequal and more insecure. It is this general pattern that has set the tone for the spread of income insecurity, although changes in social protection have played their part as well.

4 State Benefits

For the employed living in welfare state capitalism, state support long con-sisted of subsidies to consumption goods and in-kind benefits and a growing array of cash or in-kind entitlements that were important components of social income, ranging from paid sick leave and a state pension to a strong prospect of unemployment benefits if they lost their job. Back in the 1960s and 1970s, a steady expansion in the range of such benefits seemed the long-term trend.

For the core and salariat, these trends have stood up reasonably well. But many more people have found themselves in work statuses giving them more fragile entitlement. Even those in regular full-time jobs have experienced a chipping-away at sources of income security. For instance, the duration of employment required to obtain entitlement to state transfers has tended to increase, with implications for inequality not yet taken into account in statistical measures. This amounts to a cut in the state benefit (SB) share of social income.

In industrialised countries, by the 1970s many people achieved reasonable economic security as a result of the steady extension of their social rights. The state stepped in where the market failed. As long as he was prepared to labour and be loyal to factory, farm, company or organisation, labouring man could expect benefits "from cradle to grave" for himself and "his" family. As growing numbers of women were absorbed into the labour force, state transfers and services were extended to them, often to enable them to labour more effectively and "equally" with men.

Anti-discrimination laws were strengthened, protecting minorities and women, and those with disabilities, if they were in regular wage labour. Welfare states seemed to be strengthening individual security within a welfare-regulated labour market, and state benefits rose as a share of national income. Some countries were more extensive and redistributive than others, but there were advances in most of them.

Richard Titmuss originally distinguished between what he called the institutional-redistributive model, which he saw as predominating in western Europe, and the residual model, the prime case being the USA. The former was seen as relying largely on universalistic access to benefits and services, the latter on selective access. Social and labour policies evolved in different ways to reflect cultural, historical, political and economic differences. It took time for the structures to settle, and it took time for scholars to categorise their distinctive characters. Esping-Andersen differentiated what he called liberal, conservative and social-democratic welfare state regimes, depending on the extent to which benefits were intended to be redistributive, were state administered and were "decommodifying".[17] The liberal regime was close to the residual model, with selective targeting of state benefits according to per-ceived "needs". The conservative regime relied largely on "social insurance", with benefits depending on contributions, which depend on income from employment. The social-democratic regime is most closely associated with the gradual extension of social rights, and with extension of universal social services.

There have been numerous analyses of welfare regimes, with some coun-tries being identified as one type or another or as some hybrid. Some points seem clear. All welfare state systems have rested on a labourist base. The historical debate on the right to work was linked to the evolution of social insurance and with variants of social security. Two figures are identified as the defining spirits, and both had strong paternalistic leanings. For Bismarck, its originator, social insurance was a means of binding the working class to the existing social order. Although he did not set up unemployment insurance, he established the principle that the state would grant income security if a worker satisfied labour obligations and was a kind of worker valued by the state. For Beveridge, in his *Social Insurance and Allied Services* report of 1942 and in *Full Employment in a Free Society* of 1944, the design of labour-based welfare was guided by the model of a nuclear family, with male breadwinner and dependent wife. For Beveridge, women were secondary workers, and the state had no duty to diminish a husband's obligation to a wife.

In all variants of welfare state, the sexist basis has been a weakness, which could be only addressed in an *ad hoc* way, as social, economic and labour market changes resulted in political pressure to do so. As feminists have pointed out, as it did so it extended "exit from labour" rights while neglecting "exit out of family" rights.[18] Although the state benefit component of social income increased in most countries, public policy was expected to bolster both labour and the nuclear family. In the latter part of the century, it became increasingly unable to do either.

For more than two decades, welfare states succeeded in embedding the economy in society, covering what were regarded as contingency risks such as old age, maternity, sickness and unemployment. Yet the tensions gradually produced cracks. The bureaucratic nature of systems of income protection meant it was hard to respond to behavioural and circumstantial diversity, which is the essence of flexibility and economic informalisation. Statutory refinements intended to embrace more varieties of experience, such as single parenting, created more complex edifices, which were rarely transparent. They were administratively costly, and were usually unaccountable to ordinary people, as well as prone to moral hazards and adverse selection. Globalis-ation and economic liberalisation added fiscal and regulatory pressures, reminding us that Gunnar Myrdal, an important influence on the Swedish model, had recognised that the welfare state depended on an essentially closed economy model. For these and other reasons, mostly associated with ideological shifts and the global imposition of the Washington Consensus, at least since the 1970s, there has been an international trend to a hybrid of the conservative and liberal regimes – or to Titmus' residual model – involving some labour re-commodification.

The pressures that chipped away at welfare state capitalism stemmed largely from its labourist basis. As welfare provision was extended to newly legitimised contingencies, it became harder to draw a line on what merited coverage, what could be afforded and what priority to give to perceived needs. Moral, fiscal and legitimation considerations jostled for political supremacy. Recognising that disadvantage and discrimination take numerous forms, governments responded by introducing new rules or procedures. But as one practice is covered by being banned, penalised or compensated, another becomes more visible, moving up the priority list. Each adds to the cost, each requiring a bureaucratic apparatus, each tending to raise social contributions and taxes, or lowering some benefit.

The tensions on state benefit systems, due to the pressures of global-isation, labour market changes and ideological shifts of opinion, have generated a prolonged "crisis" affecting social protection around the world since the 1980s. The word crisis is overused, but the sense of threat and opportunity for change has been real. The old welfare state models should not be idealised; they had many faults, some structural. They were less redistributive than their advocates believed or pretended to believe. But the changes since the 1980s have contributed to greater income insecurity, a restructuring of social income and an increase in social income inequality linked to the new global stratification. One may see these trends through a review of what may be called the eight crises of social protection.

The Eight Crises of Social Protection

(i) The Fiscal Crisis of the Welfare State

By the 1980s, there was a widely perceived fiscal crisis of the welfare state, which spawned an impressive literature. There was a belief that affluent countries could not afford extensive state benefits, that the system was "rigid", producing a "dependency culture" that was a "burden on the economy" as well as being socially reprehensible, artificially raising un-employment. The welfare state was also seen to be failing to protect those most in need, perversely redistributing income to the middle class. Defenders of state benefits were thrown into disarray.

A sense of fiscal crisis was accentuated by the return of mass unemploy-ment, and the spread of informal and part-time employment from which social security contributions were limited. The contributory basis of social insurance was eroded or turned into a fiction, so that a rising share of social security finance had to come from tax, implying "fiscal subsidies" and seem-ingly contributing to public budget deficits, anathema to the new economic orthodoxy. A rising demand for transfers, a tendency for tax and contribution rates to take a higher share of earnings, and a tendency for those who lost jobs to face the prospect of lower incomes in new jobs all accentuated poverty traps and unemployment traps – losing more in benefits than they would gain by taking a job or labouring more in an existing low-paid job.

This gave opportunistic politicians and commentators an opportunity to claim that it paid more people to stay unemployed or to find ways of avoiding and evading contributions by clandestine labour arrangements. This in turn encouraged the state to spend more on policing the system. And high contribution rates seemed to raise labour costs (although one could argue they were passed on in lower wages), encouraging labour saving and a belief that labour-intensive production was moving to industrialising countries.

The perceived fiscal crisis also seemed to reflect an insatiable demand for healthcare improvements and a rising old-age dependency ratio, compounded by early retirement schemes that spread as a misguided response to high unemployment. And it reflected a need for high economic growth to fund improving social security, at a time when growth rates were being cut by the deflationary macro-economic policy stance of the Washington Consensus.

Essentially, the contributory basis of social insurance has been eroded, and the prospects for such a contributory basis in developing countries have faded into irrelevance. While contributions have tended to shrink, the demand for social protection has risen, and the need for it has risen even more. It has become a commonplace to refer to the low "coverage" rates of social insurance systems, and many proposals have been made to achieve an "extension" of social security, although it is rarely clear what extension would mean.

Although labour market changes and greater income inequality within countries have contributed to shrinking coverage in industrialised countries, one factor in the generalised crisis has been the growing power of capital, associated with increased capital mobility. Perceiving there is less need to compromise on social protection, big corporations have been less willing to pay contributions to solidaristic systems or to operate elaborate enterprise benefit schemes for low-income workers, putting more onus on the state. In developing countries, another factor, which has received little attention, is increased dependency on foreign aid and debt relief. This may discourage national and multinational corporations from contributing to the revenue required for adequate social protection.

Whatever the factors behind the fiscal pressures, governments have responded in ways that have cut the share of state benefits in social income, most of which have had regressive implications for the distribution of income and income security.

First, urged by the IMF, OECD and other bodies to move to "less generosity" (as if the benefits were charity) – governments have tended to cut benefit levels, by abandoning or weakening indexation, by holding down the minimum wage to which they have been linked, or by adjusting them less often to inflation, or by simply cutting the level. In some cases, this has been rationalised by reference to the "need" to cut labour costs or seemingly high "replacement rates" (the value of benefit relative to income from a job). But the latter tends to rise in labour markets characterised by widening wage differentials due to low-wage workers earning lower wages. In any case, cutting benefit levels has typically been justified on the grounds of "incentives" and the need to "cut dependency".

Second, they have made benefits and services increasingly selective (targeted). There has been a steady process of explicit disentitlement – with some groups finding they are not eligible for benefits or services – alongside a process of implicit disentitlement – caused by changes in the way labour relations are organised that have put more people in statuses that do not qualify them for state benefits.

As the tax share of the revenue needed for social protection has risen, the fiscal screw has been tightened, since governments have tried to cut social budgets. They have tightened the criteria used to determine who receives and who does not receive benefits, contributing to the global spread of conditionality and the extraordinary array of ingenious ways of deciding who should be excluded from entitlements – means-testing, asset-testing, behaviour-testing, categorical-testing, and so on. It has also contributed to the popularity of earned-income tax credits – so-called "in-work benefits" – as a means of social protection and incentive to labour.

Part of the increased selectivitiy is the piecemeal way by which governments have raised the level and duration of contributions required to secure entitlement to benefits, or to full entitlement to them. This has hit flexi-workers relative to the salariat. The main trend has been to restrict entitlement to insurance benefits and to full benefits among those still entitled to them. In terms of type of benefit, there has been a drift to means-tested "social assistance", away from universal (citizenship rights) and insurance benefits, although in some cases the fiction of insurance has been retained. There has also been a tendency to shift the contributory burden from the state and employer onto workers.

Pensions have become more labour-based. In countries with established state pensions, people without a long record of regular full-time labour have been losing, by means of the amount to which they are entitled. Disability benefits have become more selective and conditional. Healthcare has been drifting in the direction of user-pay and dualistic systems in which entitlement to free or subsidised treatment and service has been restricted or provided on a categorical basis. Unemployment insurance benefits have been whittled away.

Some countries have relied largely on means-tested schemes, led by Australia and New Zealand; others have moved in that direction, led by Ireland, the UK and USA. Even where the image of social insurance has been preserved, many people have come to rely on means-tested assistance – 7 per cent of adults in Germany and Sweden, for instance.[19] In eastern Europe, the rise in the share of the population receiving means-tested benefits was extraordinary in the 1990s, rising by more than 1000 per cent in some countries. In western Europe, the rise was also large, more than tripling in France. The share of national income going on such assistance also rose. In all types of "welfare states", the number and income share rose, so that the share of social income coming from this type of benefit also rose. By 1995, more than a third of all benefits in the UK were means-tested; in the USA between 1974 and 1994, the share of GDP going on social assistance rose by a third. Means-testing is rampant.

Also partly in response to fiscal pressures, governments have decentralised and delegated responsibility for benefits and services, shifting the cost to local authorities or to parastatal or private agencies. They have also given more attention to efficiency in the financing and delivery of benefits and services. This is not as straightforward as it might imply. Indeed, a key to the flight to selectivity is the distinction between administrative, horizontal and vertical efficiency. A policy is administratively efficient if it uses a small amount of resources to achieve its objectives. This is often measured by the ratio of staff to clients, placement rates or achievement of targets. A policy is horizontally efficient if it reaches a high percentage of the target group; it is vertically efficient if those it reaches consist mainly or wholly of those in the target group.

Policymakers have become far more interested in vertical and administrative efficiency. This has implications for the equity properties of social protection, to which we will return. But note that while fiscal concerns create pressure to make the system more efficient, selective schemes mean more complexity and tiers of decision-making. Horizontal efficiency (reaching as many of the eligible as possible) usually gives way to vertical efficiency (making sure those not eligible do not receive anything). This raises the cost of policing and monitoring and reduces the cost of seeking out those who are eligible. But it tends to be costly, because of the complexity. Administrative efficiency is particularly low in developing countries and where labour markets are in disarray as in areas of industrial restructuring, informality and "transition". So, fiscal pressures may merely reallocate costs.

Finally, besides contributing to selectivity and decentralisation, fiscal pressures have helped rationalise a major response to globalisation – the *privatisation of social protection*, in the sphere of pensions, healthcare, schooling, social care and employment services, to a greater or lesser extent. Privatisation is linked to multi-tierism – providing components of a particular benefit by different means and criteria. Both have been influenced by economic orthodoxy, political ideology, powerful commercial interests, more flexible and informal labour arrangements, and the fact that the share of affluent groups' income coming from labour has been declining.

Healthcare has become more diversified, with a tendency to shift more of the funding from employers to workers, to increased user-payment for services, to differentiate services by whether they are free, subsidised or fully paid, and to reduce direct public provision. This has been associated with an expansion of healthcare provided by firms, increasing inequality. Thus, in the USA higher-income groups are more likely to have company health and pension plans than other workers, women and part-timers are less likely to have such plans (even within job categories).

Schooling has shown similar trends, so that even where the state seems to be paying, part of the costs and responsibility have been passed to students and their families, with loans and vouchers replacing grants, and with cuts in stipends. The income security of relatively educated youth has been weakened, instilling a labouring ethic before they land in the labour market.

Pensions are the benefits that have been privatised and subject to multi-tierism most. This has been encouraged by international financial agencies, which have used conditional loans and assistance to cajole governments to move to private-funded and multi-tier pension schemes. An aspect of private-funded schemes is the claim that if people think the pension is related to their contributions, they will regard what they contribute as saving, not a tax, which will raise the incentive to labour. As such, a shift from PAYG to private funding is "commodifying", even if the main behavioural effect is to alter the timing or intensity of labour force participation over the life cycle.

If a dominant pension system is emerging, it is a four-pillar one, with a base consisting of a low public pension, perhaps means-tested, on top of which is a PAYG or private-funded compulsory scheme, topped up by an occupational pension (negotiated between firms and their workers, collectively or individually), and then topped up even more by private saving schemes. Pension reforms have influenced the restructuring of social income (cutting the state benefit component), increased income inequality and insecurity, and become part of the armoury of fiscal regulation, in that they act as an incentive and reward for regular, well-remunerated labour. In contrast to defined benefit plans, the growing type of pension, defined contribution plans (and 401(K)-type schemes), reallocate risk to potential beneficiaries, and this in itself cuts the social income of workers.

The responses to fiscal pressures have clearly had an effect on the level and structure of social income security. By the early twenty-first century, many countries seem to have managed to contain the fiscal pressures. Those budgetary deficits do not induce the fear and panic that they did a few years ago. The trouble is that the ways in which the politicians and international bodies have modified the fiscal pressures have accentuated other crises.

(ii) The Moral Crisis

The fiscal pressures and policy responses fed into what deserves to be called a moral crisis. A sentiment spread that state benefits encouraged behaviour and situations they were actually supposed to overcome, creating moral hazards and adverse selection. Some claims were fanciful and offensive, such as the assertion that teenagers were rushing to have babies so as to claim food stamps or child support. The selective schemes may to some minor extent have facilitated what was happening in any case – a decline in the conventional nuclear family. But the reforms that critics and defenders of state benefits were most inclined to adopt merely accentuated the moral criticisms, putting defenders of the labourist welfare state further on the defensive.

Contributing to the moral dilemmas were three claims, which Charles Murray characteristically described as "laws" derived from his analysis of US experience from 1950 to 1980:

- *The Law of Imperfect Selection.* As any rule defining eligibility for a transfer irrationally excludes some people, policymakers broaden target populations.
- *The Law of Unintended Rewards.* Any transfer increases the value of being in the condition that prompted the transfer.
- *The Law of Net Harm.* The less likely the "unwanted behaviour" will change voluntarily, the more likely a scheme to induce change will cause net harm.[20]

Murray and his fellow libertarians want radical cuts in state benefits, and belong to a tradition of thinkers favouring insecurity. But the perspective highlights something lost on a generation that has championed active policy, which is that scarcely any policy is passive – all policies condition and regulate in some way or another.

The perceived moral crisis initially led in the direction favoured by those who worried about a fiscal crisis – to greater selectivity and conditionality based on moving in the direction of deciding who was deserving and who was undeserving.

Moral hazards may be cited as reasons for increased selectivity and conditionality, but other hazards are generated by the reactions. New conditions of entitlement create new hazards, as well as poverty traps, unemployment traps, and other behavioural traps. Suppose a policy is made more conditional by stipulating that benefits will only be paid to those who lose their job, not to those who quit a job, on the grounds that policy should not encourage "voluntary unemployment". The condition will deter labour mobility, as well as encourage claimants to lie, scarcely the intention, but scarcely irrational in the circumstances.

Because of labour flexibility, because entry-level wages tend to be lower relative to average wages than used to be the case and because more people have to enter employment via part-time jobs, poverty traps and unemployment traps have proliferated. These encourage governments to cut benefits ("reduce the generosity") and to tighten conditions for entitlement to them. In effect, they substitute regulatory controls for wage incentives at the margin.

Above all, the moral crisis in front of us is epitomised by the willingness of policymakers and commentators to divide potential recipients of social protection into three categories:

- "the deserving poor", to be offered a residual social safety net, through means-tested basic benefits (including basic first-tier pensions);
- "the undeserving poor", offered the carrot and stick of "workfare" and/or conditional low-level transfers;
- "the transgressing poor" (those who fail and resort to unsociable behaviour), offered the stern state prepared to uphold the law in keeping public order.

This is slightly more sophisticated than the nineteenth century dichotomy of the deserving and undeserving poor, but critics would feel that the modern tendency suffers from the same shortcomings as the old tendency. Categorising people in this way is arbitrary, unnecessarily judgmental and inequitable. Its implicit use has resulted in greater income insecurity for those on the margins of society.

(iii) The Legitimation Crisis

In the post-1945 era, as the share of the population receiving state benefits and the share of national income devoted to them rose in industrialised countries, public opinion (or politicians purporting to represent it) began to question their need and their distribution. But a sense of social solidarity long made criticism rather marginal.

Initially, there were a few critics on the political left and right who worried about the paternalism of social insurance, and others who believed the benefit system did not induce "responsible behaviour" and should do so. Defenders of state benefits were put in a quandary. For social democrats it was hard to reconcile a vision of steadily extending social rights, with acceptance of a need for stronger regulatory controls. It brought out the labourist dilemma. Many found their way of reconciliation, either pragmatically – that unless concessions were made, the right would be able to mobilise enough support to dismantle the whole system – or enthusiastically, wanting to make the system more paternalistic and regulatory because of their zeal for the cleansing, integrative properties of labour. It was not well appreciated where the concessions would lead.

Other factors contributed to what deserves to be called a legitimation crisis. It was felt that the promises of the welfare state were unfulfillable, that actually schemes were ineffectual in protecting against life's contingency risks, were not redistributive, were too costly, and undermined the motivation to labour and save. Some pointed out that there were paternalistic tendencies, and an image of a "nanny state" was a convenient euphemism to put defenders further on the defensive.

Legitimation of state benefits seems to require a popular perception that those in need or distress cannot or should not be blamed for their condition. Their need must be perceived as due primarily to factors beyond their control. There must also be a popular feeling that people in need should not be expected to accept their condition, quasi-religiously, as something for which there will be reciprocity later, here or in the hereafter. There should also be a feeling that society can afford to support those in distress. Undermining that would go a long way to undermine social solidarity. Support for those in need is likely to be greater if a relatively large number of people think they could suffer a similar fate, or that their relatives could. Finally, even more opportunistically, support for benefits is more likely if the affluent believe that, if not provided, the consequences would be costly to society and to themselves, perhaps through acts of desperation, spread of infectious diseases, vandalism, or sabotage.

With the exception of the last, the above perceptions weakened in the 1970s and 1980s. Thus, a powerful lobby of ideologically motivated individuals and interest groups fanned the view that state benefits could not be afforded, that there was saturation, and so on. Assar Lindbeck, a Swedish economist and a power behind the throne in the selection of Nobel Prize winners in economics, was one such advocate. Others conjured up the euphemism of *Eurosclerosis*, suggesting an image of a society of elderly infirm folk, unable to summon up the blood. The lobby created an image of public social spending "crowding out" productive private activity, so impeding economic growth and employment generation.

Even more importantly than the new economic orthodoxy was the new stratification of globalisation. Under welfare state capitalism, labourist transfers most benefited those having regular jobs, which seemed to mean a majority in industrialised countries and what would become a majority in developing countries. Indeed, the "middle class" did build up more entitlements than those on the margin of society, and politically the welfare state evolved through the support of a middle-class and labouring-class coalition of mutual interest. The salaried did best of all. Thus, in the UK in the 1980s, the wealthiest fifth of the population received 40 per cent more of public health spending than the poorest fifth; 80 per cent more of secondary education; five times more of university; four times more in bus subsidies; seven times in housing subsidies; ten times in rail subsidies.[21]

The new global stratification means the labouring coalition that legitimised social solidarity comprise a shrinking proportion of the total, and many in the *salariat* can see that they could gain more from privatised benefits than from equivalent state benefits. So when the push for increased selectivity and tax cuts built up, defenders of state benefits were in trouble. In Europe, this was further institutionalised by the EMU agenda, by the Maastricht Treaty's rules on debt and public spending. In developing countries, the Washington Consensus demanded public spending curbs from a low base, and any path to comprehensive social protection was scrubbed out. In eastern Europe, external pressure pushed in the same direction.

Regardless of its validity or otherwise (if only because many politicians believe in it), a factor in the legitimation crisis, and accelerated restructuring of social income, is what is known as the *median voter model*. In political democracies, growing inequality, insecurity and poverty might have been expected to lead to electoral support for redistributive policies, partly on the grounds that the swing voter is in the middle of the income distribution and because the median person's income is below the mean. As the median could expect to gain from redistribution, that might lead him to favour redistribution. It does not seem to work like that, because in the era when the labourist model was eroded the conventional wisdom was that the swing voter wanted tax cuts, requiring state benefit cuts. Perhaps a reason was that the pivotal voter actually had income above the median, as the poor (often younger, less educated) were less inclined to vote. But there was also the perception that inequality and insecurity mainly hit the unemployed and detached, the already impoverished.

This was to lead to a phenomenon that gave paternalists a way to restructure state benefits. It was claimed that those at the bottom of flexible, informal labour markets not only lacked money but also suffered from "social exclusion", lacking access to benefits and facilities while being dependent on state bureaucracies for survival. For the majority of voters, "They" were not like "Us". So the sense of social solidarity and structured reciprocity that underpinned the labourist welfare state became frail. Legitimacy depended on a feeling that We give to Them today, because We may be Them tomorrow. Once that feeling weakens, the rush to selectivity and privatisation is on.

(iv) The Social Justice Crisis

The biggest global challenge to social protection systems is that, quite simply, they do no offer the prospect of income security and social protection for the poor and near-poor. There are a few rich countries where effective coverage is high, but they are a shrinking minority. At one extreme are most African and Asian countries, where only a tiny percentage of the population is covered by state-based schemes of any sort. In the middle are the "transition" countries, where often a majority is denied any realistic prospect of decent coverage. And in welfare states a growing minority is not covered, or fear that they are not. A survey in the USA found that more young people believed in UFOs (unidentified flying objects) than that they would be covered by social security later in life. Diminishing coverage, and fear of uncertain coverage, seems to be a global phenomenon.

Besides the global problem of lack of coverage – which begs a question as to the meaning of coverage, in any case – changes in social protection systems have thrown up awkward questions about social justice. For instance, a shift in priority from horizontal to vertical and administrative efficiency has implications for the equity of social policy, since it is a matter of judgment whether it is more equitable that 90 per cent of those who receive benefits are in need – implying that some who receive benefits do not meet the criteria for entitlement – than if only 80 per cent of those in need receive benefits, while nobody not meeting the criteria receive them. Many policy-makers seem more keen to prevent the "undeserving" from receiving benefits than to make sure that all the "deserving" do receive them.

In the rush to selectivity, a conflict emerges between vertical efficiency and other forms of efficiency. The more you target, the more you design criteria for selectivity, the more conditions that are applied, then the more complex the necessary procedures of identification, implementation, monitoring and auditing. In most countries, it is cynical or naïve to advise governments to adopt finely tuned targeting, given poor administrative structures, lack of information, fear and lack of knowledge among potential beneficiaries, poorly trained, inadequately paid and overburdened officials, and pervasive distrust between applicants and officials. The system will end up being highly discretionary, prone to corruption and demoralising for all concerned.

The problems are no different in industrialised countries. Targeting implies selecting those whom you think are "deserving". The narrower the target, the greater is the difficulty of identifying people correctly, and the harder the legal, administrative and practical tasks of maintaining equitable boundaries. Perversely, selectivity almost inevitably leads to arbitrariness, and this in itself may further erode the legitimacy of state benefits and services in general, and worsen moral dilemmas. Selective, conditional schemes lead to a proliferation of local rules and judgments and the quiet spread of discretion as the underlying "principle" of social policy. This is not a sound basis. Some discretion may be benign and well-intended, some judgments will flow from laziness, some will be opportunistic to benefit local officials or politicians, some will be blatantly corrupt. Yet selective social policy is always discretionary, and the more "active" the policy, the more discretionary its implementation.

Social services are the most prone to discretionary failure. They allow officials to decide whom they will meet, whom they will help, what form of help to offer, what form of monitoring, and so on. Individual case treatment is often required because laws cannot be specific enough to cover all circumstances. And means-tested and behaviour-tested transfers allow discretionary control by local authorities – in terms of interpreting, applying, monitoring and sanctioning rules – and selective oversight. The right to appeal may not always exist, and where it does it may be curtailed, costly and time-consuming.

Governments usually lack information required to make equitable judgments in designing selectivity criteria. But if motivated by vertical and administrative efficiency, they will make judgments that lead to cuts in the number entitled to state benefits. This will be compounded by the monitoring system required in selective schemes. It is oriented to disentitlement because it monitors claimants and officials asymmetrically. If a claimant makes a claim deemed to be false, he may be penalised, whereas if he does not make a claim that is valid he will lose the benefit. If an official blocks a valid claim, he is unlikely to be penalised, whereas if he paid those who should not be paid he is likely to be rebuked and penalised.

The design and application of selectivity are also shaped by statistical discrimination, i.e. making decisions based on what is typically the case or is popularly perceived as the norm. For instance, an elderly woman may receive benefits more easily and receive more of them because officials have sympathy with elderly women, or because they have parents who are elderly or because they fear being in that position themselves one day. A dirty man shouting obscenities is unlikely to do so well.

In general, complex rules may induce officials to fall back on attitudes, making judgments based on perceptions of types of client, leading them to focus on ways of exerting control over their role – "processing the client".[22] Then there are the delays that amount to partial disentitlement, even if benefits are eventually awarded.

In some countries, the drift to means-tested assistance has created such strong poverty traps that the government has introduced or extended earnings disregards, allowing some recipients to have some earned income without losing benefits, as in Australia, Belgium, New Zealand, Germany and many US states. Others have not yet gone down that road. Many have added labour tests, although these may be relaxed for groups such as the disabled and lone parents.[23] Some have linked assistance to social "integration" requirements, such as the *Minimex* in Belgium, the *Revenu Minimum d'Insertion* in France, and the *Revenu Minimum Garanti* in Luxembourg. Some have introduced or strengthened treatment conditionality, notably in Nordic countries in accordance with the localised, discretionary character of state benefits.

The trend to conditional benefits has probably reduced horizontal efficiency, because of the tendency for means-testing to result in low take-up rates. But this form of inefficiency does not count for much for those who focus exclusively on fiscal balance sheets. Even in the most well-regulated countries, studies have shown means-tested schemes have take-up rates as low as 20 per cent. In Sweden, take-up of *Socialbidrag* (a means-tested safety net benefit) may have been that low; in Germany the take-up of *Sozialhilfe* (a similar benefit) was between 21 per cent and 64 per cent; in the UK, the take up of means-tested Family Income Supplement was 55 per cent; in Japan, where means-testing was less used, the rate was under 30 per cent.[24] In the USA, only about 40 per cent of the working poor eligible to receive food stamps were actually receiving them, and only a third of eligible children receive Medicaid; both of these have been attributed to the welfare reform that cut off many people from public assistance. In eastern Europe, statistical and anecdotal evidence point to even lower take-up rates.[25] In Poland, the number of households receiving state benefits was less than half the number classified as below the poverty line used to determine entitlement.

Low take-up rates are unlikely to be random, and are likely to be lowest for those most in need or least capable of operating the system. The drift to selectivity is also likely to be systematically inequitable. For instance, because women and minorities disproportionately depend on means-tested benefits, in that they are less likely to qualify for insurance benefits, any tightening of conditionality is likely to affect them disproportionately, as is low take-up.

In spite of all the evidence about the failure to reach those in need, the march to means-tested selectivity has continued – a triumph of euphemism over fact. Low take-up and the reasons for it have created immoral hazards for policymakers and for those wedded to selectivity. They could assert that low take-up means that those not claiming benefits cannot need them. Or they could claim it is an effective way of rationing limited resources. The latter has been stated about the imposition of labour tests in rural public works in developing countries – a dubious claim, as many of the poorest will be among the least able to labour, or will have to travel furthest, while the stigma of so visibly complying will deter them and others.

If horizontally inefficient (not reaching most of those it should), such a system is also administratively inefficient. Wherever administrative systems are poor, as in developing countries and in many others, there will be large leakage costs in maladministration. For this reason, many favour targeting based on easily recorded *needs*. Yet any targeting runs into moral hazards –

making it more likely that people will enter or stay in the condition. This raises the cost of screening, monitoring, and policing behaviour. In the UK, administrative costs for means-tested Supplementary Benefit (which became Income Support) amounted to 11.3 per cent of the total spent on the benefit, and 45 per cent of administrative costs for the whole social security programme, for a benefit that accounted for only 18 per cent of social security expenditure.[26] In the 1990s, fraud and administrative error cost 16 per cent of the £80 billion annual social security budget. In short, highly selective schemes result in high administrative costs.

An adverse outcome of selectivity is a decline in the income replacement rates of state benefits in general. Formally, social assistance has given replacement rates varying from 80 per cent of average male earnings in Switzerland to under 20 per cent in some US States.[27] But this overstates the real value, because of low take-up rates and the uncertainty of receipt. Even in affluent countries, and even if one assumes a take-up rate of 50 per cent, replacement rates would have been between 40 per cent and 10 per cent – scarcely "generous". It is disingenuous for critics to claim that replacement rates are high without taking account of the probability of actually receiving them, or that they may merely reflect lower wages among those needing them.

In sum, means-tested benefits "targeted" on the poor are impoverishing and stigmatising, and are likely to be eroded because they are for the voiceless or weak groups. It is surely no coincidence that in the USA, where social protection has been divided between social security (social insurance, benefiting the middle class) and welfare (mainly means-tested), the value of welfare has fallen while the value of social security has been preserved. As Titmuss tersely concluded long ago, benefits specifically for the poor will be poor benefits.

Even in the spheres of unemployment protection and employment services a private market has been emerging. As for privatisation, there can be little doubt about the impact on social income inequality. Even where a private market is only just beginning, high-income groups have been gaining. For instance, in the spheres of unemployment protection and employment services the proficians and salariat have been taking out employment insurance, or have it taken out for them by their employers. And big firms have been offering core employees and managers generous redundancy benefit packages, capped by "golden parachute" clauses for directors and senior managers. This is part of the fragmentation of enterprise benefits, but also helps erode the legitimacy of state benefits, on which such workers do not rely.

Privatisation also has implications for the social justice qualities of social protection. Privatisation results in the individualisation of benefits, which favours the relatively insurable, and thereby increases inequality and makes economic insecurity more inegalitarian. For instance, people with chronic illnesses or disabilities often must pay more or cannot obtain private health insurance, and those in insecure jobs or living in low-income areas typically find they have similar problems. In the UK and elsewhere, private health insurance has spread. Insurance companies can screen out above-average risks, or refuse to insure them, or demand such high premiums that they cannot afford to insure themselves. Other aspects of life are also differentially insurable, including mortgage protection and the need for long-term care. And the cost of private motor insurance may be differentiated by area of residence, occupation and personal background, with exclusion clauses and premium loadings.

If one depicts insurance payments as negative income, or a tax, then the need to pay them reduces net social income, while the benefit gained from having private insurance comprises a part of social income, which higher-income groups are not only more able to afford but are also able to obtain at lower cost. So any shift to private individual insurance is a source of differential income security and inequality.

Privatisation can also produce its own poverty traps. In the UK, various cuts in state benefits encouraged people to take out loan protection insurance. But applicants for means-tested Jobseeker's Allowance found that pay-outs from the insurance were counted as income, which resulted in lost entitlement to the state allowance. In some cases, they lost more than the value of the pay-out from their insurance.

Finally, privatisation of insurable risks and benefits is likely to create an underclass of the uninsurable, unless subsidies are provided for those at the bottom of society, which would prompt new moral hazards. At the very least, the apparent shift from state to private benefits adds to the income insecurity of people who are economically disadvantaged, the already detached.

(v) The Social Dumping Crisis

With globalisation, there is a tendency, whether justified or not, for policy-makers to indulge in social policy competitiveness. Intent on attracting or retaining foreign capital, they will resort to social dumping. There are reasons for dismissing wilder fancies such as "a race to the bottom", because most interests recognise that if social protection, or labour standards, were dismantled, social cohesion and productivity would suffer. But competitive pressures are likely to lead to an international convergence around some hegemonic model, so that countries and communities with high shares of state benefits in social income are likely to cut back state benefits and the social protection share of national income.[28]

They will also shift the cost for social protection from capital to labour, which means raising the share of the costs borne by workers, through higher contribution rates, and ordinary taxpayers, rather than employers. For similar reasons, they will support partial privatisation and greater selectivity of state benefits.

A social dumping crisis is showing itself through governments justifying cuts in social protection by reference to the need for competitiveness. They have tended to cut benefits and services for those not in labour, meaning that the tendency to indulge in social dumping hurts most the unemployed and detached strata in the emerging stratification system. At the same time, also in the pursuit of competitiveness and job creation, governments have been stepping up their subsidies for low-wage labour. If paid to firms, these will keep down the incomes of low-paid workers; if paid to the workers as "in-work benefits", they will encourage firms to keep wages down and put the workers in a low-wage trap – losing benefits if they raise their wages, leaving them with little or no advantage.

Lower social protection standards and subsidies for low-wage labour are issues that should creep up the international trading regime agenda, as aspects of unfair trading practices before the WTO. But whatever the future, the tendency to indulge in social dumping has weakened the state benefit share of social income, and thereby contributed to income insecurity.

(vi) The Governance Crisis

There are several alternative governance systems for social protection. The system may be direct (without intermediaries), bipartite (through the state and employers), tripartite (through arrangements overseen by government agencies, employer bodies and trade union confederations), or what might be called civil governance (where government agencies oversee the policy in partnership with non-governmental organisations, with or without the involvement of other bodies). The system may be centralised, decentralised or multi-tiered.

Governance changes may reflect a desire to make systems more account-able and equitable or more efficient in some sense. One tendency is the policy of integrating public employment services with social protection, in one ministry. There may be cost reasons, but it risks making social protection more regulatory in character, or less concerned with the simple task of supplementing the incomes of the poor or vulnerable in society.

However, the strongest governance tendencies of recent years are what could be called *decentration* and the erosion of tripartism. The loss of strength of core workers and de-unionisation have contributed to the fading of tripartitism and variants in which workers had a strong voice, except in a few countries, where concessions have been made by unions in any case. The loss of voice by the core has in turn contributed to the loss of state benefits and services in their social income.

Decentration refers to the shifting of governance away from national level, upwards to supra-national levels and downwards to regional or local levels. Shifting part of the rule-making to an international level has unclear implications for the structure or level of social protection. Decentralisation of functions and responsibilities may have inegalitarian effects, unless countered by national policies. It tends to mean that more affluent regions can provide their residents with higher levels of benefits and better services. So, unless inter-regional subsidies are boosted, inter-regional social income inequalities are likely to grow. For similar reasons, lower-income groups of people are likely to suffer, because they tend to be concentrated in lower-income regions with limited fiscal resources.

Decentralisation historically fosters clientelism, in which localised interests can influence or control local officials and the pattern of social protection.

Unless adequate national checks and balances are implemented, the greater the degree of decentralisation, the more likely it is that social protection will be discretionary in character, selective, prone to "creaming" in allocating benefits and services, and inclined to support commercial interests and the most vociferous organisations of civil society, which may or may not be representing groups most in need.

Efficiency claims have also triggered changes in governance systems. In some countries, the desire to make services more efficient has led to the use of more market mechanisms by public agencies, turning citizens needing help into "customers" expected to buy a service. This has led to the contracting-out of social services, which in the USA has become a sphere of big business, and is spreading elsewhere.

In particular, privatisation of welfare delivery services is taking bizarre directions, and has implications for governance. In the USA, some States have contracted out their entire social protection system. Texas put out its services to tender, and the three short-listed bidders included the world's largest defence contractor (Lockheed Martin) and two other corporations with no prior involvement in social policy. There and elsewhere private firms have been awarded contracts to place welfare recipients in jobs, and are paid according to results. Such practices surely lead to "creaming", with better treatment being given to some groups and discrimination to others, and with a proliferation of paternalistic and other control functions, without any pretence at accountability. They can also lead to local or regional monopolistic or oligopolistic structures, working against the interests of "clients" or low-income groups in general. Prices of services will rise or, more likely, quality of the services for supplicants will decline relative to the quality of the service delivered to the funders or employers.

Partial privatisation has given a growing role to the vast array of "non-governmental organisations" (NGOs) or, as they often prefer to call themselves, "civil society organisations" (CSOs). These have been keen to fill gaps left by the receding role of government as provider of state benefits and services. Governments have encouraged them by providing subsidies and contracts. The model of civil society being fostered is complex, but reliance on CSOs represents part of the restructuring of social income, with implications for the income security of those who need services and financial assistance.

CSOs are, almost definitionally, self-appointed, and as such are unaccountable in any formal sense. This can be an advantage, or a cause for concern. As far as being a source of income security, their major drawback is that they can be discretionary as operators of social protection policy. However well intentioned, they will choose whom to assist, whom not to assist, and how much to assist. They raise awkward questions about representation security, to which we will return.

(vii) The Work Crisis

The desire of policymakers to roll back state-based social protection, to make it more selective and conditional, to privatise benefits and services, and to tie entitlements more to the performance of labour has created a fundamental dilemma, which could become the most subversive "crisis" of all. What should count as "work" to gain entitlement? We discuss this later in connection with workfare and the form of work society to promote. The point here is that policymakers have an awkward dilemma. Do they narrow the definition, so as to limit fiscal pressures and so as to steer people in laudable directions? Or do they broaden the definition because some of the work excluded by narrow definitions is valued, particularly given that rolling back state provision leaves various welfare deficits, most notably in the sphere of care work – caring for children, for the sick and disabled and for the elderly and infirm?

Welfare state capitalism led to a substantial growth of state-provided social services, particularly in northern Europe, where priority was given to tax-financed universalistic services rather than monetary transfers. This is part of social income. Their availability reduces dependency on private care, which has to be paid for, either directly or by reciprocity arrangements. But in the era of market regulation, selectivity, mult-tierism, individualisation and partial privatisation have also affected social services. Several models of state provision have emerged. One is the client model, in which a person can obtain a service if satisfying basic conditions, but can obtain only modest assistance. Another is the conditionality model, where a person can obtain more than basic assistance if prepared to satisfy more conditions and to go through more bureaucratic procedures. Some have described Australia and the Netherlands as operating the former model, Sweden the latter. The UK went in the latter direction with its Social Fund, since a shortage of money obliged officials to ration by discouragement.

The provision of care has been partially privatised, with a renewed expect-ation that the elderly, children and others would be cared for by relatives or voluntary organisations. Parental care has spread, as has subsidised parental care of children, cash transfers for care, income entitlement protection for those providing care, and insurance for care. In some countries, subsidies have been introduced to encourage people to care for the elderly, chronically ill and incapacitated.

The spread of payments to carers, or those receiving care, has commodi-fied this type of work, with a shift from directly provided state benefits and services to community provision and wages. Indeed, care work has become pivotal in the reorientation of welfare states, the restructuring of social income and the evolution of work. There is a growing "care deficit" in much of the world, due to ageing, rising divorce rates, single parenting, AIDS and a weakening of inter-generational reciprocities. This puts pressure on state services and encourages governments to shift to more selective schemes and private services. Multi-tierism is emerging, a mix of cash transfers from government, coupled with payment or services from charities, paid or unpaid voluntary care, and a subsidy in the form of the unpaid time of carers.

In care work, we see a more general part of the restructuring of social income – a shift from state benefits, and from family transfers, to benefits and services provided by private organisations. Some services are provided to selected groups voluntarily and freely, although recipients may have to meet reciprocal obligations. One can divide community benefits into those contractually provided and those that are discretionary. Although they may give more choice, neither provides the recipient with as much security as a universal state benefit. Care is not wholly a gift relationship, or wholly a market one. But the pressure is to make it more commercial, meaning more insecurity for anybody expecting to need it.

(viii) The Linguistic Crisis

The eighth crisis may seem peripheral to our argument, but has certainly contributed to the general direction of global reforms. Social thinking has always been afflicted by the misuse of words and phrases. But in recent years the situation in the sphere of social protection has become ridiculous. Increasingly, we see analysis by metaphor, and discussion has been blighted by a veritable babble of euphemisms.

Nobody trying to be influential can afford to neglect the art of buzzwords, and the tendency to spend time concocting acronyms has become a mild sickness. We have social scientists masquerading as consultants, and consultants posing as scientific searchers for truth. Images conveyed by simple terms are taken as reality, and words are increasingly loaded with ideological symbolism or political correctness.

It may seem innocuous. It is not. The terms used shape the policy agenda. Take just two examples. Perhaps the most influential terms in the sphere of social protection have been the *social safety net* and *active labour market policy*. In both cases, the images conveyed to the unwary are different from what they usually mean in reality. The social safety net is a candidate for most influential euphemism of the turn of the century. Who could be against a social safety net to catch all those poor victims falling off the globalising economy? The reality is that this is a disembedded notion that is actually about giving conditional crumbs of comfort for the poor. Instead of a safety net, which suggests something broad and comforting, what is meant is a targeted, selective scheme, usually based on means-testing. The notion of targeting may sound so sensible – directing scarce resources at the poorest of the poor – but a vast amount of evidence has shown that means-tested benefits rarely reach those most in need, due to low take-up, stigma, administrative inefficiencies, and so on. To advocate such schemes in low-income countries is worse than silly.

The notion of active labour market policy is equally disingenuous. The word "active" seems virile and strong, whereas its opposite, "passive", suggests laziness, a lack of initiative. Who could favour being passive if one could be active? In fact, active policy is little more than having the state telling people what they must do in order to receive some modest benefit, directing them to training or job schemes. By contrast, the much-derided passive policy entails giving funds to individuals or families with minimal or no conditions, leaving them to make choices about how to conduct their lives and allocate their resources.

Many other terms come to mind – "generosity", "undeserving", "voluntarily idle", "tax burden", "crowding-out", and so on. In short, the linguistic crisis is real. One almost feels inclined to recommend that all undergraduates should have a course to prepare them for the wiles of the wordsmiths, some of whom will be their teachers. The fear should be that the language and metaphors have helped make social benefits meaner and leaner.

5 Community Benefits

In these circumstances, individuals have to reconsider their sense of inter-dependency and reciprocity. To obtain a semblance of income security, as selectivity and conditionality grow, and as privatisation helps the upper strata, more people have had to provide services and assistance to others as informal insurance, for which they expect support if and when needed. An obvious difficulty is that such an informal system is not secure.

Part of any remuneration system is the pattern of community support, including family transfers and broader support networks. With increased income insecurity associated with labour market flexibility and economic informalisation, and with the changing character of state provision of transfers and services, there has been a global trend to greater reliance on community benefits, which has been insufficiently integrated into economic analysis.

The situation begins with several paradoxes. One is that a source of human tragedy in countries undergoing a "transition" from state socialism to capitalism has been that, as a result of several generations in which informal networks of support were effectively wiped out, there has been a vacuum when they were most needed, when state benefits had not arisen or were being emasculated. Perhaps the most poignant instance is in Uzbekistan, where many more Russians than native Uzbeks have died prematurely from hunger, illness and stress; this has been attributed to a lack of extended family support for Russians living in those communities, even though their relative job incomes were long much higher.

In the wake of the Asian economic crisis, although one should not belittle the hardship, it was found that while money incomes plunged, rural networks enabled the population to absorb part of the shock. But urbanisation, industrialisation and the nuclearisation of households meant a weaker support system than would have been the case a generation earlier. Much the same could be said of what has been happening in industrialised countries. The role of the family in providing benefits has shrunk, both inter-generationally, because of diminished capacities and because of weaker linkages, and laterally, because households are smaller, often consisting of single individuals or couples living in informal relationships. Similarly, the church has fallen away as a source of succour, simply because more of us have become non-religious. So the irony is that while more community support is needed, the capacity of traditional communities has diminished.

Here comes the still largely uncharted surge of civil society organisations (CSOs). One can interpret part of their growth to their provision of community benefit, through mobilising charitable funds and through the voluntary work undertaken under their name. To some extent, they are expected to fill gaps left by the erosion of state benefits, enterprise benefits and fixed wages. We still do not have a reasonable picture of the extent to which they counteract the growth of income insecurity from other sources. We do know that millions of people work for CSOs, some for wages, some voluntarily. They are providing a growing range of social benefits and services, including medical care, education, training, kindergarten care, cultural services and housing. We should not romanticise this trend, or presume that it is either good or bad. We will consider what is required in the final chapter. But so far one must incline to the view that, relative to state benefits or contractually agreed enterprise benefits, they represent a more insecure source of social income.

A related global trend is philanthropic capitalism. This is an intriguing means by which the CB component of social income has grown. It is being fostered under Third Wayism and, more systematically, by compassionate conservatism. Essentially, the elite and some others find they have so much income and wealth that they can disburse millions of dollars to charities of their choice. Some of this trickles down to those picked out, deliberately or otherwise, as the deserving poor. One need not question the donors' motives, and individually one may admire their gesture. However, it increases the community benefit component of social income and boosts the discretionary part of it. If it can be given discretionally, it can be taken away discretionally – and that is part of income insecurity.

6 Fiscal welfare

The shift in the incidence of taxation has also contributed to the growth of income insecurity, in that labour is being taxed more heavily, capital less so. As indicated earlier, this reflects the impact of globalisation and the international effect of such momentous reforms as the abolition of with-holding tax on foreign investment income in the USA in 1984, which led to the sharp fall in the tax on capital. By one way or another, the effective tax on capital has withered, while the tax on labour has risen, absolutely as well as in relative terms.

To compound the twist to income inequality, the incidence of subsidies has shifted in the opposite direction. Subsidies for consumer or wage goods and services have been reduced or removed, denigrated as labour market distor-tions. But there has been a huge growth in subsidies to capital, in the form of tax holidays, low-cost credit, and direct transfers to induce foreign direct investment. According to the orthodoxy, this is not a distortion, but an incentive to boost economic growth and create jobs. The security of capital income has been improved, while the income security of those who rely solely on wage income has been diminished.

At the other end of the spectrum, the important trend is in the use of fiscal measures to provide social protection and be part of the regulatory apparatus. We discuss this later as part of Third Wayism. Suffice it here to note that any shift to tax credits or "earned income tax credits" along the lines of what has become the main social policy in the USA increases the monetisation of social income. Although the overall effect on income inequality is unclear, it shifts it in favour of low-paid wage earners and away from those outside wage employment.

7 Restructuring Social Income

In sum, under the impact of economic liberalisation, "globalisation" and labour flexibility, the structure of social income has become more insecure, largely because of shifts to more variable and uncertain forms of income, and more unequal. Overall, recalling the pattern implied by the preceding era of statutory regulation, one could guesstimate that the median changes taking place in the various regions of the world are as in table 4.2, where a plus sign implies a rise in the relative contribution to total individual income, a minus sign implies the opposite. Where both a plus and a minus sign are given, one surmises that part of the growth of income differentiation is due to a shift in one direction for some groups and in the opposite direction for others.

What table 4.2 suggests is that in most of the world there has been a shift to money wages and a shrinkage in the average share provided by state benefits and services. Most significantly – and this is an educated guesstimate rather than a statement based on substantial statistical information – for income security there is increasing reliance on private provision (personal investment and saving) and community support (voluntary provision), or increased need for those sources to fill voids opened up by the diminishing public provision.

The disaggregation of table 4.2 is not as revealing as when we consider what is happening to the five components of social income for the distinctive socio-economic groups in the emerging global stratification. Let us conclude with this.

If one divides societies and the international economy into the seven strata described earlier, one can see that the top three are increasingly

Table 4.2. Guesstimated trends in components of social income since 1970s, by region of the world

	W	EB	SB	PB	CB
Africna	−/+	−/+	−	0	+
Western Europe	+/−	+/−	−	+	+
Eastern Europe	+	−	+/−	+	+
North America	+/−	+/−	−	+	+
Latin America	+	+/−	−	+	0
South Asia	0	?	−	+ ?	0
South-East Asia	+	+	0	+	−

detaching themselves from national tax regimes, statutory regulations and state-based social protection, while the bottom three are being detached by explicit and implicit disentitlement to state benefits and services, particularly the unemployed and detached lumpen elements. One may say that the top three strata are detached by fortune, the bottom three by misfortune. The analytical device may also help us to picture the growing inequality of *social income* and the associated deterioration of economic security.

Table 4.3 is an interpretation of what anecdotal evidence and reports suggest are the main sources of social income received by the separate strata, or the sources on which each group relies for survival (whether or not they receive them). The asterisks indicate the main sources of income for the higher-income strata; the blanks imply that the source is not applicable, or that no guess on aggregate trend seemed reasonable.

The table's final row indicates what seems to have been the global trend for the source of income specified by the column. Thus, relative to other elements (and often in absolute terms), on average the base wage (W_b) has tended to decline as a source of social income, the flexible part of the wage has been rising, income from private savings and personal investment has been rising sharply, and so on. The +/− sign in the final row means that the source has been rising for higher-income groups, falling for others. Table 4.3 presents a picture of a general shift from relatively secure to relatively insecure sources of social income.

Table 4.4 complements table 4.3, in that it indicates how the seven strata typically experience the various forms of labour security. Thus, for example, *proficians* have high (or above-average) levels of income security and skill reproduction security, being in control of their own activities, but typically have no employment or job security. *Core workers* have some employment security (although diminishing), have relatively high work security and above-average entitlement to enterprise and other benefits. All three strata below the core have less of all forms of labour security, which represents a loss of social income that is not easily measured in conventional income terms. By contrast, while those above the core have gained in most respects, there is a trade-off for those contemplating clinging to a life of the salariat or

Table 4.3. Trends in sources of social income, by socio-economic status

Stratum \ Source	Wb	Wf	FT	LT	NWB	IB	C	Is	D	PB/K
Elite										***
Proficians		*				+	+			*
Salariat	*	+			*	*	+	+		+
Core	+	+			+	+	+	+		
Flexiworkers		+	+	+			+	(+)		
Unemployed		+		+			+	(+)	+	
Detached				+			+		+	
Global trend	−	+		+	+/−	+/−	−	−	+	*

profician. Some would call it part of the risk society. The problem is that some people can avoid taking risks more easily than others, and some will find they have to enter the risk economy when then they did not wish to take the risk of being a risk-taker. One may regard this as the ultimate un-insurable risk.

Although one may quibble with these tables, they are a way of interpreting what is happening to income and income security. Socio-economic fragment-ation has produced a situation in which those in – or identifying with – the top three strata feel increasingly detached from the state social protection system, and are thus less inclined to defend its principles of social solidarity. The bottom three strata feel deprived, detached by disentitlement to benefits long offered to core workers, to whose ranks they had aspired. To them, there is no solidarity on offer, and to talk about solidarity would sound like a sick joke. The pervasive detachment and lack of social solidarity have contributed to the loss of legitimation of the welfare state.

The image of socio-economic stratification coupled with the classifications of informal activities and forms of flexibility outlined earlier may be useful for assessing the relevance and applicability of policies intended to give social protection and security, and for assessing the limitations and apparent lack of general appeal of systems of social protection promoted in the twenieth century.

8 Concluding Points

Income insecurity is a structural characteristic of globalisation and flexible, informal labour markets. It goes with the growth in inequality around the world. The latter has accompanied the spread of "democracy", and it has been suggested that in some countries, notably in Latin America, high-income groups have supported democracy in return for acceptance of the greater degree of inequality.

Statistically, the full extent of insecurity and inequality can only be captured piecemeal, with various changes complementing others, none of which by themselves would create a societal sense of insecurity but which

Table 4.4. Forms of labour security, by socio-economic status (expressed relative to the global average for each form of security)

Stratum	Labour market	Employ-ment	Job	Work	Skill Reprod.	Income	Benefits	Represen-tation
Elite	+	+	+	+	+	+	+	0
Proficians	(+)	–	–	–	+	+	0	–
Salariat	+	+	(+)	+	(+)	+	+	0
Core	0	(+)	0	+	0	0	+	+
Flexiworkers	–	–	–	–	–	–	–	–
Unemployed	–	–	–	–	–	–	–	–
Detached	–	–	–	–	–	–	–	–

taken together do so. This is why subjective perceptions of insecurity, as revealed in opinion polls, can be greater than can be gleaned from individual indicators and can be so puzzling for those who look at just one or two statistical trends. Monetary income inequality may have stopped growing in some countries, but the changing incidence of social income may have increased social income inequality, imparting correspondingly more insecurity.

Social security (in the European sense) has become part of social and labour regulation policy, used to steer people to behave in certain ways and not others. This represents a loss of security. More than ever before, the notion of social insurance is a misnomer, particularly in areas such as unemployment, as considered later. Countries with complex welfare states have shifted from universalistic social protection to selective, means-tested schemes and to pluralism in the financing and provision of social protection that make reference to social insurance somewhat bizarre.

In doing so, they have contributed to labour *re-commodification*, in which social income has been restructured, with money wages becoming a larger share of total social income, and state benefits a declining share. Incomes are being re-monetised. Benefits based on citizenship rights have been eroded, or converted into conditional entitlements, while enterprise benefits have become more polarised, less available for lower-income workers. Almost everywhere, there has been greater reliance on local and community networks for support, to replace declining state and enterprise provision. In most places, it is not clear that there is the capacity to provide that alternative support, although "civil society" organisations are trying to do so.

In sum, income insecurity has been intensified, by the shift from fixed wages to more flexible wages, by the shift from universal to selective and discretionary state benefits, and by the greater need for voluntary help. By the beginning of the twenty-first century, there were signs that the era of market regulation was coming to an end. The insecurity was worrying too many people, and the politicians and the bevy of political advisers and think tanks were beginning to sense the unease. Perhaps when the voters stay at home, they will realise that income security is the essence of a participatory democracy and real freedom.

5

Ageing: Time Bomb or the Spark of Good Society?

1 Introduction

Across the world, ageing and pensions have become the subjects of intense and controversial debates. In most places, they have been clouded by commercial, political and economic undercurrents that have had little to do with the simple process of finding ways of providing an adequate income for those who have "retired" from the labour force. Ideological crusades have particularly characterised the debates on pension reform in Latin America and eastern Europe, with countries in the latter region intent on emulating policies introduced in Chile and elsewhere, commonly pushed by outsiders, notably the IMF and World Bank.

Indeed, one's position on pension reform has almost been a touchstone of one's position on the political spectrum. Contributing further to the intensity of controversy, heavy lobbying by powerful commercial interests has scarcely contributed to objective assessments of the options for improving income security and human development. We have a spectre of pension fund capitalism, not just in Anglo-Saxon countries, but also increasingly in most of the global economy, being led by huge corporations that want the elderly market to be opened up everywhere. These are overwhelmingly dominated by US multinational corporations, which took advantage of the long bull market in the USA to acquire major UK and other pension funds. They have dominated the direction of pension reform in the era of globalisation.

This chapter has the modest objective of indicating the issues surrounding the pension reform debates. An underlying premise is that the "pensions crisis", as popularly depicted, is not primarily about the pension system but about the political, social and economic changes taking place around it. The significance is, of course, that the direction reforms take will have a powerful bearing on the type of society that will emerge during the early part of the twenty-first century.

2 Demographic Time Bomb?

Ageing is conventionally seen as a problem, and particularly as a threat to public pension systems and national economic growth. The popular image is of a bunch of elderly folk, frail, on walking sticks or cluttering up overburdened hospitals and old-people's homes while a dwindling proportion of the population is labouring to support them. There are reasons for being cautious about accepting this alarmist imagery.

We must begin by reflecting on what is meant by "ageing". The conventional way of looking at the situation is to point to long-term changes in the ratio of those aged 15–64 to those aged 65 and older. This reflects *individual ageing* (people living longer on average) and *population ageing* (due to declining fertility coupled with increased longevitiy). Due to declining fertility after the "baby boom" generation, the annual intake into the "prime age" bracket has only recently begun to fall in most industrialised countries. But because of increasing longevity among older people, the old-age dependency ratio has risen steadily. After about 2010, in most industrialised countries that ratio is scheduled to rise quite sharply. There might be a medical breakthrough to raise it further – and demographic forecasts used by insurers have traditionally consistently underestimated the rising life expectancy – but otherwise we can be confident that the rise will be close to that forecast.

The demographic figures are clear. In 1960, across all industrialised countries the population aged 65 and over was equal to about 15 per cent of the working-age population. By 2030, the figure will probably be 35 per cent. In 1960, men could expect to live about 68 years with 50 of those years being in employment. Now, men can expect to live about 76 years, with merely 38 years being in employment. Any likely change in fertility will make little difference to this trend. In western Europe, there are about 22.4 persons over 65 for every 100 persons of working age; this is expected to rise to 32.3 in the next twenty years.[1]

Another well-known feature of the long-term trend is the changing pattern of labour force participation, which might even be called early ageing. The second half of the twentieth century saw female participation rates rising everywhere, while male participation rates declined for all age groups, and not just for older men, although they fell most for men in their 50s. This means that the effective dependency ratio has risen by more than the purely demographic ratio. It is generally argued that the labour market marginalisation of older men should be reversed. How to do so is one of those much-discussed big questions of social policy. But it must not be overlooked that while male labour force participation rates have fallen – and for those over age 60 the fall has been substantial – female labour force participation has risen, and this includes women in their 50s.

There are also two aspects of what might be called the de-ageing of society. First, on average in industrialised countries older people are on average healthier than used to be the case, and consequently are able to be more active for longer and are able to maintain a high level of consumption relative to their income, if only because they can travel more. One implication is that more of the elderly are likely to want to do some income-earning work well beyond either the "early retirement" age or the standard retirement age. Probably far more are doing so without that being recorded.

Second, older people are more likely to want to do some labour force work because the pattern of income-earning opportunities has been changing, with more flexibility meaning more variety of work options to suit individual preferences and capacities, because fewer young workers are coming onto the labour market, and because the rise in female labour force participation has reached the stage of coming mainly from older women. So, although the image is still one of older worker marginalisation (the main story of the 1980s and 1990s), barriers to the economic activity among older workers are probably coming down.

One senses that ageism in the labour market is actually weakening, paradoxically at a time when pension reformers and politicians are calling for measures to reduce ageist discrimination. While policies could accelerate the process, the task may be easier than would have been the case a decade ago. The barn door is already open.

3 Pensions: Basic Economics and Emerging Issues

The stylised facts are as follows. Public pensions have been under fiscal pressure because of rising old-age dependency, longer life expectancy among pensioners (and more contributors reaching pension age), erosion of worker and employer contributions, and higher and longer-term unemployment. None of this has made PAYG pension systems unaffordable, contrary to what many commentators have claimed or assumed. For example, according to Howard Glennerster in countries such as France, Germany and Japan, governments have been "promising their future elderly populations state pensions that cannot be remotely met from present taxes and social security contribution rates".[2] This is unproven. But the alarm is real. For instance, in November 1999 the European Round Table of Industrialists, representing over forty leading EU companies, described the European situation as a "time bomb" threatening Europe's competitiveness. Demographic research for the Centre for Strategic and International Studies in Washington DC even suggested that the ageing is much greater than official forecasts, claiming that life expectancy will rise more than in the recent past, rather than less.

The projected growth in the "cost" of pensions as a share of GDP in various European countries gives some support to this alarmist vision (table 5.1). But what is remarkable is that countries have had very different levels of pension costs, and some have managed to sustain a level more than twice that projected for the UK at its projected height.

One cannot dismiss out of hand the possibility that part of the pressure to roll back public pension schemes is a reflection of vested interest. After all, reducing pension "generosity" (a loaded euphemism for what some observers might call adequacy) is in the interest of those who make profits out of pension funds or who wish to do so. This is one reason for making sure that objective, accountable and independent evaluations of alternative options are made and for making good governance of any pension system a high priority, such that *all* interests are taken into account in the design, implementation and evaluation of pension schemes.

Table 5.1. European pension costs: time bomb? (projection as a % of GDP)

	1995	2000	2010	2020	2030	2040
Belgium	10.4	9.7	8.7	10.7	13.9	15.0
Denmark	6.8	6.4	7.6	9.3	10.9	11.6
Germany	11.1	11.5	11.8	12.3	16.5	18.4
Spain	10.0	9.8	10.0	11.3	14.1	16.8
France	10.6	9.8	9.7	11.6	13.5	14.3
Ireland	3.6	2.9	2.6	2.7	2.8	2.9
Italy	13.3	12.6	13.2	15.3	20.3	21.4
Netherlands	6.0	5.7	6.1	8.4	11.2	12.1
Austria	8.8	8.6	10.2	12.1	14.4	15.0
Portugal	7.1	6.9	8.1	9.6	13.0	15.2
Finland	10.1	9.5	10.7	15.2	17.8	18.0
Sweden	11.8	11.1	12.4	13.9	15.0	14.9
UK	4.5	4.5	5.2	5.1	5.5	5.0

Source: Financial Times, 23 November 1999

In that context, we can summarise the main objectives of reformers, without subscribing to their validity, or order of significance:

- to reduce fiscal pressures on pensions, due to ageing, rising old-age dependency;
- to reverse the labour market marginalisation of older workers;
- to overcome the tendency for some pensioners to be impoverished, while many others have "over-generous" incomes in retirement.
- to cut national insurance contributions in the interest of improving industrial "competitiveness" and labour market flexibility, so promoting employment.

Whether or not the pressures amount to a crisis, they have induced responses that have curtailed pension entitlements in one way or another – and look likely to curtail them further in the near future. Many of the changes have eroded the insurance principle little by little. The possibility that the morality of the responses will become more tendentious is a cloud on the horizon.

Actual responses have been of two types – incremental or radical. Although all are familiar to participants in this debate, it might be useful to recall the various measures that are on the reformers' table.

Incremental Options

- *Raise the retirement age.* This is happening in many countries. In the UK, the retirement age for women has been raised from 60 to 65, as it has in Greece; in Sweden it was raised from 65 to 66, in eastern Europe, the rise has been much greater, largely because it was relatively low in the 1980s. Raising the age further is the preferred option of several lobbyist groups, such as the European Round Table of Industrialists.[3] The Japanese Government announced in 2000 that it intended to raise the retirement age. The UK's *National Association of Pension Funds* (NAPF) has called on the Government to raise the retirement age from 65 to 70. Merrill Lynch (the giant US asset management organisation) estimated that if the retirement age were raised by stages, the old-age dependency ratio would be stabilised (table 5.2). One objection to this is that it would amount to "moving the goalposts", since people paying earlier would have planned on the basis of a known retirement age. To counter this objection, the NAPF has proposed that there should be a 15–year "wind-down" period before it comes into effect. Another objection is that this would persist in treating the life-cycle in the conventional rigid three phases (school, work, retirement). It may respond to fiscal pressures, but not to the desire for lifetime flexibility. One variant of the proposal would be to make the adjustment automatic, by making the retirement age dependent on current adult life expectancy. One difficulty is that since men and women have different life expectancy this might have to be taken into account by either taking the male life expectancy as the yardstick or having separate retirement ages – perversely implying that women's pensionable age would be *above* that of men. The former option would presumably be preferred.

• *Lower the income replacement rate of state pensions.* This too has been happening. One obvious objection to this route is that, in effect, it reneges on previous commitments. Persons in their 40s and 50s, in particular, could have contributed or saved on the presumption that their pensions would be a certain level. To change the level as they approach the goal line smacks of moving the goalposts. So, if this is among the most transparent responses, it is also among the least fair, and is probably politically unappealing. There has been an international tendency to break the link between economic growth and pensions. In the UK, indexation is now to prices rather than earned incomes, and the state pension has fallen to 20 per cent of national average earnings, which was largely responsible for the fact that pensions fell from 4.8 per cent of GDP in 1981 to 3.7 per cent in 1996, in spite of an increase of over one million pensioners. In

Table 5.2. Impact of raising the retirement age in the European Union

	1990	2000	2010	2020	2030
% of population of working age					
Where retirement at 65	66	66	67	63	60
Increased retirement age scenario*	66	68	70	67	66
% of population of pensionable age					
Where retirement at 65	14	15	16	20	23
Increased retirement age scenario*	14	13	13	16	17
Pension contribution as % of average salary after increases in retirement age	13.76	12.75	12.38	15.92	17.17

Note: *Effect of raising the retirement age to 66 in 2000, 68 in 2020 and 69 in 2030
Source: Merrill Lynch

other countries, the basic pension has fallen in relative terms, widening the gap between the minimum and average pensions. This has scarcely helped redress socio-economic inequality.

- *Increase contributions rates*. A difficulty with this route is that, *ceteris paribus*, in some countries the rate would have to rise to very high levels in order to balance costs and benefits. The most drastic case is Italy, where it would have to rise to 48 per cent of average wages if the pensions budget was to be balanced by 2030. In late 1999, the rate was 33 per cent. Raising contributions rates is likely to be politically unpopular, although in an era in which politicians are loath to raise taxes, this may be easier than raising revenue from taxation. Ironically, many national pension systems have come to rely increasingly on general taxation and less on employer and employee contributions. And there has been a shift from employer to worker contributions. The combination of these trends has probably reduced the redistributive character of public pensions.

- *Increase the number of years of contributory employment to qualify for a "full" pension*. This has been happening in various countries. The number of years of employment used to calculate the amount of pension has risen in such countries as Austria, France, Portugal, Spain and the UK. The upward trend has been prolonged and considerable. Consequently, the number of years of employment required to obtain a full state pension has risen steadily. In 1960, for industrialised countries on average, a contribution record of 13 years sufficed to obtain a full pension. By 1985, that had doubled. It continued to rise in the 1990s, so that within the EU the number of years for a full pension ranges from 35 in Greece and Spain to 48 in Ireland. This is surely moving the goalposts off the pitch.

- *Increase the number of years prior to retirement for calculating earnings-related pensions*. This ruse is fairly transparent, although it also prompts questions about the nature of the social compact. To be moderately equitable, it should surely be changed only for those further from age of retirement than the newly stated number of years.

- *Index pensions to prices rather than to earnings*. This is what the UK Government did in 1981. If pensions are linked to earnings, they rise with economic growth, tending to increase fiscal pressure more than if they are linked to price rises, since prices have risen by less than money incomes. However, the UK's experience in the two decades following the change shows that it results in many more pensioners being impoverished, finding their pension falling further behind average incomes and only having it raised in moments of fiscal looseness, usually just before elections.

- *Make early retirement harder or less financially attractive*. This is widely advocated, and has happened, putting into reverse policies introduced in the 1970s and 1980s as a means of lowering unemployment.

- *Give incentives to older workers to remain in employment*. This is not, or should not be, the same as making early retirement harder or less attractive. One way of encouraging people to continue income-earning work is simply to reduce the marginal tax rate on earnings by pension-age persons. In the

USA, in 1999 President Clinton and several Republican Congressmen proposed that all pension recipients aged over 65 should be allowed to earn as much as they wished without losing any pension.[4] This may have an indirect beneficial effect on the budget, since the older workers will pay tax if they declare the income. However, the main positive effect of that move should be that it would not distort decisions on whether or not to work. A second benefit might be that, if it is true that more active people tend to live longer, longevity should rise. That is scarcely going to ease pressure on pension funds.

- *Make pensions rise by more for each year worked in contributory employment after retirement age than for each year of such employment below retirement age.* Often those who work beyond retirement age have not obtained a substantially higher pension when they eventually retire. Making additional years of employment have a stronger positive effect on subsequent pension levels would have the virtue of inducing behavioural change by relying on financial incentives, and would thus be more equitable than the more arbitrary device of rigid rules and regulations limiting access to pensions or measures to reduce pensions for those who have contributed on the expectation that they would receive a higher level.

- *Extend and promote the combination of partial retirement, partial pension.* This has been popular. In Finland, for instance, receiving a partial pension is possible from the age of 56; in France and Germany, government subsidies facilitate gradual retirement from age 55. This sort of reform also has the virtue, or could have, of relying on incentives to induce behavioural changes rather than on more punitive or rigid aspects of pension systems.

- *Compel people to save more.* This is the Singapore route, and is central to private funded schemes. In Singapore, the government forces workers to save 40 per cent of their earnings, most of which can only be tapped when they retire. Other countries have contemplated following suit, and some analysts have proposed it in the UK.[5] It is an example of state paternalism. Its advocates claim that it would ensure savings for old-age because many people are short-sighted, and would boost economic growth by increasing savings. However, there are objections. First, a high forced savings rate would have a similar effect on the propensity to labour as a high tax rate, affecting work incentives. Second, and more importantly, it would interfere with individual preferences. Some people wish to consume more now, and spend less later; some have the opposite tendency. The state could not decide which is preferable without indulging in arbitrary paternalism. Some people would be required to save more than they need or desire to save. A third consideration is that research has shown that many pensioners over-save during their working lives if one assumes that smoothing consumption over the lifetime is a rational objective. Increasing savings at earlier ages would make the matter worse.

- *Allow workers to transfer pensions across national borders.* To some extent this does occur. It may not be seen as a reform to lower fiscal pressure. However, as a measure to promote labour mobility it might raise older worker employment, thus indirectly lowering unemployment and the demand for public transfers and early pensions.

- *Reduce or remove tax breaks on savings for pensions.* One could use the extra tax revenue from this move to help pay for a basic state pension. There is no evidence that pension saving is in need of a fiscal incentive, especially bearing in mind that those likely to be saving are middle-income or upper-income earners, whose pension income replacement rates have been high.

- *Allow pension funds to invest in national or foreign equity markets more easily.* In some countries, allowing pension funds to invest where they wish in order to obtain a high rate of return might reduce fiscal pressures. This is happening by one means or another in any case. The debate in the USA about what to do with the social security "trust fund" will have a lasting effect on what is adopted as the norm in the rest of the world. In booms, equities yield higher returns than Treasury bonds, allowing pension funds to accumulate more with which to pay pensions, but they do involve greater risks.

- *Co-ordinate tax and regulatory treatment of pensions internationally.* This has been a major policy dilemma in the European Union. An orderly system would presumably be a more stable one, and costs could thus be reduced. But it is unlikely to make a vast difference to the fiscal and labour market pressures.

- *Allow more international migration.* This is one response that many rich countries are reluctant to take, or at least to any large extent. The United Nations called on Japan, facing the most striking ageing process, to let more migrants into the country, but enthusiasm has not been great.

This list of options is far from complete. What it suggests is that it would be grossly simplistic to focus on just one or two options to the exclusion of others. Although practical policymakers may not be doing so, popular commentary often presents the situation as if there were straightforward and stark choices.

4 Multi-Tierism

All of the measures mentioned in the preceding section can be described as incremental. But perhaps the main response has been the reform of pension systems in the direction of funded schemes, and in particular to multi-tierism. Actually, it is hard to identify any model pension system, because in most countries a hybrid has long been in place.[6] But during the 1980s and 1990s there was an international trend to a mixed contributions-and-assistance pension structure (table 5.3). The changes have continued, led by the major reform in Sweden, and more tentatively in Germany and Japan.

In the international arena, the World Bank's *Averting the Old Age Crisis* in 1994 was notable for its huge cost, its unbridled advocacy of radical reform in the direction of individual fully funded schemes, and its timing, for it came at a time when the ideological zeal for public spending cuts and

Table 5.3. Paths towards mixed contributions-and-assistance pension systems in western European and Anglo-American countries, mid-1990s

Type of scheme	Tax-financed minimum pension	Minimum plus compulsory contribution-based (dual mandatory system)	Subsidised voluntary schemes	Compulsory contribution-based
First pension schemea	Australia, Canada, Denmark, Iceland, Ireland, New Zealand, Norway, Sweden, UK		Belgium, France, Italy, Spain	Austro-Hungarian Empire, Finland, Germany, Greece, Netherlands, Portugal, Switzerland, USA
Pension structure in 1996	Denmark,[b] Ireland,[c] New Zealand	Australia, Austria, Belgium, Canada, Finland, France, Greece, Iceland, Italy, Norway, Netherlands,[d] Portugal, Spain, Sweden, Switzerland, UK, USA		Germany[e]

Notes: [a]Some countries adopted a mixed approach from the beginning, as in Sweden in 1913
[b]With almost total coverage of occupational pensions and small-flat-rate contribution-based pension
[c]Minimum pension for employees is contribution-based
[d]Mandatory membership in 62 of 83 industry pension funds supplementing minimum pension from 1980
[e]With standardised social assistance. Periods of higher education and registered unemployment, as well as up to three years of child-rearing, count as contribution periods. Pension rights are split between spouses in case of divorce
Source: Overbaye, 1997, op. cit., p. 108

privatisation was at its zenith. The World Bank has also devoted much money and technical advice to the effort to induce governments to reform their pensions in that direction, particularly in central and eastern Europe. Although one should be hesitant about mentioning a family scrap, it is notable that the most strident critique of the World Bank's approach came from its own Chief Economist. Although he resigned from that post after completing his three-year stint, he had lambasted the reform agenda in a characteristically trenchant manner.[7] Others have pointed out the large fiscal costs of a transition from a PAYG system to a fully-funded one.[8] And many have pointed out that the risks and uncertainty increase for the poor and for those in precarious jobs. Here is not the place to try to summarise the debates.[9] But three points are worth making, all related to the labour market flexibility and socio-economic stratification trends.

First, if there is going to be a global trend to multi-tier systems in which a mandatory funded tier is to be a rising part of the total, what should be the anchor of the system? There is a fear among some observers that the thrust of reform in the direction of "social safety nets" and the "reduction of the burden of pensions" implies lower pensions for the poor.[10] Presumably, there should be a floor, so that everybody in society receives a basic pension of some sort. In the twenty-first century, one hopes there is no place for a system that envisaged a category of undeserving elderly poor disentitled to any public transfer.

What should the basic pension be? And on what basis should it be calculated and distributed? The main options are a flat-rate guaranteed citizenship pension and a means-tested basic pension. Means-testing (and other "targeting") has become popular with governments, and all over Europe the number of people dependant on means-tested benefits has increased enormously. Questions persist about low take-up rates, the stigma, administrative costs, the costs relative to the savings supposedly gained from such systems, moral hazards (pensioners living just above poverty impoverishing themselves in order to gain a pension), and poverty traps (people being discouraged from doing some income-earning activity because they fear losing their basic pension). There is also, or should be, a concern that policy in this direction is guided by something close to cynicism: The welfare loss to

Table 5.4. Employer-sponsored defined contribution schemes

| | Percentage of employer-sponsored plans that are DC | | Typical contributions as a percentage of salary | |
	1998	*2003*	*Employee*	*Employer*
Austria	10	30	15.0	5.0
Belgium	45	60	5.0*	10.0*
Czech Republic	100	100	2.0	0.5
Denmark	90	95	4.0	8.0
Finland	0	2	n.a.	n.a.
France	40	50	2.0	3.0
Germany	10	12	0.0	4.0
Greece	40	50	0.0	5.0
Hungary	100	100	1.0	5.0
Ireland	32	45	4.0	6.0
Italy	80	90	1.5	1.5
Netherlands	5	8	4.0	8.0
Norway	0	2	n.a.	n.a.
Portugal	15	20	0.0	3.0
Spain	50	65	2.0	6.0
Sweden	50	75	0.0	8.0
Switzerland	50	60	5.0**	9.0**
UK	25	35	2.0	4.0

Notes: *Or 1% and 2% if salary is below social security ceiling
         **Or 4% and 8% if contracted out of state earnings related pension scheme
Source: William Mercer

pensioners of the moral hazards and the consequences of the pension trap are economically insignificant, so that they can be ignored. To the extent that this thinking is occurring, it is deplorable.

By contrast, a guaranteed citizenship pension would not only ensure that all elderly people would have basic income security with dignity but would minimise administrative costs, while facilitating more flexible lifestyles in which those capable of engaging in income-earning work, and wanting to do so, could engage in such work without being penalised. If we want to promote a work-based society in which the poor and educationally less well-endowed can indulge in their work enthusiasms into old age, then moving in this direction should be a high priority.

Second, a multi-tier pension system means that most people will be primarily interested in preserving the value and security of contributions-based tiers. If the system works reasonably efficiently, the majority will be concerned almost exclusively with those tiers and regard the bottom tier as of marginal relevance. This raises the awkward question related to the legitim-ation crisis of social protection. If the bottom tier is only of importance for those in the bottom three strata of society, and if they do not conform to the model voter, will there be a tendency to allow the real value of the bottom, state tier to wither? The answer may be that this is precisely what will happen, especially if the social solidarity principle has been eroded.

Third, a multi-tier system in which private schemes predominate poses major challenges for regulation and governance, which are linked to the previous points. The sheer size of pension assets, and their rapid growth as shown in table 5.55, make this more than a marginal issue. Even staunch advocates of privatisation acknowledge the need for strong government

Table 5.5. European pension assets, 1998–99

	% of GDP		1998
	1998	*1999*	*($'000)**
Austria	4	12	1.0
Belgium	10	12	2.5
Denmark	89	108	31.2
Finland	31	41	7.9
France	6	4	1.6
Germany	12	13	3.5
Ireland	43	47	9.7
Italy	19	20	4.3
Netherlands	141	141	35.5
Norway	24	31	8.9
Portugal	10	10	1.2
Spain	4	5	0.7
Sweden	90	107	25.3
Switzerland	105	117	40.3
UK	86	101	21.0

Note: *Per capita
Source: William Mercer

regulation.[11] The risks and uncertainty for contributors are substantial, and are greatest for the most vulnerable, those who are the "near poor", which include most flexiworkers and the more fortunate of the unemployed and detached. These are least likely to be well informed, least likely to be able to afford losses from misguided investments or to be able to maintain regular or adequate contributions over a prolonged period.

Pensioners and the state cannot afford to allow pension funds to be reckless in their use of investors' funds, and they are unlikely to favour a highly fragmented pension fund system, because an industry characterised by numerous small funds would tend to be an unstable one, with many failures jeopardising pensioners' incomes. So governments will always wish to regulate pension funds in some way. A quite different concern arises from the tendency of pension funds to operate in a "pack" or "herd" fashion. If, for instance, the main pension funds all invested mainly in "tracker" funds, those following something like the FTSE, their size would mean that investment would be concentrated in a small range of firms.

The state of debate on privatisation of pensions and multi-tierism is such that a major stocktaking is required. The World Bank, the OECD, the ILO and the International Social Security Association all conducted lengthy reassessments in the 1990s. However, they did those at a time of major reforms and restructuring, in an atmosphere of controversy and acrimony. It is perhaps appropriate to put pressure on all those bodies to carry out a joint review of theories and evidence in the light of the many reforms carried out not just in Europe but all over the world in the 1990s. This might be something like an international Commission – a real case of global multi-sectoral governance, to produce not a set of directives but a balanced assessment of the advantages and disadvantages of all the options. Smaller countries, and emerging market economies, deserve that service from the international community.

At the national level, governments have been looking for ways to provide security for members of occupational pension schemes. In the UK, the government found that in 2000 one in seven final-salary pension schemes were not in a position to honour obligations to employees if the firm went bankrupt. The proposal to set up a "bail-out" fund might appeal to those concerned for pensioners, but can be subject to the same moral hazard criticisms as mentioned for social protection schemes.

5 Concluding Points

The struggle to reform pensions across the world is far from resolved. But the debates and trends are strong guides to the underlying tensions induced by globalisation and more flexible labour markets. Pensions are becoming a means of polarising income security for a quarter of the lifetime of the average citizen in a growing number of countries. Clearly, income insecurity will be greater for those whose working lives have been dogged by ill-luck or by misguided choices.

As governments have been driven towards some variant of multi-tierism, concern for those at the bottom of society should become the highest priority. There must be a guaranteed basic pension, not one made contingent on satisfactory form-filling, bearing in mind that a vast amount of empirical evidence shows that such procedures will result in many being denied benefits, even though they are entitled to them. Beyond that, such is the power of pension funds that they require transparent, democratic governance and regulation, if only to limit their oligopolistic practices against the interest of the citizen. And beyond that, most excitingly, a range of new policies and institutions are required to make pension systems more flexible, so that they become a vehicle for lifetime lifestyle diversity. Public policy has barely begun to face this challenge, although it is surely one of the most exciting areas of socio-economic policy ahead.

In the latter part of the twentieth century, older workers were among the hardest hit by the spread of more flexible and insecure labour markets. Among the signs of this was the fact that it was their average employment tenure suffered the sharp declines. For instance, for men aged 55–64 in the USA it fell from over 15 years in 1983 to just over 11 in 1998. And they were most likely to suffer sharp income declines through job changing, often enforced on them. But the lot of their successors in that age group could be somewhat better, and a harbinger of exciting changes in working habits.

The average age to which a majority of people could expect to live will probably rise into the late seventies in many countries of the world during the first decades of the twenty-first century. A person aged 60 could expect to live another 25 years. Work will not stop at some standard age. It is mildly subversive that people living longer could be the means by which the labouring basis of twentieth-century social security is defeated. The older citizen, if assured of a pension, could work in real freedom, and increasingly can be expected to want to work on his or her enthusiasms, at a pace and intensity that suits personal desires and capacities. Contrary to the alarmist nonsense about "time bombs", ageing could be a great liberating force, promoting work, real freedom and flexible working that will spread down through the younger groups. Grey power could be about much more than marginalisation.

6

End of Unemployment Benefits?

1 Introduction

Social policy is notoriously struck by images. During the twentieth century one image above all dominated thinking about labour market policy – the dole queue, a long line of men, hands in pockets, mostly with caps, queuing forlornly in the early morning rain for a meagre hand-out to enable them to survive in unemployment as they competed with each other for jobs that were not there. There were a few women, but they were not regarded as "bread-winners"; they were left in the shadows of economic and social policy. It was all those unemployed men who took the headlines and who worried governments, with their dirtiness, incipient violence and awkward voting habits.

From the 1930s onwards – and significantly not before then – the world rushed to measure the number of unemployed. Doing so has not been easy. But if they were to be helped, the state had to know how many of them there were. As the traumas of the Great Depression faded, policymakers in industrialised countries turned their attention to making schemes of income support for the unemployed more rational and equitable, according to their way of seeing reality. Two basic questions dominated their thinking. Who should qualify? Who should pay?

The first question seems to have an easy answer – the unemployed. Yet defining these is far from easy. What about the person who apparently chooses to become or remain unemployed? Or the person who has not been employed before or for a long time? Or the person who withdraws from the labour force because she sees no prospect of a decent job?

The *second* question also seems easy to answer – the employer should pay, on the grounds that he can afford to do so and is ultimately responsible for making the employed redundant. Merely stating that answer highlights its inadequacy.

The basic questions for a while seemed interesting but not too problematical. *Assuming* Full Employment, one could have a system in which modest "insurance contributions" could be levied on firms to pay for the small number of workers subject randomly to "frictional" involuntary unemployment that amounted to no more than Beveridge's famous "temporary interruptions of earnings power". But then reality ruined this comforting image.

Two sets of factors ruined the image. Probably first chronologically, social protection policy became part of development policy. None of the orthodox assumptions looked remotely true in developing countries, in contexts of rural non-wage labour, casual informal activities in urban slums and relations of production that were quite unlike the model of big bureaucratic, stable firms and public organisations that until the last quarter of the century seemed to be the coming norm. Clearly the main problems in developing countries were absolute poverty and chronic inequalities, in which impoverished "underemployment" was more pervasive than open unemployment. The official "discovery" in the early 1970s of the "informal sector" – a euphemism that was to have a long life – turned attention away from the Ricardian-Lewis model of surplus labour being absorbed gradually into the "formal sector" in which statutory protective regulations and social security could operate.

The other set of developments concerned what has become subsumed in aspects of globalisation. Mass unemployment – and a lot of long-term unemployment lasting for a year or more – returned to industrialised countries, while more flexible and informal labour markets meant that full-time, regular and stable wage labour ceased to be the overwhelming norm. More importantly, policymakers could no longer comfort themselves with the image that stable full-time labour was the norm, or in the case of developing countries was becoming the norm. At the same time, a revolution in economics destroyed the comforting notion that the closed economy system underlying Keynesianism and the extension of welfare state capitalism meant that macro-economic policy could and would maintain Full Employment. Henceforth, unemployment was attributed largely to the behaviour and expectations of workers and employers. In a crude sense, the new orthodox economics regards unemployment as largely "voluntary", due to behavioural and institutional rigidities. This has profoundly altered both policy attitudes and the statistical measurement of unemployment.

In this context, we have to ask what makes unemployment so special. As commonly defined, unemployment is a condition (being without work), a desire (for work), a need (income from work), and an activity (seeking work). If someone satisfies one of these criteria without the others, he is unlikely to be classified as unemployed in the standard sense of the term. Yet defining or measuring any of them is notoriously difficult. A woman in a village without any income-earning activity will spend her days doing something we would normally call work. I may do some gardening or read economics, so have work. But I may also seek a job, without wanting one, merely needing the income. It is easy to think of combinations of the four criteria where one or more of them are not satisfied. Should only those who satisfy all four be called unemployed and become the focus of public policy?

This leads to another awkward question that has come to prominence since the 1980s. Why focus on providing income security for the unemployed in particular? The standard answer stems from the model of social security, which emerged in industrial societies to suit industrial societies. This is seen as a system for providing income security to deal with the contingency risks of life – "sickness, maternity, employment injury, unemployment, invalidity, old age and death; the provision of medical care, and the provision of subsidies for families with children".[1] In other words, unemployment is a contingency risk, for which insurance cover should be provided to give social security for those who labour. But is not the person in chronic (or even temporary) "underemployment" just as "deserving" of income security? Why should we give income support to someone with zero hours of work last week and not to someone who did two hours?

Of course, these questions have been answered pragmatically to some extent over the years, and the answers have been incorporated in the design and refinement of poverty-ameliorating schemes and income supplements for the working poor. Yet they have not been answered fully or adequately. Perhaps the biggest question of all at the beginning of the twenty-first century is:

> Could and should the insurance approach to income security be sustained in the light of economic, labour market and social policy developments?

With good reason, most people regard unemployment as a negative experience, with adverse consequences for income, status, morale and "social integration". However, there is a view that unemployment should not be seen in this light, or at least not just in that way. It can or could be a period of "investment", a source of regeneration or re-energising, a useful passage in life for reflection and redirection. For some people – and it does not have to be anything like the majority for the point to be valid – it can be a positive experience.

Is it socially just to give someone in that position an income while not giving it to a person working 30 hours a week at a sewage plant or high on a construction site? The trouble with posing such philosophical questions is that they lead to very familiar normative dilemmas. For many analysts, they lead to words like "deserving" and "involuntary". Public transfers, it is said, should be given only to those who conform to all four of the criteria used to define unemployment and only if they behave in socially responsible ways, became unemployed involuntarily and show in various ways that they are among the deserving poor rather than the "undeserving". The cry is that "there are no rights without responsibilities".

Others – critics from diverse philosophical traditions – feel uncomfortable with this reasoning. Who can know what is best for someone else? Who can justify paternalism as the guiding principle of social policy? Local bureaucrats and tightly defined rules to weed out the nominally undeserving and voluntarily unemployed are likely to result in many type A and type B errors – excluding many of those who should be included, and including many who should be excluded, at least by the rules. Arbitrary, discretionary, inequitable and inefficient outcomes can be assured.

In that context, the issue can lead in one of two directions. It can lead in the direction of workfare (offering income-earning jobs to those prepared to accept them, refusing income to those who do not). Or it can lead to a de-linking of income security from labour force behaviour altogether. One might try to combine these two approaches, stopping half-way in each case – not too much stick, just enough carrot. But both lead away from the main approach that shaped the growth of welfare state capitalism in the middle decades of the twentieth century, namely unemployment insurance benefits.

2 Unemployment and Income Security

Before considering policies used to provide income for the unemployed, it may be useful to recall the disaggregation of the individual's social income, and consider what sources of social income can be received by an unemployed person. This can be expressed as follows:

$$SI = SP + (UI + UA + D) + (S + PI) + FT + LT$$

Where *SI* is social income, *SP* is severance pay, *UI* is unemployment insurance benefits, *UA* is unemployment assistance (means-tested), *S* is savings, *PI* is private insurance, *FT* are intra-family transfers, and LT are local community transfers, including any income from charity or non-governmental organisations.

In a stylised way, one can see that the poor (including most people in developing countries) usually have to depend on at most three of those sources – discretionary benefits, means-tested assistance and family-community transfers.[2] By contrast, a middle-income worker may be able to rely on enterprise benefits in the form of severance pay (lump sums paid on being made redundant) plus unemployment insurance benefits and private transfers. Higher up the scale, a person becoming unemployed is likely to rely purely on private means under his or her control. Thus, one can see that those near the bottom of society rely much more on precarious *forms* of income support, as well as having lower amounts.

Although data are hard to find to substantiate the claim, what seems to be happening around the world is that the unemployed have to depend increasingly on the most precarious forms of income support – means-tested assistance, discretionary benefits and whatever community or family support they can obtain. This is the context in which to assess recent policy trends.

3 Policy Frameworks for Unemployment

There are three main models of social protection for responding to unemployment. The first, and long the dominant way of thinking, has been called the *social solidarity paradigm*. Underlying this model, unemployment is viewed as a contingency risk that we all share, to different degrees. The basic argument is that a mandatory insurance system would pool risks. Because of market failure, in which those with a low probability of unemployment will not voluntarily take out insurance because its cost will reflect the average, higher probability of making a claim, and because the disadvantaged could not pay for the higher insurance rates that they would have to pay if they did so individually, the state must require compulsory insurance in which risks are pooled, enabling the state to afford to compensate those who have the misfortune to become unemployed.

A complication with this model is that probabilities come into play all through the system. Some of those who become unemployed drift into a chronic condition of long-term, anomic idleness, so that unemployment is a means by which individuals and groups suffer "social exclusion", being cut off from normal society and adopting deviant behaviour as "outsiders". Adherents of this paradigm believe these people need to be socially integrated, and that the state has a duty to help them to achieve "moral integration". A variant of this paradigm is that private rather than public agencies should assume responsibility for this integration.

A second approach might be called the *contractual exchange paradigm*. According to this, as long as due process and legal property rights are assured and equal, inequality of economic and social outcomes are acceptable, merely reflecting social differentiation and the division of labour. The appropriate way to achieve social integration and overcome social exclusion is to ensure fair contractual exchange based on individual property rights and to prevent discriminatory barriers to social and economic mobility.

A third approach might be called the *citizenship rights paradigm*. This sees group monopolies as restricting access by "outsiders" and protecting good opportunities for "insiders". Socio-economic stratification and labour market segmentation are seen as the primary sources of social exclusion. In this model, citizenship rights are seen as the means of overcoming stratification and detachment. Unemployment is part of a continuum, and need not be regarded as a special status.

With these alternatives in mind, there are six *main* means of improving the economic security of the unemployed and achieving their "social integration":

1 *Unemployment insurance benefits* – where contributions are paid, or credits provided, to earn entitlements to compensatory income, normally by the state (1a), but possibly by a private agency (1b).
2 *Unemployment assistance* – means-tested and/or asset-tested assistance.
3 *Labour market policy* – state-provided combination of training and/or jobs coupled with income transfers, for both participants and others. This includes "public works" and emergency employment schemes.
4 *Workfare* – the more usual variant of (3), in which the unemployed are obliged to take a training course or a job provided or subsidised by the state, in return for an income transfer.
5 *Employment or wage transfers* – a sum or money or tax credit paid either to the worker on being hired or, more typically, to the firm hiring the unemployed. These include so-called "in-work" benefits intended to "make work pay".
6 *Citizenship income grants* – an unconditional basic income paid as a citizenship right to all, including the unemployed.

Table 6.1. Political line and policy preferences

Political line	Primary paradigm	Policy preferences
1 Social democracy	Social solidarity	**1a**+2+5
2 Libertarianism	Contractual exchange	**1b**+2
3 "Compassionate conservatism"	Contractual exchange (+social solidarity)	1b+2+**4**+5
4 "Third Wayism"	Social solidarity (+contractual exchange)	1a+2+**4**+5
5 Economic democracy	Citizenship rights	**6**+3+1(a,b)

Of course, there are variants of all six of these policies, and there are some ingenuous proposals that combine elements of two or more of them.[3] Nevertheless, if one thinks of the three paradigms and the six possible approaches, one can predict the policy mixes that will be promoted by the political philosophies that look likely to compete for dominance in the first decade of the twenty-first century.

There may not appear to be much difference between these six approaches. But to highlight the differences stemming from the philosophical/political stances, the primary policy in each case is shown in bold. One may hypothesise that at least in the near future international discussion will be dominated by debate between advocates of "compassionate conservatism" and adherents of Third Wayism – or whatever each ends up being called.[4] Each relies on unemployment insurance and assistance benefits, backed by variants of workfare and employment and wage subsidies.

With this at the back of our minds, let us consider the standard approach to the provision of income security for the unemployed – insurance benefits.

4 Unemployment Insurance Benefits

For most of the twentieth century, there were two main means by which the unemployed were provided with some income security – unemployment insurance benefits (UI) and unemployment assistance (UA). In most countries, the latter was seen as a residual, a means-tested system, with benefits determined by financial need. Most industrialised countries presented an image of reliance on insurance benefits, supposedly provided as an entitlement acquired as a result of the payment of contributions by employers and/or the workers themselves.

A third means by which the unemployed acquired some income security was through transfers from family, kinship or the community. Throughout history this has always been the main source of support, and has continued to be the main – and usually only – source in developing countries. According to the welfare state model of development, they were expected to decline in significance with "development", and in the post-1945 era they did so.

However, since the mid 1970s the expected trend towards insurance benefits has gone sharply into reverse. This is so much so that it is a misnomer to call almost any existing unemployment benefit system an "insurance" system. The question for any observer should be: Have we seen the end of unemployment insurance?

Potentially, unemployment insurance benefits have at least eight functions, and a major drawback of them is precisely that because they are expected to fulfil several roles, some of which are in contradiction with others, they have been susceptible to political manipulation and endless tinkering. Rare is the Minister of Labour or Social Affairs who leaves the system as he or she found it.

Like most forms of "social protection", their design has been motivated by conflicting notions of social protection. The most conventional line is that they are intended to be compensatory, that is, covering for the contingency risk of job loss. Another line is that such benefits fulfil a social solidarity function, redistributing income to those who are unfortunate enough to be losers in a dynamic economy. Another is that they help to achieve macro-economic stabilisation. This role as a Keynesian stabiliser has gone out of fashion, but it is still sometimes mentioned. The essential point is that by providing income to those who have lost their earnings, such benefits prevent a decline in aggregate demand. A non-Keynesian might see that as a disadvantage in that it prevents unemployment being a macro-economic stabiliser through curbing inflationary pressure.

Another line is that unemployment benefits have a labour mobility function, making workers less resistant to losing or leaving their jobs, and encouraging and facilitating the rational movement between jobs and local labour markets, making employers less reluctant to declare workers redundant if their job is not justified economically, and giving workers some income security in which to search for suitable work. A related argument is that they have an income floor function, giving income to ensure that there is a strict limit to "downward risk".

Another is that they help individuals smooth their life-cycle consumption and savings patterns – a perceived effect rather than a deliberate objective. A seventh objective, which has become increasingly significant, is to provide incentives to labour, and in particular to do so in the legitimate, economic mainstream from which taxation and social contributions can be collected.

Finally, they also have a labour regulation function, being concerned about strengthening the incentive to labour in jobs and penalising the slothful. Unemployment benefits have always had this double character – a means of providing social protection and a mechanism of labour regulation. It is this that has allowed politicians to tinker with them with endless sophistry. Numerous generations of politicians have had a veiled tendency to divide those out of work into the "deserving" and the "undeserving". In every age, the fear of "the scrounger" has been brought into public debates on what the state should do. This underpinned the 1834 Poor Law in Great Britain, which specified that the deserving destitute could be identified by their willingness to perform unattractive labour, in what came to be known as the "workhouse". These were to be provided with survival assistance. This punitive approach has never been far away from reformers' minds. Thus, when unemployment insurance was introduced in Britain in 1911, two conditions were applied, ostensibly to safeguard against abuse and to legitimise the benefits – the unemployed had to be "available for work" and were not to have left their jobs "without good cause". These conditions have dogged unemployment benefits ever since.

Political and social considerations have influenced the directions taken. Entitlement conditions have been particularly erratic. For instance, in Britain, the requirement that a certain number of insurance contributions had to have been paid for entitlement was relaxed after 1918, because it was politically impossible to leave the millions of ex-soldiers and others who had worked in the war merely dependent on inadequate poor relief. Then, with high unemployment in 1921, the condition was inserted that a person had to be "genuinely seeking whole-time employment", and in 1924 the condition was added that the person had to be "making all reasonable efforts to secure employment". After six years of social suffering associated with the arbitrary application of these rules, the work-seeking test was removed. For some time, entitlement conditions were relaxed, and this continued in the post-1945 period.

In that era of statutory regulation, unemployment benefit systems spread around the world, although in most developing countries they were regarded – quite rightly – as impractical. In state socialism countries, they were regarded as unnecessary, since unemployment was ruled out, leaving the unemployed to be described as "parasitic". In welfare state countries, Full Employment was presumed to be the permanent state of things. Benefits were needed only to cover "temporary interruptions of earnings power". They could be paid from social insurance contributions, leaving only a small minority of unfortunates to be assisted by social assistance of some kind.

Then the rollback started. From the 1980s onwards one can detect a strong trend towards meaner and leaner systems. This was well under way when the state socialism countries began their rush to introduce benefit schemes, beginning with Hungary in 1986, most others after 1990. The trouble was that they were doing so when the type of system they were introducing was under strain almost everywhere.

The reasons were partly a reflection of the economic circumstances, partly a result of labour market changes and partly ideological. Whereas Keynesians, who dominated thinking from the late 1930s until the mid-1970s, attributed unemployment to a deficiency of aggregate demand, and thus the responsibility of the state, the supply-side economics revolution of the 1970s and 1980s attributed unemployment to a combination of the behaviour of job-seekers and firms, the impact of regulations and institutions (rigidities), and the character of social protection schemes (distortions). The subsequent persistence of high levels of unemployment and the spread of substantial long-term unemployment gave credence to those who claimed that much of that was voluntary. Even though there was no evidence that this was the case, there was a clamour to reduce "the generosity of unemployment benefits" and to tighten the conditions for entitlement. There was a logical contradiction in believing two positions simultaneously – that unemployment was a contingency risk, to be covered by an insurance scheme, and that unemployment was at root voluntary.

The clamour to reduce benefits was accentuated by the perception that there was a fiscal crisis. This reflected the economic orthodoxy, which stated that public deficits should be cut and that public expenditure should not only be cut but be shifted to so-called "human capital" policies. Part of this meant legitimation of the euphemism of "active labour market policies" rather than "passive" policies, which were taken to include unemployment benefits.

The quiet onslaught on UI systems has been relentless. To appreciate what has been happening, consider the main options. An unemployment benefit scheme could be purely insurance-based – you pay according to how much you think you can afford and how much you want to receive. The obvious problems with such a system are:

- Who should pay? Should it be the employer, whose actions could be deemed to determine the probability of the person becoming unemployed, the government, whose macro-economic policies could be said to influence the probability as well, or the individual worker, who bears the risk of becoming unemployed?
- How can a scheme designed to provide income security prevent the moral hazard that, since becoming unemployed results in receipt of an income, there will be an incentive to become or remain unemployed?

The Contributions Issue

For a long time, the most common answer to the first of these questions was that the employer should pay all or most of the contributions, while the worker could receive only a proportion of the income he would lose from losing employment *and* be constrained by conditions of entitlement that block the moral hazard, i.e., prevent the person from becoming or remaining voluntarily unemployed. In practice, this mix has proved extremely hard to translate into an efficient and equitable system.

Consider the funding options, and in particular the question of who should pay the contributions. It could be the employers, the workers or the government, or some combination of all three. If the employer pays the whole amount, then as long as unemployment is low and the claims are correspondingly small, the cost is likely to be only a small proportion of total labour costs. But if actual or anticipated unemployment is high, and if a large or growing proportion of employment is not covered (as is likely to be the case with more flexible or informal labour markets), then the contributions rate is likely to high. This is especially likely if a high proportion of those becoming unemployed are either young workers just entering the labour market without a contributions record, or workers returning from a period outside the labour force.

Since the 1970s, unemployment has been high in most parts of the world, and a high proportion of the unemployed have not been covered by regular contributions. Because of more intense competitive pressures for international trade and investment, and the increased demand for transfers due to high unemployment and a higher incidence of poverty, all of which have tended to force up contribution rates, economists, employers and numerous commentators have bemoaned high "non-wage labour costs" represented, in part, by social insurance contributions. The claim is that those limit employment, and that high non-wage labour costs drive more of the employment into the illegal or grey zone. This is one reason for a shift that has taken place around the world, in which workers themselves have paid a growing share of total contributions while a growing share of funding has come from general taxation.

The fiction of an insurance system has become clearer. The political desire to cut taxes has meant there have been attempts to make employers and workers bear most of the contributions. But here arises what might be called an immoral hazard. If the combined contribution rate is high, the worker and employer each have an incentive to avoid or evade payment and split the difference, especially if they think there is a low probability of needing or expecting to receive an unemployment benefit, or if they could allocate the money to a private insurance scheme or to savings. And as workers value certain income in the short term more than possible income at some future unknown time, they are likely to opt for the private arrangement. Doing so could leave them exposed to income insecurity, dependent on social assistance or a discretionary benefit. Low-income earners are most likely to fall into this trap, since they are least likely to be able to take a long-term approach to economic planning.[5]

The Incentive Issue

Unemployment benefits are expected to fulfil the potentially conflicting objectives of providing income security and providing incentive to look for and take income-earning activity. The extent of income security reflects entitlement and access to benefits, their duration and the income replacement rate – all of which are hard to estimate in advance and are rarely known or understood by anybody prior to unemployment. What principle of income security should they seek to follow?

The basis could be either a flat-rate or an earnings-related, or contributions-related, scheme. The latter has the appeal of financial equity. But it jeopardizes the social solidarity principle, since it reproduces inequalities in employment. A flat-rate system in its extreme form would provide a given level of benefit regardless of past income or amount or number of contributions. But what should determine that level? This has generated endless debate. The administrative-economic difficulty has been to find a level, or set of levels, that provide adequate income security for the unemployed coupled with reasonable incentive to find or accept available jobs.

In practice, just as most systems have become mixed in terms of contributions, so most have become mixes of flat-rate and earnings-related benefits. And the calculation of replacement rates has become complex, variable and often extremely hard to fathom. Many countries now have a range of amounts that can be received, dependent on past work experience, demographic characteristics, duration of unemployment, and so on. Thus, just to give one example, in the Netherlands the rule has been that the unemployed can receive up to 70 per cent of previous earnings but for those who have had very low income or none at all, the minimum amount they can receive has been 70 per cent of the statutory minimum wage.

One change has been to reduce the level of benefit over the course of the period of unemployment, as a means of influencing behaviour and as a deterrent to "voluntary" unemployment. Thus, in France in 2000 the employers and trade unions earnestly discussed the idea of paying a higher benefit at the beginning of a spell of unemployment, reducing the amount as the period lengthens. The rationale is that the prospect of a cut would discourage the unemployed from prolonging their unemployment. The drawback is that a tapered scheme penalises the less competent and the socially vulnerable groups, who are the most adversely affected by unemployment, and is thus regressive. It is a form of selectivity, and it would be hard to administer equitably.

A preoccupation among policymakers and analysts has been the famous unemployment trap, whereby somebody taking a job finds that they lose almost as much income in lost benefits, or possibly as much or more, as they gain from the job in terms of earnings. This tendency has been compounded by the existence of wage supplements for duration in employment paid in many firms and organisations. Commonly a new job pays significantly less than the job the person left, so that if the replacement rate is linked to past earnings, the individual may face what is in effect a marginal income tax rate of close to 100 per cent.

Besides being unfair and contrary to the intentions of workers or policy-makers, this encourages immoral hazards. The unemployed person has a strong incentive to take a job without declaring it, which an employer might be content to allow because he does not pay contributions and does not run into regulatory constraints.

While the incentive issues have been widely discussed, in practice many governments have taken the easy option of cutting replacement rates, or have tried to do so by reducing the maximum amount or duration of benefits. In doing so, they have gradually converted unemployment benefit systems into regulatory and paternalistic policy. To appreciate this, it is worth reflecting on the three sets of pressures that have eroded the original premises of unemployment benefits – fiscal, moral and legitimation. All three have lessons for any country contemplating the introduction of insurance-style unemployment benefits.

The Three Crises of Unemployment Benefits

In the 1980s and 1990s, in industrialised countries social policy was shaped by the fiscal crisis discussed earlier. Politicians and economists suddenly found – or claimed to believe – that they could not afford to do things they had been doing. The sense of crisis was mainly the outcome of mass unemployment, the new poverty, and more flexible and informal labour, which were associated with a decline in contributions and a rise in the demand for benefits. The squeeze induced pressure to cut the level and duration of benefits, raise contribution rates and tighten conditions for entitlement. The new economic orthodoxy added pressure to this by arguing that tighter fiscal policy would control inflation and boost economic growth.

A moral crisis has been slower to emerge. It has been building up, and may dominate public debate over the next decade. It stems from labour market developments and from the responses that have been taken by social scientists and a host of new-style politicians on the left and right of the political spectrum. Unemployment benefits were built up for industrial labour markets consisting overwhelmingly of full-time, reasonably well-paid workers, with only a tiny proportion of them needing such benefits while "frictionally unemployed". In such circumstances, there is unlikely to be pressure to tighten conditions for entitlement to benefits, because the number of people who might be "voluntarily idle" is small. In the post-war era, the labour market enabled the benefits system to operate reasonably well. Because it was presumed that a spell of unemployment would be short, that average earnings were rising, and that those losing jobs would be able to obtain others that would pay about the same, the benefits provided income replacement rates that were reasonably adequate and did not have strong disincentive effects to take jobs. These conditions never existed in developing countries, or in depressed regions of some industrialised countries. But even in affluent countries, long before the end of the century, none of those presumptions were justifiable.

As unemployment rose in the 1980s, in most countries the average duration of unemployment increased, the number (if not the proportion) of long-term unemployed grew, more of the unemployed had no employment history or at least not a recent one, more had not built up insurance contribution records because they had been unemployed or in some flexible, or shady, form of labour, and many more had low pre-unemployment wages. So, more of the unemployed who managed to qualify for benefits appeared to have high replacement rates. The resultant moral dilemmas could be expressed as follows:

> Should the replacement rate be lowered to provide a greater incentive to take available jobs, at the cost of reducing the income security of the unemployed? Or should the replacement rate be maintained (or lowered only moderately) while conditions for entitlement to benefits are tightened, maintaining income security of those who qualify but risking disentitling some in need? Or should the action be elsewhere altogether – raising entry-level wages or giving marginal wage subsidies or tax credits (or tax holidays) so as to raise the net incomes of those who enter jobs or start some own-account work?

Debates around these moral dilemmas have been hindered by the use of euphemisms and loaded language. It is surely inappropriate for highly paid economists, commentators or officials of international financial agencies to call for a reduction in the "generosity of benefits". If it is an insurance-based policy, it should be compensatory. If you insure a car you expect to receive the value of the car if it destroyed in an accident. If insurance companies said they were going to reduce the "generosity" of repayments, you would be scandalised. And it is dubious to claim that the problem is one of "voluntary unemployment" on the *presumption* that they are not taking "available jobs". It is also inappropriate, or worse, to base policy on anecdotal images of individuals not rising from bed in the morning to jump onto their bicycle in search of a career and fortune.

The debates on so-called generous benefits and voluntary unemployment have taken many turns. Some commentators have even claimed that cutting unemployment benefits would help the unemployed because it would induce pressure on employed workers to lower wages, thereby raising labour demand. This is speculative. Cutting replacement rates on an *ad hoc* (and non-compensatory) basis does explode the insurance principle. In the face of such actions, a person who pays contributions, or has them paid for him, does not have a known benefit to cover a known risk or one that at least can be estimated. Moreover, cutting the value of benefits risks more of the unemployed drifting into poverty.

The moral dilemmas have also been increased by reforms designed to make it harder to be "voluntarily" unemployed. In doing so, a very old euphemism has returned – the distinction between the "deserving poor" and the "undeserving". We will come back to that later. We merely assert here that it ultimately rests on subjective and often arbitrary judgments.

One moral dilemma deserves more attention than it has received. If the unemployed believe that they are being treated reasonably and fairly, they are more likely to be "honest" in their response to the system of benefits. If there is reason for trust, people are more likely to conform to the rules. One source of trust erosion is the arbitrary or discretionary nature of many rules, including the rule that an unemployed person can receive benefit income only if he or she is not earning anything from work. Doing a few "odd jobs" could lose all benefits. This poverty or unemployment trap is likely to seem unfair. So, the unemployed will feel morally justified in concealing earnings. Some governments have allowed for some "earnings disregard". But that merely erodes the basis of the UI scheme. Where is the line to be drawn?

Albeit related to the moralising tendency, a third dilemma that has arisen since the 1980s constitutes a legitimation crisis. As with many forms of public transfers, the political legitimacy of UI benefits has depended in part on the perception by enough people that they might need the benefit at some time and that they would be able to depend on it if they did. Legitimation also depends on the existence of a sense of social solidarity among a large proportion of the voting population, and it depends on whether the winners in society, those with a very low probability of becoming unemployed, fear the threat of agitation or retributive violence by the losers if they do not receive some compensatory income for their misfortune.

In the past quarter of a century, although it has never been anything like random, the probability of becoming or remaining unemployed has become increasingly non-random. People with certain characteristics – lack of quali-fications, age, gender, disability, race, etc. – have much higher probabilities than others. One can stretch the *median voter* thesis too far, but if people feel they themselves have a low probability of being unemployed, they are likely to vote for politicians promising to cut benefits. If they think that even if they were to become unemployed they would have a low probability of experiencing long-term unemployment, they are also likely to favour cutting the duration of benefit entitlement.

So, with more stratified social structures – the strengthening of winners-take-all, losers-lose-all society – a growing majority of the electorate will have little direct interest in the income security of the unemployed. Smugness rules. The jobless are not Us; they should take responsibility for their lives. It is unfortunate, but they should make themselves more "employable", or the authorities should help them to do so. This is popular rhetoric at the beginning of the twenty-first century.

Legitimation or its absence also derives from hegemonic images. If the unemployed are successfully depicted as the victims of de-industrialisation, or industrial restructuring, or a recession, or the "Asian crisis" or some other external event, then it will be easy to sustain the legitimation of a scheme for giving income security. But if unemployment is systematically depicted as laziness, voluntary behaviour due to the "generosity of benefits", then popular support by the median voters and others could trickle away. Something like this has been happening in many parts of the world, although there is no convincing evidence that unemployment is predominantly voluntary.

No doubt one could give a twist or two to these interpretations. But the fiscal, moral and legitimation pressures have induced numerous changes in the type and structures of conditions for entitlement to unemployment benefits. These deserve scrutiny because our judgment on their fairness or otherwise should go a long way to determine what form of policy is desirable or feasible in the flexible and informal labour markets that are spreading across the world.

5 The Conditionality of Unemployment Benefit Schemes

To appreciate the operation of most unemployment benefit systems that are based on unemployment insurance, it is instructive to consider the various steps that lead in its direction. Figure 6.1 shows the process by which anybody in employment could become unemployed. The process is not as simple as is commonly presumed.

For example, it is not valid to treat the act of becoming unemployed as "voluntary" or "involuntary". The terms "quit", "dismissal" and "made redundant" are vaguer than they might seem. I may be employed as a legal specialist and be bumped into a job as an office cleaner. If I subsequently leave the firm in disgust or shame, would you call my departure voluntary?

Figure 6.1. From labour surplus to labour market marginalisation

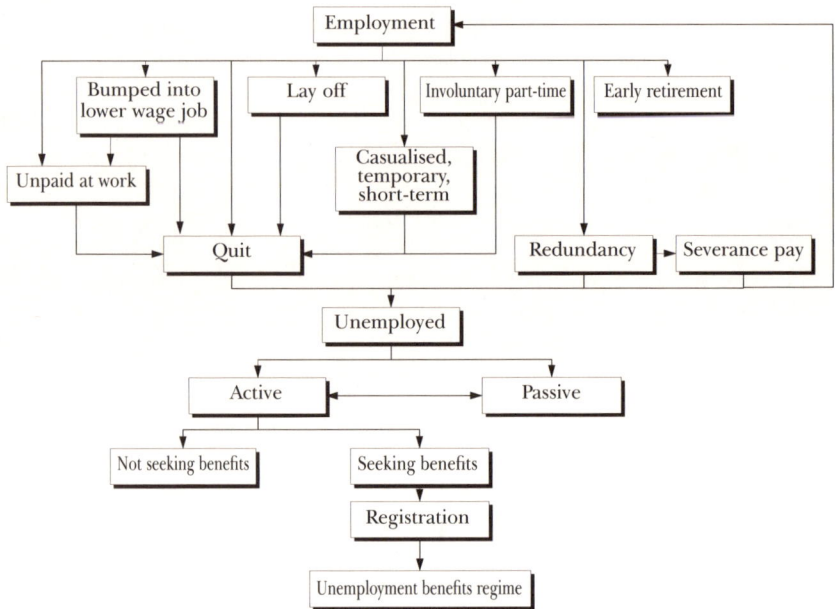

Or take the situation that has been widespread in eastern Europe over the past decade. If a firm stops paying wages ("wage arrears") or tells you to stay away from the factory until required ("unpaid administrative leave"), and then after several months you quit in despair, would you regard this as a voluntary action that deserved to be penalised in any way? What about the woman who "quits" because of the sexual attentions of an office colleague? To call this voluntary is a misnomer in common language, but it could easily be construed as such by an employment office. Unfortunately, the distinctions have proved remarkably important in the operation of unemployment benefit systems.

Figure 6.1 also shows the two behavioural responses to becoming unemployed. A person could start looking for income-earning activity immediately or could withdraw into passivity. Should the latter response be regarded as evidence of voluntary idleness? Only if one can answer with close to certainty that this would be the case could one justify disentitlement to benefits.

Finally, note that even if the person becomes active in the job-seeking sense, he or she may not apply for benefits, for reasons of pride, stigma, fear, ignorance or lack of interest or need. This throws up a moral dilemma that is too rarely considered: Should benefits be offered to a person even if he or she has not applied for them? One could suggest that those who do not apply cannot need benefits very much. But this is unproven. Minorities or those who have suffered most in their dealings with officials are among those who may not apply, from fear or from ignorance. Women may be less likely to apply, but there is no reason to presume that they do not need the income as much as men do.

Now consider figure 6.2. This is an attempt to display the process by which, once unemployed, a person could attempt to obtain unemployment benefits. Every element displayed in the figure comes into every benefit system, even though in many cases the designers of the system may not have made a conscious decision on every element. The process is well known, although rarely considered systematically.

The basic point is that any individual becoming unemployed faces a series of obstacles to the acquisition of benefits. In the early schemes, the conditions were relatively few. This is certainly no longer the case. The upper half of figure 6.2 refers to the initial application for benefits. The person has to sum up the energy and courage to go to an office to register, no easy task in many countries, especially in a large one with limited and costly public transport. Once there, he or she in effect has to pass a series of tests by satisfying prescribed conditions for entitlement. They are not in any particular order, so figure 6.2 should be regarded as merely illustrative of the process. However, there are certain conditions that are much more rigid and standard than others. Consider the tests in turn.

Age Test

First of all, they have to satisfy the age test. The usual rationale is that a person has to be within a certain age range to qualify for benefits. This is always going to be subjective and even arbitrary to some extent. To massage down the unemployment claims and even the recorded unemployment, some governments have lowered the upper age for entitlement and/or raised the initial age, and many responded to the high unemployment in the 1980s and 1990s by putting older workers into early retirement or disability status.

Employment Record Test

Presuming the unemployed pass the age test, they usually have to pass some employment record test. This means that they must prove they have paid insurance contributions for so many months or years over a recent period, or have had them paid for them. Increasing the required length of employment record and shortening the period in which the required number of contributions must have been paid have been ways of eroding entitlement. In some countries, employment in certain statuses does not count, and in some youths are excluded from entitlement simply because they do not have any employment record. There is no standard rule, and no rule would be any more socially just than another.

Some countries have excluded certain types of economic activity from building up entitlement to benefits. Those who have been self-employed are sometimes deemed to have not built up an employment record. This has been the case in Ireland, Portugal and Spain among EU member countries.

Figure 6.2. Entering the unemployment benefits regime

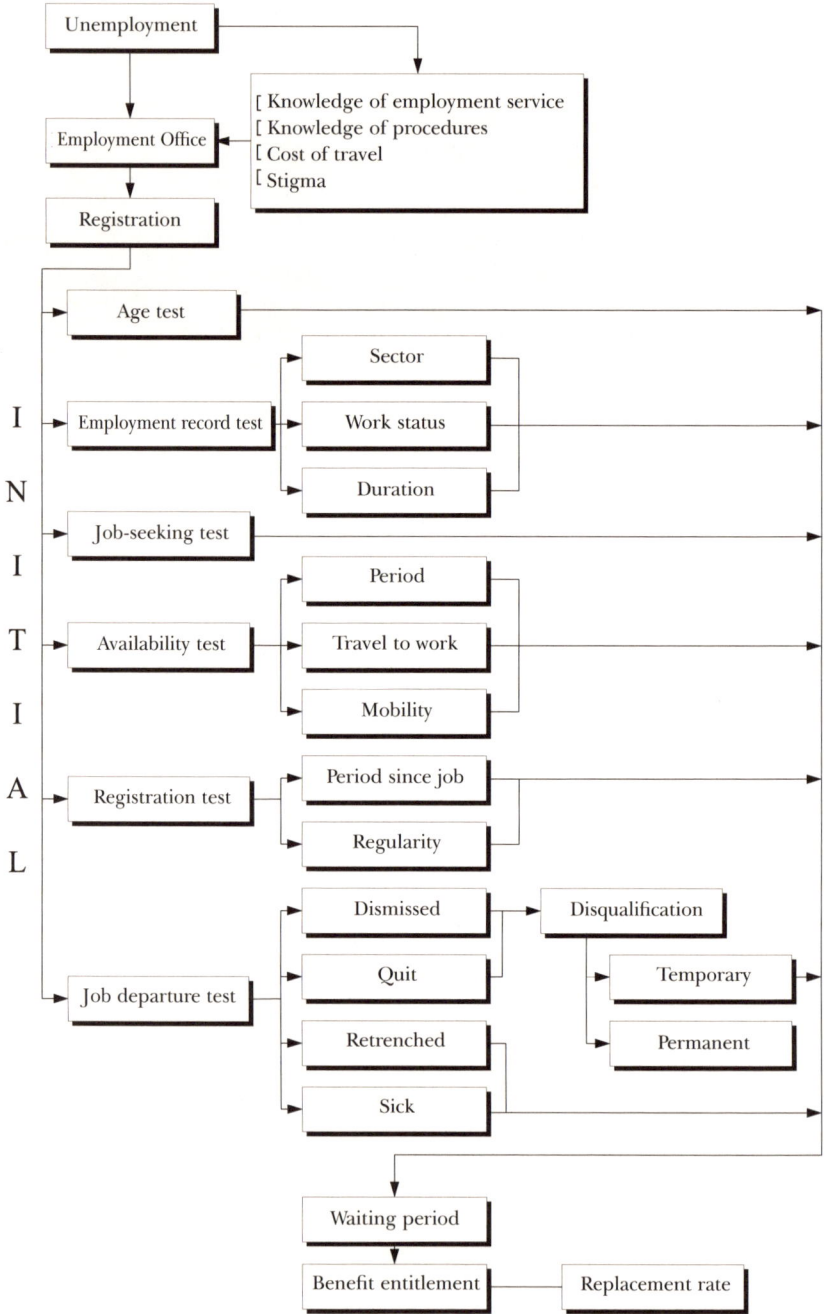

In most eastern European countries, the self-employed have been excluded from entitlement. And it has also been the practice in some developing countries that have introduced UI schemes, such as Algeria, Argentina, South Africa and Tunisia.

The rationale may be that it is hard to determine when someone is doing the work classified as self-employment, and it is difficult or impractical to collect contributions. However, there is no equitable argument for excluding the self-employed from entitlement to unemployment benefits. And in developing countries such a rule would effectively mean that the UI scheme could only apply to a privileged minority of workers. It would not be a source of social solidarity because most of the non-beneficiaries would be more impoverished than the beneficiaries.

Whatever the pragmatic fiscal reasons for any employment or contributions record test, application is likely to be arbitrary. Many anomalies are likely. Suppose the rule is that the person must have been employed for six of the last twelve months in order to qualify. This would mean that someone who worked part-time for six months would qualify, whereas someone who worked full-time for five months would not. Such a rule would be inequitable. Yet this is what happens. Given the growing flexibility and informalisation of economic activity, this sort of rule may have been responsible for an increasing number of unemployed being disentitled to benefits.

The employment continuity requirements in western Europe have varied considerably.[6] But the differences are small compared with the diversity of rules that have been introduced in central and eastern Europe, often steered by foreign advisers seemingly more keen to control fiscal commitments than with providing adequate state transfers for the unemployed. In Bulgaria, the person must have been employed for at least six of the past twelve months; in the Czech and Slovak Republics, it has been at least twelve in the past three years. So someone in Bulgaria employed for seven months in the past year would receive benefits while someone in the Czech Republic who worked for just as long would not. In some countries, the amount of benefit has depended on the duration of past employment. In Latvia, entitlement to full benefit has only been achieved if the person has paid the social tax (associated with employment) for at least five years. And in Azerbaijan, full entitlement has required proof of employment for at least ten years.

No employment record rule is demonstrably fairer than any other, and any rule introduces inter-personal inequity. What is apparent is that there has been a tendency to increase the required duration of past employment and to shorten the period in which the selected number of months of employment must have been worked. These two trends tend to result in greater explicit disentitlement.

In some countries, the past employment or contributions record test has been applied on the basis of a formula linking duration of contributions to level or duration of benefits. This has been adopted in developing countries. For instance, in Argentina the benefit can be received for four months if the employer had made contributions for the person during the year before the start of unemployment, and can be received for twelve months if the contributions had been made for the past three years. In other countries, there have been variants of this rule.

Less noticed by commentators is that during the 1990s the employment record test tended to become more differentiated, with special rules for the self-employed, part-time workers, youths and so on. This trend may reflect a growing perception of diversity of labour force patterns, but it also makes the rules increasingly arbitrary.

The insurance contribution principle may be reasonable if everybody who has a job is in regular employment and there is something like Full Employment. But there is nothing particularly just about a rule that says, for instance, that if you have been employed for eleven months and lose your job, you should not receive benefits, whereas if you were in a job for twelve months you should receive them. If I insure my car and after six months am hit in an accident that is not my fault, it would be a useless insurance if I only had coverage after twelve months of driving and paying.

Job Departure Test

The next barrier is the job departure test. In many countries, those who "quit" employment or who are dismissed for disciplinary reasons (whether proven or not) can be disqualified from entitlement to benefits, either for an initial period or for the entire time in which they are unemployed. The usual justification for this condition is that it discourages frivolous job-leaving. In practice, it impedes labour mobility. One might even describe it as a version of workfare, in that the threat of disentitlement may force workers to stay in jobs that have inadequate wages or working conditions.

The job departure condition too has been tightened, dramatically so in the UK in the 1980s. A person deemed by local employment service officials to have left a job without good cause was initially disqualified from receiving benefits for six weeks. This was first lengthened to 13 weeks, and then to 26 weeks. Such changes can have impressive effects on the official unemployment rate. The practice in the USA is even more drastic. Most US states have disqualified all those who quit their job "without just cause" for the entire period of their unemployment. In other countries the rule has varied widely; in Germany, someone has been disqualified for twelve weeks, in others the period has remained short.

Whatever the specific rule, the job departure test is inequitable. It introduces arbitrary decisions and leaves too much to the personal discretion of local employment service officials. The distinction between quitting and other forms of departure from employment is often very hazy. Personal interpretation usually comes into play, as in the case of the ending of a fixed-term or temporary contract. Subjective dilemmas are awkward. Many workers do not like to admit that they were pushed out because they were not wanted. It is easier to say "I left" rather than "I was pushed out". Yet a little white lie in one direction could result in disentitlement, whereas a little one in the other could gain them a benefit.

The job departure test has been a particularly severe source of income insecurity in eastern Europe. In countries such as Russia and Ukraine, millions of workers have been placed on administrative leave, without pay or with merely a token payment.[7] If they quit their non-paying jobs in despair they not only lost entitlement to severance pay but also lost entitlement to unemployment benefits. So, millions of eastern Europeans have been in the absurd situation of being trapped in a nether region between employment and unemployment – counted as employed but in reality unemployed, without any source of income security.

That may seem extreme and reflect a "transition" phase. However, in flexible labour markets everywhere, the job departure test could only be applied on a discretionary basis. And once disqualified, a person would surely be less inclined to return to face the process of seeking entitlement. The irony is that policymakers typically argue that labour mobility is essential for dynamic efficiency, but at the same time permit rules that penalise voluntary action to put that into effect.

There is also likely to be a waiting period before an applicant can receive an unemployment benefit. This could be a week or more. Where it involves a return visit to the employment office, with the queuing and re-interview, the stigma, discomfort and cost are all likely to deter a few timid people from the process. In any case, the wait means that for a proportion of the time in unemployment there is no benefit.

Job-seeking Test

The second round of disentitlements starts with the job-seeking test. This is usually regarded as reasonable, and it is common that the person must search "actively" for a job in the past week or two weeks. Where applied, this may cause problems of interpretation. There is not much point in searching for jobs when there are none available. There is also scope for bureaucratic discretion. The rule may allow abuse, allowing officials to intrude into the private lives of claimants. There have been instances when governments have tightened the rules or the application of them, demanding proof or questioning the motives and veracity of claimants who are already sure to be feeling insecure.

In the UK, the job-seeking test was a source of suffering and bitterness in the 1920s, which led to a prolonged distaste for the condition. However, it was reinstated under the Social Security Act of 1989, which once more placed the onus of proof of active job-seeking on the unemployed, strengthening the discretionary power of local officials. It is widely believed to have chipped away at the number of claimants and recipients of unemployment benefits, and the condition was applied with increasing rigour and vigour, with checks and interviews becoming the norm. The regulatory nature of the so-called unemployment insurance benefits became more transparent. Other countries also tightened this condition during the latter part of the twentieth century, with Australia leading the way with "activity agreements" and Job Search Allowances, which replaced unemployment benefits in 1991.

The job-seeking test makes it a strange use of words to describe un-employment benefits as "passive" policy. They are regulatory, and have become increasingly so. The test may seem reasonable because it could identify those who are not unemployed, perhaps justifying the extra expenditure on identifying fraudulent or "undeserving" claimants. It may help legitimise unemployment benefits among the voting public. It is unclear whether the saving covers the cost of the policing. The checks are supposed to overcome the moral hazard entailed in an insurance benefit that implicitly subsidises someone who becomes unemployed. But there is a moral hazard of sorts for officials operating the scheme. Is not the test, and the fear of having officials snooping into their lives, likely to lead some unemployed, in a vulnerable stage of their lives, to withdraw a claim, even if fully entitled to it?

Available-for-work Test

The next step is the available-for-work test. In most cases, there is a rule that the unemployed person must be available to take a job at short notice, which may be as short as 24 hours or may be a week or longer. The shorter the specified period, the more likely that it will be a source of disentitlement. The person may also have to give a commitment to be prepared to travel to take a job or even to move to another area to do so. There has been some tightening of such conditions in some countries.

However defined, the availability condition always risks being arbitrary in application. In the UK, the rule was tightened steadily in the 1980s, particularly in 1988, when the unemployed claimant was required to fill in a form with eighteen questions. Any wrong answers resulted in a suspension of entitlement to benefits. If the Department of Employment subsequently supported the suspension, the person was declared unavailable for work and thus ineligible for benefits. The intentions were clear, as shown by a circular sent to benefit managers around the country:

> A claimant must be able to accept at once (or at 24 hours notice in certain specified circumstances) any opportunity of suitable employment. This also means not just being ready to take a job, but taking active steps to draw attention to their availability for work. A claimant must not place restrictions on the nature and conditions (such as pay, hours of work, locality, etc.) they are prepared to accept which would prevent them from having reasonable prospects of getting work.

How academics, commentators, bureaucrats or politicians can continue to make a distinction between so-called "active" and "passive" policy in the light of rules such as this is a testament to the power of euphemisms. This is a prescription for behavioural control through insecurity. It gives discretionary powers to local officials. The rules were tightened even though evidence collected after the availability-for-work rules were tightened in the mid-1980s through "Restart" interviews, which showed that two-thirds of those suspended from entitlement were subsequently found to have been wrongly barred. But one does not need to cast doubt on motives. The rule is too subjective for comfort.

Job Refusal Test

Related to it is the job refusal test. The common rule is that a benefit recipient must accept a job if offered by an employer or through the employment exchange. In some countries, a person is allowed to decline one job offer but not more, in others they are obliged to accept the first offer. In some, the person can decline a job below the skill level of his or her past job, in others they must accept almost any job. This is the problem. Who decides, and on what basis should such a decision be made? The rule invites bureaucratic, paternalistic intrusiveness, and presumes that a local official knows better than the job-seeker what is best for him or her. It is hardly the norm that local officials are highly trained and experienced enough to be able to define what is "suitable" for an individual that they meet for the first time over a counter.

The intrusiveness and arbitrariness of this rule are likely to be particularly acute if employment exchanges are under pressure to demonstrate efficiency by demonstrating high and rising "placement rates". This has become a common tendency.

The job refusal test has been tightened in many countries in recent years. In many, refusing even one job results in disentitlement, and in some even refusing a job requiring fewer qualifications than possessed by the person or paying a wage lower than the person's last wage can do so. In the UK, in which the job refusal test has long been used, the 1989 Social Security Act stipulated that most unemployed, after a short period, were no longer entitled to refuse a job on the grounds that the wage was low. In Australia, entitlement rules were amended to require the unemployed to accept even a temporary job if offered. Such moves would seem to encourage labour casualisation and could even undermine the person's subsequent entitlements to benefits if employment continuity or duration rules apply.

Training Refusal Test

A variant of the rule is what might be called a training refusal test. Again, this is part of the paternalistic approach. With governments favouring "active" over "passive" policy, the rule may be that a person refusing a training place offered by an employment exchange will face disentitlement. One consequence of this may be that some of the unemployed drop out of the pool of benefit claimants – and from being counted as unemployed – simply because they do not wish to go into a labour market training scheme, or believe that they will be pushed into one. We have no idea of how many unemployed react in this way, which makes it hard to attribute the "disentitlement" to the training refusal rule *per se*.

Unemployment Duration Test

Next is the unemployment duration test. In most countries, UI benefits are paid only for a limited period, such as twelve or six months. The rationale is that income security is provided while a person seeks employment, which is expected to be a short period. A time limit is supposed to concentrate the mind on taking a job. The orthodox reasoning is that if unemployment benefits are provided for a long period, it could induce voluntary idleness. But if they are only paid for a short time, that could induce the unemployed to make poor long-term decisions, perhaps rushing into the first available job, which may be inappropriate for them and thus lead to repeat un-employment, perhaps even resulting in their disentitlement to benefits on the grounds that they "quit" the job "voluntarily". Or they could take temporary jobs that offer no chance of building up entitlements or skills before a new spell of unemployment strikes. It cannot be presumed that a short duration benefit regime lowers unemployment.

In some countries, maximum duration of entitlement has been made a function of the level of unemployment, either cyclically, as in the USA, or according to some predetermined level in the area in which the unemployed person is residing, as has been the system in Poland. If living in an area of "crisis-level" unemployment, the person has been entitled to twelve months of benefits; if not, entitlement has been for six months. Such a rule is supposed to reflect the fact that when overall unemployment is high, there is a tendency to take longer to find employment. However, it discourages mobility from high-unemployment to lower-unemployment areas, and it is inequitable. Why should someone in an area with 9.9 per cent unemployment receive half the benefit of someone in an area with a 10.1 per cent level? However pragmatic the rule, it offends any principle of distributive justice. Both are unemployed, and if the person in the higher-unemployment area has more skills, he would probably have a higher probability of finding employment than the other.

Paradoxically, with higher levels of unemployment in the 1980s and 1990s, many governments reduced the duration of entitlement to unemployment benefits. The Netherlands, Switzerland and the UK were among western European countries to do so. In the UK, it was reduced from twelve to six months with the replacement of unemployment benefits by the Jobseeker's Allowance. In Switzerland, in 1996 those aged under 50 had the maximum duration cut from 400 to 150 days, after which they had to participate in a workfare scheme if they wished to receive a benefit.

The tendency to reduce duration has been strong in central and eastern Europe. At the beginning of the 1990s, most countries allowed for up to twelve months, often with a declining level of benefits during the course of unemployment. Since then, the maximum has been shortened, often to six months, as in Belarus, Bulgaria, the Czech Republic, Estonia, Kyrgyzia and Lithuania, or to nine months, as in Latvia, or to a system with declining levels over successive months, as in Moldova and Romania. Ironically, the reductions occurred as unemployment rose, and were accompanied by increasingly selective and complex rules. In Bulgaria, duration of entitlement was made dependent on age and on duration of past employment. In Slovakia, if the unemployed were aged 15–29, maximum duration was set at six months; if aged 30–44, it was eight; if aged 45–49, it was nine; if aged 50 or more, it was twelve months. One may comprehend the rough logic, but it represents a rough sort of justice.

The Result: Creeping Disentitlement

In sum, a complex set of conditions have been developed to determine entitlement to unemployment benefits. There has been a powerful international trend to make it harder for unemployed people to obtain them. And in the process the uncertainty of entitlement has increased, implying that even in industrialized countries unemployment has been associated with greater income insecurity. In terms of figure 6.2, after all the conditions just listed has come the use of means tests or asset tests. This practice has normally been applied to unemployment assistance rather than to insurance benefits, but in a few countries the distinction has disappeared, as in Australia since 1987.

The simple and undeniable fact is that probability of entitlement to unemployment benefits has declined globally. For instance, in the UK between 1979 and 1988 no less than 27 measures were introduced to cut benefits, compared to four that benefited the unemployed.[8] In the USA, where conditions have always been tight, the situation has long been that only a minority of the unemployed actually receive unemployment benefits. In the 1980s and 1990s, the average fluctuated between 30 per cent and 40 per cent. In most so-called "right to work" states, the figure has been lower, with less than 20 per cent in states like South Dakota and Virginia.[9] This might make the labour market more "flexible", but clearly the system *per se* is not providing income security for the unemployed.

Studies in the USA have shown that declining coverage by unemployment benefits has reflected several factors. One is the shift away from manufacturing, where employment involving regular contributions has been more the norm than in other sectors. This is important, for it may be that unemployment insurance benefits only work reasonably well in economies in which manufacturing labour predominates. Other factors included changes in state programmes, in which base-period earnings requirements and income-based denials for benefit were increased, while eligibility conditions were tightened.

The subsequent introduction of taxation of unemployment benefits reduced their value, and thus acted as a disincentive to claim them. During the 1990s further changes made entitlement even harder to obtain. In most US states, the current situation is that the unemployed must have been employed for at least six of the past twelve months to qualify for minimum benefits, with other states stipulating that the person must have received at least a specified amount of wage earnings in the past year. In 1989–90, fifteen states raised the level of earnings required to qualify for a minimum weekly benefit, and thirty-nine increased the amount required for maximum benefit.

Another trend in the USA during the last part of the twentieth century was stricter application of disqualification rules. One study found that of the "monetarily eligible" initial claimants for UI benefits 24.3 per cent were disqualified – 5.9 per cent for supposedly not being able to work or for not being readily available for work, 6.8 per cent for leaving a job "without good cause", 4.1 per cent for being fired for misconduct, 0.3 per cent for refusing "suitable work", and 7.2 per cent for other reasons.[10] The trouble is that in many states, once disqualified – perhaps for quitting a job – the unemployed cannot receive benefits for the entire period of their unemployment.

Entitlement to UI benefits has become harder in many other countries as well. According to government reports, in the 1990s alone eligibility conditions were tightened in Austria, Canada, Denmark, Finland, France, the Netherlands, New Zealand, Norway, Spain, Sweden and the UK. Tighter job availability requirements were applied in Belgium, Canada, Denmark, Germany, Italy, the Netherlands, New Zealand, Spain, Sweden and the UK.

The decline has meant that in many countries only a minority of the unemployed receive unemployment benefits. This is not a new phenomenon. By the late 1980s only 30 per cent of the unemployed in Spain were receiving benefits, in France 39 per cent, in western Germany 55 per cent and in Sweden – supposedly the model of universalism – only 68 per cent. If you take the European Union overall, by the mid 1990s only two out of every five unemployed were receiving unemployment benefits (table 6.2). This actually considerably overstates receipt of insurance benefits because the figures include those receiving only unemployment assistance (means-tested). But if we accept the figures as upper limits, we should have a clearer picture of the "generosity of unemployment benefits".

Table 6.2 indicates that in EU countries, where entitlement and recipient rates are higher than elsewhere, the share of active unemployed receiving unemployment insurance or assistance benefits ranges from over 80 per cent in Belgium to less than 8 per cent in Greece and Italy. In most countries, women were less likely to be receiving benefits. But these figures overstate the probability of receipt of benefits. According to EUROSTAT data, if we count all the unemployed, including those wanting but not currently seeking employment, in 1996 less than 20 per cent were receiving benefits.

In eastern Europe, the situation is more peculiar because in some countries, including the two largest, most unemployed are not registered at employment offices and accordingly do not receive unemployment benefits. If they are registered, probability of entitlement is now high in Russia. But entitlement does not necessarily mean receipt, since many *oblast* employment services have not had the funds to pay. Even if 80 per cent of the registered received benefits, since three quarters of the unemployed were not registered, that would imply only about 20 per cent were receiving benefits.

In other countries, there was a sharp decline in the proportion receiving benefits – in Bulgaria to 23 per cent in 1996, in Latvia to 47 per cent, in Poland 52 per cent, all well down from the levels in 1992. In several countries, such as Armenia, the figure fell to less than 15 per cent. The experience with the introduction of unemployment insurance schemes

Table 6.2. Unemployed receiving benefits, European Community, 1992–99 (percent of active unemployed receiving)

Country	1992	1993	1994	1995	1996	1997	1998	1999
Austria	n.a.	n.a.	n.a.	63.1	68.9	65.9	69.7	74.2
Belgium	83.8	83.3	84.5	81.1	82.6	80.3	77.9	66.3
Denmark	79.9	82.6	64.2	65.4	55.1	59.0	61.9	62.6
Finland	n.a.	n.a.	n.a.	67.6	60.4	55.7	53.3	51.6
France	45.0	45.0	46.5	43.6	43.6	44.2	43.6	42.4
Germany	60.2	64.6	66.0	63.2	68.0	73.0	73.5	74.2
Greece	7.1	6.7	7.1	8.1	5.8	6.4	8.0	n.a.
Italy	4.6	6.0	7.0	5.8	5.1	5.7	5.1	n.a.
Luxembourg	30.8	21.0	36.0	37.9	36.5	27.2	25.9	29.3
Netherlands	36.9	41.3	45.0	40.8	42.2	38.4	32.4	31.2
Portugal	18.7	25.9	25.3	27.9	25.5	25.3	21.8	28.4
Spain	29.7	31.3	28.1	23.5	20.4	19.1	17.4	16.6
Sweden	n.a.	n.a.	n.a.	70.3	68.7	66.0	63.6	55.4
UK	62.3	62.5	59.9	56.4	55.6	48.9	38.9	40.6
Total	41.8	43.1	42.0	40.0	39.7	39.2	37.8	37.1

Note: Calculated from data supplied by EUROSTAT

countries in central and eastern Europe may be closest to what could be expected to occur if they were introduced in 'middle-income' developing countries. The experience in reaching the unemployed is not encouraging.

6 The "Generosity of Benefits"

Now consider the difficult issue of income replacement rates – the income value of unemployment benefits relative to average earnings. The task is not easy, since the national formulae used are complex, variable and rarely comparable across countries. The OECD has made a valuable effort to measure and monitor replacement rates, but the resultant database is correspondingly complex.[11]

There are several difficulties. First, one must distinguish between gross (before tax) and net replacement; there is often a substantial difference. Second, the figures as presented give the impression that all claimants receive their entitlement, which is often not the case.[12] Third, average replacement rates over a prolonged period of unemployment often differ from initial replacement rates. Some commentators exaggerate the "generosity" by citing the rate for the first month, *after* the waiting period, which is when the rate is at its height.

According to OECD data, average gross replacement rates in the mid-1990s varied from less than 20 per cent in Japan, the UK and the USA to 71 per cent in Denmark. The latter was an outlier, since the next highest was the Netherlands, with 46 per cent. The unweighted overall average was 31 per cent, which was a little higher than in the early 1960s. In some countries, the rate had risen, in some it fell or stayed about the same (Belgium, Germany, Japan, New Zealand, UK and USA). Across industrialised countries as a group, there had been a convergence in gross replacement rates.

The apparent rise may in part reflect a tendency for the tighter eligibility conditions to exclude those with relatively low replacement rates. If they were expressed as an average for all the unemployed, they would be lower. Another factor in the apparent rise is the fall in average earnings of those most likely to experience unemployment. The appearance of constant or rising "generosity" of benefits may be due to lower incomes received before unemployment. To put the point bluntly: if your past earnings were $1 a day (which is why the job ended) and the benefit you are given is $1 a day, your replacement rate would be 100 per cent. But if you need $5 a day in order to survive, the 100 per cent replacement is hardly "generous". This is left out of the following, but it adds to the strength of the argument.

Net replacement rates are higher than gross rates in most countries, and probably these are more relevant for assessing income security and behavioural responses, because they refer to what the unemployed would "take home" relative to what those with average earnings would take home. According to OECD estimates, net replacement rates in the mid 1990s varied

Table 6.3. Average gross and net unemployment benefit replacement rates, industrialised countries, 1995

	Replacement rate	
	Gross	Net
Australia	27	31
Austria	26	–
Belgium	42	59
Canada	27	43
Denmark	71	81
Finland	43	59
France	38	55
Germany	26	54
Greece	22	–
Ireland	26	37
Italy	20	19
Japan	10	45
Netherlands	46	69
New Zealand	30	39
Norway	39	62
Portugal	35	–
Spain	32	49
Sweden	27	67
Switzerland	30	62
United Kingdom	18	51
United States	12	16

Source: OECD Database on Unemployment Benefit Entitlements and Replacement Rates

from a low of 16 per cent in the USA and 19 per cent in Italy to a high of 81 per cent in Denmark, followed by the Netherlands with 69 per cent (table 6.3).[13] The unweighted average for eighteen industrialised countries for which there were comparable data was about 50 per cent.

In some countries the value of unemployment benefits has fallen because they have been linked to the minimum wage, which has been allowed to decline. This has been the case in the Netherlands, where unemployment benefit has been set at 70 per cent of the minimum wage, payable for up to six months for those without earnings-related benefit entitlement. In the UK, in the 1980s earnings-related supplements to unemployment benefits were abolished, and the new Jobseeker's Allowance gave a low replacement rate.

It is in the context of the evidence on replacement rates and entitlement probabilities that we should consider a popular view that western Europe, in particular, has been suffering from "structural unemployment" due to "the generosity of unemployment benefits" and "welfare dependency". This view has been stated categorically by the International Monetary Fund in several of its annual *World Economic Outlook* reports, and by others.[14] It is hard to accept.

By way of conclusion, we may estimate the unemployed's income security index, or the probable income replacement rate. For this, we need three ratios – the probability of claiming, conditional on being unemployed, the probability of being entitled to and receiving benefits, and the income replacement rate. None of these is easy to measure, and the data available are not adequate. Because we do not wish to exaggerate, the assumptions made in the following tend to overstate each ratio.

For illustrative purposes, we concentrate on EU countries. It is assumed that the percentage of unemployed who were "active" measures the unemployed's probability of claiming benefits. Since this may have a selectivity bias, we adjust the figure by adding half the difference between the percentage active and 100 per cent.[14] We also need the beneficiary ratio. We saw earlier that on average about 33 per cent of the active unemployed receive benefits, although this varies enormously, being lower for women. The third ratio is the hardest to estimate. The data available are for all unemployment benefits, including assistance, which gives an upward bias. Another problem is to decide on the duration. It is inappropriate to take the replacement rate for the first month of unemployment, or an average rate over a five-year period of unemployment. So, we take the gross replacement rate as a percentage of average earnings for a single person and for a married man with a "dependent wife" (sic) during the first twelve months of unemployment. The average and standard deviation for married men with "dependent wife" are shown in figure 6.3.

Using the three ratios we can estimate the average unemployed person's income security index. For Belgium, for example, in the mid-1990s a married man would have had a probable replacement rate of 0.8 multiplied by 0.84 multiplied by 0.38, giving a figure of 26 per cent of average earnings. A man in Germany would have had slightly less. These levels are

Figure 6.3. Average gross replacement rate at 100 per cent of average earnings during first year of unemployment, with dependent wife, OECD countries, 1961–97 (grey area showing standard deviation in replacement rates across OECD countries)

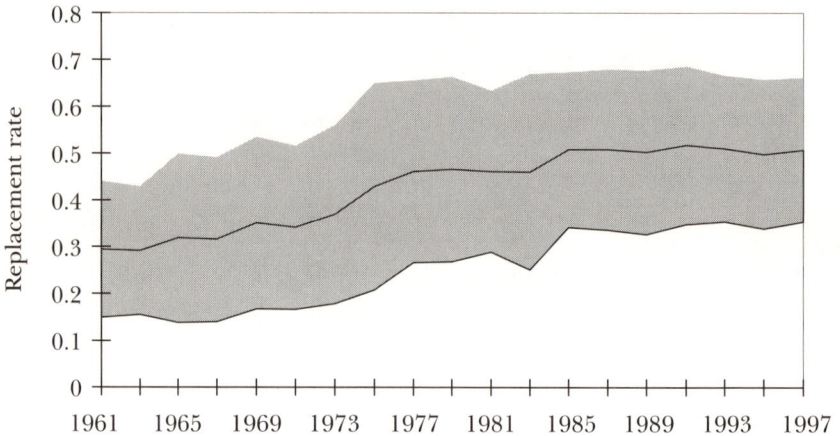

Source: OECD Database on Benefit Entitlements and Gross Replacement Rates, 1998

scarcely conducive to voluntary unemployment and are impoverishing. The value of this index is approximately what the modal person must expect from becoming unemployed.

The fiction of unemployment insurance is exploded by these figures. And to talk of excess generosity of unemployment benefits in this context is mildly distasteful. The subjective terms "generous" and "generosity" should not be used.

Alternatives to Unemployment Benefits

The bulk of this analysis has focused on a critique of the practicalities of unemployment insurance benefits. The thrust of the argument and evidence is that they suffer from serious flaws that make them unpromising for developing countries and for highly flexible labour markets of the type emerging in industrialised and developing countries. We will conclude with brief reference to several alternative approaches.

7 Unemployment Assistance

Is unemployment assistance an acceptable alternative to unemployment insurance benefits? The appeal to some economists, commentators and politicians lies in the view that this is the way to *target* on the needy *and* save money, showing good fiscal husbandry.

With the possible exception of Germany, in most industrialised countries labour market changes and tighter conditionality have contributed to a strong drift away from UI to means-tested unemployment assistance. This too has been subject to a steady process of additional and tighter conditionality. And as with insurance benefits, the value of unemployment assistance has tended to fall, as in the Netherlands, for example, where it has been set at 70 per cent of the minimum wage, which itself has fallen in relative terms. In a few cases, means-tested assistance has become the base of the system for giving income to the unemployed.

The biggest drawback to unemployment assistance is that means-tested schemes have low take-up rates, i.e., only a small proportion of those entitled to assistance actually applies for or receives them. In industrialised countries, there is a vast body of evidence to support this claim. In developing countries, the take-up rates are likely to be even lower, since the lack of administrative capacity will be coupled with a lack of knowledge of the existence of such schemes, an inability to afford the transport to distant and ill-equipped offices and other practical obstacles.

Some economists argue that if people do not apply for a benefit, it must mean that either they do not need it or they know they do not deserve it or qualify. There is no justification for presuming that these are the reasons for non-take-up. More likely, fear, lack of knowledge, stigma and other psychological and financial barriers are the factors.

Means-testing also intensifies the unemployment trap. At the simplest, this arises because if you are not earning anything you receive an income in the form of a benefit. As soon as you start earning, all or part of the benefit is taken away. To counter this disincentive to take a job, some schemes allow for a modest amount of earned income before the benefit is lost. In other countries, tax credits or a wage subsidy exists to "make work pay". But the unemployment trap tends to remain, if somewhat ameliorated.

Another serious problem arises if the means test (or income test) is applied on a family-unit basis, as is common. In this case, an unemployed man with an income-earning wife may be disqualified from all or part of unemployment assistance, in some cases making it financially advantageous for the wife to become unemployed as well or to leave the labour force. Call this a moral hazard or a market failure if you wish. The means test could raise unemployment, although if the wife "quit" her job she might not be counted as unemployed because she might not be entitled to benefits because she entered unemployment without what the authorities would regard as "good cause". It was for such reasons that, even controlling for other influences, wives of unemployed men have had a lower labour force participation rate than other married women.

Perversely, means tests may have contributed to the feminisation of the lower end of labour markets. Those with entitlement to unemployment benefits are likely to be in an unemployment or poverty trap, since they could lose more than they gain by taking a low-wage or part-time job. The poor, in particular, cannot easily afford to take a long-term view to such jobs – by seeing them as stepping stones into higher-paying employment. So it would be rational for them to take the benefits, while women and others without entitlement to benefits took the available jobs. This tendency may have become much stronger because the trend to more flexible and informal labour markets means that many jobs have lower wages than those that are disappearing or from which the unemployed have come.

Unemployment traps associated with means-tested assistance encourage some to remain unemployed "involuntarily", some to work informally to evade taxes and escape being penalised by loss of benefits. They may also be a disincentive to saving, since savings are often taken into account in determining benefits.

Means-testing and other forms of selective screening are always partially discretionary. They allow local officials control over people by "processing the client", as one famous study of local bureaucracy put it.[16] Officials will fall back on standard attitudes to type of claimants. What is insufficiently appreciated is that selective policy is always discretionary. The more "active" the policy, the more discretionary its implementation. Social services are the most discretionary, since they allow officials to decide whom they will meet, whom they will help, what form of help to offer, what form of follow-up, what form of monitoring, what form of sanction, and so on.

Means-tested and behaviour-tested transfers allow discretionary interpretation of rules and procedures, including selective oversight. The right to appeal against the judgment of some clerk (well-intentioned or otherwise) may not exist, and where it does may be limited, costly or time-consuming. A few moments of assessment will surely convince most observers that complex testing in a low-income country or region simply will not work with any degree of fairness or efficiency.

8 Other Options

Workfare, considered in chapter 8, is the most paternalistic means of attempting to provide income security to the unemployed, and derives its rationale from a revision of the social solidarity paradigm combined with the libertarianism underlying the exchange entitlements framework for social policy. The opposite of this is the citizenship rights approach, in which everybody is granted a guaranteed basic income as a right of citizenship, without any labour-related condition. The arguments for and against moving in this direction are considered at length later.

9 Work Insurance

Earlier, when outlining the main options for responding to the challenge of income security for the unemployed, one direction for reform was omitted, deliberately. In part this was because it has yet to crystallise into a coherent view and in part because it potentially could go in the direction of the labourist line of unemployment insurance and other schemes listed under the first five options or in the direction of citizenship income and security based on work.

A challenge over the first decade of the twenty-first century will be to escape from the view that labour markets will or should correspond to the norm of the industrial model in which the life stages are divided into three phases (childhood, labouring life, retirement) and economic activity is divided into three forms (employed, unemployed or economically inactive (sic)). Work activity is becoming more diversified, because more people are combining different activities at any one time and over their life and because some forms of work that people have performed over countless generations are finally being recognised as work, with use value if not exchange value.

Combining work activities has always been the norm in developing countries. It is also now becoming more common and recognised in industrialised countries. People are less likely to say they are either employed or self-employed – they are both, at different times of the day or week or year. There has been reference to "feigned self-employment", with the suggestion that people are lying or concealing their true status for tax or other reasons. What may be more significant is that conventional terminology and statistics may be inappropriate for the more flexible, informal work system that is emerging.

The image of the "portfolio" worker may seem fanciful or exaggerated. But the space exists for complex work statuses, for working while training for something else, for doing community work while doing care work, and so on. And so is the scope for occupational deconstruction and reconstruction. The diversity of work statuses need not be chaotic. If people are bundling competencies in ways that suit their needs, capabilities and aspirations – which they have always done, although the social and technical divisions of labour have concealed the reality – the challenge is to find policies and institutions to facilitate that and ensure adequate security for those working in this mould.

The emerging diversity poses challenges for social protection policy. One way of putting it is that the system must move away from the traditional model of social security based on the notion of contingency risks to one based on something like endogenous risk. A dynamic economy and a dynamic society, and dynamic individual human beings, are those in which its members are encouraged to take constructive risks. This means that many forms of risk are partly a matter of choice.

To put this in terms of the currently orthodox language of moral hazard is dubious, because it conveys a negative judgmental connotation. To give a simple example: I may think it is rational, for my longer-term occupation, to decline a job now that might appear to be "suitable". The implicit judgment in a system in which anyone turning down a suitable job loses entitlement to unemployment benefit is that the person is choosing to be unemployed voluntarily. Therefore the behaviour is not a risk for which insurance cover is warranted. This is not good enough.

So, one type of problem is that it is extraordinarily difficult to decide between voluntary and involuntary unemployment, and it may be advisable to avoid using either adjective. Another is that the nature of risk in a flexible work system is more akin to the working pattern norms in developing countries than to those in industrial society that Beveridge and his generation of social policy designers envisaged. The main risk is unstable and unpredict-able income coupled with unstable and unpredictable need for income. Included in this is the risk that one's competencies and carefully nurtured "skills" will suddenly become obsolescent.

Some economists have seen employment insurance – or as some have called it, wage insurance – as the answer to this predicament.[17] The appeal is that it could be the means for smoothing income and could deal with manufactured or endogenous risks. A failing of unemployment insurance is that it penalises a certain type of risk taking and "rewards" only those who are not working. The concept of employment insurance opens up more flexible possibilities. Its drawback is that it focuses on only paid employment. While an advance on UI, it still leaves out those who are doing work but not labour. The challenge will be to see whether this can be incorporated into such a scheme, perhaps by giving credits for periods when forms of work other than income-earning labour are being performed. Another challenge posed by consideration of this type of reform is the need to devise a system for income security that covers the whole spectrum of work activity. Some analysts have proposed this sort of policy for dealing with the standard transitions in economic life of individuals – between school and employment, employment and unemployment, employment and retirement, and between various working time arrangements.[18]

What is also required is a policy framework for providing basic income security for simultaneous combinations of activities and types of work. The continuum is considerable between those who are almost entirely involved in non-income earning work and those who are almost entirely involved in income-earning work. The optimum scheme for income security should facilitate diversity of productive and useful work, including flexible work schedules.

10 Concluding Points

Images shape policymakers' attitudes, and of course they use images to shape the public attitude in directions that they wish to go. The image that predominated after the 1930s was of the unemployed struggling for dignity, involuntarily unemployed. The image that has been encouraged in recent decades is one of voluntary unemployment, "dependency" and "scrounging": They are not "us", and "they" should be more like "us". Stereotypes are ideally suited to an age of time pressure and sound bites.

That aside, one must conclude that it is unlikely that unemployment insurance benefits have a viable or even desirable future. More flexible labour markets and extensive economic informalisation make standardised schemes based on the behavioural presumptions used in UI increasingly discretionary, arbitrary, intrusive, inefficient and inequitable.

Even in industrialised countries, insurance benefits now reach only a minority of the unemployed. The drift to means-tested assistance and the lack of benefits altogether for many of the unemployed has reflected high unemployment, tighter conditions for entitlement and a process of implicit disentitlement due to the trend away from regular, full-time employment. As a result, once more, to be unemployed is usually to face substantial and growing economic insecurity.

The fact that governments feel able to make changes to the benefit conditions and levels of income provided at will and with short notice has undermined any claim that they are compensatory insurance benefits. To enter a scheme under one set of conditions only to see them change from day to day is scarcely consistent with any notion of insurance. Rules may be essential for the viability of an unemployment benefit system, but they are arbitrary, shaped by images of a norm of some type.

Unemployment benefits have become more transparently part of the regulatory apparatus, seeking to control and influence people's behaviour, expectations and aspirations. To call any existing unemployment benefit scheme "passive" policy would be a misnomer. Similarly, few schemes deserve to be called "generous", and it ill becomes economists to use such words to describe schemes in which only a minority manage to obtain any benefits.

The steady process of restrictive reforms that has been taking place since the 1970s has affected socio-economic security more generally. They create greater insecurity among those anticipating or fearing unemployment, so lowering subjective employment security. And they are likely to have contributed to the weakening of workers' representation security, fear having made workers less likely to support independent, adversarial trade unionism.

Unemployment insurance benefits may also have become a source of income inequality. For example, in many countries (not all) income replacement rates for men have remained higher than for women. In the 1990s, this was the case in countries such as France, Germany, the Netherlands, Portugal, Spain and Sweden. One reason for this is that women have been unable to build up insurance contributions and because the means-tested schemes on which they have had to rely have tended to adhere to a traditional "bread-winner" model.[19] Above all, women have had a lower probability of receiving unemployment benefits.

In sum, unemployment insurance benefits suffer from several severe limitations. They limit choice, by tending to restrict legitimate activity to full-time unemployment or employment; they limit solidarity because only a minority are effectively in the system and because it only accepts a certain range of behaviour; they limit income security because many of the unemployed fail to qualify; and they limit competence enhancement because they constrain mobility. With respect to this last limitation, bear in mind that if the conditions include the need to demonstrate regular job-seeking and availability for jobs at short notice, a person is likely to be restricted in attending courses of learning.

Finally, as long as unemployment benefits continue, several practical principles should be strengthened. First, there should be strong pressure to ensure that regular statistics on the incidence of entitlement and receipt of benefits are collected and published by government authorities. These should be disaggregated by gender, since there is anecdotal and statistical evidence that women are less likely to receive benefits, even when they are entitled to do so. And they are also less likely to secure entitlement to benefits. Similar concerns arise with ethnic minorities, migrants and other socially vulnerable groups.

Second, it may be advisable to keep administration of unemployment benefits (or other forms of income transfer) separate from administration of employment or labour market services. The stigma of one may make it harder for some to apply for the other. And the administration of "career guidance" should not be muddled with the provision of income for those in need. They require different skills.

Third, income security policies should be kept separate from labour market policies, that is, policies to promote employment and to make the labour market more efficient or equitable. Mixing up objectives is likely to undermine the effectiveness of all policies. This extends to images. One drawback in considering them together is that they are seen as coming from the same source and are thus seen as in competition for limited resources. The image that money spent on unemployment benefits is "crowding out" funds for policies to improve labour market efficiency, training, or job promotion leads politicians and commentators to claim that benefits must be cut so as to make more resources available for "active" measures. Any such coupling is deplorable and ultimately to the detriment of those in the margin of the labour market.

7

The Paternalistic Consensus

1 Introduction

In the 1990s, the prescriptions and models that had been so assiduously promoted in the era of market capitalism came under increasing criticism. Although its principal spokesmen seemed impervious to the concerns, the evident failings became more widely accepted. This was demonstrated most conspicuously in a series of electoral defeats for politicians and political parties wedded to market capitalism. Besides the electoral rejection of the neo-liberal experiments pursued in various industrialised countries, there was the protracted and disastrous failure of attempted reform in the Russian Federation (and the less noticed failures in other countries in the region), there was the Mexican crisis in 1994, and there was the Asian crisis in 1998. All chipped away at the public credibility and legitimacy of the economic orthodoxy.

2 A Crumbling Washington Consensus?

The human species does not like to be subject to a social Darwinism based on the ethics of greed and the survival of the fittest defined in terms of market success or failure. "Greed is the best development tool", Larry Summers, the US Treasury Secretary, told a group of South Africans in May 2000. Although this is the essence of the neo-liberalism that lies at the heart of the Washington Consensus, it leaves too much out for comfort. It is a licence to pursue individual gain opportunistically, and identifies development with individual self-possession. It legitimises a motive that is inherently selfish and inegalitarian. It gives no space for sharing or for values, of reproduction, of community. This sense fuelled the disquiet that built up in the 1990s.

The criticisms reached a high pitch in Seattle in late 1999, when many thousands of protesters from all around the world disrupted the proceedings of the World Trade Organisation. The momentum was sustained in further disruptions at the annual meeting of the IMF and World Bank in Washington in April 2000. Less momentously, but perhaps in its way most dramatically, Jo Stiglitz, who had resigned under pressure from the post of Chief Economist, and as one of the Vice-Presidents, of the World Bank at the end of 1999, launched a tirade against the IMF and its policies, which winged its way round the world on the internet, much to the delight and amusement of the many critics of the Washington Consensus and the international financial institutions. The retorts and denigration were swift and vitriolic, showing how narrow and personalised the debates had become. But the tensions reflected the difficulty of persisting with a perspective that seems to offer the losers little respite.

Then in May 2000, the co-ordinating editor of the World Bank's *World Development Report* resigned in a huff, claiming that others were messing around with his draft Report, with the intention of altering the line that income redistribution was desirable for development to one that gave overwhelming weight to economic growth. Observers were entitled to be a little sceptical about all this, since the draft Report had been widely circulated, and was scarcely radical, while it is part of the normal process for a draft to be subject to comments and modifications to make it more consistent with the main line being taken by the institution. Nobody would be so naïve as to take on the job without knowing that.

Nevertheless, these were signs that all was not well with the packaging and thrust of the orthodox approach. This further emerged in the World Bank's Development Conference held in Paris in June 2000, one of those glamorous occasions when prominent politicians mixed with prominent economists at great expense. The trouble was that in that forum, predictably, the debate narrowed to whether or not economic growth was all important, whether or not the state should take responsibility for education and health services and whether or not free trade was good in all circumstances. The more basic criticisms are that the orthodox policies have tended to foster inequalities and economic insecurities, that the international financial agencies and the international capital markets are non-accountable, and that these have been growing in economic and political influence. And beneath all that is a more fundamental human reaction, a feeling that the type of society and the modes of social and individual behaviour being encouraged and rewarded by global capitalism are not particularly attractive.

The disquiet was taken into the streets of Prague in September 2000, when disparate groups sloganised against the IMF and World Bank during their annual meeting. It was a discordant noise, which gave establishments everywhere ample opportunity to mock. Some of the reaction was placatory. But it was hard to take seriously assurances that the major new objective was people's "empowerment". For over two decades, the policies supported and often imposed by these agencies to cut the "power" of collective agencies, from trade unions to protective statutory regulations. These empowering mechanisms were lambasted as rigidities, as numerous reports by those agencies stated. Now they say it is vital to "empower".

We live in a time in which politicians and analysts are in awe of financial capital. Economic news and economic policy are dominated by what happens on stock exchanges. Absurdly wealthy individuals lure Presidents, Prime Ministers and sundry aspirants to their fireplaces, and major commercial institutions have truly impressive power. Private pension companies have assets that in some industrialized countries, such as the Netherlands and Switzerland, are larger than the GDP, and in others that situation will soon arrive. The size and reach of huge financial corporations give them an ability to use exit options to obtain acquiescence from weak or potentially weak governments. In effect – to play on the ideas of Hirschman – the ability to use exit gives them a stronger voice, because they have no loyalty to any nation state. And should a politician deviate from an acceptable path, re-election could prove difficult.

There is no need to express this reality in class terms or in Marxian analysis. The reality is hard to deny, and we need to start constructive thinking from that basis. The strength of financial capital is driving distributive policy, driving social protection policy and driving the development of regulatory regimes.

There is a dissonance in the international debates and manoeuvring, between the rhetoric of a "war on poverty" – with world bodies and con-ferences setting exemplary targets for achieving unprecedented reductions in poverty rates and improvements in most other things – and the practice, with those targets being pitched just far enough away so as to suggest meaningful objectives and not too far away as to be too distant to worry current policymakers and leaders or to induce scorn from critics. The dissonance reflects a perceived need to say that policies designed to establish market mechanisms and boost economic growth are the most or only effective means of reducing poverty. This reached a new crescendo at the Millennium Summit of the United Nations, where for three days Presidents and Prime Ministers of 150 countries committed themselves to splendid targets for the year 2015.

During the era of globalisation, the extent of poverty scarcely improved, and income and wealth inequality grew, between and within countries. The disquiet these trends have generated is global, regional, and national in character.

At the global level, there is a crisis of governance. Many feel uncomfort-able at the imposition and hegemony of a paradigm, and the presumption that this should not be questioned, because it might somehow lead to support for protectionism. There is also unease about the extended use of increasingly tight conditionality in the provision of international financial assistance. And there has been criticism about use of IFAs to seek the transformation of supposedly-independent societies and economic systems. Both are highly paternalistic and are regulatory in intent, even if some of their leading advocates claim that they favour deregulation and free markets.

Even more frightening, there has been talk about making the World Bank the world's "knowledge bank", a most paternalistic idea. Yet a source of global crisis is precisely the lack of transparency, accountability and demo-cratic governance in the powerful agencies of global regulation. To think of one setting itself up as the arbiter of knowledge is to bring Big Brother somewhat closer.

The really crucial issue is finding ways of securing accountable governance. For unless the voices of diverse social interests are part of the governance of these agencies, all the defensive rhetoric about "listening" and "participation" that has emerged since the criticisms of the Washington Consensus became part of the streets will be a waste of time.

At the regional level, there is growing concern that regional blocs, such as the European Union, ASEAN, NAFTA, MERCOSUR and SADEC, will indulge in competitive moves to harmonise standards and regulations. The *harmonisation* around flexibility, fiscal policy and social protection policies raises questions about the subordination of rights and standards to the dictates of competitiveness.

At the national level, there has been an attempt to add onto the Washington consensus a new concept – "social capital". This almost infinitely elastic concept is a reflection of a failure at the core of the model underlying the Consensus – a lack of any sense of representation or of agency to safeguard against the insecurities that come with individualisation. It is also a way of trying to re-legitimise the state. In the same vein, the orthodox school has also been trying to legitimise a role for "civil society" organisations.

A further paradox chipping away at the Washington Consensus' credibility is that economic crises are just as likely to affect "well-managed" as "poorly managed" economies. Small economies that open their capital account and, for whatever reason, grow fast are likely to attract capital inflows that are large relative to their GDP. But success of this sort breeds problems, because a slight deterioration in economic growth or political stability may lead to mass capital flight. Capital volatility causes price and income fluctuations, which dampen growth, all of which make governments of such countries acutely oriented to the good will of the international capital market and the international financial agencies, thereby constraining their independence in social policy, particularly anything redistributive in character.

The globalising economy seems to thrive on crisis. The new millennium began with a pervasive fear of insecurity. At one level, there is the fear that the forces unleashed by global capitalism are out of control, and are so strong that a series of destabilising developments could tip the world into a great crash that would make the events of 1929 seem minor. Many think that the institutions of global governance could contain such crises. Others think that local crises are induced deliberately and used to induce restructuring, forcing recalcitrant governments to adopt policies of economic liberalisation, open capital accounts and strong individual and corporate property rights.

A bigger source of crisis is the distributional unease, the sense that globalisation is associated with a widening gulf between the winners and losers, and between the minority in secure positions in a few centres of global capitalism, who see great opportunities, and those in many parts of the world, who see only the constraints. This is the globalisation paradox. There is a claim that globalisation and new technologies give so much more choice, and there is a feeling that there is a narrowing of choice for many governments. This is the control mechanism of global governance. And many people do not like it – and nor should they.

Another dilemma is the *mobility paradox* of globalisation. The orthodox view has been that globalisation is about liberalisation, and that freedom of capital mobility is essential for economic dynamism. Hypocrisy has stalked the rhetoric. Imagine internationally open labour markets. Where are most of the millions of impoverished surplus workers? No mainstream politician or economic liberaliser advocates free and unrestricted labour mobility, facilitated by tax holidays, guaranteed rates of return and so on. The politics of the Washington consensus and globalisation are inegalitarian between the right to free movement of capital and of labour.

All in all, it is somewhat remarkable that the essence of the Washington consensus model retained its appeal and hold through the 1990s, except that it takes more than criticism to replace a paradigm – it takes an alternative to do that, an alternative model capable of addressing the questions being posed when the prevailing paradigm cannot do so. It was precisely a lack of an alternative that made so much of the 1980s and 1990s so intellectually frustrating, and politically rather unattractive.

Yet a new consensus was emerging that was attempting to respond to the worst excesses of global market capitalism while retaining the labourist ideals of the twentieth century. It deserves to be called the Paternalistic Consensus.

3 Third Wayism: Labourism's Rigor Mortis?

What the noise in Seattle, Washington and Prague signified was a recognition that the era of market regulation was running up against the insecurities and inequalities that were beginning to threaten the sustainability of a global system of open economies. The fragmentation into winners – the Davos-meeting elites, hyper-active proficians, cosy salariats – and losers – the flexi-workers, unemployed and lumpenised detached – demanded greater concern for the preservation and strengthening of the social and ecological fabric in which the economic forces were being unleashed. Into this vacuum came something close to a new paradigm, known to its advocates as the Third Way.

The notion of the Third Way has had a chequered history. All sorts of beginnings have been sighted. Perhaps the most distinguished variant was that offered by the Swedish social democrats after the Second World War in developing and applying the "Swedish model" or the Rehn-Meidner model. For several decades, this third way between capitalism and state socialism was admired by social democrats almost everywhere. Memories fade, and it has been replaced by a vague combination of ideas trumpeted by some leading politicians and their think-tanks and advisers. Several social commentators present themselves as the father of the approach, and several national leaders have associated their career reputations with it.

Roy Hattersley has commented, scarcely sympathetically, "If the third way really exists, it is technique, not ideology". This is moot. It looks very much like ideology clothed in technique. In what follows, an attempt will be made to present the essence of the Third Way. Because of its amorphous character, any such representation will be criticised for not being faithful to something or other. That is the nature of any living organism. It never is what it was, and it never was what it is – or will be. This is perhaps why even its leading personalities lost faith in their own slogan, and in early 2000 there was an attempt to replace the label with *progressive governance*. This new term seems no clearer, and we will use the more familiar term.

Although it is hard to characterise, Third Wayism seems to have a core set of policies, backed by some characteristic euphemisms, which drive its policy agenda. A full and fair statement of those should be found among its advocates. The following seem to be the primary ingredients.

Minimum Standards

The Third Way is committed to social integration, and favours policies and institutions that promote employment, seeing this as the way of maximising opportunity and for achieving a more just distribution of income. But it recognises that more open economies and flexible labour markets leave more people, even those with jobs, receiving too little income. Accordingly, a minimal statutory floor of protective regulations is required, including a statutory minimum wage. This is part of its strategy to "make work pay". As noted earlier, the reality around the world has been that minimum wages have declined or been converted into a differentiated instrument giving less protection for groups that have most needed it. There are also reasons for doubting their effectiveness in flexible labour markets. Nevertheless, they do provide a yardstick for individual and collective bargaining.

A minimum wage has been coupled with support for a floor of protective regulations, including support for a core set of labour standards along the lines of the ILO's Declaration of Fundamental Principles, consisting of seven core standards to which all member countries must subscribe. This runs into tensions around linkage with trade, which contributed to the failure of the Seattle round of the WTO negotiations. Usually, supporters of core standards in industrial countries have lobbied for a formal link, demanding that all countries should be obliged to meet them. To governments and commercial interests in developing countries, this seems to require them to move to standards attained in industrialised countries "prematurely" and they have attacked the demands as quasi-protectionist and unfair. Advocates in industrialised countries, and trade unions in most parts of the world, have claimed that refusal to abide by minimum standards amounts to unfair competitive advantage.

Ironically, while demanding minimal core standards, Third Way supporters seem to accept several forms of *social dumping*. This is a great dilemma for the early years of the twenty-first century. Implicitly or overtly, they seem to accept the need to roll back social protection coverage or "generosity" as a means of increasing competitiveness, and the need to weaken protective regulations in the name of flexibility. There has been much talk about whether or not there is a "race to the bottom" as a result. There is not much evidence that anything as drastic as that is taking place, or is desired by anybody. However, there does seem to be an acceptance of a trend towards some convergence in which the strong protective levels achieved in welfare state capitalist economies are somewhat eroded. Third Wayists do not seem to have given much attention to finding ways of achieving a race upwards.

Competitiveness

Third Wayism starts from the premise that globalisation is a fact of life and that governments must ensure that their policies and the behaviour that they facilitate are compatible with the realities of globalisation. This means that everybody must become "competitive". In this they echo readily the ironic advice of one member of the elite, an influential multinational businessman, Percy Barnevik: "Workers of the world, compete!" It is not just the Communist Manifesto that is the target of such a gibe. It is the old-style notion of capital-and-labour and the sense that labour does not have the capacity to struggle against global market forces – except against its counterparts in other countries.

Competitiveness became a new rallying cry. It means more than the simple matter of cost, quality and efficiency. It means *credibility*. If one's credibility is in question, long-term commitments will not be made. If the country's monetary policy lacks credibility, financial markets will react adversely so that borrowing will be more expensive, capital flows will tend to be shorter-term, foreign direct investment will be more hesitant and will "require" (or demand) more subsidies, tax holidays and the like. The economic "fundamentals" may be adequate, but the magic of credibility is required to create a stable macro-economic environment. Credibility ultimately requires *capital security* – the assurance that financial investors will be able to earn, retain and transfer their profits and assets unhindered.

Competitiveness has become a yardstick for so much at so many levels. At the level of regional blocs, we hear that our region – the European Union, MERCOSUR, ASEAN, NAFTA, or whatever – must be more competitive than theirs. At this level, there have been attempts to do what Franklin Roosevelt, Keynes and others had hoped to be a primary function of the United Nations and Bretton Woods system after 1945, but at the regional level rather than at the global level, which is to take labour rights and standards out of international trade. Regional harmonisation has been a means of regulation. If you harmonise and standardise something you are obviously limited in using it as an instrument of competitiveness. But if there are substantial differences between regions, labour standards will remain spheres of competitiveness.

The same cry has been used at the national level – our country must be more competitive than theirs. We must be more flexible, or at least be as flexible, and so on. The competitiveness agenda has predictable outcomes. Thus, fiscal policy was once used for distributive purposes and for curbing inflationary pressure. Now it has been turned far more into an instrument for boosting cost competitiveness (and, as argued later, behavioural regulation).

There is also the euphemism of "fiscal competitiveness", a term that seems to mean that tax rates should be lowered to some international norm and that there is some idea of a norm in the structure or incidence of taxation. Implicitly, it seems to mean moving towards what is done in the USA.

Taxes on capital are still being cut, by governments made up of political parties that historically grew as representatives of "labour", and they have shifted taxes to labour. For instance, in July 2000 the German Social Democratic government managed to pass a tax reform, against conservative opposition, in which the top income tax rate was cut from 51 per cent to 42 per cent (by 2005), and the main corporation tax rate was cut to 25 per cent in 2001, from its previous level of 40 per cent; capital gains tax on the sale by companies of shares in other firms was cut for 2002. Fiscal policy was being used unashamedly to increase national competitiveness.

Subsidies for firms have also been used increasingly as a means of enticement of foreign direct investment and a means of tilting the attractiveness of a country to portfolio investment, being one indicator of a "business-friendly" economic environment. Subsidies to workers (labour) and working consumers are regarded as "distorting" and are therefore condemned as market unfriendly and a brake on competitiveness. Subsidies to capital are not treated to this type of criticism.

The notion of competitiveness has been used to drive down tax rates, and is also used to rationalise cuts in social protection policy and for rolling back protective and pro-collective regulations. And at the level of the individual, we are all urged to be more competitive, leading predictably to the latest euphemism of the era.

Employability

Credibility and competitiveness blur into the notion of employability. This has been a distinctive contribution of Third Wayism. Our country must become more competitive, which means that our workers must become more employable. This variant of supply-side economics puts the onus firmly on workers to upgrade certain skills to make them more attractive to potential employers, particularly multinational corporations. Being attractive means not just being able to demonstrate and apply technical qualifications. It means having the "right" attitude, being able to communicate and being flexible and adaptable. And it means committing oneself to "lifelong learning".

All of these behavioural and attitudinal characteristics require institutions that can produce or induce them. So, unions have to be encouraged to become partners in the national drive to be competitive and have to co-operate with socially responsible employers. Thus one can see the nucleus of a renewal of the notion of a social contract – a partnership based on employability, credibility and social responsibility. The advocates talk of new euphemisms here, such as "benchmarking" and "soft convergence", which seems to mean moving towards what is found or advocated in the USA.

This perspective amounts to much more than technique, because it is rooted in an ideological position, which is that class antagonisms are finished and irrelevant in the context of globalisation (and more incidentally in the context of the fall of the Berlin Wall and the effective collapse of state socialism). The message is an image that is a cross between war and sport. We are all stakeholders of our country, united in a drive to be competitive with "their" country. Policies and institutions must be made to correspond to that imperative.

As part of this, it is accepted that there should be labour market flexibility, partly because this is what employers want, partly because the perception that the country's labour market is flexible will add to the country's credibility in international financial markets, and will thus help to attract that scarce foreign direct and indirect investment. Flexibility means many things, as noted earlier, but in this context it means mainly that the growth of real wages adjusts rapidly to demand and that employment protection or employment security is modest, and is perceived by commentators and financial markets to be modest. In other words, Third Wayism accepts and even rationalises employment insecurity and income insecurity.

Part of this push for flexibility involves a reduction in labour costs, and "non-wage labour costs" in particular. This can be achieved by raising productivity, by lowering the wages that employers have to pay, by changes in work organisation, by making it easier for employers to operate flexible work schedules that increase utilisation of their plant, machinery and service networks, and by redesign of fiscal policy to reduce overhead costs. Fiscal ingenuity is a key to Third Wayism, as will be explained shortly.

The emphasis on labour flexibility also amounts to a modern form of labour (re-)commodification. Workers who lose employment security lose a form of income that has some monetary value. They may receive a higher money wage, but this must be put alongside the loss of actual or prospective employment security. Similarly, the acceptance of flexibility, and such practices as unlimited hours contracts and other intensified working schedules, means the diminution of personal control over time, in the amount at one's own control and in the predictability of its availability. The surrender of time control may be a derived outcome of Third Wayism's fascination with competitiveness and employability.

This has regressive implications, because a cut in labour security implies a loss of social income, while owners of firms and those receiving profit-related income will receive more income, simply because of the increased flexibility. The Third Way response to the claim that greater labour flexibility results in greater insecurity and loss of social income might be that there are ways of compensating people that would not impinge on competitiveness.

Third Wayism has a complex perspective on monetary and fiscal policy. As far as monetary policy is concerned, the tendency has been to go one stage further than the reverse-Keynesianism of the 1970s and 1980s, not only accepting that the state cannot use macro-economic policy to stimulate aggregate demand in the interests of promoting employment, but believing that the central bank should be independent of government. This is one area where the surrender of control is regarded as a virtue.

As far as fiscal policy is concerned, the Third Way position seems to be based in part on the premise that public provision of universalistic social protection is neither feasible nor desirable. The welfare state needs to be trimmed because it is "bloated", because non-wage labour costs are made excessive by an extensive mix of public transfers and services, because of "middle-class capture", such that a disproportionate amount of the transfers and social services go to the affluent, and because it does not help achieve the "social integration" of those most in need in society, the disadvantaged, the long-term unemployed and so on. For these reasons, social protection must become more selective, through use of means tests and forms of social assistance targeted at the poor.

As is well known, the trouble is that means-tested benefits create poverty traps and unemployment traps, whereby many of the poor and unemployed who wish to take jobs or work longer consequently lose benefit income that is almost as much as they gain from earnings (effectively having marginal income tax rates of near 100 per cent). To circumvent these traps, the main Third Way response is to turn increasingly to in-work benefits – giving additional income to those who take or remain in low-wage jobs. The solution may seem simple – something like an earned-income tax credit, which in the USA has become easily the largest income transfer mechanism and which is becoming so in some other countries, notably the UK and Canada. It seems that the Third Way strategy would be to complement tax credits with employment subsidies. These two fiscal measures together make a neat combination.

These may not be enough. Suppose the fiscal carrots do not entice the unemployed and poor to the labouring table. Suppose the jobs on offer are wretched, onerous, stigmatisng and lacking in those qualities that workers are expected to learn. There is no escape from these dilemmas for Third Wayists. Fortunately for them, there is a way out, which stems from their ideological premise. This is that there should be no social rights without social responsibilities. Their view is that you cannot expect the state – your fellow citizens – to pay their taxes to support you in times of need unless you meet your social responsibilities. This position has been given the name of the *reciprocity principle*.[1] This is the heart of Third Wayism, and the New Paternalism that guided it. It leads to some strong policy conclusions.

According to Tony Blair, it is equality of individual worth that is required – "not equality of income or outcome, or simply equality of opportunity. Rather it affirms our equal right to dignity, liberty, freedom from discrimination as well as economic opportunity."[2] He has claimed that individuals have responsibilities in return for social rights, which he calls "the covenant at the heart of modern civil society". Critics would say that this bypasses the awkward realities of conflicts of interest. Apparently one of Blair's favourite theologians, Hans Kung, the dissident Catholic and founding head of the modestly named Global Ethics Foundation, has expressed one outcome of this way of looking at society in a pithy way:

> "Human dignity consists of both, to have rights and responsibilities. If someone just does not want to work because he is lazy, then it is not a fundamental human right to be lazy and to be protected in his laziness."[3]

A Catholic is by training and by inclination a paternalist. The appeal to authority comes easily. Yet words such as "lazy" and "responsibilities" are not easily defined. A humble person would not prejudge what constitutes another person's laziness or responsibilities. Who gives me the right to say whether or not you are lazy, let alone take action to take away some right because I decide that you are lazy? Any presumption that I have such a right would be sheer impudence.

Active Labour Market Policy

It should be no surprise that one well-known adviser to the UK Government openly advocated "compulsion" to help the unemployed to be reintegrated into mainstream society. Compulsion could be seen as the end game of one of the most influential euphemisms of the era – "active labour market policy". We consider this at length in the next chapter. But the essence of it concerns a belief that people need to be socially integrated, and it needs the state to intervene to achieve this.

The notion of active policy began life as part of the Swedish (third way) Model in the 1950s, meaning counter-cyclical policies to take workers out of the labour force in recessions, into training schemes mainly or public works, and then reducing the numbers in such schemes as the economy picked up. Later the term was converted into an approach for socially integrating the unemployed and detached, inculcating responsible commitment to labour. During the 1980s and 1990s, it became a powerful euphemism. As noted in chapter 1, the words "active" and "passive" are loaded. But advocates of the virtues of active policy seem impervious to all the criticisms – the displacement and deadweight effects and much else. It has been extended by each new generation of policymakers, with a tendency towards more reliance on wage and employment subsidies intended to induce employers to hire the less employable. What is most revealing is the silence of the new technocrats on the role of the participants in determining and controlling the policy. Unless their Voice is prominent, what does active policy mean?

Welfare Pluralism

The Third Way approach to social protection is hard to characterise, but seems to rest on a belief in selectivity in which the state guarantees minimum income security through greater reliance on means-tested targeted benefits than was the expectation at the height of the welfare state era. Its rationale is defensive, in that it sees the need to justify social protection on economic grounds, trying to make sure that "social protection is a productive factor", as was the title of a major EU conference held in Portugal in early 2000. Behind the scenes, advocates will argue that unless concessions are made to the libertarians, the loss of legitimacy of state systems will grow. By accepting this premise, they can argue that either levels of benefits and services must be cut, or conditions for entitlement must be tightened. Although they have also allowed some of the former (or accepted previous cuts, as in the spheres of unemployment benefits and pensions), Third Wayists tend to prefer the latter. And they can do so with a clear conscience because they regard tighter conditionality as essential to oblige the poor, unemployed and "work shy" to take jobs.

All the criticisms of means-testing and behaviour-testing of benefits remain to dog the Third Way agenda. Ultimately it encourages a culture of moral hazards and "learned deception", in which applicants for benefits become "clients" and in which poverty traps and unemployment traps and savings traps persist. To try to circumvent these, various in-work benefits have been introduced to assist in the transition into jobs and the tighter conditionality has been used to cajole people through the traps.

Above all else is the use of fiscal policy as an integral part of social protection, through earned income tax credits. This has become the biggest social transfer system in the USA, and has spread to western Europe, led by the UK. Essentially, this is the other part of the strategy to "make work pay", since as long as you have a family designated as the norm for coverage and as long as you have some earned income you can obtain a supplement to your income if it is low, which tapers off as your earned income rises. It is essentially a negative income tax. Clearly, it is labourist in intention, since it is tied to actual performance of an income-earning job. But as argued in the final chapter, it creates the basis for an integration of tax and benefits that is more radical than its main Third Way supporters would want.

The final part of the social protection strategy seems to be partial privatisation of social services and provision of benefits to what are called civil society organisations. These are being encouraged or required to perform functions that state agencies long performed. This was noted earlier as an outcome of reforms of social protection in the 1980s and 1990s, but it seems to have become part of the overall strategy. This leads to a new variant of the approach.

4 Compassionate Conservatism

At the turn of the new millennium, Third Wayism represented the main response to the failings of the era of market regulation. It was the social democratic response. Meanwhile, not to be outdone, on the political right, there has been a tendency to move away from the extreme libertarianism into the centre ground of compassionate conservatism, or compassionate capitalism. The difference between this and Third Wayism is a matter of degree or balance, not substance.

The notion of compassion seems to imply a sort of privatised paternalism. Third Wayism also tends to have them, but religious undertones are much more prominent in compassionate conservatism. There is recognition that in highly competitive market economies there are many losers. The proponents accept this as socially just, and adhere to a belief in equality of opportunity, and to the apparent need to improve *human capital* as the means of producing more winners, thereby limiting income inequality. But in their model there will still be those who drift out of the mainstream into an anomic or violent existence of social exclusion.

These must be reintegrated, in a way that is consistent with the ideology of their model of society. The preferred answer, logically enough, is to privatise social services and give private agencies the tools to operate a paternalistic role. It is here that some very old religious tactics are to be given a new lease of legitimacy. We enter the realm of philanthropic charity, where civil society is brought into the mainstream of governance and social regulation.

Part of the process of privatising social protection is by the encourage-ment of philanthropy by the affluent towards deserving groups and interests. In July 1999, George Bush suggested that, if elected President, he would increase tax incentives by $8 billion to encourage more charitable giving to "faith-based" organizations and other community groups. He added: "In every instance where my administration sees a responsibility to help people, we will look first to faith-based organizations, charities and community groups."[4] The amount proposed was substantial – about 10 per cent of the estimated future budget surplus not attributable to social security, with proposed tax cuts taking most of the remainder. The pledge is unlikely to be forgotten. The intention is to give tax credits for individuals giving contri-butions to "faith-based" charities service providers and to introduce lighter regulations for them.

Although there may be a constitutional barrier to these particular initi-atives, they comprise part of the agenda to privatise social protection, through fostering a particular form of community benefit (CB). The bodies set up by churches, synagogues and mosques are behaviour-control institu-tions. It is a Third Way response, based on the premise that dysfunctional social beheaviour is what traps people in poverty and "social exclusion". But whereas a left-of-centre Third Wayism would wish the state to shape behaviour, a right-of-centre Third Wayism would delegate that to its favourite moralising institutions. One anticipates that with the change in administration in the USA, the privatisation trend will accelerate. It is doing so elsewhere as well.

5 Conclusions

"The certainties of one age are the problems of the next."
(Richard Tawney, 1938)

Coincidentally, the first years of the new millennium is a period in which Tawney's rueful aphorism should be engraved on our minds. He was witnessing a world plunging into a dark madness of inhumanity, when the old order and the institutions built to sustain and legitimise it were crumbling pathetically in the face of barbarism. Karl Polanyi soon after wrote his *The Great Transformation* which saw welfare policies as making a market economy function and embedding the economy in society. The welfare state, which he and so many others saw as the means of doing this, lost its capacity to do so in the face of global economic forces in the last few years of the twentieth century.

Third Wayism is oddly appropriate for an era of disembeddedness. Its euphemisms and metaphors are rootless, or ahistorical. It is paternalistic and directive, scarcely promoting the values of a radical progressive tradition. Why should people purporting to belong to a radical, progressive tradition tell workers *en masse* that they should become more employable, be more flexible, become more competitive? When politicians call for lifelong learning, do they mean the creation of an ethos of creativity and development among the poor, or do they mean a lifelong treadmill of acquiring new sets of tricks in order to be competitive? Unless they are setting up institutions in which ordinary people have control, we should be suspicious of the motives.

Third Wayism has been said to be the political position of the new middle-class, or the "bobos". In our terms, it seems to be an attempt to appeal to the growing groups of proficians and flexiworkers, as well as being acceptable to the *elite* who are assured that policies and institutions will be put in place that promote and facilitate a competitive open economy, and globalisation, with emphasis on incentives for risk-taking and on deterrents to other types of social behaviour. As such, it has a chance of success politically, since it appeals to a growing coalition of interests that could make up a voting majority. Paternalism has always thrived on a limited range of solidarity and reciprocity. But it does not answer the human need for collective agency and structured reciprocities that respect the needs and aspirations of all interest groups.

8

The Road to Workfare: Route to Integration or Threat to Occupation?

1 Introduction

Rulers have always worried about those on the margin of their society disturbing their social peace. Globalisation, as we have seen, produces its few winners and many losers, and among the losers are the unemployed and the lumpenised detached from the mainstream of society. Most of these are poor, in both senses, lacking income and being poor at functioning in a competitive dynamic society.

In chapter 6 it was suggested that three paradigms have dominated thinking about responses to unemployment and marginalisation – the social solidarity paradigm, the contractual exchange paradigm, and the citizenship rights paradigm. Adherents of the first two have been drawn inexorably towards what has been called workfare. Behind that lies a new orthodoxy. This has three variants, reflecting a search for legitimacy for a long-practised paternalism. The first is that "active" labour market policy should be expanded relative to "passive". The second is that "workfare" should replace "welfare". The third is that "welfare-to-work" programmes should become the core of welfare systems.

Active policy derives from Swedish social democracy, workfare sprang mainly from libertarian roots, and welfare-to-work from a centrist bloc of social democrats, liberals, moderate conservatives and Christian democrats. It is probably fair to say that the choice of term has reflected a difference of emphasis on incentives or obligations. Whatever the term chosen, the approach can be summarised in two imperatives – the State should place those on the margins of the labour force in jobs (or job training), or induce them to take jobs, while the unemployed should be obliged to take such jobs. In practice, the objectives have been more complex. Often, explicit objectives have been combined with others pursued through it and complementary policies, one being to reduce childbearing by unmarried teenage women.

Although its adherents like to use the word "new", workfare has a long tradition. It was enshrined in the English *Poor Law* of 1536 dealing with "sturdy vagabonds", and in the French *Ordonnance de Moulins* of 1556. The most famous precedent was the 1834 *Poor Law Amendment Act* in Great

Britain, a "targeted" system designed to reach only the "deserving" and the desperate poor. If a person wanted support he had to agree to work in a workhouse run by the local parish, which according to the Poor Law Commissioners was to be "the hardest taskmaster and the worst paymaster". The work had to be harder than that performed by independent labourers, and thus not competitive with them. From 1834 onwards, the practice was to give "relief" in return for labour, but because workhouses could not deal with all those in need, the authorities also operated an "outdoor labour test" as a deterrent to potential claimants.

This was modified at the end of the nineteenth century with municipal relief works, and then the *Unemployed Workmen Act* of 1905 became a precedent of another form of "targeting", providing labour for the merit-worthy unemployed and not for those regarded as undeserving of assistance, those deemed to lack "good character" and not "honestly desirous of obtaining work". Capturing the establishment view of the time, Winston Churchill blustered in 1909: "There is no reason why people should wander about in a loafing and idle manner. If they are not earning their living, they ought to be put under some control." He, like his current day successors, muttered less about the loafing of the idle rich.

The themes of helping the deserving and deterring the poor from applying for benefits figured prominently in reforms of the late twentieth century. Even though extensive testing for conditionality and screening have proved ineffectual labour regulations, governments have never given up the ideas that guided those early initiatives. Indeed, resort to some variant of workfare has coincided historically with periods of transition, when the economic basis of society has been out of step with the regulatory devices inherited from a period of relative stability. Above all, workfare and welfare-to-work belong to the paternalist tradition, and must be assessed as the labourist solution to the crisis of insecurity. It may not be hyperbole to describe workfare as the great social experiment of the late twentieth and early twenty-first centuries. Its success or failure will determine social and labour market policy for decades to come.

2 The Workfare State?

If flexibility means diversity, and if there is the sort of stratification described earlier, then the outcomes must include a greater problem of social exclusion or a perceived need to ensure "social integration". These are dangerous notions, but workfare is seen as part of the answer. We may define it as the obligation to take labour, or a course intended to lead to labour in return for state benefits, where the payment is less than the market wage and where the terms of employment are inferior to those in comparable jobs in the 'open' labour market.[1]

The notion of workfare is a euphemism that has had a mixed review, with even strong proponents finding it advisable to be cautious about use of the word. The later euphemism of "welfare-to-work" conveys the message its proponents want – helping the socially excluded to escape from dependence on state benefits into jobs.

A hidden message is that "we have to be harsh to be kind". One might depict it as the micro-analogue of "shock therapy" – and wonder at the psychological basis of the images that motivate the perspective. In the following, we use the word workfare to cover all schemes that require individuals to take jobs or training courses if they wish to receive some state benefit or service. There is a blurring between unemployment insurance and assistance, between means-testing and actual and prospective behaviour-testing. The trend appears to be that individuals must satisfy conditions that relate to their past behaviour, their current behaviour (and to their attitudes) and their future prospective behaviour. This three-dimensional refinement of the notion of reciprocity has not attracted the attention it deserves.

There are arguments for and against workfare, or welfare-to-work schemes, which are considered in this chapter. What is clear is that since the 1980s, in both industrialised and industrialising countries, governments have moved policy towards workfare and away from reliance on insurance benefits for the unemployed. The trend has gone furthest in the United States, led by states such as Wisconsin and converted into national legislation with the Personal Responsibility and Work Opportunity Reconciliation Act in August 1996. The UK's welfare-to-work orientation has taken this route in a major way – with the characteristic euphemism of a New Deal – and one can detect elements of it in many European countries, as one can in Australia, New Zealand and several developing countries, where Chile took an early lead. In France, in 2000 the main employers' organisation placed it at the heart of public policy debate.

A question is whether the reforms are turning the so-called welfare state into the workfare state, moving decisively away from universalism and towards reliance on behavioural entitlements, rather than earned-income and insurance-based entitlements. There is little doubt that this is what many advocates of workfare want.

3 Workfare Schemes

The term workfare originated in the United States in the 1960s, notably with the Federal *Work Incentive Programme* (WIN). The practice spread after 1981, when Federal legislation enabled States to establish welfare-for-work programmes. By 1986, twenty-nine States were running variants of workfare schemes for beneficiaries of the Aid to Families with Dependent Children scheme (AFDC). In the 1988 Presidential election all major candidates advocated a workfare policy of some kind. A move in that direction was the 1988 Family Support Act, designed to encourage job-seeking by lone mothers. By the mid 1990s, through "waivers" allowing experiments with deviations from AFDC rules, most states were operating a workfare scheme, often given a grand name that gave politicians credibility and made critics seem churlish – such as GAIN (Greater Avenues for Independence), SWIM

(Saturation Work Initiative Model), New Chance, Wisconsin Works, Quantum Opportunities, and Express to Success.

In the 1980s and 1990s, the rhetoric surrounding workfare moved from work-for-benefits to preparation-for-self-support-while-on-benefits, to "term limits". Most US States developed schemes by which, if recipients did not want to forfeit all or part of their welfare cheques, they had to choose between taking a stipulated non-contractual job (i.e., one without an employment contract providing normal employment protection), attending "job-hunting classes", and returning to school or undertaking full-time training. State schemes varied considerably, but in 1990 a Federal welfare reform confirmed a national trend towards workfare.

This culminated in the Personal Responsibility and Work Opportunity Reconciliation Act in August 1996, which ended the Federal commitment to provide aid to the poor, shifting responsibility back to the States. It also limited entitlement to welfare benefits to a maximum of five years in a lifetime, obliged recipients to accept designated jobs after two years, banned legal aid to legal immigrants, and cut food stamps. AFDC was converted into TANF (Temporary Assistance for Needy Families). As a result of these changes, the Government anticipated that Federal spending would fall by $56 billion over six years.

The objectives were to cut public spending, to reduce poverty, and to alter the behaviour of the poor, particularly poor women with children perceived to suffer from "welfare dependency". Capturing the regulatory objective, President Clinton told the National Governors' Association in July 1996:

> Anyone who can work must do so. We'll say to welfare recipients: Within two years, you will be expected to go to work and earn a paycheck, not draw a welfare check.

The Administration had merely built on state initiatives over the preceding decade. Among the most interventionist states, Wisconsin introduced a Pay for Performance Scheme in 1994, under which welfare recipients had to choose between (i) transitional work, (ii) community service, (iii) trial jobs lasting up to three years, and (iv) subsidised private employment. Wisconsin introduced a pilot scheme, known as "Work-not-Welfare", in 1993 by which AFDC benefits were denied to those who did not accept an assigned job or enrol in a training programme. In return, the State guaranteed a cash supplement to reach the AFDC level if the wage fell below that, and paid for full-time childcare, transport to work and job-placement assistance. This arrangement was to last for up to two years, after which there was no resumption of benefits. This has been called the "two years and you're out" condition.

With workfare has come a complementary trend towards "learnfare" and "trainingfare" aimed at teenagers, whereby non-employed youth can receive income support from the state only if they attend school or a training course. Such a scheme has been operating in Wisconsin, and has been presented as a stage in the development of a "social contract" between teenagers and society.[2]

Another aspect of the reforms has been the targeting on "unmarried" or "single" mothers, a group in society which was demonised in the 1990s. The main measure directed at them has been the Family Cap, whereby in New Jersey, Wisconsin and some other states, an unemployed single woman conceiving a baby while receiving welfare payments cannot receive extra benefit for the child. This was the first time that the positive link between the size of benefit and number of children has been broken. Wisconsin has also operated a Bridefare scheme, which supposedly as a scheme to cut teenage pregnancies halved child benefit for a child born to an unmarried teenager. Finally, under the US welfare reform, unmarried teenage parents on welfare must sign a Personal Responsibility Contract in which they agree to stay at school or live at home.

Another feature is devolution of welfare policy to the states, primarily through "block grants", often to counties within States. This reduced the Federal Government's responsibility, although States were instructed to cut welfare rolls by 50 per cent between 1996 and 2002. Some central regulations have been made. Most importantly, married parents were to be allowed only two years of welfare at most, and welfare recipients were to be required to increase the weekly hours they work in jobs each year or start to lose benefits. States not meeting those targets will receive less Federal cash. Thus the devolution was scarcely delegation of responsibility, although laws in some states have been tougher than the Federal law. Very quickly, many states required TANF recipients to work before the two-year time limit was reached, and some had imposed work requirements from the outset of receipt of benefits.

Workfare has since spread in Europe, partly through the tighter con-ditionality and the drift to means tests and poverty tests. The trend began in the 1980s, notably in the UK, with measures such as the *Employment Training* and *Restart* schemes, but also in Germany, with the Federal *Social Assistance Act*, in Sweden, with its *Youth Teams* scheme in particular, in Denmark, in Italy and elsewhere.[3] Elements of workfare have become common. In the Netherlands, the unemployed had their benefits cut if they refused a training place considered necessary by a local authority official. In Germany, in 1998 the government introduced a package in which local authorities were to provide jobs for some long-term unemployed receiving social security payments. If they refused their benefits were cut. In Finland, a "rehabilitation" act was passed with similar motives. Some countries outside Europe have moved in a similar direction, as in Australia where a "work for dole" scheme was introduced in 1997, targeted on those aged between 18 and 24.

In the UK, in 1996 a pilot scheme was tested in two areas, under which the long-term unemployed received 13 weeks of job-search training followed by 13 weeks of compulsory job experience, for which they received unemployment benefit plus £10 per week. The scheme was hastily expanded before any evaluation. In 1997, the new Government announced a plan to introduce a four-choice scheme for 250,000 young unemployed – (i) six-month subsidised private job, (ii) six months with a non-profit organisation, (iii) paid full-time study, (iv) a place on an environmental task force. The

Chancellor also announced plans to introduce a £75–a-week tax rebate for firms hiring an adult who had been unemployed for more than two years. Originally a scheme for 16–24 year olds who had been unemployed for more than six months, by 2000 it was clear that it was intended for others as well. By then, the New Deal was being described as one of the great successes of the Government's first three years, reaching its target of 250,000 placements.

The USA, UK and Australia may have gone furthest towards workfare as a pillar of social policy, but the trend is a global one. It is a labourist and paternalistic response to a crisis of labour insecurity. Given its appeal and the implications for social and labour policy, it is worth considering the arguments used to justify workfare or something like it.

4 Arguments For and Against Workfare

The following should not be taken to imply any order of presumed significance of the arguments, although some issues are more important than others. Although evidence comes mainly from the USA, the discussion is intended to refer to the international drift to workfare as a regulatory instrument of social and labour market policy.

Workfare as Social Reciprocity

Workfare is based on a claim of reciprocity – the view that social rights are conditional on labour obligations. According to its advocates, rights should be matched by duties, which is the essence of citizenship. This argument has adherents on the political right and left. Thus, Gorz argued for an obligatory duty to perform a specified social service to match the right to a basic income grant from the state.[4] And in the UK New Labour defenders have criticised Anthony Crosland and others for favouring redistribution without being prepared to press beneficiaries to have a sense of duty.[5] According to Marquand, "If rights are not balanced by duties, why should the rich make sacrifices for the poor? If collective provision is not a means of moral improvement why should those who are not in need pay taxes to pay for it?" (p. 24). In Australia, in 1996 the Minister for Social Security claimed that "the community has indicated very clearly that it is concerned people meet all their obligations when receiving taxpayer-funded income support because they are unemployed."[6]

There are two counter-arguments against this position. First, the right to do something can only be a right if there is a corresponding right not to do it. Workfare threatens that principle of justice, compromising choice and freedom. The proponents' point that the right to income should be matched by the duty to labour can be seen as an unbalanced reciprocity, since the insistence on duties threatens to stigmatise prospective recipients and so encourage them to forgo their rights. Rights are meaningful only if individuals are able to exercise them. For those without resources, this can be done only by belonging to a group that provides the collective strength to overcome their vulnerability. Proponents of workfare link it to the notion of citizenship; but citizenship must be universal and equal. Why should the supposedly idle poor be forced to take directed work while the "idle rich" are not? If it is desirable to empower the poor to participate as "active citizens", that is an argument either for doing so for everybody or for decoupling income support from labour market activity, not for workfare.

Another counter-argument is that the presumption of balanced reciprocity is unfair because for those on the margins of society, there are not fair opportunities or the prospect of them. Unless the state can guarantee fair and equal access to all forms of job, one cannot justify a claim for reciprocity. If there is less than Full Employment – even defined as a level of unemployment consistent with minimal frictional unemployment – more people would be looking for jobs than could have them. In other words, if one accepts there is involuntary unemployment, imposing an obligation that citizens should take jobs or lose entitlement to transfers is unfair, because the condition for fairness of opportunity does not exist.

The dilemma of inadequate opportunity has been the primary justification for the view held by some advocates of workfare that there must be a guarantee of a job or its equivalent. This has been called "fair workfare" or "new workfare", and has been adopted as the position by many who would not call themselves libertarians.[7] But this way of resolving the dilemma upsets some libertarians, because it offers the prospect of large numbers of people having continued dependency on the state. This was behind the "two years and you're out" rule in the US welfare reform, and the move in that direction in the UK, with increasing reliance on supposedly "random" inspections.

Charles Murray put the rationale most starkly, in stating that social policy should encourage "independence" and allow "better people" to receive their "merit" because "they deserve more of society's rewards".[8] Unfortunately, according to him, "Government cannot identify the worthy, but it can protect a society in which the worthy can identify themselves." The worthy, apparently, identify themselves only if the government does *not* guarantee jobs. Only if this condition exists will a government encourage self-sufficiency and basic liberty, enabling deserving, merit-worthy citizens to make most effective use of opportunities.

It is easy to caricature this line of reasoning as heartless. However, Murray concluded that it shows "no lack of compassion" and expresses "the principle of respect", because it conveys a message to people that they have responsibility for themselves. In our terms, they have self-control. The difficulty with this rationale for unconditional workfare is that it presumes that the conditions exist for individual responsibility and basic opportunity, ignoring discrimination, ill luck and injustice. The notion of "worthy" or deserving is at root just as paternalistic as any form of dependency that libertarians condemn with such gusto.

Adherents of so-called "fair workfare" claim,

> "An obligation to work should be contingent on the availability of work. Furthermore, even when employment is available, children should not be penalised for their parents' unwillingness to work, and therefore family caps are not justifiable."[9]

While agreeing with the second assertion, and that it would be unfair to impose an obligation if there were no "work" available, the statement still begs many questions. What sort of work? What amount of time should an individual be allowed to spend in seeking a job before having to meet the "obligation"? One can only answer such questions arbitrarily. Gutmann and Thompson claim "the opportunity principle is consistent with imposing an obligation to work on able-bodied citizens" on the grounds that citizens are "mutually dependent, each obligated to contribute his or her share in a fair scheme of social cooperation". But what is a "fair scheme"? What is the "share" that each is obliged to contribute? Does a property speculator who receives millions of dollars contribute his "fair share" to society? Who asks him to make this contribution?

Fair workfare implies that the poor and disadvantaged should be obliged to contribute, while those born with wealth or who gain it by other means have no such obligation, and do not have an obligation bestowed on them by somebody they do not select for the task. Decision-makers are rarely those for whom such decisions are made, and they would surely fail the Rawlsian test that, behind a veil of ignorance, they would be prepared to put themselves in their place and choose workfare.

The morality of the moral rationale for workfare is confused or disingenuous. It is hard to remain straight faced about a scheme that refers to an entitlement requiring duties from the poor while providing subsidies to firms so that they can hire labour and increase their own income. Subsidies to a relatively affluent group might be justifiable on pragmatic grounds (although they have a poor record as employment generators, due to high deadweight and substitution effects). But they should be subject to the same moralising as used for workfare. In short, the reciprocity argument for workfare is both disingenuous and inequitable.

Workfare as Promoting Functional Citizenship

Another very popular claim is that workfare increases the ability of government to improve the functioning of its citizens. One workfare advocate, L. M. Mead, argued that "to improve social order" government must use benefits "to require better functioning of recipients who have difficulty coping".[10] He defined functioning as the ability to discharge "social obligations" such as learning, working, supporting one's family and respecting the rights of others. He claimed that US welfare programmes meant the recipients'

> place in American society is defined by their need and weakness, not their competence [to discharge those obligations]. This lack of accountability is among the reasons why non-work, crime, family break-up and other problems are much commoner among recipients than Americans generally.

In such circumstances, workfare would transform welfare from means-tested entitlements into reciprocal obligations between society and individuals.

Critics might retort that it is questionable whether the state should presume to turn individuals into "functioning citizens" by obliging poorer groups to do specified activities. There is little evidence that lack of accountability is a major cause of crime and so on, and it is not clear that any such relationship exists. In a breathtaking statement, Mead asserted, "far from blaming people if they deviate, government must persuade them to *blame themselves*" (p. 10, emphasis in original). Why should the victim of a mishap, whether by ill luck or because he lacks the particular knack of obtaining or holding the type of job on offer, be encouraged to feel so blameworthy? Can it really be the duty of a citizen to feel responsible and culpable for every personal mishap? One wonders too at the desirability of benefits being used to "inculcate values".

Mead and others have argued that the recipient of state transfers should have obligations in return. This focuses exclusively on individual obligations and reciprocity, neglecting collective aspects of reciprocity. As one critic pointed out, ". . . obligation implies mutual responsibilities, and Mead fails to ask what we in our organized capacity as government . . . owe in return".[11]

What are the collective obligations to citizens? If the state does not provide the means or services to ensure social participation, integration or the acquisition and maintenance of skills, surely collective reciprocity is undermined. The possibility of economic participation must be created if the language of mutual responsibilities and obligations is to be respectable.

Advocates of "fair workfare" link citizenship with labour obligations. In a passage that deserves to be quoted at length, Gutmann and Thompson assert:

> In our society having a job is a necessary condition of what has been called social dignity – maintaining the respect of one's fellow citizens. (Having a job of course includes being a homemaker in a family where others have a job outside the home.) The point is not merely that having a job shows that you can take care of yourself; more important, it shows that you are carrying your share of the social burden. What your fellow citizens think of you in this sense should matter.[12]

This justification raises difficulties. Many people have dignity without having a job, just as many who have a job lack any social dignity. Put the claim to a simple test. I am a sewage cleaner; you are a lawyer. Whether in my eyes or yours, in what way would my job give me social dignity? One could insert many other jobs in place of sewage cleaning. Similarly, once you allow "homemaking" to count as a job, there is no reason to exclude any activity that has use value for the individual. And why should someone be accepted as having a job if they were "homemaking" when others from the household were in jobs outside the home, whereas they would not be counted as in a job if they were "homemaking" if no household member had a job? The next sentence is also unclear. Someone may have a job that did not provide enough on which to live, and as already emphasised, it is unclear what carrying your share of the social burden means. Does the amount of time spent working for wages matter, or the type of job?

It may seem unfair to dissect a particular text. But this was an attempt by two well-respected analysts to present a justification that goes beyond euphemisms and platitudes. Their text merely shows that the functional citizenship argument is paternalistic and suspect, if only because the terms are arbitrary and hazy.

Workfare increases the stigmatisation of the poor, who are subject to pressures and scrutiny, as well as discretionary judgments by officials who may not be trained to make such decisions fairly. Even if they were, the imposition of obligations should raise a question about the contractual justice of the transaction. The person is in a vulnerable position, dependent on the goodwill of the caseworker. To talk of the relationship reflecting a "new social contract", as commentators have described workfare, is to imply that it is a free contract entered into voluntarily. It is difficult to envisage how this dependent relationship strengthens functional citizenship.

Workfare is paternalistic control, with many signs that policing of the poor's behaviour is part of the process. For instance, in 1995 New York's Work Experience Programme began with insistence that applicants for welfare benefits had to be fingerprinted in order to satisfy tight tests for eligibility. Such treatment humiliates and stigmatises, and would make most people fearful about applying. It is no use defenders saying that such action is not part of workfare, since a mix of pressures, threats and sanctions is the essence of workfare. They must justify those pressures.

In the UK, successive governments have tightened the scrutiny of the poor, in the process changing their image, from being citizens who have a right to and need for income to one of a dirty, dysfunctional bunch of scroungers.

Workfare as Combating Dependency

Another claim is that workfare identifies real need for assistance by imposing a work test. This is based on a presumption that incentives do not work for the poor, a view supported by evidence that there were only marginal changes in labour supply in response to income maintenance experiments of the 1960s. Thus, it was argued, those who do not wish to work or to take jobs on offer cannot need the income very much. From this we soon arrive at controversial notions of "deserving" and "undeserving" poor. Debates in the USA in the 1980s and 1990s became embroiled in this dichotomy of dubious pedigree. A compromise proposal was to give those deemed unemployable, such as mothers with young children, a higher guaranteed income, and therefore less incentive to take paid employment because of the implicitly high marginal tax rate (poverty trap), while those regarded as employable (e.g., husbands) should have a low, means-tested entitlement coupled with a work obligation. Such distinctions between the employable and unemployable are somewhat subjective, and become arbitrary and inequitable.

The problem, according to workfare advocates, is that welfare recipients lose the will to work and sink into a state of dependency. As noted earlier, some go further, opposing "new-style" workfare precisely on the grounds that it does not remove dependency. They support workfare as a threat, to ensure that welfare recipients seek and take jobs or training promptly. According to Mead, "The dependent poor appear to react more strongly to *requirements* to work than incentives . . .".[13]

Critics of workfare believe the claim that the long-term unemployed or other recipients of transfers are immersed in a "dependency culture" are exaggerated. For example, an evaluation of workfare in Massachusetts found that a majority of long-term unemployed men put on workfare could have found employment without the "work experience" imposed on them.[14] And many studies have shown that the poor want to work just as much as the non-poor.

One might argue that social security systems have eroded forms of social solidarity and induced forms of dependency.[15] But workfare does nothing to recreate such solidarity. By turning parts of the population into workfare targets (those designated as employable and thus, implicitly, undeserving) and others into welfare recipients (those designated as unemployable), a false dichotomy between those expected to be productive citizens and those expected to be unproductive is intensified.

The dependency-combating argument put forward by workfare proponents is double-edged. Why stop at the poor? What about middle-class dependency, which is considerable? In many countries the more affluent strata are dependent on tax relief that allows them to contract enormous debts, such as mortgages. Many middle-income earners are dependent on fiscal welfare.

The anti-dependency lobby has pushed for greater selectivity in social protection and for grants to be converted to loans, on the pattern of the UK's Social Fund, giving the poor "emergency" loans, not grants. Supposedly, this encourages the poor to manage their own budgets and obliges them to take jobs. This reasoning goes with support for workfare, especially since giving loans to those who cannot pay may be seen as a way of turning paupers into debtors as well, at which point workfare advocates can depict the work obligation as a way of repaying the financial obligation. This is punitive, because it sees the poor as being where they are by their own actions. The dichotomy of deserving and undeserving has dogged social policy through the ages. As Alexis de Tocqueville recognised, it is practically impossible and inequitable to "separate unmerited misfortune from an adversity produced by vice."[16] Workfare adherents have yet to demonstrate that de Tocqueville was wrong.

It is often not the case that those receiving benefits are in a state of "dependency" suggested by popular accounts, dependent on benefits, unable and unwilling to seek or take employment. In the USA, contrary to the image of women living on AFDC benefits for years without employment, most recipients did not depend totally on them and many cycled back and forth between jobs and welfare.[17] The common problem has been that they take jobs that do not last long, or are forced to take inappropriate jobs, or cannot afford to remain in them, and so end up returning to "welfare". But if it is not a cultural aversion to work that is the cause of the marginalisation, a paternalistic or coercive policy is misdirected.

There is one further variant of the anti-dependency justification for work-fare to be considered. One libertarian claim is that, because the objective of social policy should be to make people personally independent, guaranteeing jobs for welfare recipients is unjustifiable, because it would create a new form of dependency and reinforce a culture of poverty. This sophistry poses a challenge to paternalists. It is for them to answer.

Workfare as Restoring the "Work Ethic"

One claim voiced strongly by workfare advocates is that workfare would inculcate or restore the "work ethic". Some go further, saying that the welfare system *should* cultivate labour discipline and that since other social institutions already exist to do that, such as churches and schools, there should be no objection to one more institution doing so. In the UK, for instance, some prominent economists have argued that, since general schooling has been advanced by compulsion, so should post-school vocational training, for all teenagers.[18] Why stop there?

Opponents are unimpressed, claiming that workfare is misguided because implicitly it blames the victim, in assuming that the target group lacks a "work ethic" and needs to be compelled. The problem may be a poverty trap, with prospective earnings from jobs being less than the value of the benefit, as was the case in all US states in the mid 1990s.[19] Or it may be non-work barriers to taking a job. Many AFDC recipients had constraints, such as disability, drug or alcohol problems, housing difficulties, low skills, health limitations, disabled small children or elderly parents.[20] A third of unemployed welfare recipients in the USA report lack of childcare as the reason for non-employment.[21] One in seven have health impediments stopping them from working.[22] For many people the problem is a lack of appropriate opportunities, or a lack of access to facilities to unblock a barrier to employment. Others may want or be able to work only so-called non-standard hours.[23] Moreover, if workfare leads to a proliferation of artificial, "unreal" jobs, it may actually weaken a work ethic among those forced to take them.

Creating or restoring a work ethic through workfare smacks of social engineering. The apparatus and institutions set up to oversee workfare could be transformed easily into mechanisms of coercion. This is not to attribute such intentions to most workfare advocates; their motives should not be impugned just because a coercive intention is the motivation of a few. However, many observers have concluded that as workfare spread in the 1980s and 1990s, so compulsion gained primacy over incentives. As it gives discretionary power to local bureaucrats, it must lead to subjective judgments in "workfare offices". It depends on sanctions, and in practice the onus of proof of appropriate behaviour is put on the unemployed or other needy individual, who may be inarticulate or unable to prove legitimate activity.

Workfare regulates individual and group behaviour and leads towards directed labour. It therefore undermines the right to work, a point to which we shall return. At the very least, it is paternalistic. According to a review supportive of workfare,

Often a state puts job-hunting welfare recipients into a job club, a sort of therapy group in which peers offer motivation and moral support. In San Diego, when a job club member tells the group she has found employment, the group leader, a social worker, rings a cowbell.[24]

Paternalism has also been revealed by the tendency of workfare proponents to condemn "non-directive" schemes on the grounds that they encourage beneficiaries to undertake training only for jobs they would like, which apparently results in them working fewer hours than before because the training prepares them for work "beyond their reach" rather than for "the more menial jobs actually available to them".[25]

Such language should make both libertarians and egalitarians uncomfortable. If nobody wants such menial jobs, either the wage should be raised or the jobs should be automated, or ways should be found of doing without them. Conversely, if many workers want to do some types of attractive work, then the wage of such jobs should be allowed to drop relative to that of menial jobs. In other words, one should not criticise the non-employed if they respond to market signals by choosing their own way to reintegrate. Mainstream norms are not necessarily universally valid. Workfare is a form of regulation that "integrates" lower-class people in a way they may not like.

Workfare as Cost-Reducing Social Policy

One advantage claimed for workfare is that the labour obligation will reduce the cost of the welfare system by generating extra output and hence tax revenue. Directed work, it is also claimed, reduces caseload costs, including those arising from the administrative need to check that benefit recipients are seeking, and are available for jobs.

Critics retort that the financial advantages of eliminating a few "scroungers" from the benefit rolls is small compared with the social and economic cost to needy claimants, and that in practice where real, productive jobs are involved workfare participants tend to displace workers in regular employment, thereby leading to additional costs. Such displacement effects were observed, for example, in evaluations of the San Diego workfare experiments.

The claim that workfare can reduce welfare expenditure is also dubious, because enforcement and other administrative costs may deter effective implementation.[26] To be efficient, workfare requires costly institutional reform, because of a need to merge welfare and labour market agencies. An alternative, also costly in public expenditure, was followed in some schemes in the USA, where local agencies responsible for them have contracted out the work-related activities. That raises questions of public accountability and quality control. Workfare evaluations have rarely taken account of these, or of deadweight and displacement effects, so they have given an upward bias to the estimated benefit–cost ratios.

In the USA, in the years after the welfare reform of 1996 many people dropped off welfare rolls. The difficulty is to know what explains the drop, since it continued a longer-term decline. Between 1993 and 1997 the number dropped by nearly 3 million. In May 1997, the White House's Council of Economic Advisers attributed 40 per cent of the fall to economic growth and 31 per cent to policy changes, including earned income tax credit for low-income workers, increased child support collections and spending on daycare for children of welfare mothers. But the Council Chairwoman, Janet Yellen, admitted they did not know what had happened to those who had left welfare, adding, "Are we pushing more people into poverty by revamping welfare programmes? We just don't know until there is more research."[27] Studies since have concluded that a large proportion dropped off welfare and out of the labour force as well.

"Diversion programmes" in most US States have commonly required welfare applicants to search for jobs for up to six weeks before they can start receiving benefits. In New York city, "Job Centres" have made applicants go through five appointments, with a financial planner, an employment planner, an intake worker and twice with an anti-fraud investigator, as well as experience the joy of a "home visit". This is really guilty until proven innocent. It is perhaps not surprising that apparently acceptance rates for benefit fell sharply after this process in social improvement was put into effect. In the country overall, one study concluded that about 40 per cent of those who left the welfare rolls did so because of sanctions.[28]

In the UK, the government in 1996 claimed that its pilot workfare scheme resulted in a 20 per cent drop in the number of registered unemployed claiming benefits, which was twice as many as had found jobs. The government interpreted the decline to detection of benefit fraud, claiming that it "flushed out of the system people who have been cheating."[29] But there was no check on whether people withdrew for that reason. After that, the policing of benefit claimants was tightened still further.

It is generally accepted that workfare is "expensive", but the overall cost may be moderated because, as a result of the stigma and unpleasantness of what is on offer, the financial costs may be less than anticipated simply because fewer claim or gain entitlement to benefits. But the direct costs should not be equated with social costs. The additional income insecurity among potential beneficiaries of state benefits may result in more need for financial support later.

Workfare as Cutting the Black Economy

Workfare, it is suggested, will diminish the black economy, because it makes it harder for welfare recipients who are actually working – but outside the taxable economy – to obtain benefits. To this, critics might respond that workfare cannot make much of a dent in the black economy, since most of those in it are also employed in other jobs. Empirical studies have shown that those with regular jobs are more likely than the unemployed to have such informal work as well.

Perhaps workfare schemes reduce the extent of petty, undeclared informal work by the poor, but in the absence of convincing evidence to the contrary one can presume that the effect is of minor significance. It could be beneficial if the threat of obligations brought some part-time employment into the legal economy. But it could end some casual income-earning by preventing people from continuing the work or discouraging them from persisting with what they know is illegal; the result might be that their income insecurity would be overwhelming. Often the reality is that the poor do casual jobs in the evenings, at week-ends or when they find the time, whereas for family or other reasons they could not do paid jobs at "standard" times or on conventional work schedules.

Workfare as Restoring Equity in Welfare

According to supporters, workfare is more equitable than orthodox welfare. The reasoning starts from the premise that any individual's full income consists of both money and leisure time. With conventional state transfers, recipients without time-using obligations effectively receive more than many low-wage earners, whose lost "free time" can be equated with forgone in-come. Related to this is the claim that it is unfair that, with conventional welfare, some people are paid benefits for not doing unpleasant jobs when others are doing them for wages.

To critics, this smacks of sophistry. If it were accepted that the full income of welfare exceeds the monetary value because of hidden leisure, it would help to justify an unconditional transfer, because it implies that poverty and unemployment traps that exist with means-tested schemes are even worse then income comparisons suggest.

Workfare proponents also claim that it strengthens the family unit by stressing responsible social behaviour by employable adults, a theme given prominence during passage of the US welfare reform. However, it is surely unfair to penalise a whole family or household by withholding benefit because one or other parent does not fulfil some behavioural condition for benefits on which all family members rely. And the surmise that "learnfare" for teenagers subjects families to economic insecurity and stress has been widely reported. Rather than strengthen the nuclear family by imposing behavioural norms, workfare may erode it by increasing internal tensions. That is surely not equitable.

Workfare as Legitimising Social Transfers

An overtly political justification for workfare is the claim that the imposition of work on welfare recipients enhances political support for welfare programmes in general. It also demonstrates to others, including potential employers, that those "on welfare" are really employable. However, rather than attract support, workfare may weaken public endorsement of state social protection in general by stigmatising the poor and encouraging a perception of "them-and-us". It undermines a principle of citizenship, which is that everybody should be treated on an inclusive, equal basis.

Finally, workfare is unlikely to be effective because no group directly involved favours it. Participants try to avoid it or resent being in it; officials in workfare agencies prefer to have willing clients and so are loath to force claimants to take menial jobs, public authorities and firms are reluctant to employ participants because they expect such workers, even if subsidised, to be unreliable, have high turnover and require close supervision; trade unions resent them as a threat to their employed members' jobs, pay and benefits; and other workers feel threatened by the presence of workfare placements because they fear being displaced by lower-paid substitutes or having over-time, working hours or promotion prospects reduced.

Workfare as a Means of Poverty Reduction

Supporters also claim that workfare raises participants' longer-term income above what they would otherwise receive. This may be true for single-parent families; one early US study suggested that participants' subsequent in-come was higher than that of those who remained on welfare.[30] But it also indicated that income gains were insufficient to lift them out of poverty, or remove them from eligibility for welfare transfers. Later studies also showed that the income gain was small, that only short-run effects were measured, and that subsequent incomes of two-parent families were actually reduced by workfare.[31] One concluded that it was unrealistic to expect that pushing recipients into the type of job they could expect would lift them out of poverty.[32] Then several years after the Federal welfare reform, the National Conference of State Legislators reported that while many of those who left the welfare system had jobs, most remained in poverty, and the jobs were unstable.

There is also an indirect sequence of effects to be considered, since the jobs usually envisaged by workfare proponents have low productivity, status and pay – cleaning streets, sweeping leaves, being maids or waitresses, and so on. Most do not enhance the probability of good employment and do little to reverse the structural tendency to marginalise a substantial proportion of the labour force. If the poor pushed into workfare slots see little chance of thereby joining the mainstream, coercion cannot lead to self-reliant indi-vidualism, let alone higher long-term income.

There are other reasons for doubting that workfare is an efficient means of reducing poverty. A large-scale workfare scheme introduces distortions into the lower end of the labour market. It will probably give overwhelming emphasis to maximising the "placement rate", to the detriment of genuine skill development. Cheap labour undermines better labour, leading – as observed even in Sweden – to substitution/displacement effects and a weakening of the bargaining position of lower-status, lower-income groups among the employed.

Another effect is that US workfare schemes have resulted in many non-employed women being placed in jobs with very low wages, without health benefits, sick leave or paid vacation. This was shown to be the case for three-quarters of those placed under the GAIN scheme in California.[33] There is also evidence that the wage displacement effect may be stronger than the employment displacement effect. Thus, placing recipients in jobs by giving them a "grant" below the going wage appeared to result in substantially lower wages among the low-paid workforce.[34]

The overall effect on poverty depends on outcomes that are unknown prior to the policy coming into operation. This is unlike social protection as usually perceived, whereby the vulnerable, near-poor and poor are given prior assurance of income security. The poverty effect of time limits and work obligations depend on the income received in the jobs, the costs of taking and remaining in jobs, the income mobility potential of those jobs and the effect on the poverty of others in or potentially in jobs taken by workfare participants. The overall effect must take into consideration the impact not just on those on workfare but on low-income groups in general.

The effect on participants themselves depends crucially on the costs of jobholding, and in the USA these have been shown to be a cause of many participants leaving jobs and returning to claim benefits.[35] The cost of childcare, transport, clothes, processed food and so on, quite apart from loss of other transfers or informal support from relatives, friends or non-governmental organisations, may easily make low-wage jobs an impoverishing experience.

For the near-poor, taking a job may tip them from a subsistence equilibrium into financial crisis. They may take a low-paid job, losing entitlement to benefits, in the hope that initial costs are an investment that will be worthwhile when the income rises in the longer term. In this frame of mind, they build up debts, only to find their hopes – perhaps induced by their social caseworker – are ill-founded, leaving them with unsustainable debts. At least one study has found that many women who went from welfare to jobs ended up sinking into debt.[36] This form of poverty trap has received insufficient attention.

The ability of those relying on welfare support to find jobs at all is also questionable. Although it will take several years before full evaluation of the US welfare reform is possible – and by 1998, several multi-million dollar research projects were underway – research based on workfare experiments, the profiles of the target population and official job projections is not encouraging. Not only is the wage displacement large but, as one careful study concluded, "alarming numbers of low-income families may face sanctions or benefit cutoffs as a result of the time limits mandated by the 1996 welfare legislation".[37]

In the USA, the notion of "time limits" is meant to be a shock tactic, or what its advocates call "tough love". A concern is that many will not be able to meet the criteria, and will be made destitute. The rhetoric opens social policy to the awesome prospect of a credibility "shoot-out". Suppose after two years, and more dramatically after five years, millions of citizens are unable to satisfy the workfare criteria and cease to be entitled to welfare benefits. There is a strong prospect that this will be the case. If the state then started to make exceptions to meet desperate cases, the policy's credibility and its fragile residual fairness would be undermined. If it did not give way, the consequences for the poor would be terrible.

Other countries moving down the same road may benefit from the US lessons. It was blessed with fortuitous circumstances given the extraordinary fact that the workfare policy launched in 1996 was "fund capped". The welfare budget was declared in advance, involving a $56 billion cut up to 2002. But the number of claimants over that period could only be forecast contingently. If the economy slowed, the number would rise, which would strain the diminished block grants. Some observers expressed fears about this, and some states no doubt operated a more restrictive regime as a result of the uncertainty. Although the continued economic growth into 2000 enabled the policy to continue, the conditionality opened up the prospect of politicising social policy beyond any economic or social rationale.

A similar sort of distributive twist had already arisen by 1997, in that as a result of concentrating on placing welfare recipients in jobs, in some States resources had been diverted from childcare for the working poor to pay for the placements, jeopardising the ability of the employed poor to stay in jobs.[38] This outcome is likely when policy focuses on one group and when job placement is the primary concern.

Another potential source of impoverishment is the relationship between the statutory minimum wage and the level of transfers. In 1997, it was decided that workfare participants were covered by the *Fair Labour Standards Act* of 1938, entitling them to the minimum wage. This caused consternation. For relatively low-income States, such as Alabama, since the existing welfare payments were equal to less than half the minimum wage, the ruling meant that the cost of placing workfare participants in jobs would more than double. If the state could not meet the requirement to place welfare recipients in jobs, its block grant would be reduced. The debate centred on what counted as the minimum wage. The outcome could be crucial for the effect of workfare on poverty in general.

In assessing the effects, what is most striking is that workfare was launched with no evidence that it would reduce poverty, and some evidence that it would make it worse, in spite of rhetoric to the contrary. By early in the new century, preliminary evaluations left the picture no clearer.

Workfare as the Answer to Unemployment

A commonly stated rationale for "welfare-to-work", workfare and "active labour market policy" is that it would reduce not only unemployment but the NAIRU. Workfare has been depicted as reducing unemployment not only directly but by discouraging welfare claimants from registering as un-employed jobseekers and by encouraging employers to offer more low-wage jobs.[39] Related to this is the argument that workfare is needed because most unemployment in affluent societies is 'voluntary', primarily because the poor do not like the type of jobs they are able to obtain and repeatedly quit in the hope of finding something better.

This argument does not stand close scrutiny, partly because the voluntary unemployment claim is based on dubious or unverified assumptions. In any case, to reduce unemployment by discouraging genuine claimants from registration is scarcely a legitimate policy. To do so merely intensifies the poverty of those not satisfying the conditions for support. This has, for example, been reported as the outcome of the UK's policy change making teenagers eligible for housing benefits only if they joined the government's *Youth Training Scheme*, which led to more homelessness and other adverse social consequences.[40]

A related claim is that workfare removes the "unemployment trap", i.e. the fact that with most systems unemployed people taking low-paying jobs face what are effectively very high marginal tax rates, losing benefits as their earned income rises. Some economists favour workfare partly because they believe that marginal income tax rates *should* be higher at the lower end of the scale, on the grounds that the better off should be given more incentives because of their higher productivity, whereas the lost output of the poor discouraged from working by high tax rates would not matter much. On this reasoning, workfare is a way of avoiding the unemployment trap.

Not only is this argument dubious theoretically (the substitution effect may offset the income effect), but the rationale is inequitable. That aside, if removing the unemployment trap were the objective, an unconditional income transfer would surely be a preferable alternative.

Another criticism of workfare as a means of combating unemployment is that it may actually raise frictional unemployment. Almost by definition, workfare participation interrupts the unemployed's job search, and so may increase labour market inefficiency. It is difficult to search for the type of work you want, or think you might be able to do, if you have to participate in a workfare scheme at the same time. Indeed, evaluations of male AFDC-UP (Unemployed Parents) programmes in the USA found that workfare delayed labour market re-entry. In Baltimore, for instance, there was a vibrant "living wage" campaign in the 1990s, led by churches and trade unions, with the objective of raising wages of the low paid. Campaign leaders claimed that the higher wages lowered labour turnover, because workers were enabled to afford to stay in jobs, whereas workfare reversed this, threatening to raise frictional unemployment as well as income insecurity.[40]

A more standard criticism of workfare is that it fails to reduce unemployment by much, because of substantial employment displacement effects, or substitution effects (placing people in posts instead of others already in or previously in those jobs), as well as because of deadweight effects (placing people in jobs in which they would have been placed anyhow). Although these are often regarded as the most serious drawbacks of workfare, they are introduced at this stage to emphasise that they are not necessarily the major criticism, even though many advocates attempt to defuse this criticism almost to the exclusion of addressing others.

In any case, obliging the unemployed to take jobs could have the effect of displacing others in similar jobs, and studies have suggested that the displacement could be so large that the net effects on employment and unemployment are modest. There is also evidence that many unemployed are obliged to take jobs that would have been created for them anyhow or that would not exist, and need not be done, were they not obliged to perform them.

An example of displacement, although hard to attribute directly to work-fare, is what happened to employment in New York's Parks Department. Having reduced employment by over 40 per cent, half by dismissals, over a three-year period, the department deployed 6,000 "Weps" (participants in the Work Experience Program, a workfare scheme) at lower cost. The fact that the lay-offs preceded the deployment of Weps made it possible to claim there was no displacement, yet surely this is what it was.

In a tight labour market, as in the USA during the period when workfare was extended, the displacement effect may not appear very significant, although it is unfair to those displaced and to those denied a proper waged job. However, when unemployment is high, displacement should be regarded as a primary aspect of economic and social evaluation of work-fare.

In 1998, under its *New Deal* welfare-to-work scheme, the UK Government obliged some unemployed youths aged 16 to 24 to work for six months in the "voluntary sector". This was ironic in that it meant making some do jobs that others did voluntarily. The unemployed were to receive their benefits, if entitled, plus a small grant. The effect on unemployment would be modest if there were substantial displacement effects, and the adverse effects on the services could be considerable if reluctant or inexperienced unemployed created friction with volunteers working alongside them, leading to an erosion of the charity's reputation or capacities.

Workfare as Moderating Wage Inflation

Workfare, it is further claimed, puts downward pressure on wages and thus boosts employment indirectly. This should be seen in context. Proponents usually stipulate that those put on workfare should be paid only the equiv-alent of their welfare benefit or that plus a supplement to cover their costs of employment. Often they suggest that workfare should pay less than the lowest-level jobs. This has been the usual situation in the USA.

There is probably something in this claim. But besides raising problems of equity, surely using workfare to reduce wages at the lower end of the labour market distorts market mechanisms. As indicated earlier, workfare is a means of lowering the wages of the low-paid, and is thus a mechanism for achieving downward wage flexibility and intensifying the labour market segmentation, since it applies predominantly to low-wage workers.

Workfare for Developing Skills

Workfare schemes have been presented as a means of enhancing skills, through direct training or through the work experience, thus making participants more employable and favouring the social reintegration of marginalised groups. The "employability" theme was asserted repeatedly in the USA in the mid 1990s and in western Europe in 1997.

The counter-claim is that workfare generates few skills, since – if linked to skill development at all – the type of jobs involved provide little more than "orientation" or "work preparation" training, rather than training for a craft or occupation. Such training may boost the employment chances of some but marginalise others, by causing firms to substitute workers with "formal" certification for those with informal but valuable skills. In any case, training schemes should surely attract workers by their intrinsic worth; the training should be perceived by trainees as improving their "skill". A workfare scheme may actually reduce the participants' capacity or desire to undertake appropriate vocational training.[42] Those obliged to take low-level, static jobs have less time and energy to pursue occupational education or training. Even at the lowest levels, unless there are incentives for firms and workers to make skill development part of the workfare scheme, the result is more likely to be de-skilling. On-the-job training may yield reasonable economic returns. However, given the low schooling of many welfare recipients in the USA, off-the-job training would be required to enable them to take and remain in jobs.[43]

Workfare presumes that social integration can be achieved by doing a "job", sometimes under the "professional guidance" of some local official. One can think of many jobs that offer little prospect of doing any such thing. It also presumes an answer to an unclear question. It presumes that what needs to be reformed is people's behaviour rather than the institutions supposed to serve them. For example, one form of workfare – obliging teenagers to attend a school or training institution in return for welfare benefits – described as "learnfare" in Wisconsin, is a case of a response to an unclear problem. Perhaps teenagers do need discipline, though critics might feel uneasy about beating them into compliance with a social security stick. But are policy-makers sure that is the problem? Suppose schools are teaching subjects that are not relevant, or not appropriate to those expected to study them. Should a high drop-out rate be attributed to cultural background, to teenagers' behavioural traits, or to the schools? The point is that judgments about school attendance are not a reliable basis for deciding whether an individual deserves income support.

The possibility that workfare would have a skill displacement effect has received little attention. Those combining training with employment on their own initiative, or even with assistance from others, could be discouraged if there were an influx of others provided with comparable training, if the expected earnings from that type of job declined or if opportunities to use those skills appear to worsen.

Workfare relates to another structural aspect of skill development, close to the spirit of this book. The thinking that led towards workfare is that it is justified because of welfare dependency and behavioural deficiencies on the part of the poor and unemployed. It focuses on the supply side, directly and indirectly lowering the reservation wage and distorting the labour market. The message is that the unemployed or other recipients should alter their behaviour and attributes. The state may help, with a conditional grant or loan, or with advice or job-seeking assistance. The motives may be bene-volent. However, the policy alters the labour market in a way that lessens pressure on firms to make jobs an avenue to occupation. There is less need to make jobs attractive and a source of skill development if applicants are driven to accept whatever is available through fear and insecurity.

5 Conclusions

In the 1980s, it was predicted that workfare would be the reaction to growing labour market flexibility and the fiscal pressures that were leading to a flight to selectivity in social security systems.[44] This has materialised, and is likely to continue for a short time. It is the ultimate policy of labour control. But it has several drawbacks – it is judgmental, paternalistic, erodes real freedom, is socially divisive, and may block forms of social and economic participation, such as voluntary community service, since workfare officials could claim that the person would not be searching for wage employment and would not be available at short notice, and therefore should not be classified as un-employed or receive benefits. The conditionality erects barriers to social participation, community involvement and social integration. Ironically, it could prevent people from participation, rather than induce it.

A central message has been that industrialised societies cannot afford extensive social protection, public pensions, public health care, public housing and so on. Hardly anybody has had the temerity to challenge this orthodoxy. The presumption or belief that extensive welfare cannot be afforded has been linked to the apparent dictates of globalisation, to the implied need for greater national competitiveness, and to the need to reduce public budget deficits (as in the case of targets set for monetary union under the Maastricht Treaty). But the rollback, or "reorientation", of welfare has also been advo-cated as a desirable objective by libertarians, on grounds of social justice and as a pragmatic means of "reducing welfare dependency".

Workfare is a labourist response to the crisis of social and economic insecurity. It stigmatises the poor by associating certain activities with prior failure and by eroding the right to income security even further than recent labour market developments have done. It is coercive social policy, and is a morally soft option. When the paternalistic family was seen as the norm, women were expected to stay out of the labour force, so that labour con-ditionality was not regarded as reasonable. Now the norm is that women should be in wage jobs, so paternalism dictates that women, even with young children and without a regular partner, should be obliged to take jobs. The application of norms to social policy is surely misguided, whichever norm is popular at the time.

By contrast with workfare, transfers without work-related obligations would separate the government's social responsibility for basic income security from the individual's personal responsibility for developing skills and a "lifetime" sense of occupation, which in the coming era will consist increasingly of individual bundles of skills, interests and experience rather than predeter-mined, standardised packages.

Workfare represents a move away from the social insurance principle without strengthening the right to work or income security. It is the outcome of moves away from universalism, and the drift to "targeting" and selectivity, since means-testing and work-testing turn recipients of social protection into a category easily stigmatised by the majority. The drift to selectivity prepared the ground for workfare because politicians could play on the sentiment that the median worker or taxpayer is paying for the support and training and education of others.

Ultimately, workfare is an exercise in discretionary social policy. The case worker or personal adviser – or whatever politically correct euphemism is used to describe those hired to guide those perceived to be suffering from social exclusion – is able to decide who is treated, who is put aside, who is sanctioned and who is encouraged. The labour requirements placed on applicants provide ample opportunity for local officials to impose sanctions. There are layers of opportunity – failure to keep appointments, unwilling-ness to do as one is told, resentment of counselling, refusal to undergo medical examinations, and so on. Think of all those "personal responsibility agreements" introduced in the USA since the mid-1990s. However hard you try to avoid the conclusion, this is social engineering.

One need not criticise the motives of those who advocate or try to put this policy into effect. Assume their motives are well-meaning and that they want to see the social integration of their fellow citizens. They see the tramp, the drug addict, the shambling pitiful human being living in a cardboard box – and they want to help resurrect a life. But why stop there? In the end, what they advocate is organised clientelism. What is interesting is that those who have been the most insistent advocates of workfare and its extensions have been singularly silent about the need for representation security for those in the workfare queue. Unless the "client" has an effective Voice, how can he or she avoid injustice?

Workfare derives from a strange concept of mutual obligation – strange because it is not clear that "mutual" or "obligation" can be satisfactorily defined. In the more flexible societies that are emerging, behavioural diver-sity should be facilitated, rather than curtailed by mechanisms designed to pressurise the poor to conform to some state-determined norm. Workfare neither addresses the structural features of labour markets that intensify marginalisation, nor enhances the prospects of more equitable outcomes. It is an unpromising road to take.

Workfare separates the progressive mind from the classical liberal mind. The progressive believes in ordinary people, believes that they can find their own way, and believes that the state must equalise the conditions in which each person can develop his or her craft or occupation. The liberal thinks that the poor are somehow dysfunctional and lost souls, who need rescuing so that they can be like us. For the liberal, charity is given as part of a marketable bargain. The progressive is inclined to think that assistance should be given without the humbug.

9

Basic Security as Reviving Equality

1 Introduction

If workfare is the final twist of labourism, combining paternalism and a multi-tier approach to social integration, it is time to look to the philosophical foundations of an alternative strategy. What should be equalised in a Good Society of the twenty-first century? Every modern theory of distributive justice has started from the position that there is something that should be equalised. For liberals, it has always been equality of opportunity. For socialists, it was something close to equality of non-ownership of the means of production. For modern social democrats, there have been wriggling attempts to avoid the term altogether.

Yet although during the era of market regulation there was an undercurrent of unease, which surfaced in a concern to reduce "poverty", and a rearguard defence by a few economists determined to prove that reductions in income inequality raise economic growth, issues of distributive justice (unlike procedural justice) were pushed to the margin of political, economic and cultural discourse. It was as if the word "equality" were tarnished beyond redemption by the horror of state socialism. Yet there are signs of a new awakening, best captured in a desire for a gentler pace of life, strong limits on polluting aggrandisement and commercial greed, and a horror at the ecological damage that is visibly mounting. The public outbursts may be incoherent, but distributive justice is beginning to creep up the agenda of popular concerns.

The starting point should be that distributive justice requires that everyone in society should have basic security and self-control. Equal basic security implies that there should be equal freedom from morbidity, sustainable self-respect, and equal freedom from controls. There should also be equal good opportunity to develop one's competencies, or Sen's functionings.

A Good Society is a just society. All modern theories of justice begin with the premise that everyone should be treated as equal in some respect. The essence of the claim in this book is that the Good Society would be one in which freedom, security and self-control would be part of the equalisandum (that pursued as the bundle of social needs to be equalised as far as possible). This seems consistent with John Rawls' magisterial *Theory of Justice* and with extensions by liberals *and* egalitarians.

A common starting point is that justice requires equalisation of advantages that are the consequence of circumstances and traits for which an individual could not be held responsible. There are several ways of refining this. Thus Arnesan postulated that justice requires "equality of opportunity for welfare", and Cohen put it as "equality of access to advantage". It is just as important to emphasise that justice requires equality of self-control and equality of basic security. Everybody needs a stable base. A fear spreading around the world is that social progress was arrested when flexibility came to mean insecurity, and when more people found themselves feeling structurally isolated, without social responsibilities beyond themselves and their immediate family, and without the assurance of assistance from those around them. Individualism seemed to be a prescription for unbridled opportunism and the morality of the marketplace. This induced more fragmented societies of groups detached by fortune or by misfortune, in which legal controls, complex systems of auditing and increasingly detailed contracts were required to check rampant opportunism and a pervasive lack of trust.

It is against this background that basic security and self-control should be seen as the prerequisites for a just society. Rawls in his *Theory of Justice* emphasised that justice depends on the provision of "primary goods" and the Difference Principle, i.e., that a just society should maximise the bundle of primary goods available to the least well-off in society. These cover basic liberties, including freedom of association, freedom of movement and choice of occupation, and the social bases of self-respect. Although Rawls gave little attention to it, primary social goods must surely include security in which to pursue "a rational plan of life".

Sen refined this by arguing that distributive justice requires equalisation of capabilities, not primary goods, where capabilities comprise opportunities and competencies.[1] For Sen, the focus should be on the means for escaping morbidity, for being adequately nourished, achieving self-respect, participating in the community and being happy.[2] Income should not be equalised because, for example, a disabled person needs more than someone else to achieve the same level of functionings. Recognising that slaves, housewives, the unemployed and the destitute tend to have "cheap tastes", because of their deprivation, justice requires concentration on improving individual functionings, rather than incomes. Sen recognised a trade-off between distributive objectives, which left him open to the charge that he does not have a coherent theory of justice.[3] However, to include self-control and security as basic functionings would be consistent with Sen's work.

Dworkin rejected welfare equalisation as the appropriate principle of social justice, on the grounds that equalising everybody's welfare would justify giving more to those with expensive tastes.[4] He claimed that justice requires an equal distribution of a bundle of resources, but because resources include "native talents" that are unequally endowed, he proposed that compensation be provided for inequalities in circumstances over which individuals are not responsible, but not for those due to their exercise of preferences. He thus integrated the notion of "responsibility" into egalitarianism, by allowing for types of inequality due to the exercise of preferences and actions for which individuals are responsible, and with which they identified at the time decisions were made. He believes there is a collective duty to correct for "brute luck", which deals out talents and handicaps unequally.[5]

Cohen added another caveat by demonstrating that justice requires fraternity, circumstances in which the talented are encouraged to be not purely self-regarding, and are prepared to compensate and support the less talented.[6] This is significant, because if social groups become more detached from each other in terms of their relative security and life-style, the sense of fraternity or community will be eroded, just as having some groups control the activity and advantages of others must erode it. Policies and institutions are required to safeguard fraternity, as both a social goal and a matter of individual justice.

While egalitarian theories have wrestled with what should be equalised, the era of market regulation ushered in libertarianism, which sat comfortably with the "revolution" associated with the Chicago school of law and economics. The libertarian theory of justice was articulated by Robert Nozick in his influential *Anarchy, State and Utopia*, published in 1974. The central thesis of this profoundly inegalitarian theory is that justice is not concerned with outcomes but with processes by which individuals interact. For Nozick, there should be "justice in acquisition" and "justice in transfer", and these determine entitlements.[7] As long as persons or firms acquire something legally, they are entitled to it, and nobody has a right to infringe their ownership. This allows monopolies, rejects redistributive taxation and state transfers, allows labour market discrimination and accepts the operation of labour controls, while asserting that any infringement on "self-ownership" is an injustice.

Libertarianism gives overwhelming priority to liberty, but gives negative liberty too much authority, that is, freedom from interference, so rationalising consideration of actions limiting freedom. Libertarianism neglects the need for an equal opportunity principle. By contrast, egalitarianism respects liberty as a constitutional principle, but sees a need to limit it to allow for equal opportunity and other forms of equality.

Libertarianism has greatly influenced social and labour policy since the 1970s. It is based on the notion of "self-ownership" and the doctrine of entitlements. Derived from Millian liberalism, self-ownership amounts to the view that everyone possesses (or should possess) full and exclusive rights of control and use of himself or herself, and his or her competencies and capacities. As such, nobody owes any service or product to anyone else unless he or she has contracted to supply it to someone.[8]

Libertarianism draws on a view expressed by John Locke justifying private appropriation from nature, subject to leaving "enough and as good in common for others". Critics point out that there should be no presumption that natural resources were "unowned" prior to private acquisition; one could presume they were "jointly owned" or "communally owned". They have also criticised the principle of justice in acquisition, based on Rawls' argument that there is no right to income when that is due to *luck*, whether genetic or environmental.

Both egalitarians and libertarians have come to recognise that respons-ibility must figure in the theory of justice. But unlike libertarians, modern egalitarians have differentiated responsibility according to whether or not the individual could reasonably be said to have control. Roemer's scholarly review of theories of distributive justice concluded that there are philosophical difficulties to be resolved in treating responsibility. However, we may conclude that justice requires that everybody should be provided with basic security and a situation of self-control in which to form preferences responsibly and in which to take actions that are not induced by social situations in which they would not choose to find themselves. Without basic security and self-control, a demand for responsibility seems eminently unfair. *Real* freedom requires a rock of security – or it is the liberty of the outcast.

In this, there may be advance to be gained through Cohen's idea of midfare, which is what one enjoys from one's functionings (capabilities). We might say that midfare – unlike welfare and workfare – requires that individuals be provided with the basic freedoms, including self-control and basic security, in which to act and decide with social responsibility. Sen's critique of Rawls for focusing on primary goods amounts to a plea to equalise midfare across persons. As such, justice depends on equalising access to advantage.

The conclusion is that a just society requires policies and institutions that enhance self-control and basic security. These objectives are compatible with both egalitarianism and libertarianism. Moreover, following Rawls' Difference Principle, distributive justice requires that policies should improve the position of the worst off in society, which can only mean increasing their degree of self-control. A just society would be one in which policies were regarded as just if and only if they reduced the difference between the insecurity of the least advantaged and the remainder.

This leads to a reconsideration of the idea of security, and what sort of security we should desire for a Good Society. One may assert that subject to incentive and dynamic efficiency constraints, distributive justice depends on equalising economic security. Yet some forms of security are neither wanted nor desirable. And as stated at the outset, one may have too much or too little security. This is why we should emphasise that basic security should be the pillar of a good society. Extensive security without rights is an image that reminds us of heavy-handed state control. It fails. State socialism showed that. Rights without security is symbolic of market regulation and welfare residualism. It fails too. Basic security with rights is the desirable objective – building liberty from basic security. As a former Prime Minister of Spain noted, "When security is lost, the sense of freedom becomes weak and fragile".

2 Policy Decision Principles

Equality of opportunity should be interpreted as the equal opportunity to pursue one's self-determined occupation, defined in terms of a bundle of competencies and aspirations linked to work over a lifetime. Occupation is the positive core of work. It requires self-discipline and a progressive content – as befits human development – and a regulatory framework to limit opportunism and dilettantism.

Freedom to pursue occupation requires basic security, which implies economic security and freedom from controls. The former is easy to accept – one must have a guarantee of subsistence by one means or another in order to be able to take decisions in developing one's capacities. The latter seems harder to justify. Some would see no need for freedom from controls to be part of basic security. They might cite the "contented slave" objection, i.e., the view that people may place themselves under the control of somebody as a means of obtaining basic security, or as a means of overcoming vulnerability, so avoiding having to make awkward or risky decisions. Although this is an awkward issue, suffice it to state that social and political rules cannot be derived from a belief that human beings would opt for slavery. Justice requires policies and institutions that provide adequate security and self-control, in which every individual can make rational choices – the essence of real freedom.

We could describe our approach as a position of complex egalitarianism. In telegraphic form, distributive justice requires basic security for all, equal opportunity for occupational security, and voice representation security, to ensure that the vulnerable and all interest groups are taken into account. In addition, it is necessary to have two policy rules. The first is based on the Rawlsian Difference Principle:

> Policies and institutions are just if and only if they reduce (or do not worsen) the insecurity of the least secure groups in society.

There is a resonance to this principle in the Swiss national Constitution. In its preamble, it states "that the strength of the community is measured by the well-being of the weakest of its members". Policies and institutions should be judgd by whether or not they improve the well-being of the least secure groups, and that means ruling out as unacceptable any policies that worsen their insecurity.

In addition, security requires freedom from controls (except for those required to prevent individuals doing harm to others). Accordingly, the second policy decision rule could be formulated as what might be called the Paternalism Test Principle:

> Policies and institutions are just if they reduce the controls limiting the autonomy to pursue occupation of those facing the most controls, and are just if they do not impose controls on anybody that are not imposed on the most free groups in society.

The Good Society of the twenty-first century will offer everybody basic security coupled with strong Voice security, so that group and individual interests can be protected and enhanced and coupled with mechanisms that redistribute economic surplus. How would this appeal to the seven strata in the emerging global social stratification? For example, what would such a formula offer to the proficians, or the salariat? The answer may be something like the following.

We should be able to accept a core principle that gives basic security, because we want our children to have as good a starting point in life as anybody else. This appeals to opportunistic altruism, because in a competitive, individualistic society, most people will not know where they would come in the spectrum of occupational security. With increasing life expectancy, even the middle class will move into middle age before wealth inheritance could give them income security. So, a floor offers the assurance, which would not exist otherwise, that the children of even the economically secure will be protected. The floor itself should be differentiated to counteract natural ill luck. Those with special needs will always be determined to some extent randomly, through accidents, ill health, disability, poor choice of partners, etc. They need extra to provide basic security.

It is relatively easy to recognise and accept the need for supplements for categories of need, and special voice mechanisms for them. The middle class – the salariat and proficians – will also favour redistribution of surplus, because they will be net beneficiaries, even if they see a loss of labour income security and employment security. The vision that one is presenting is one of individualism backed by collective support for social solidarity, and this individualism is based on moving towards a flexible life image, legitimising all forms of work and allowing for flexible careers. Those from the middle class have been enabled to learn and possess several competencies, and the image of flexible life and flexible work goes with that.

3 A Strategy for Distributive Justice

What would be a feasible strategy for distributive justice that placed work and occupation at the centre of society, appropriate for the flexible open economies that characterise the era of global capitalism? The sensible way forward is to erect a system based on three principles – basic income security (so that choices are made in real freedom), universal representation security (voice), and the Security Difference and Paternalism Test Principles. The objectives should be equality of security and good opportunity for all, coupled with equal liberty for all. If liberty comes from self-control and security, the strategy must satisfy those principles and promote dynamic efficiency.

Neither of the main twentieth-century development models offered all these conditions, and nor has the era of market regulation. A failing of state socialism was denial of liberty coupled with subordinated security, which stifled incentives and personal development. The failing of welfare state capitalism was less pronounced. It promoted liberty and security through citizenship rights and a welfare state underpinned by social protection that was never as universal as its advocates liked to believe. For a while, the norms on which it was based were sufficiently widespread to make the system functional and amenable to marginal extensions to cater for other situations.

That is no longer true. Above all, single-adult and single-person households have become common. For instance, in the Netherlands since 1975 the number of one-person households has more than doubled, and by the 1990s more than one-third of all households had only one person. Some call this "the great disruption", attributing it in part to the welfare system.[9] More problematical, it accords with the pursuit of individual freedom.

Social individualisation has accompanied more individualised employment and more flexible, insecure labour markets. Means-tested, work-tested benefits and workfare erode liberty by regulating behaviour. Even if one dislikes the apparent sloth of one's neighbour, once policy goes down the road of directing and controlling the activity of the victims and the vulnerable, the liberty and opportunity of others will soon be threatened. Paternalism is never benign for long, since unless it carries an implicit threat of coercion, exercised from time to time, it loses credibility.

In developing an alternative strategy for distributive justice – to re-embed the economy in society and reduce insecurity – the following premises and stylised facts must be taken into account.

First, reforms must build on the recognition that the character of production and distribution is creating socio-economic detachment, materially and psychologically. Most of those in positions of status, influence or leadership, or who anticipate being or who desire to be in such positions, feel more comfortable in being detached from the poor and disadvantaged in society than used to be the case. The tenuous solidarity between the "middle" and "working" classes, between "them" and "us", was partly an emotional one built on a sense of common history and social identity. Now "we" see a fragmented, IT-driven, globalising society where more of the affluent could echo Napoleon's immortal quip, "Je suis un parvenu", living a trajectory that flashes by without roots or solid ties of reciprocity. The detaching character of relations of production in global capitalism undermines the sense of balanced reciprocity on which all societies have depended.

If social and economic progress are to be in step – if the economy is to be re-embedded in society – the socio-economic distance between groups, particularly between people as workers, must shrink. This would create the basis of solidarity, a coalition coalescing around a feasible redistributive agenda. The perception of distance has tended to preclude such a vision, and until such a coalition arises, fear will not change sides again to the extent that representatives of the privileged see egalitarian redistribution as desirable.

Second, the strategy must recognise that in a globalising, flexible economy, a growing number of jobs will not offer adequate earnings to provide a viable social income for the individual. Also, inequality is growing due to the rising returns to capital and the diminishing capacity of progressive taxation.

Third, statutory protective regulations are weakened in open flexible economies, as are traditional voice mechanisms. A system that lacks effective regulation cannot provide basic security and good opportunity. Distributive justice will depend on achieving a better balance between the forms of labour regulation (statutory, market and voice) and on reducing faith in market regulation, so that statutory regulation can more effectively establish basic standards of decency while there are adequate measures to promote *voice regulation*, which means mechanisms to enable *all* groups to put pressure on the powerful to redistribute gains of growth.

Fourth, privatisation of social policy will continue, making it likely that the selectivity will intensify insecurity and strengthen paternalistic social policy. With flexible labour markets, income security cannot be provided by complex formulae and systems of entitlement based on intrusive work-tests, means-tests and the like. Simplicity, transparency, equity and efficiency must be the principles.

Fifth, the strategy must secure political and social legitimation. In the era of market regulation, the legitimacy of welfare state policies has been eroded, in part because an increasing proportion of the benefits has gone to the middle class, because the drift to selective, conditional schemes has revived the distinction between the "deserving" and "undeserving" poor, because selectivity reduces the constituency identifying with particular schemes, and because increased conditionality has resulted in stigmatisation and what might be called distributive justice failure, due to large numbers of those who should be entitled being excluded or not reached.

Sixth, the strategy must facilitate flexibility, and above all lifestyle work flexibility. In this regard, it should take account of the limitations of statutory working-time reductions, which means primarily cutting hours in paid jobs. Ironically, this is proposed as a means of generating employment – reducing some people's as a means of increasing others'. There may be reasons for cutting hours, but since some would want to work longer for more income, the policy could lead to restrictions on long workweeks, leading to rigidities, coercion and even punitive taxes.

As a response to unemployment, working time reductions would have little effect in part because part-time working has spread already. The likelihood is that substantial cuts in working time would lead more of those in regular jobs to take additional part-time jobs. If those in regular jobs have, on average, more skills and contacts than the unemployed, cutting working time could increase the unequal distribution of paid employment. And if working hours were cut, whose hours would be targeted? It is hard to cut the working time of many professional and salaried workers, because they need to work intensively to stay in touch with technical and social developments. Labouring part-time is not without costs in a system oriented to full-time participation. If it were the working time of manual workers that was cut – and this is the image – anything less than full wage compensation would worsen inequality.

None of this means that cutting time spent in labour is undesirable. Liberation from labour remains a legitimate objective in so far as it is compatible with an increase in personal autonomy, or self-control, and as long as it is accompanied by an improvement in income security. The challenge is to find ways of enabling people to adjust their working time flexibly according to their needs and workstyles, without endangering the survival or dynamic efficiency of firms in which they work.

Bearing these premises in mind, the principle that must underlie any feasible redistributive strategy is that it should enhance personal security and allow a social sharing of the proceeds of technological advance and capital, while promoting a ecologically and socially sustainable rate of economic growth based on adequate incentives to work, save and invest. In the following sections, three complementary policy directions are considered, which together offer a feasible strategy for distributive justice based on the principles and objectives stated earlier.

The Right to Income Security: Citizenship Income

> . . . the plan we are advocating amounts essentially to this: that a certain small income, sufficient for necessaries, should be secured to all, whether they work or not, and that a larger income – as much larger as might be warranted by the total amount of commodities produced – should be given to those who are willing to engage in some work which the community recognises as useful.
>
> (Bertrand Russell, 1918[10])

If one accepts that a Good Society must involve greater self-control, security and good opportunity to pursue occupation, then basic income security would be a necessary condition. The challenge is to find a feasible way of providing this for everybody in society. The idea that everybody should receive a basic citizenship income as a *right* has a long history. Some find it in Thomas More's *Utopia*. It certainly guided Thomas Paine in his *Rights of Man* and explicitly in *Agrarian Justice*. Since then it has attracted philosophers, prominent economists, religious thinkers, and others. It has also had its critics from across the spectrum. In the twentieth century, advocates owe much to Denis Milner, who elaborated a scheme during the First World War, and passed on ideas to James Meade, G.D.H. Cole and other sympathisers. Since the early 1980s, a considerable literature has grown up.[11] Supporters have included those from the political left and from the right.[12]

In a sense, all countries that ratify the United Nations' Universal Declaration of Human Rights are committed to the principle. Article 40 of the Declaration is clear:

> Everyone has the right to a standard of living adequate for the health and well-being of himself and his family, including food, clothing, housing and medical care and the necessary social services, and the right to security in the event of unemployment, sickness, disability, widowhood, old age or other lack of livelihood in circumstances beyond his control.

Others have found their own ethical justification. In the following, the basic proposal is stated, followed by a review of the standard objections and primary advantages. Before turning to the specifics, it is worth recalling Albert Hirschman's perceptive assessment of the reaction to every progressive idea.[13] He observed that there are claims of futility, that is, that it would be ineffectual; of jeopardy, that it would endanger other goals or accomplishments; and of perversity, that is, it would have unintended consequences that would undermine the benefits. This sequence of objections has been the common reaction to proposals that everyone should be provided with a basic income, even among those who vehemently proclaim that poverty should be combated by all means possible.

The long-term objective should be to establish a right to a basic income for every individual, regardless of work status, marital status, age or other income. It would be given as an individual right. It would not require any past or present labour performance, nor would it be made conditional on any labour commitment. The thrust of the idea is to give income security that is not based on class or labouring status but on citizenship. It would give income security based not on judgmental decisions about "deserving" and "undeserving" behaviour or status, merely on the need for, and right to, basic security. However, it would be a modest security, so as to give incentives for work and for sustainable risk-taking.

Before considering the pros and cons, two important caveats should be emphasised. A citizenship income must not be understood as a panacea. It is only part of a distributive strategy that would be consistent with globalisation and flexible product and labour markets. Without other components, it would be ineffectual. And one should think of moving in the direction of citizenship income security, not imagining that such a scheme could be introduced overnight. Only crises such as war or a depression facilitate such a radical shift. We should think of gentler ways forward.

Citizenship is the unifying principle of society, and for real citizenship ordinary people must be able to impose order on chaos, as Norberto Bobbio has put it, which requires that insecurity be limited. To strengthen citizenship is to help in the institutionalisation of tolerance. A citizenship income would be a means of strengthening the sense of citizenship. If social policy is a tool of democracy, as it should be, a citizenship income would help strengthen the democratic basis of society.

One moral justification, with a long and distinguished pedigree, is that we all have an equal right to the inheritance of social progress. Paine, with his *Agrarian Justice*, published in 1797, was one of the earliest proponents of a minimum income as a right of citizenship. This went forward in the welfare proposals in the *Rights of Man*. He argued that property is an acquired not a natural right. His religious argument was that the earth was jointly owned by all, given as a "garden" rather than something to cultivate for a land-owning elite. For Paine, the fruits of property should be shared through entitling everyone to an adequate income.

At the time of Paine, a person doing hard work would have earned about 4 per cent of average real earnings in the USA today, implying that about 96 per cent of the increase in earnings over the two centuries has been attributable to historical inheritance of technological development. Who has the right to the inherited contributions to technological knowledge? Take Bill Gates, with a fortune of $9 billion in 1995, about $20 billion in 1996, over $40 billion in 1997 and $50 billion by March 1998. As someone put it, he made a pebble of a contribution to a Gibraltar of technology. Yet he put the touches to a long process that turned the product into a money-spinner, so that his income has multiplied to such an extent that not only is he the richest person in the world but his income grows almost exponentially. Paine, and his followers, would have regarded it a matter of social justice that everybody should have shared in the fruits of technological progress, particularly as applied to the productivity of land. This is the inheritance justification of citizenship income.

Another moral justification is the claim, which has preoccupied some philosophers, that citizens have a right to equal liberty to pursue their life plans, as long as they do not harm others. Another argument, undeveloped so far, is that the objective of social policy should be equalisation of security and self-control. Without those, there can be no equal basic opportunity, which Rawls and other philosophers have accepted as the basis of social justice.

Another attractive perspective is that it accords to a view of justice that behind a veil of ignorance and through deliberation ordinary people are likely to find reasonable. The difficulty is finding a way of achieving those conditions. One important analysis achieved this.[14] It set out to determine what principle of distributive justice people would support through social laboratory experiments. It put groups of people together behind a veil of ignorance in that they were not informed of the task in advance, were told they would not know where they would be in the spectrum of income distribution, and were requested to decide collectively which principle of distributive justice they supported. They were given four options:

1 setting a floor constraint (an income below which citizens could not go);
2 the Rawlsian Difference Principle (maximising the lowest income);
3 maximising average income;
4 setting a range constraint (a range for individual incomes).

The experiments were carried out across Canada and the USA, and covered people with different backgrounds and values. Overall, 77.8 per cent chose the floor constraint. The choices emerged from deliberation, discussion and the exercise of impartial reasoning induced by the experimental conditions. The floor constraint was the only principle that gained support as discussion proceeded. Note that the institutional arrangement made a difference. In effect, the voice mechanism makes a difference to the choice of a principle of distributive justice. A sensible deduction is that if the institution represents a narrow interest, it would tend to opt for a competitive stance to secure more for its group, whereas a broader association that brought in the community's voices – of the street, the fields and the homes as well as of the factories and offices – would bind round the floor constraint principle *and* the Difference Principle, the latter being more relevant for structural change.[15]

Another finding was that once the veil of ignorance was removed, so that individuals were allowed to opt for whatever principle they wished once they could take account of the fact that they would not be direct beneficiaries of the floor constraint, a majority still opted for that principle. The authors concluded that "the source of the stability seems to be far less individualistic; it seems rather to be the result of the emergence of the social acceptance and bonding engendered in the discussion and choice".

In the light of these considerations, the proposition here is that a basic citizenship income is justifiable on the basis of two principles, subject to three constraints. The first, well-known Equal Opportunity Principle is:

> EOP: Each person should have equal opportunity to pursue a conception of the good life.

The second might be called the Occupational Security Principle:

> OSP: Each individual should have an equal good opportunity to pursue their idea of occupation.

The constraints are what might be called the Non-Harm Constraint, the Sustainability Constraint, and the Incentives Constraint:

> NHC: The rights under EOP and OSP are conditional on the activities not doing harm to the welfare or good opportunity of others.

> SC: The Citizenship Income giving OSP should not impair the sustainable living standards of the community.

> IC: The Citizenship Income should allow for adequate incentives to work, save and invest.

This summarises the rationale for a citizenship income. The criticisms can be split into moral, political and economic. The main moral objection is the claim that people should receive income only if they make a corresponding contribution to society, usually interpreted to mean paid labour. Some deny that a citizenship income would be socially just because it would deny the principle of reciprocity.[16] A lazy person would receive income that would come from income generated by a person who "works" and "contributes" to society. Benefits should be matched by contributions. This they see as linked to the principle of opportunity, which should guide "individual responsibility". As Gutmann and Thompson put it,

> To demand income but to refuse to work is to make a claim on one's fellow citizens that they may reasonably reject.[17]

Leaving aside the questionable words "demand", "refuse" and "claim", consider this proposition dispassionately. Throughout history, society has allowed and legitimised non-reciprocity, and has functioned deliberately on the basis of non-reciprocity. The ancient Greeks had leisure and income and freedom for themselves, rather less for their slaves; feudal societies have rested on landlords and their kin receiving high incomes without conspicuous work from them; capitalism has always existed with a leisured elite, with vicarious consumption by relatives of the affluent (memorably evaluated by Thorsten Veblen), and with inherited wealth and the transfer of valuable gifts that have no relationship whatsoever to the individual "contribution" of the recipient (except in cases connected with age, beauty or some such quality). Gutmann and Thompson, and others taking their position, condemn unconditional income for the poor but are silent on the wider ramifications of applying the supposed principle of reciprocity, particularly to those who inherit wealth or are provided with privileged access to elite schooling. Is there not something unseemly about preaching the reciprocity principle – telling the poor that to be entitled to poverty-level benefits they must meet objectionable obligations – when the top 1 per cent of the citizens are receiving more than the bottom 40 per cent put together, or when the 400 richest people in society have a net worth equal to the combined GNP of India, Bangladesh, Nepal and Sri Lanka, as has been the case in the USA?

If one were to apply the reciprocity principle consistently, one should be drawn to Paine's justification for an unconditional basic income – which may be called the social inheritance principle, that everybody should have an equal share of the economic surplus generated by past generations. This is associated too with Herbert Spencer's argument made in 1851 for a universal endowment derived from each person's right to a fair share of the natural resources (or land). That runs into other difficulties, considered shortly, but it is more distributively just than a policy of requiring the poor to labour in return for a modest benefit while not requiring others to do anything in return for receiving a much higher income.

Gutmann and Thompson's position is also unclear about what counts as "work". A person might believe that for the long-term pursuit of occupation and personal development, a part-time wage job coupled with home-based unpaid work and study, coupled with voluntary community work and caring for dependants, might be beneficial for a while. One suspects that such a course of action would be condemned by the labourist for not making a contribution, ruling out the person from entitlement to an income transfer from the state. If not, then one must accept that any line between what is deemed "work" and what is not will be arbitrary. It is surely preferable to err on the side of liberty rather than on the side of paternalism.

What divides those who support a citizenship income and many of those who oppose it is the labourist bias. On the one side are those who, citing the reciprocity principle, argue that there should be entitlement to income security only based on social insurance (the rest is charity). This means that, except for the incapacitated, only labour counts, so that one only "earns" entitlement if one pays taxes, in the past (pensions), recently (unemployment benefits, etc.) or in the near future (youth labour-force entrants). Non-taxpaying work does not count. On the other side are those who believe that there are many forms of work besides paid labour, and that it is unjust to give income security only to those in jobs. Most of those doing labour could not survive without the unpaid work of carers, most of whom are women. The economic value of such work is enormous.[18] Yet social insurance rests on the premise that such work is worthless and undeserving of income entitlement. Not only housework is excluded from the labourist calculus. There is also the vast amount of social, political and community service work done in all societies.

Thinking about the timing of reciprocity also shows the labourist bias. Implicitly, those who cite the "reciprocity principle" have in mind that anybody wanting a state transfer should labour now in return for income later. On their own terms, there should be nothing to stop the rule being reversed, so that people could receive income now for the promise of labour, or the stated intention to perform labour, later. If one accepts this reversibility rule as inherent to a fair principle of reciprocity, one must deal with the nature of the underlying bargain. Since one cannot foresee all circumstance that might prevent desired behaviour from becoming actual behaviour, labourists might reject the reversibility rule on grounds of uncertainty. Thus, the paternalism would show itself more openly.

A related argument against an unconditional basic income is the following:

> Citizens who decline to work are in effect refusing to participate in a scheme of fair social co-operation that is necessary to sustain any adequate policy of income support. Society's capacity to secure a basic income for needy citizens depends on economic productivity, and economic productivity depends in turn on citizens' willingness to work.[19]

Familiar objections come to mind about the type, timing and amount of "work". In addition, this presumes the existence of a "scheme of fair co-operation", which is debatable. If one accepts that most people are denied self-control, one might question the fairness of whatever "scheme" is supposed to characterise society. If a growing number of people, through no fault of their own, are exposed to unchosen insecurity, then fair social co-operation cannot be strong. In the fragmentation that flexible labour markets and open economies generate, co-operation is weaker than in the solidaristic society presumed at the height of welfare state capitalism. It is also more asymmetrical. While the poor are supposed to labour in dreary jobs, in return for modest conditional protection, elites and others detached at the upper end of the income and status spectrum receive the protection they need to live comfortably and to retain their income and wealth, even if they do not contribute to the "productivity" of the country in which they reside.[20] By contrast, a basic income would in a small way compensate for the economic and technological requirements of an "unfair scheme of economic co-operation".

Gutmann and Thompson argue that if citizens "choose to spend their life surfing at Malibu, they cannot reasonably expect their fellow citizens to support them".[21] Among the responses is that all who live affluently benefit from the work of previous generations, who have created the infrastructure and technology to enable them to live well, so that everybody should have the opportunity to live better through working and earning higher income. Those who receive a basic income might find it impossible to live the multi-dimensional existence of occupational security if they chose to dissipate their youth in surfing or reading books. However, it is not demonstrably true that doing either of these apparently leisurely pursuits is more undeserving and exploitative than working in an office making tea for the boss or doing some other labour activity that presumably counts as "contributing" to society.

Moreover, some of the great contributions to social, artistic and technological progress have come from individuals who have dissipated their
youth or idled away a period of their life. This is not to justify this or
any other lifestyle, merely to question the legitimacy of making any a
priori judgment about what is or is not "deserving". It is to oppose the
paternalistic twitch.

In discussing workfare, we had to confront the issue of "obligations", and
criticised the libertarian view that the poor have specific obligations.
Defining the collective obligations of the state has exercised the minds of
many thinkers. One approach has been to suggest that we (the collective) are
responsible for those who are vulnerable to our actions.[22] Given the
increased technological and social integration of society, people have become
more dependent on, and therefore vulnerable to, the actions of others.
Dependence relations have become more abstract and distant, giving rise to
"secondary responsibilities", which can only be discharged by the welfare
state. If we define vulnerability in terms of socio-economic participation, it
leads to a familiar justification of the welfare state:

> If full participation in our societies is conditional upon a person's being a
> minimally independent agent, then morally we must not only serve the needs of
> those who are dependent upon us but also do what we can to render those
> persons independent. . . . [The welfare state] secures for them the sort of minimal
> independence that is required for them to participate in the other market and
> quasi-market sectors of their society.[23]

Not any more. The drift to selectivity and workfare precludes that. Indeed
the reasoning is a good justification of moving towards basic income security.
It justifies protecting the vulnerable and preventing vulnerability.

Another justice-based argument against the labourist fiction of reciprocity
is that liberty and justice require opportunity for occupation. If the economy
does not provide enough good opportunities, it would be more reasonable to
compensate those denied opportunity rather than to penalise them. Unless
one could be sure that there were adequate good opportunities, some people
must be excluded. Anybody objecting to that reasoning on the grounds that
it is vague should be reminded of the extraordinary vagueness of the claims
of "obligations" and "reciprocity".

There is another justification for the principle of good opportunity. Only
then would there be adequate pressure for the bundle of characteristics of
jobs to change towards opportunity for the pursuit of occupation. If a woman
can refuse to labour for a very low wage in an onerous job in unsociable
hours, such jobs will disappear or their character will be changed or the
wages will rise until some workers find the characteristics attractive enough
to take that type of job. Changing job characteristics into those compatible
with the pursuit of occupation should be an objective, instead of forcing
people to take the unattractive dead-end jobs because of penury. It is part of
the paternalistic twitch to claim that there is "structural unemployment" that
must be rectified by overcoming the "lack of skills", through "training". How

often do politicians, bureaucrats and economists say that jobs must be changed to suit workers' skills and aspirations?

The economic objections to a citizenship income have been that it would be too costly and would undermine the labour market by reducing labour supply. The issue of cost can be answered in several ways. One could refer to priorities, and argue that if the egalitarian principle is accepted the policy should be given sufficiently high priority in the allocation of public resources. Another is to consider the feasibility of converting existing social transfers into a basic income, or a partial basic income with needs-based supplements, keeping tax rates constant. Calculations done in several European countries show that a partial basic income could replace social assistance and insurance-based benefits without having to raise taxes.[24] Such calculations are actually too onerous, since they ignore the potential of altering labour market behaviour favourably. If means-testing and behavioural regulations were reduced, poverty traps, unemployment traps and mobility traps would be reduced, so more people would be encouraged to enter the legitimate economy, generating more tax revenue, through social contributions and taxes. Further cost-saving would come from a reduced need to "police" the poor, reducing the practice of checking to see if they "deserve" income support, so reducing the public cost of a huge administrative service. These issues should be taken into account, as should the cost of the subsidies given to firms to create "jobs" as a means of reducing state transfers.

An ingenious way of approaching the costing issue has been proposed by Philippe Van Parijs, who has argued that the Equal Opportunity Principle implies that each person is entitled to an equal share of external wealth, which can be equated with an unconditional basic income.[25] The external wealth for the tax base for financing a basic income consists of natural resources, private bequests and inheritances and "jobs". His argument for including "jobs" is that they are assets, in that they are in short supply and determine chances of a good life. There will always be involuntary un-employment, because some unemployed would be prepared to work for less than the prevailing wage, which is above the market-clearing level, due to efficiency considerations and turnover costs that firms want to avoid. If there is involuntary unemployment, those in jobs receive an employment rent, which should be included in the tax base for financing a basic income. One might object to the "jobs assets" perspective, in that many jobs are neither chosen nor compatible with occupation. Nevertheless, those who regard jobs as the source of welfare and midfare should accept that a tax on jobs (supposedly a privilege) to compensate those denied the privilege could help to pay for a citizenship income. *If* one accepts that jobs are assets, this reasoning has much to commend it.

Other costing exercises begin by postulating a suitable basic income and then estimating what income tax rate would be required to pay for it. Excellent research has been done in this vein in Ireland.[26] This concluded that a realistic basic income could be financed if the average and marginal rate of income tax were 48 per cent. A former Taoiseach (Prime Minister), Garret FitzGerald, welcomed the findings and concluded that obstacles to

change were political rather than fiscal.[27] In the UK, Meghnad Desai, drawing on work by Holly Sutherland, has estimated that if a citizenship income
were introduced instead of Jobseeker's Allowance (unemployment benefits),
the state pension, Income Support and Family Credit, leaving other state
benefits unaltered, a basic income of £50 a week could be financed with a
standard income tax rate of 35 per cent.[28] Not only is it affordable at this
rate, but it is moderately progressive, in that the primary beneficiaries would
be those households in the bottom decile, with more moderate gains for
those in the next three deciles, while the highest income decile would be the
loser, albeit only moderately.

Two aspects not taken into account in such exercises mean that the costs
are overstated. A citizenship income would save on administrative costs
because it would simplify the complex schemes, make them more transparent and reduce the amount of intrusive enquiry. And it would reduce
poverty and unemployment traps (to be discussed later), thereby inducing
greater labour supply and encouraging those involved in the grey economy
to enter the legal, taxpaying mainstream of society

The cost issue is also related to the view that a citizenship income is an
appropriate redistributive instrument for the era. In many countries, it could
be linked to privatisation. Thus, although it might appear that a basic
income for eastern Europe would be impossible because of the stagnation,
the scope for moving in that direction may exist because social expenditure
is still a high share of GDP, and because there is a windfall gain to be realised
by the state through "privatisation", providing income that could be used to
enable the state to honour a form of social compact.

One criticism is that it would conflict with a minimum wage. Indeed, some
have vehemently opposed the idea because they claim it would lead to less
pressure to secure an adequate minimum wage. But a basic income would
strengthen pressures to raise wages at the lower end of the labour market,
since it would help those exposed to low wages to resist with more strength.
In any case, there is nothing to rule out having a minimum wage *and* a
citizenship income. As for reducing the pressure for a minimum wage, in
recent years there has been rather little pressure, to little effect.

A related argument concerns social insurance, since some commentators
have depicted citizen's income as an alternative to social insurance. There is
no reason for this to be the case, although social insurance in practice has
not been providing protection to the poor and vulnerable. The counter-
argument is that since a basic income would provide modest income security,
it would strengthen their ability to bargain or hold out for more reasonable
wages. A statutory minimum wage will be ineffectual if most of those in
competition at the bottom end of the labour market are so desperate that
they have to take whatever job is offered, unless the regulatory authorities
are more effective than is likely.

A basic income would enable some to take low-paying jobs that were low-
paying because the activity was low-productivity or because the person had
only limited capacity to be productive, perhaps due to age or disability.
Wages should be a labour market issue, concerned with efficiency, incentives,

demand and supply. The only way for wages to be adequately protected is through collective voice in the labour market coupled with sufficient income security to enable people to make choices. In any case, a citizenship income could allow for wage flexibility, if that were required to raise employment or for other reasons, and it was for that reason that just before he died the Nobel Laureate James Meade advocated a basic income coupled with wage flexibility to achieve Full Employment.[29]

Another criticism is one raised by Lawrence Mead. He decried US welfare programmes because they gave benefits without expecting much in return, which he claimed eroded the individual's will, inducing apathy and incompetence, which is why he favoured workfare. His thesis has been criticised on empirical grounds, but it suffers from theoretical shortcomings as well. There is no reason to presume that a transfer giving modest unconditional income would induce apathy and incompetence. Indeed, by giving people more self-confidence derived from a sense of security it may do precisely the opposite.

Another criticism is that "young people might be encouraged to opt for a basic income and to drop out of school prematurely and uncertificated".[30] However, rather than a drawback, this could be an advantage, since it would focus decision-making on the quality of schooling. It would encourage firms to make entry-level jobs more attractive, rather than dull and alienating as so many of the available jobs must be for potential drop-outs from schools. It is paternalistic to presume that people should be discouraged from dropping out of school rather than to make schooling more attractive, and to make it easier for the poor to attend and complete school.

Some supporters of basic income worry about the likelihood of it generating sufficient support to make it politically feasible. Among concerns are the following. People are attached to social insurance; many would fear they would lose from a shift towards a basic income; "loafers", the idle and "surfers" should not be subsidised; tax rates would have to be too high; the change would be too radical to be feasible; and the civil service responsible for administering the existing tax-cum-welfare system would oppose the change because it would threaten its size and security.

Some of these arguments are variants of Hirschmann's predicted reactions to all progressive ideas. The major obstacle is political – politicians and others are reluctant to dispense with the comforting rationalisation of social insurance, that it is a system for matching risks and benefits. They are also reluctant to move away from the superficially appealing idea of "targeting" by means tests. They will continue to resort to the slogan that nobody should receive something for nothing. Partial moves in the direction of a citizen's income are all that one could reasonably expect in the near future. This was recognised by early advocates of the French Revenue Minimum d'Insertion and by those making similar proposals in the Netherlands and elsewhere. But change can be achieved more speedily than many presume. Only a few weeks before the RMI was sprung on a surprised French public during a Presidential election, government advisers and officials were sceptical that such a move was feasible.

Some believe that it would be impractical to shift to a citizenship income because it would be too radical for people to accept. Some proponents respond by talking about stumbling towards a good idea, that it would not be introduced at once, and could be introduced as a partial basic income or by gradually loosening the conditionality for income security. In some respects, tax and benefit reforms in the 1980s and 1990s, such as the US EITC and the UK's Family Credit, have been creating elements for such a system. In Alaska they have launched such a scheme, with remarkable success. And in several industrialising economies, such as Brazil and Argentina, pilot schemes have been introduced that are seen by their advocates as steps towards an unconditional citizenship income. By 2001, in over forty Brazilian cities, mothers of young children were being given a basic income on condition they sent their children to school. Studies showed that this had the quadruple advantage of combating poverty, improving the independence of poor women, combating child labour and increasing school attendance.

One bloc traditionally opposed to the idea is the union movement, as was apparent during the Kreisky Commission hearings in the 1980s. However, unions are changing, and the influx of more women and the growing concern for women's work patterns within unions have begun to change this attitude. For instance, unions in the Netherlands have taken a more constructive attitude to basic income in part because the independent Women's Federation, part of the Dutch Trade Unions (FNV), has been interested, as has the Food Workers' Union, which has supported the proposal.

Another worry, sometimes expressed by supporters of trade unions, is that an unconditional income would sever the solidarity between the employed and those dependent on income transfers from the state. Associated with this is the view that the income differential between those in jobs and the unemployed should be large, so that labour receives a "proper" reward. This is the reaction of those who wish to control workers and reflects a paternalism that is atavistic and inappropriate for the type of flexible economy that is emerging.

A common claim from the political "left" and "right" is that it would subsidise voluntary unemployment. One response is that many work activities other than paid labour are socially valuable and should be legitimised in a civilised society. Another is that involvement in learning, training or recuperation may be just as "productive" in the longer term as labour, for the individual and the community. Above all though, there is evidence that a majority of people want to work, and express the opinion that they would wish to continue to do so even if they had an assured income. In the British Social Attitude Surveys, for instance, three of every four respondents responded positively to the question:

> If without having to work you had what you would regard as a reasonable income, do you think you would still prefer to have a paid job or wouldn't you bother?

Between 1984 and 1993, the proportion responding positively increased.[31] Some have interpreted this as supporting Full Employment while claiming that a basic income would undermine the desire to work. This is inconsistent. In fact, it suggests that a basic income would *not* undermine the desire to work.

The strongest argument in favour of moving towards a basic income is that it would provide a basis for free choice on activity mixes between productive and reproductive activities. If one is optimistic about human aspirations and behaviour, freedom of choice will lead to more skill acquisition and more creative and productive endeavour, rather than "loafing". Basic income security would lessen the tendency to ignore social costs or environmental considerations in the pursuit of employment. There would be less resistance to closure of obsolescent, polluting factories and machinery, often kept going solely to protect costly jobs. Claus Offe has argued that it would also facilitate an ecological critique of unbridled industrialism.

To some, a basic income seems so radical that it is impractical to advocate it. However, in a piecemeal way fiscal and transfer policy has been moving in that direction, particularly with the US EITC and moves toward a negative income tax. The labourist intentions of tax credits or wage subsidies, and their limitations, make them questionable as liberating and redistributive instruments in an era of growing flexibility. However, they have established a fiscal basis for moving towards a citizenship income. Opposition will soften as it is realised that the elements for such a system are taking shape. Tax credits are a negative income tax; the spread of wage subsidies bolsters the low paid. The main remaining condition is labour. Why should those who do low-productivity, low-status jobs receive a tax credit (payment) when those doing voluntary social work, caring and so on do not receive anything?

The main motivations for tax credits have been to induce people to shift from reliance on benefits, or to "make work pay" for low-earning families, and to strengthen the family unit. That still leaves the benefits system dualistic in character, with measures for those out of employment and measures for those in employment. Moving towards a basic income would reduce this dualism.

A citizenship income might also reduce gender inequality. Under existing selective systems, women tend to receive less and have greater difficulty in obtaining entitlement to benefits. An individualised system of citizenship income would remove this inequitable form of gender inequality.

A basic income would strengthen the right to work, while weakening the obligation to labour. It could give substance to the notion to "freely chosen" employment, and both recognise and encourage work-related activities that are socially and personally "useful" without being standard employment. Some advocates of a citizenship income, such as Tony Atkinson, recognise the difficulty of obtaining legitimacy by proposing a participation income guarantee, where in return for a basic income every adult should agree to participate in society.[32] This seems reasonable, although what is intended is suitably broad – paid employment, self-employment, education, training, caring for dependants, old-age or disability retirement and job-seeking unemployment. It would be difficult to define what constitutes social participation without being arbitrary and inequitable. By all means let us express the idea in terms of participation, since it opens up the debate on what constitutes work in flexible twenty-first-century labour markets. It would make it easier to legitimise politically, as long as safeguards favoured liberty and security, rather than paternalism and social control. And the rule should apply to everybody, so that the poor and rich had an obligation to perform community or voluntary work, not just the poor.

With or without a participation component, a basic income could limit the growth of the detached stratum, or "underclass". It would improve social integration by reducing the stigma associated with being "out of employment". It would also give income to those performing types of work other than those counted as labour. Millions of women (mostly) spend much of their lives as carers. Unpaid, they save the state and employers part of their labour costs, in providing a back-up part of social income. If the imputed cost were added to existing social expenditure, the net cost of a basic income would be further reduced.

A citizenship income would also reduce the state's directive role in regulating economic and social behaviour. It would be a blow against bureaucratic paternalism. It would facilitate personal experimentation with work, allowing people more security in which to take risks, and be a defensive measure against any "welfare backlash". The challenge is to find ways of mobilising an alliance of social and economic interests to support this move.

It would also put pressure on enterprises to improve work organisation, because greater income security would strengthen the position of those demanding better working conditions. It would tilt the balance in favour of better conditions, since employers of low-paid labour would be encouraged to improve the attractiveness of jobs, as they would have to attract workers rather than rely on financial necessity.

One reason for favouring an individual citizenship income is the individualisation of economic and social relationships. The share of single-person households has grown almost everywhere. Most welfare state policies have been based on a nuclear family household. Because of social diversity, administration of social policy has become increasingly complex and discretionary. A couple receives less than two individuals, so that there is a moral hazard, giving a premium to those living separately or to those who can appear to be living separately. A household-based welfare system paradoxically encourages single parenting, which incurs extra social expenditure. For instance, in 1997 a single unemployed person in the UK received about £48 per week with an extra £30 for an "adult dependent"(husband or wife). Thus the couple would have been better off by £18 if they had separated.

No other system offers the prospect of removing poverty in flexible labour markets. We have seen that social protection has drifted towards selectivity, more conditions for securing and maintaining entitlement, more conditions applied to the period after entitlement has been established, tighter definitions of categories "at risk", a greater policing character in the application of conditions, greater onus of proof of entitlement placed on potential claimants, more intrusive policing of "scroungers", more scope for discretionary judgments by local officials, more cost or barriers to appeal against disentitlement. If one accepts that this is what has been happening, one should ask whether the existing system is compatible with security, freedom or self-control. It is intrusive, paternalistic, directive and inegalitarian.

Reducing means-tested benefits could also check the growing "illegality" of economic activity. If, as is the case for many people in the late 1990s, the poor can only avoid high taxes by working in informal activities, and if they can retain entitlement to state benefits only through concealment of such activities, then the base of the welfare state will continue to shrink. A citizenship income would be consistent with flexible labour relations, where avoidance of the appearance of income earning is easier, tax evasion more likely, and so on. This is not a marginal issue. A report by the European Commission in 1998 estimated that undeclared jobs accounted for up to 16 per cent of the EU's GNP, and over 20 per cent in some countries. Overall, it may account for over 20 million "jobs" or about 15 per cent of total EU "employment". The bureaucratic instinct is to condemn this as the "black economy" and to try to prevent it.

A CI would reduce the poverty trap and unemployment trap. These are more important in flexible labour markets, in the context of the drift to means-tested transfers, notably those based on the household as the tax-paying, benefit-receiving unit. Means-testing entails high marginal tax rates on the income of the poor, which create poverty traps and so boost the shadow economy. Some economists believe it is better to lower marginal tax rates for high-income earners and raise them for low-income earners because if that reduces the labour supply of the latter, it would not matter much because they have low productivity. This view is unedifying, but one suspects that more mainstream economists subscribe to it than care to admit it.

With conventional means-tested benefits, once a person enters the wage system he loses heavily. If an unemployed worker relying on insurance-based, earnings-related benefits were to take a part-time job, loss of unemployment benefits and means-tested supplements could mean that he would face a "tax" rate of up to 100 per cent or even higher, implying that he would be irrational to take such work. It is to overcome such circumstances that officials resort to the regulatory stick, with workfare, "job refusal" tests for entitlement to benefits, in-work tax credits, and related measures.

There are essentially two alternative options. The first is a negative income tax, conceived by Milton Friedman in 1962, which guided the development of earned-income tax credits. At low earned incomes, the "tax unit" (family) receives an income subsidy, which tapers as earnings rise until it starts to pay tax. This removes the worst of the poverty trap. But it has the drawback of being family-based, being paid after the accounting has been done (so being received after the need has arisen) and only going to those in income-earning activity. A basic income would achieve the same result except that it would avoid those three drawbacks. With this, everybody receives a basic gross income and is taxed proportionately on *all* earned income.

Even a partial basic income must have a liberating effect on labour market behaviour, encouraging mobility, more varied lifestyles, combinations of part-time jobs and own-account work, and periods of training interspersed with partial labour force participation. Whereas advocates of workfare and "active" labour policy speak of integration and obligations, and rely on directive regulations and sanctions against those who do not want the options offered them by kindly employment exchange officials, a citizenship income would rely on incentives and opportunities to strengthen socio-economic integration. Liberty would gain, paternalism lose.

A CI would help transform one outgrowth of the labourist society – the notion that life is split into three parts – school, work, and retirement – and that idleness by those over age 60 is a sensible norm, while idleness at any other age is deplorable (lazy, irresponsible, anti-social). Many older people want to work and are blocked or discouraged from doing so, whereas many younger people would like "to parent" or to study or to idle for a while, but cannot do so for fear of stigmatisation.

One way of moving towards a CI would be through a system of social drawing rights. This would give all citizens a personalised account of entitlements. Individuals could build up their SDRs through participating in school (*n* points for each year attended, perhaps), community work, paid employment, care, voluntary service (overseas or in the local community), which would give them rights to income or leave from work (*sabbaticalisation*). This

---

A Citizenship Credit Card

The desire to cut public spending and improve efficiency has led to social protection targeting, selectivity, rationing of benefits, privatisation, multi-tierism, a shift in the incidence of contributions, user fees and a remonetisation of welfare. The administration of all this is enormously expensive, with much churning of taxes and benefits, with form-filling, a vast amount of paper work and auditing. Meanwhile, electronic technology has created the potential for an *integrated* system, as with the French *Carté Sante*, the German *Versichertenkarten*, and the US Federal Electronic Benefit Transfer Task Force, set up at the initiative of Vice-President Al Gore. This could lead to a citizenship welfare card. Everybody would have individual needs-based entitlements to different social benefits and services on top of a basic amount for their self-determined basic living needs, which they could spend each month as they chose.

Something like this will happen before the twenty-first century is very old. Thoughts about the implications should start sooner. The shift to citizenship welfare will require advisory voice mechanisms, to represent the low-income and ill-informed so that they can make rational decisions. The basic credit must be allied to voice to produce just outcomes.

relates to Gosta Rehn's idea of a *time bank*, although it should also have points for disability, for childbearing, and so on.[111] It would be a form of saving for those earning income, and a form of social income for those not receiving an earned income.

In sum, except for paternalists, and those who believe that society requires inequality or who fear the poor having freedom from labour controls, a citizenship income scheme should have appeal. At this stage, moves towards that ideal should be favoured over moves away from it. Instead of hostility to such moves, more effort should be devoted to finding ways of making that feasible. Perhaps in the end it will be called one of the most basic rights of all.

The great news is that it is no longer a dream of a few unorthodox thinkers. One can see the pieces falling into place, often in spite of the opposition by those making them. Each time in-work benefits are extended, they move tentatively towards a citizenship scheme. The UK's new Working Families Tax Credit does not make sense restricted to "families", and should be extended to childless couples and single people. Once you have done that, and recognising the cost and complexity of operating a conditional, selective system, it should make sense to reduce conditionality and make the system simpler and more transparent. And then you are nearly there.

Distributive Justice through Economic Democracy

Another component of a redistributive strategy in flexible labour markets must be some form of capital and profit sharing, in the spirit of economic democracy. A premise is that income accruing to capital and to those making technological advance has been rising, while the income going to labour is lagging. As noted earlier, taxes on capital are becoming less effective and are being cut as a result of globalisation and other forces. And there is a global trend towards "flexible" pay systems based on individualised profit sharing, profit-related pay, performance-related pay and so on, which widen earnings differentials. Ordinary workers and their families and communities are left behind, as well as the unemployed, flexiworkers and lumpenised elements in society. At the bottom, the design of fiscal policy to "make work pay", through tax credits, amounts to a gesture by comparison with the tax cuts and subsidies that have benefited those high in the income scale.

While the detached are left out of the growth process, economic control is being concentrated in the hands of a few institutions, or even a few individuals. In some countries, private pension fund managers and other financial institutions own most enterprises. Pension funds and insurance companies own over 75 per cent of UK public companies. Control is not so concentrated elsewhere, but the global trend is to more concentration. This has pushed firms to maximise dividends, and fuelled stock markets in New York, London and elsewhere, generating the huge portfolio capital flows. Unless capital dispersion occurs, those financial institutions will continue to redistribute income from stakeholders within firms to outside shareholders.

The response to all this should be a search for ways to achieve at least the equivalent redistribution as in the era of welfare state capitalism, while not undermining investment incentives. Ideally, the policy would also stabilise global capital mobility, which means there would have to be a better balance between short-term profit maximisation and longer-term profitability and dynamic efficiency.

Using a euphemism of the time, the most feasible option for reversing the divisive growth of inequality is to incorporate workers, unions and their communities into the economic mainstream as stakeholders, to enable them to share the surplus with those currently gaining from capital, while enabling all groups to have an effective voice in decisions on work, investment and distribution. This implies some form of profit sharing and corporate governance restructuring.

Research has shown that profit sharing can have beneficial economic effects. Although some profit sharing schemes have been merely a method of facilitating wage flexibility and pooling risks in firms with high wage flexibility, it encourages longer-term investment, rather than dispersion of profits to external principals, shareholders not directly involved in production. It encourages training by firms, boosts productivity, can improve employment, and can improve income distribution. Many benefits can be gained, if the design of the surplus sharing is appropriate.

The majority view among economists on employee ownership has ebbed and flowed, with some contending that it undermines efficiency, others that it soon reverts to standard hierarchical systems, others that it fosters dynamic efficiency and equity. Events have shaped the intellectual climate. For example, the success of United Airlines after its workforce assumed majority ownership in 1994 gave confidence to those who believe it could be part of a redistributive strategy. From being a sick company, United soon outperformed its rivals. Similarly, the spread of Employee Stock Ownership Plans (ESOPs) has enhanced the legitimacy of profit sharing, although these are really a deferred, defined-benefit contributory pension system. Nevertheless, by 1997, about 10 million US workers in 10,000 firms were part owners of their firms through ESOPs.[34] They have encouraged functional flexibility, boosting dynamic efficiency. Some companies have even provided workers with stock in return for concessions on working practices. This might be a positive form of "progression bargaining" or "investment bargaining". It gives a hint of how conventional control functions could be diffused.

The key research findings are the following:

1 Employee ownership coupled with participatory management has advantages over conventional shareholder ownership. In terms of employment and sales growth, the *combination* of participation and employee partial ownership works better than one or other taken alone.

2 To be a mechanism for redistribution, it must be some collective profit sharing, since individual profit sharing accentuates inequality. Profit-sharing in which only top managers receive profit shares not only widens

inequality, but induces managerial caution. Research has indicated that while it is good for top executives to have equity stakes in their company, they may grow excessively cautious if their stakes become too large.

3 Minority employee ownership, as with US ESOPs, is associated with increased stability for firms, making it less likely that firms will go bankrupt, or be taken over and be subject to asset stripping.[35] A growing number of firms put blocks of shares in the hands of their employees as a way of protecting themselves from hostile take-overs. Sizeable shareholding by employees in their own companies is also associated with greater employment stability.

4 Employee shareholding is not more likely than traditional capital–labour relations to induce shirking where labour input is complex.

5 Claims that efficiency is reduced by stakeholder governance, where control rights are shared between workers and shareholders, are unproven. Indeed, there is evidence that it can raise dynamic efficiency. The criticism that employee ownership would induce shirking because of the difficulty of monitoring (known as the 1/n problem) is undermined by the tendency of surplus sharing to induce mutual monitoring by workers, who all stand to lose or gain by each other's efforts. Workers also have an interest in putting pressure on management to be efficient. Governance mechanisms that break down hierarchical management, such as employee-involvement programmes, work better in raising productivity if combined with employee ownership or profit sharing.[36]

6 Stakeholder ownership can promote efficiency by reducing adjustment costs, by making management claims about crises more credible, thus making workers more amenable to compromises, and by making management claims that workers would share in the benefit of changes more credible. Minority employee ownership improves efficiency, restructuring and equity.[37]

7 Economic democracy would promote skill reproduction security, since it would imply that in a downturn for a firm there would be fewer layoffs and more income sharing, so that workers' investment in firm-specific skills would be protected, giving them more incentive to acquire those skills in the first place.[38]

8 Economic democracy would be more effective if statutory or other regulations overcame potential externalities. Unless most firms adopted principles of stakeholderism, the likelihood of free riding and opportunism would be high, so that, for instance, in a recession firms that cut short-term costs by laying off workers might gain competitive advantage over those that did not.[39] This is a case where statutory regulations (perhaps fiscal) would promote dynamic efficiency and equity.

9 To prevent profit-sharing or stakeholder firms from reverting to conventional firms dominated by external blockholder principals (banks, pension funds, etc.), there must be a mechanism for ensuring that all stakeholders have voice regulation over the allocation of economic surplus and the timing of its realisation.

As with citizenship income, conditions for economic democracy are emerging in bits and pieces. "Stakeholder capitalism" and individualised profit sharing, which widen economic inequality, could evolve into collective forms of capital sharing. This is where the literature on corporative governance overlaps with consideration of new forms of labour regulation and social policy. Capital sharing must become broader than company-level profit sharing because decentralised production and flexible labour markets mean that, with company profit sharing, those in high-technology, high-value-added, high-profit firms would accentuate their advantage and relative income security. If only a few high-tech, high-profit firms adopt profit sharing, the result could be greater inequality in society and within the workforce.[40] Flexiworkers, the unemployed and the detached would be left out.

A redistributive strategy will require communal profit sharing, by which some of the profits of firms making profits would go into local social investment and "social security" funds. This should combine incentives to investment and work with tangible forms of redistribution. The surplus sharing system must embrace the intermittently employed flexiworkers and the community around the firm. Among the benefits would be a reduction in income inequalities between those in and out of employment, and a reduction in the social pressures on those not in jobs to play the role of socially responsible citizens. Firms would benefit from an enlarged pool of skilled workers, given increased in-firm training and greater social pressure to make the training available for the community's benefit.

In this, as in so many spheres of social policy, the 1990s was a period of experimentation. We can appreciate what is required, without being able to see the ideal system. This is why it is welcome that an international Federation of Employed Shareholders was established in 1998. One of its primary tasks should be to monitor the numerous experimental stakeholder schemes, and the means by which worker shareholding can benefit communities, firms and workers. An example of communal profit sharing emerging from more traditional institutions was an initiative taken by the St. Petersburg trade union federation. In 1993, it encouraged workers to invest their privatisation vouchers in an investment fund, which was used to invest in enterprises in the region to yield a return for ordinary people *and* to induce the firms to adopt practices that the unions wanted for the benefit of their members. Although scarcely an auspicious case, this was an attempt to combine redistribution with increased voice representation.

One idea, associated with James Meade among others, is to have two types of shares in registered firms, one giving voting rights in control over the firm's decisions, one giving only income-earning rights. An alternative and perhaps more promising route would be to limit the controlling voice of certain types of shareholder to issues of concern to the interest they represent. For example, to ensure the community was taken into account the local authority might have a bloc of shares, which could be used only for voting on spheres affecting community development and the environment, not on allocative decisions within the enterprise. In this spirit, shares belonging to specific stakeholders should be non-tradable, since one purpose would be to ensure continuing voice representation security of different interests.

Communal profit-sharing would strengthen the sense of community and citizenship. The challenge is to give voice to groups that would check winner-takes-all mechanisms. Progressive tax has lost force. Yet unless inequalities are addressed, distributive justice is impossible. A governance structure involving democratic control over the identification, monitoring and allocation of economic surplus could ensure a balance between competing claims. But stakeholder democracy must also incorporate the Difference Principle, meaning that checks would have to prevent powerful combinations from taking most of the profits for themselves. Similarly, if control were concentrated in the hands of any one type of shareholder, that interest might opt for short-term, high-return investment, distributing dividends quickly to a few institutions. This would have adverse consequences for others, including actual and potential workers in the firm and the local community. The challenge is to ensure that all stakeholder groups have a strong voice in governance, and that sustainable investment coexists with sustainable redistribution to insecure workers and the surrounding community.

There is, of course, a strong connection between a basic income and capital sharing. Several people have proposed capital grants for every citizen, derived from the idea proposed to the French Directoire in 1796 by Thomas Paine.[41] One variant would be to give everyone reaching a certain age, say 18, a one-off grant of £10,000, which would enable them to invest in their further schooling, or to invest in a business or acquisition of tools or premises. A strong point about this type of idea is that it offers a "preventive" approach to social protection, rather than merely an *ex post* top-up of income for the poor, which is what social insurance and assistance benefits do at best. However, it may be inequitable between age groups, since if one were to receive the lump sum when investment opportunities were good, one would benefit relative to those who received it in a recession. A flow of income rather than a lump sum would also reduce the risk and consequences of folly, bad luck or simple error.

Firms of the Future: Stakeholding and Good Labour Markets

> The only people who work this hard are people who want to. The only people who want to are people with enough freedom to do the things they want to do. Netscape is a company that consciously undermanages.[42]
>
> (Handy, 1998)

> Today's leaders understand that you have to give up control to get results.[43]
>
> (Waterman, 1994)

What should be the legitimate role of "markets" in a Good Society? They perform the valuable functions of allocative efficiency and information generation. The less attractive features are that they generate unequal outcomes and are based on intrinsically unattractive motivations – greed, fear, insecurity, opportunism, withholding information and obtaining control over others, usually to take advantage of them. Markets are also not good at generating dynamic efficiency. They do not create the incentives to be co-operative and creative, and these are essential for successful firms, economies and societies.

Labour markets function in and around "firms", whose practices help shape society, as well as the production and distribution system. If there is to be distributive justice, firms must be vehicles for it, and must create communities and be communities. They must become places of human development, which is different from places where people are treated as "human resources", an ugly notion.

Good firms should move away from twentieth-century notions of control – whether Tayloristic, bureaucratic or paternalistic. The fad of "re-engineering", and the earlier notion of "human relations" theory associated with the Hawthorne experiment, continued in the tradition of administrative control, inducing people to behave in ways that managers want. A goal should be to break distinctions between controllers and the controlled and to replace them with ideas of partnership, citizenship and stakeholdership. Yet if the firm of the future will replace the language of engineering, control and hierarchy with one of partnership and community, *all* groups in firms must have equal and meaningful voice. If unions have too much power, it might jeopardise the firm's efficiency and profitability. If outside shareholders have too much, they might suck out dividends and turn the firm into a short-term profit-maximising shell. If managements have too much control, they will pay themselves too well, emphasise short-term profit and be opportunistic. If all the preceding have too much power, the outside community could suffer from environmental neglect, other externalities and loss of social income.

The literature on firms and management has been a growth industry in recent years. Debates have raged over the merits and demerits of "shareholder value" and "stakeholder value", "loyalty" and "trust", "social responsibility" and much more. Rare is the management consultant who has not invented several buzz words. Basically it is about repositioning ideas of security, flexibility and dynamic efficiency in the context of a growing range of organisational and management-style options. It is because options are greater that policymakers should wish to identify and promote practices that are compatible with a combination of dynamic efficiency, profitability, extension of human capabilities and distributive justice. Of course, firms exist in local, national and international spaces and labour markets are broader than encompassed by the firm. Practices of a good firm must be complemented by policies and institutions to provide security and flexibility in the surrounding labour market.

Concern about institutional structures has been inadequately addressed by mainstream economics. Supply-side economics gives institutional concerns minimal attention, is hostile towards collective entities, and favours liberalisation and privatisation of economic and social policy. For it, firms exist for one purpose only. As the father of the orthodox approach, the

Nobel Prize winner, Milton Friedman, put it, "The social responsibility of business is to make a profit".[44]

In this reasoning, enterprise performance and adjustment to market forces would be assisted by the removal of regulations, i.e., statutory and institutional mechanisms, notably protective labour regulations, including minimum wages, employment protection, labour codes and unions. This adheres to the Chicago school of law and economics, in which the guiding principle is "Pareto optimality", leading to the view that regulations are justified only if they promote economic growth and if some people gain while nobody loses. The perspective can be summarised as stating that firms should be freed from social responsibilities and should focus on maximising shareholder value. As the consultancy firm Price Waterhouse put it, "The management of a business must have one prime focus: maximising the value of its equity".[45]

In contrast to the Chicago school, the following starts from the Difference Principle that, assuming an institutional framework providing for equality of opportunity and equal liberty, distributive justice improves only if a change in a practice improves the position of the "worst off" or most vulnerable groups. A second principle guiding the analysis is: The powerful need protecting from themselves.

Less abstractly, an alternative to the orthodox perspective is one that looks to regulations, institutions and incentive-structures to encourage human development, while recognising that reasonably flexible markets are essential. The starting point for constructive thinking is the need to create conditions for competition "regulated" to ensure that it is based on competition between strong partners who are simultaneously rivals and co-operative. Such competition must promote equity and dynamic efficiency, which is derived from having rivals that are strong. Managers may not like having strong, well-informed negotiators sitting opposite them, and vice versa. They may not like the prospect of having to sit opposite them again and again. But these conditions are the best because those involved are best placed to know when to compromise and when to press the other side to improve their efficiency and competence. By the same token, societies are dynamic to the extent that their organisations reflect internal pressures to be equitably efficient.[46]

What is a Good Enterprise? The notion of "good" conjures up images of socially decent, which may prompt scepticism from neo-liberals. Accordingly, it must be stated that a good enterprise must be compatible with dynamic efficiency and profitability, for without efficiency it will not be economically viable. The notion also conjures up images of paternalistic corporatism, as does talk of "best practices". Overcoming paternalistic control is essential.

Defining a good firm is not easy. A sweatshop does not contribute to the human development of those required to work in it, and an economy of sweatshops would not do well on human development generally. Nor would working in polluting, dangerous, noisy, hierarchically controlled factories. On this most would agree. Yet what *is* wanted is harder to determine than what is *not*. To make progress, we might construct an ideal type of a firm that would contribute to distributive justice and promote occupational security. Elsewhere an attempt is made to define and measure what is called a Human Development Enterprise (HDE), that is, a type of firm with exemplary practices and mechanisms in terms of the following:

- skill reproduction security,
- social equity,
- work security (health and safety),
- economic equity (income security),
- democracy (representation security).

Human development involves all those dimensions. People need to develop and refine work skills. We need equitable treatment, in which discrimination based on non-changeable human characteristics is a denial of human rights. We need a fair distribution of the income generated by the efforts of workers, managers, employers and those working on their own account. And we need voice in the work process, recognising that absence of democracy there is a denial of democracy in general.

Left out are other dimensions of stakeholder responsibility. A Good Firm is surely one that yields a reasonable return to shareholders and one that does not pollute or have other costly externalities. We will not discuss these issues here, although they should be integrated into the proposed approach, and are part of the new stream of thinking around corporate ethics and socially responsible investment.

It is consistent with other analyses. In 1996, Kleinwort Benson Investment Management launched a "Tomorrow's Company" investment fund and portfolio service, which was to lend to firms that maintain five good relationships – with investors, employees, customers, suppliers and the community. Kleinwort estimated that companies that had done well on these five outperformed the national all-share index over a substantial period. Its managers believe that backward-looking financial measures such as return on assets or profitability do not capture the key issue, and that it is accounting truism that the most profitable time in a firm's life is the period between the moment it stops investing and the moment when it goes bust. Essentially, the investment fund had concluded that broadening the role of companies was compatible with dynamic efficiency. Implicitly, they were also recognising that because of externalities, there would be no automatic tendency for socially responsible firms to predominate without inducements.

The HDE idea is also consistent with proposals such as the "mutual gains" enterprise in the USA.[47] It is also suited to an era of emphasis on incentives to good practice rather than sanctions against bad. If "labour standards" are obligatory and rigid, even those who support them will do so with reservation. Some will pay scant attention to the sins of others in case their own sins, real or imaginary, are exposed to scrutiny. By contrast, rewarding good practices and shining the light on exemplary cases would be in keeping with mature social cultures.

The approach also corresponds to advanced management thinking, epitomised by top companies in the USA and elsewhere. Firms that put the interest of their workers first appear to perform better.[48] And firms that give relatively high priority to "objectives beyond profit" over the long term tend to outperform those that focus more exclusively on profits.[49] There are also positive externalities. Thus, economically democratic firms are likely to promote democratic behaviour outside them. There is evidence that skills learned inside firms improve participation in the wider community.[50] One need not turn this into an ideological battleground. Rather one should seek ways of refining the approach to secure a consensus, and foster communities of economic security, bearing in mind the "network externalities" that would come from firms adopting good employment systems.

So far, empirically, we have applied the HDE to inauspicious cases, in east Asia, eastern Europe and South Africa. It would apply more easily in the USA or western Europe. In the USA, Robert Reich, the former Secretary of Labour, has proposed that firms failing in their "responsibility" to maintain jobs should pay more tax. If that meant using sanctions rather than incentives, one could anticipate opposition and a lack of consensus on promoting good practices that way.

What constitutes an HDE could be decided by negotiation, legislation, or by a combination. The way it has been measured is merely illustrative. In east Asia, indicators were included to measure employment security, i.e., comprising an index to measure whether the firm gave workers employment protection as good as or better than the average. Firms relying on casual, temporary or contract labour to a substantial extent were regarded less favourably than those that gave most of their workers regular employment contracts. If one extended the idea to include elements of *labour market security*, one might give positive value if the firm gave relatively long notice in retrenchments and reasonable redundancy payments, and give value to firms that had "social plans" ready to assist workers affected by structural adjustment or employment cuts.

One reason for emphasising incentives to good practice rather than sanctions against those who do not measure well is that more flexible production systems mean there are many inherently risky small firms on the technological frontier. They tend to have short dynamic lives. For instance, "silicon valley" has thrived in part because small firms have risen and closed quickly, the economy's success being built on their high failure rate.[51] Such "flexible re-cycling" may be an integral part of the future production and labour market process, just as "flexiworkers" and unattached "proficians" (respectively with low-skill and high-skill competencies in varying work statuses) will be part of it. The HDE leaves out such phenomena. This is why it must be complemented by community-level voice mechanisms and income security.

This leads to a challenge for those wishing to promote something like the HDE. It depends on the existence of viable voice mechanisms. In most countries, traditional unionism is on the wane, yet enterprise and economic democracy cannot be envisaged without strong representative organisations.

There is a need to re-examine alternative forms of union, as long as ways can be found to overcome well-known drawbacks and as long as unions can cross sectoral and occupational boundaries in securing members. In south-east Asia, where the HDE idea was first applied, a positive value was given if the union was an independent rather than an enterprise union. For both workers and firms, independent unions had advantages, although enterprise unions were better for workers than no union. The reason for concern about enterprise unions is that they tend to be co-opted, if not set up by management to pre-empt independent unions.

A similar ambivalence exists in the USA about "employee involvement programmes"(EIP), which are an alternative to unions or a means of eroding worker interest in them. Yet enterprise unions and EIPs (or equivalents) are spreading, while craft and industrial unions are shrinking. The old-style "craft" was an ideal of a past age. Now, industrial unions are facing the fate of craft unions, and industrial solidarity is under pressure almost everywhere. Increasingly, loyalties cross craft and sectoral boundaries, and workers identify more with their local community – to the extent that they identify with anything.

For the HDE to be viable, worker representation of some sort is essential. The more representation is autonomous, the more meaningful the voice. We need to identify Voice mechanisms offering the best prospect for democracy. The literature on socially responsible companies has neglected the tendency for "good employers" to turn into "paternalistic employers" and into more Orwellian creatures of 2004. Consider a book on "successful" US companies. *The Economist*, without irony, summarised its main message:

> Successful companies put a huge amount of effort into turning new recruits into company men and women, sending them on in-house training courses (both McDonald's and Walt Disney have their own "universities"), influencing the way they speak and dress,and encouraging them to spend time with other company people. Procter and Gamble, a consumer goods company, ruthlessly rejects applicants who do not conform to the "company type". Wal-Mart, a discount retailer, gets new recruits to raise their right hand and swear to smile at their customers, "so, help me, Sam". Until recently IBM expected its workers to wear white shirts. "Nordies", as the employees of Nordstrom, a retail chain, happily call themselves, start every day with the collective chant: "We want to do it for Nordstrom".[52]

This is not too attractive. It is a powerful argument for independent voice regulation, for economic democracy that can constrain the tendency to go from management to manipulation, from incentives to coercion.

4 Equality of Voice: Reviving Representation Security

For distributive justice, social or collective voice is essential, alongside a system for enhancing individual rights. Basic security is hard to envisage unless the vulnerable in society have their voice to represent them, in challenging alternative knowledge and to bargain on their behalf. Imagine a society in which no organisation was allowed to represent anybody in their dealings with others. The strong would tyrannise through their presence, while the weak would see shadows in everything they did. Imagine the opposite extreme – one big collective body in which all our interests were to be represented. Been there, done that, would mutter a Romanian, Russian or sundry others.

What is required now more than ever before is a system that embeds a structure of voice mechanisms, each of which embody those well-rehearsed values that have entered the vocabulary of governance – democracy, account-ability and transparency – as well as an ability to develop their knowledge, recognising that this is not just a technical matter that can be left to experts. Above all, representative organisations potentially give individuals and groups the opportunity to obtain or retain self-control, via collective security.

For most of the last century, it would have been unremarkable to claim that collective representation is essential for economic security. Trade unions were expected to provide that for the common man (and woman). Early in the twenty-first century, social opinion and workers' opinion are less certain. Loss of faith has much to do with the reasons for the widespread represent-ation insecurity. But the rationale for collective representation remains. What is needed is a structure of governance systems to correspond to globalisation and flexible labour markets, beginning at the international level, in which the voice of workers (in the broadest sense of that term) is strengthened at each level.

In the workplace, among developments seen by some as offering forms of representation security are team-based production and what in the USA are called "employee involvement programs" (EIPs). The former bypasses unions, and leaves workers without effective voice. EIPs are associated with non-union firms, their drawback being that they leave hierarchical power relations unchanged.[53] Management set up channels for workers to express concerns, but procedures for making complaints scarcely protect workers in non-union plants.[54] By themselves, EIPs do not offer representation security.

Some US analysts have sought the ideal in independent local unions (ILU). Those were established in the wake of the Wagner Act, which made it an unfair labour practice for an employer to dominate, interfere with, or provide financial assistance to a union. Difficulties include their financial *vulnerability*, and a tendency to suffer from the "golden handcuffs" technique of management. They are relatively democratic because their officials come from a smaller community. But they may have insufficient clout to force themselves into boardrooms to shape corporate strategy. ILUs have also been compared unfavourably with industrial unions, on the grounds that the latter desire to take wages and standards out of the sphere of "competition" by standardising them in an industry or occupation. But industrial unions cannot do that any more, for with globalisation and flexibility, they cannot set effective rules on labour practices.

The erosion of representation security provided by unions and neo-corporatist structures prompts consideration of what type of voice institution

could emerge for flexible labour markets. Some analysts argue that globalisation requires "global solutions" and "global identities". This is too abstract.
What is required is something closer to what Benedict Anderson has called
"imagined communities", beyond notions of class or state.[55] But they must
be real, in holding groups together. The need for institutional security
means that forms of collective bodies suitable for flexible labour systems
must evolve to replace old forms that cannot provide the individual forms of
security needed or other aspects of distributive justice. For this, a network of
citizenship associations must give voice to all those faced by insecurity.

To be effective, voice regulation must be based on incorporating those on
the margins of the labour market and on the margins of society. They too
must be part of the shadow of the future. They must be given voice in the
institutions of labour market regulation and social policy, and they must be
taken into account in regulatory and redistributive decisions. Today's insiders
must understand that in flexible systems tomorrow they may be outsiders.
What this means, in short, is that in the emerging flexible economies, multi-
partite structures must displace atavistic institutions better suited to early
industrial society.

Mancur Olsen, among others, captured a crucial point in asserting that
dynamically efficient societies require a series of social bargains, since for
legitimacy a competitive market economy depends on social co-operation.[56]
Arthur Okun famously stated that there was an "invisible handshake" in
society alongside Adam Smith's "invisible hand" in market transactions.
Unfortunately, in the era of market regulation and globalisation, the imagery
of handshakes is rather less credible than in the previous era, largely because
of the social detachment and fragmentation.

Of all forms of labour security, the most crucial are representation and
income security. The only way of reversing the insecurity and socio-economic
fragmentation is that statutory regulation, increasingly unprotective and
directive, must be buttressed by stronger voice regulation. Representation
security implies that participants in the labour market must have a secure
capacity to bargain and to influence the character of work, to have a strong
voice to ensure that distributive justice is pursued. Without that, all forms of
labour security will be jeopardised.

With the welfare state presumption of a closed economy gone, and downward pressure on social income increasingly global, there has been an effort
to revive the Keynesian idea of a social clause in international trade, as part
of WTO rules. One core standard would be freedom of association, the
objective being to limit "unfair competition". Ruling elites in developing
countries are opposed to a social clause, while employer organisations are
scarcely enthusiastic. The prospects of unions resisting the pressure of
beggar-my-neighbour competitiveness arguments are not promising. But it is
essential to convince employer representatives everywhere of the Polanyian
imperative that it is in the interest of economic stability to establish an
international framework of social decency, with scope for scrutinising those
abusing their position. That is part of the process of re-embedding the
economy in society.

In some industrialised countries, there may be resistance to regulation competitiveness. The European Union has been trying to develop a minimum framework of "good employment practices" for member countries. The European Trade Union Institute has been pushing for consultative works councils and employee participation schemes for all companies, giving impetus to resistance to use of differential regulations. And some national unions are forging international links that cater for labour mobility. For instance, the UK's GMB signed a membership agreement with IG Chemie in Germany to enable their respective members to enjoy union rights in each other's country.

These are signs of adaptation and new strategy. Nevertheless, the need is for greater voice regulation of labour market relations. Representation security must be the basis of any strategy for distributive justice, and the form should foster dynamic efficiency and a trend towards economic equality. However, unions have limited experience of bargaining to enable workers to obtain capital, which should be a priority, and they have difficulty responding to flexible labour systems.

Industrial unions are inappropriate in flexible labour markets in which a growing proportion of workers have no long-term commitment to specific industries or large occupational groups. Craft unions have long been weak, and in some countries shrinking industrial unions have been merging into big general unions. But this would increase the alienation of unions from actual and potential members, who understandably equate bigness with bureaucracy and social distance.

The one form to show resurgence is the company union, due to the fact that it has been the main form in east Asia, notably in Japan, the Republic of Korea and Malaysia. It has spread to Chile and Mexico, and is spreading in Europe. "Company unions" rose to prominence in the USA in the 1920s, as a paternalistic ('welfare capitalism') alternative to the struggle between anti-union employers and national unionism. The New Deal temporarily resolved the conflict by ushering in the era of statutory regulation, by favouring "tripartism" and welfare state policies. Since then, company unions have had a bad name in American industrial relations. Yet in the 1990s, in the wake of the AFL-CIO's institutional weakness, pro-union advocates reconsidered company unions, notably in the 1994 Dunlop Commission Report.

In a survey carried out for that Commission, over half the workers had no workplace representation, and while 63 per cent said that they would like to have more influence in workplace decisions, few workers wanted a union – 48 per cent of blue-collar workers, against 38 per cent who did not want one.[57] In manufacturing, 47 per cent said they would not vote to join a union. Yet most workers favoured a type of employee organisation to give them more influence in the workplace. This led the Commission to recommend that workplace non-union employee participation schemes should be legalised to cover production issues, product quality, safety, health, training and dispute resolution "as long as they do not allow for the rebirth of company unions".

There is debate on the relative effectiveness and impact of industrial and enterprise unions. Evidence from Japan and east Asia suggests that enterprise unions achieve less for wages than industrial unions but are more successful in promoting employment security for their members. It is awkward for critics that economies with enterprise unions have been dynamic, have promoted functional flexibility and have had favourable employment records. It also seems that enterprise unions do provide scope for voice regulation, at least at the workplace.

These interpretations should not be construed as a recommendation for enterprise unions. Their limitations are that they are likely to be little more than instruments of management, thus justifying pejorative epithets such as "pet unions", and are likely to favour "insiders" over "outsiders" to a greater degree than industrial unions, encouraging current members' employment and income security by fostering the dualistic character of employment that has characterised Japanese enterprises. Even in Japan, enterprise unions have not appealed to flexiworkers.

So, while industrial unions have declining appeal and effectiveness, enterprise unions merely promote functional flexibility and employment security for core workers. The scope for representation security in flexible labour markets appears bleak. One can see what is needed – institutions that can resist pressures of co-option, promote dynamic efficiency and have a redistributive effect beyond the confines of individual firms. Are there any germs of hope?

Well, perhaps. It lies in the emergence of all those quasi-representative "non-government organisations", in what has been called a "global associational revolution".[58] These do constitute a transforming phenomenon, and more of them are taking on global form, with "international" in their titles. Although they are often romanticised as "organs of civil society" and "social stakeholders", they do contain the potential for a progressively radical role. In terms of flexible labour relations, what is needed is a movement that brings together bodies representing local groups of employed and those at the margin of the labour force to bargain over distributional, security and production issues.

What might be called community unions or citizenship associations could be the most effective way forward if distributive justice is to be pursued. Traditional unions must recognise that their long-term representative capacity will depend on their appeal to flexiworkers and those on the labour force margins. Only if they organise workers of all types in communities will they be able to put effective pressure on local networks of firms.[59] The agenda of community unions would differ from that of enterprise unions, giving higher priority to social income issues, including environmental protection and shared entitlement to benefits by those in regular and non-regular employment, and from industrial unions, in that they would give less emphasis to money wages relative to other components of the social income.

Community unions would offer a better prospect than others of promoting democratically exemplary practices within firms, because they would comprise a wider coalition of workers. They should also develop a governance role in rapidly growing employment agencies, where they could limit the potentially adverse effects and strengthen the potentially beneficial effects of the flexible employment that they offer. In this respect it is moderately encouraging that in the USA, there have been attempts (e.g., in Baltimore and New York) to organise the new workfare labour force, to try to limit substitution effects and secure equal wages and benefits for workfare placements.

In this vein, the *Jobs With Justice* (JWJ) movement in the USA tried to foster ties between trade unionists and community, senior citizen, student, consumer, environmental and religious organisations, creating a national network of workers' and social rights activists.[60] Set up in 1987, it grew on principles of reciprocity – everyone joining having to promise to participate in others' struggle for rights at least five times a year. Based on local coalitions, the JWJ was determined to remain an informal movement, uniting interests of workers and those working for other interests. Although it seems to have gone into decline, it may have been a harbinger of citizenship associations. Among others are worker advocacy groups such as Working Today in New York and Working Partnerships in Silicon Valley, trying to represent the interests of flexiworkers. They also included substantial organisations in some developing countries, such as the SEWA in India, which has about 300,000 women members doing "informal" work of one kind or another.

Several terms are jostling for attention to describe these new forms of representation, such as social movement unionism and associational unionism.[61] Perhaps ideal would be one that conveys links between worker interests and those of the local community, and that stresses the sense of citizenship solidarity. Whatever they are called, associations combining the functions of representing people as workers, as consumers and as citizens could overcome a dilemma highlighted by Cole long ago, when he commented that "a person requires as many forms of representation as he has distinct organisable interests or points of view".[62]

The idea of multiple forms of representation, coupled with multiple forms of stakeholder in firms, relates to the multi-tierism of social protection. The emerging structure of firms is dispersing power and control across quasi-autonomous units, reducing direct control. The hollowing-out of enterprises and shrinking of "head offices" encourage partnership rather than hierarchy. The forms of representation will have to match the inherent flexibility of those developments.

Community unions would offer the best prospect for creating that vital factor in redistributive justice – the shadow of the future. For effective representation, those facing each other over the metaphorical bargaining tables must have the strong prospect of having to deal with each other again and again for the foreseeable future.

Union-type organisations could also play a role as employment agencies, or as "employee mutuals", independently or in combination with commercial firms, giving workers voice representation in what should be non-profit organisations. The mutuals could offer training courses, perhaps sub-contracted to specialist agencies, and could offer employment services to workers according to their aspirations and skills. This would be compatible with external labour flexibility and the inability of traditional unions to cover flexiworkers effectively.

Before the era of welfare state capitalism, unions in some industrial economies strengthened job security by controlling labour supply. Often, they controlled job content through apprenticeship schemes that they helped to design and regulate. As corporations became large, oriented to securing a loyal labour force, they took over these functions. Now, with firms outsourcing and downsizing, splintering and "re-engineering", those functions may pass to market institutions and agencies. Probably these will be profit-making bodies. But it is an opportunity for representative associations to emerge, not just lobbying for protective regulations but trying to control the labour supply and conditions of employment.

A pivotal role in flexible labour markets will be played by intermediary agencies linking firms with workers. Only if workers' represesntatives are part of the governance of such intermediaries will their interests be enhanced. In this context, it is significant that middle management is being squeezed, and to some extent are being replaced by external intermediary controllers, public and private agencies. Voice representation in both could be a countervailing power. Similarly, Voice is needed in all institutions of social protection. Given their awesome economic power, pension fund managers should be required to have a governance structure that gives real Voice to all interests. It is not sufficient that firms should subscribe to codes of good practice. This issue came up in the US debate on what to do with the trust fund of the social security system. If the trust fund could invest in equities, it was likely to be subject to political manipulation. This led to defensive proposals to set up an independent board to oversee bidding by firms to manage the fund's investments. This would not be enough because the Voice of all interests should be involved, before and after managers are chosen.

Voice and the New Controllers

The desired character of voice mechanisms can be appreciated by considering labour market trends. The employment function is becoming more indirect, with intermediaries being labour controllers. Governments are cutting direct provision, integrating social and labour market policies and privatising social service delivery. In the USA, companies are taking over the functions of determining recipients of state transfers, delivering them and integrating welfare beneficiaries into jobs.

Integrating social protection and employment policy increases the paternalistic character and control function of both. This is what is happening, so that the labour market is changing from employer–worker to employer–agency–worker, where the agency may be a public or private employment agency. There may be one intermediary or several. Whose interests do they serve? If the caseworker acts as mediator with employers, landlords and others, the person becomes dependent on the caseworker's skill and attitude. The intermediary is a new form of labour market intervention, and is subject to all the usual principal–agent dilemmas.

A case is America Works, a firm that places welfare participants in jobs and gives supporting services. It may be a valuable firm. But it is partial controller, partial representative of the participant. The locus of trust and loyalty shifts to the agency-worker relationship. The agency is supposed to be a job-seeking service, a job-retention service, a social worker, job-training adviser, and perhaps something else as well. It is also a commercial operation, and understandably would want to place workers in any job and put pressure on its "placements" to remain in jobs even if they did not like them and wished to leave. There is a structural conflict of interest. Only organisations representing jobseekers and workers could resolve this.

Privatisation of employment services will accelerate the evolution of the "profession" of employment agent, something like an estate (or real estate) agent. This involves a heady mixture of psychology, social policy with knowledge of benefit systems, social work, training, community health, counselling, para-legal service and personnel practice. It is not clear whose interests such a profession represents. But already, as befits a "profession", there have been claims that only those licensed to do so should be allowed to practise.

There are commercial and political pressures to emphasise their role as paternalistic controller, as part of the workfare agenda, making them agents to maximise job placement rates. There is the countervailing public service function. But the clients most likely to influence employment agents will be potential employers, particularly if firms pay for their services. To complicate the incentive structure further, government authorities may push them to maximise placement and job retention rates, and offer subsidies and grants to encourage that. If so, employment agents will become part of the labour control system, even though many taking up the profession will be intent on providing a public service and have impeccable values. The market pressures are just too unbalanced. To counter this, public authorities should regulate the governance of employment services and ensure voice regulation by those who use them. Only then could the paternalism and opportunistic treatment of vulnerable clients be combated.

Unions have also begun to participate in the privatisation of social policy and develop as commercial entities in competition with private firms. As aspiring service agencies, some have started to provide free life insurance, legal services, car insurance, discount travel, discount car hire, credit cards and household insurance. In the Netherlands, the major trade union federation has been issuing Traveller's Aid and Shopper's Advantage cards. In the USA, similar practices have spread.[63] In the UK, the stakeholder pension has been a factor arresting the unions' decline in membership.

Unions are almost becoming individualistic insurance-oriented mechanisms for selective protection, and promoting consumption. This may attract and retain members, but it must remain peripheral to the objective of being a powerful voice for promoting occupational security and distributive justice. The voice of workers and those on the margins of labour must be incorporated in the design and delivery of social protection – or re-incorporated in some countries. This could be a feature of new pension systems. Such avenues might strengthen the workers' voice, as long as the voice of all groups is incorporated, including those on the margins of society.

Presuming that for some time selective social protection will continue to be provided by complex formulae and systems of entitlement based on intrusive work tests, means tests and the like, community-level associations could give voice to those dependent on the good will of government officials or their private agents. They could dispense aid and advice, just as unions traditionally did so. But there is another role citizenship associations could play. Representative associations shape how people formulate and adhere to principles of distributive justice. If they bring together people from "many walks of life" and allow all strata to be heard, deliberative democracy may generate support for universal basic social and economic rights. A lesson from the justice experiments cited earlier was that group deliberation strengthened support for the floor constraint (effectively, a basic income). Groups foster deliberation around competing knowledge, and in the process can induce a sense of social solidarity. And surely in communal associations notions of deserving and undeserving would soon yield to the perception of the basic similarity of the human condition.

Privatisation of benefits and services has encouraged civil society organisations to fill gaps left by receding governments, just as the restructuring of enterprise benefits towards more polarised systems does so. But the model of civil society being encouraged risks turning representative interests into regulatory interests, in part through a spread of a "contract culture", whereby what are nominally charities receive money from government in return for taking responsibility for certain social tasks.

It is claimed that NGOs have a comparative advantage in making transfers to the poor, because they have better information, more local contacts, lower administrative costs, and are less likely to be corrupt.[64] But the evidence is mixed, since many have flourished as rent-seeking devices, documented in both industrialised and developing countries. We lack a vocabulary for what has been happening, although a typology along the following lines could characterise the multitude of NGOs:

- ANGOs – These are the Altruistic NGOs, the ideal type, in which those involved are highly motivated by morality or concern at a threat to a particular interest. These NGOs are those we admire, filling a void in caring for or representing people or social causes such as the environment. They are instruments for social solidarity as well as for human and natural development.
- GRINGOs – Government-dependent NGOs. These may also start as ANGOs, but become profit-making bodies through taking and becoming dependent on government contracts, in some cases becoming quasi-civil servants, at less cost to the government and with less accountability.
- BINGOs – Business-dependent NGOs. These are bodies which, however they start, become largely dependent on grants, contracts or donations from business corporations, which in turn are often intent on deflecting criticism or on appearing as "good corporate citizens".
- PINGOs – The type of NGO that is almost entirely dependent on a well-endowed Philanthropist, often being merely an expression of vanity.

- PONGOs – Political NGOs. These are basically political front organisations posturing as worthy social bodies.
- LINGOs – Labour-based NGOs, typically derived from a trade union organisation, providing services to members. ("If you can't beat them, join them").
- FANGOs – Foreign-aid dependent NGOs. These are organisations offering services, mostly in developing countries, for which they seek foreign-aid funds, often ending up importing systems and practices from a specific donor.
- WANGOs – World Bank-dependent NGOs. These may not start as dependent on grants from or projects with the World Bank, but once involved become dependent on such funds in order to operate and maintain staff. Unwittingly or otherwise, they may become delivery services for Bank policies. They have flourished in developing countries and in eastern Europe, in particular.
- MINGOs – These are Mafioso-type NGOs, which have also flourished in a few countries.
- RINGOs – These are religious NGOs or "faith-based organisations" which some governments see as the type to be encouraged as a mechanism for delivering social policy. They eagerly take money from government agencies, and in return provide conditional aid, usually with a light or heavy dose of proselytising.
- ENGOs – Evangelical NGOs, the type that is not just religious but is operating to extend membership and conversion to its particular creed. They run local social services in some countries, openly linking access to benefits to membership, and often control local politics.
- INGOs – These are the men, or less commonly women, whom one might meet in a train station or in a business lounge of an airport, who, when asked what they do, say, "I am an NGO".

One is being only mildly facetious, because the moral hazards of the global associational revolution are too great for comfort. Vested interests can play on the emerging "contract culture", so that NGOs soon become dependent on funds from governments, from the World Bank or some other financial agency, or from a large corporation intent on being "socially responsible", or from corporate or individual philanthropists with their own hobby-horse to ride. These boides do not give the basic security that comes from rights. The immoral hazards as well as the moral ones are too big for comfort. What is required is basic security based on some notion of community, not the family, because of its fragile state, but democratic civic associations.

We have made few references to discrimination and disadvantage in labour markets. These thrive on fear and insecurity. Socio-economic detachment and fragmentation encourage selectivity of social and labour policy that is discriminatory. Basic income security would enable the vulnerable to oppose those who use discrimination as a mechanism of control. Strengthening voice regulation through communal organisations could also do so. The efficacy of quotas and paternalistic statutory regulations is fading. No doubt they will continue, but they are less effectve and more stigmatising in flexible labour markets because they can be circumvented or used in distortionary ways. Individuals must have rights, and the wherewithal to pursue them if discrimination and group-based disadvantage is to be tackled.

In all of this, there is need to accommodate differences, value diversity, and dissolve differences. Preventing discrimination does not amount to treating everybody alike, as so many labourist policies and statutory procedures have done, in effect if not in intention. Recognising and facilitating diversity of needs and aspirations is essential if a flexible economic system and labour market is to be based on security. The just forms of security are those that undermine discrimination by strengthening fraternity and a sense of community.

5 Concluding Reflections

A Good Society will ensure that everybody has sufficient security to enable them to have a decent existence and pursue their sense of occupation. Distributive justice is about the distribution of security just as much as about the distribution of income and the balance of control and freedom. The security that is required is a combination of basic income security, without which there is no real freedom to make rational choices and without which survival is jeopardised, and strong voice representational security, for without voice the vulnerable will always be in danger of losing their income and other freedoms.

The failing of the dominant development models of the twentieth century was the primacy given to labour market security. Yet beyond basic income and voice security, what is ultimately required is occupational security, the good opportunity to pursue creative work in developing one's competencies. It is to this that we turn in the final chapter.

10

Reviving Work and Occupation

1 Introduction

We have made a mess of work by making an ideal of labour. Most people want to work, yet most have to labour. The distinction between work and labour is crucial, since making labour the fulcrum of twentieth century societies led to the new paternalism at the end of it.

All societies legitimise some forms of work and not others. The twentieth century was unique in romanticising wage labour and employment. Its main ideologies portrayed "the worker" as someone, usually a man, who received a "pay packet" and whose interests needed to be protected. The welfare state and state socialism were built on labour. And conventional statistics portrayed work by means of the labour force approach, which was introduced in the 1930s in response to the political needs of the Depression and the Keynesian focus on open unemployment. In this final chapter, an attempt is made to shift the focus to work and occupation.

2 The Labour Force Approach

Although most countries lacked figures, the twentieth century began with the world being mapped by statistics conforming to the labour status approach. Albeit crudely, the figures found in censuses and other surveys were suited to a perspective in which class was the main prism, and in which the social and detailed division of labour was presumed to be easy to portray. The population was disaggregated by main usual labour status, not current activity. The idea of identifying "gainful workers" not only concealed most women from sensible classifications, but meant there was no measure of unemployment or employment. It was this latter deficiency that undermined the approach in the 1930s, leading to what became the labour force approach, which soon became legitimised around the world.

This approach, with its neat division of the adult population into employed, unemployed and "economically inactive", always distorted the picture of work in society, and everybody with any knowledge of labour statistics knows that several arbitrary decisions are taken in dividing the population into those "in the labour force" and those out of it. The approach is deeply sexist, yet the schema has persisted with only minor revisions and only muted opposition.

It is inappropriate for developing countries, yet policymakers, donors and statisticians have eagerly exported it to those countries, sometimes as a sign of modernity. It is inappropriate for flexible labour systems, yet dissatisfaction has not yet led to reform. Everywhere, the images it sets up, or perpetuates, encourage a distortion of labour and social policy. Above all, it is oriented to a labourist social protection system. If you are doing an activity that counts as labour force work, you will be given entitlement to state benefits (or more of them); if not, you will probably be disentitled to them.

The labour force approach must be reformed. To appreciate the most glaring deficiencies, consider the three meanings of the term "labour force". For statisticians, it means "the economically active population", which means those doing or seeking (or in some variants of the term, wanting) income-earning activity. For economists, it typically means the proportion of the population that is supplying labour. In popular language, the labour force is the employed, those actually labouring, so that those only wishing to do so, the unemployed, are excluded from the picture.

Often the meanings are mixed up, and the rationale of inclusion or exclusion is unclear. For instance, a landlord may be included in the first notion, if he does 'economic activity' collecting his rents; he is unlikely to be included in the available labour supply, and would not be included in the third notion. Similarly, with the first meaning, ambiguities arise from trying to define "economic" and "non-economic". And whereas labour supply is a flow, the labour force is treated as a stock by statisticians. This has led to confusion. In making refinements to the simple concepts over the years, statisticians have introduced criteria that relate more to labour supply, that is, a flow of labour, which can be measured validly only in terms of some opportunity income. For example, with a measure of the labour force that includes people who declare themselves "available for work", it is not clear what this work would be. You may be available for $1,000 a week but not for $200, to be Prime Minister but not a sewage worker.

A difference between the labour force approach and the other notions is that they are closer to earlier traditions. The Physiocrats, early demographers and classical economists all had conceptualisations closer to it than to the labour force approach. In different ways, they distinguished the "productive labour" force from the "non-productive". For the Physiocrats, only agricultural producers were productive, whereas for political economists adhering to the labour theory of value, productive labour was that intending to yield a surplus for accumulation. Some twentieth-century extensions of the productive–unproductive distinction attempted to separate "reproductive labour", that is, work done to reproduce labour power, which may generate surplus. This approach has minority appeal nowadays. The "gainful worker" approach was also closer to the second notion of labour force than to the statisticians' current approach, since it tried to identify those in specified work statuses.

The conventional notion of labour force was a child of Keynesian economics, and the concern to measure unemployment. It makes no distinction between productive and unproductive labour, excludes some activities because they do not generate an income, and excludes some income-earning activities on an arbitrary, moralistic basis. It is "sexist". It excludes housework, done mainly by women. This has been widely criticised and poorly rationalised over the years. But what is the basis for excluding a prostitute or gangster from the labour force? The formal definitions of economic activity cannot be used to justify such exclusions.

Figure 10.1 presents a version of the labour force approach. The terms in capital letters are not usual features of labour force statistics. The main point is to recall the way of thinking and the edifice involved. The approach begins by dividing the population into the adult "working age" population and the rest; this is purely a convention. Those in the working age are divided into "active" and "inactive", though many inactive are "discouraged" or "potential" labour force participants. Then the active are divided into employed and unemployed, and the "employed" into self-employed, employers, wage workers and unpaid (family) workers. One might suppose that the unemployed should be divided into groups according to availability for specific work statuses, but they are not; the work status categories are over-simplifications.

The difficulties are partly "aggregative", partly conceptual. Taking the "population at risk" as the point of departure, at each stage of the dis-aggregation arbitrary decisions must be made to complement conceptual

Figure 10.1. Modified labour force approach (abbreviated)

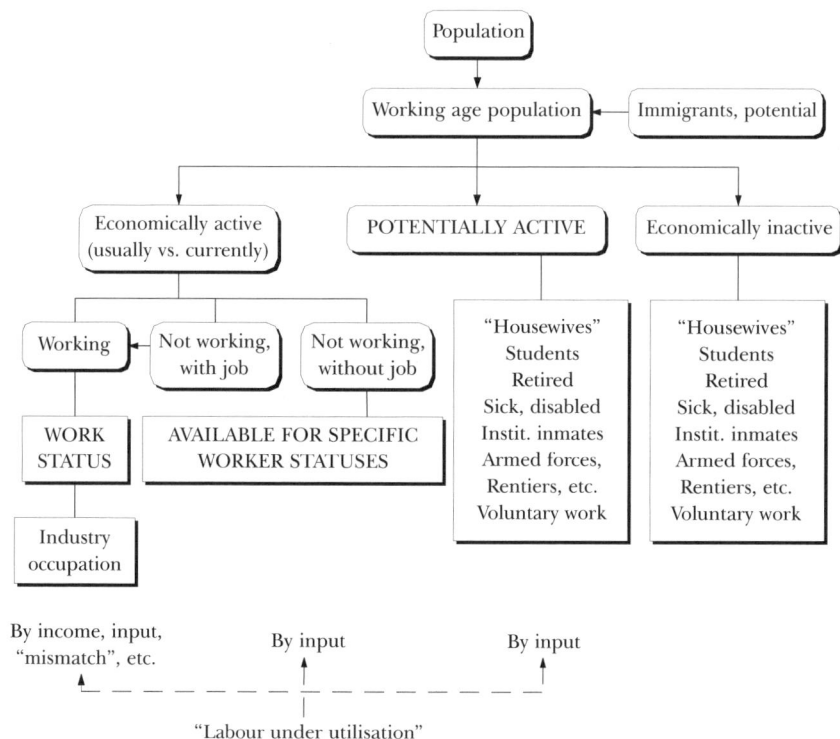

decisions. Thus, a proportion of the population at risk is excluded from "working age population" but is "economically active" in reality. To give just one example: the conventional retirement age in some countries is 60; those employed above that age are counted as employed, but if they lose their job and search for another, they may be excluded from unemployment and the labour force.

Some of the economically active, such as many migrants, are not included in the population at risk. Some with a labour status but not working may be included as employed (such as those on "lay-off"), others excluded. Then, there are problems of category "priority", with multiple statuses and so on. Should someone cleaning shoes for two hours a week and searching for employment for 38 hours be called employed or unemployed? Normally, he would be classified as employed. This is a statistical convenience, no more.

It is an *ad hoc* edifice, however neat its formal presentation. In its defence, it gives an image of reality useful for policymaking and those who wish to give a broad-brush picture. However, its deficiencies are substantial for low-income countries, for flexible labour systems and for social structures that do not correspond to the model of society that prevailed in the mid-twentieth century. It is reasonable only for societies based on male full-time industrial labour. That is why the "gainful worker" approach prevailed before, based on occupational status and social class.

In many countries, including state socialist and developing countries, some economists have claimed there is no labour market. Yet, almost all countries have been collecting supposedly internationally comparable labour statistics. In numerous reports and books, the percentage employment rate in a central African country, for example, is presented alongside the percentage employment rate in the USA or Germany. The unemployment rate is shown as lower in a middle-eastern country than in France, lower in Ukraine than in neighbouring Hungary. Most economists and commentators seem content with such data. They convey an image, and if there is unease about comparability, it is usually reserved to concern over measurement differences. Some observers criticise the concepts, but usually criticisms are relegated to footnotes to show the points are noted. Then everyone goes on much as before.

The statistical representation of labour and work needs to be overhauled. If occupation and flexible lifestyles are to become the focus of concern, a synthesis of the gainful worker and labour force approaches is needed. Just as the former was disembedded from the twentieth century concern for the labouring man, so the labour force approach is disembedded from a society in which informal work, multiple statuses, occupational diversity and flexible lifestyles predominate.

3 Work versus Labour

Most people want to work, by being creative, active, caring for those they love, and helping others whether altruistically or in the expectation that they will be helped when they need help. The human being wants to build, to make and to understand. Above all, we use work to become, to extend ourselves. The motivation comes from our conscious and unconscious drives, from our culture and from our history.

Before we go further down that familiar track, consider the notion of labour. It rather than work became the fulcrum for policies and political rhetoric throughout the twentieth century, and it is labour that led to the state paternalism that was sweeping the world as the new century began. Etymologically, the roots of the word labour are negative. It is derived from the Latin (*labor*), implying toil, distress and trouble. *Laborare* meant to do heavy, onerous activity, and medieval use of *labeur* was associated with agricultural activity, typically with a plough. The French word for to labour, *travailler*, is derived from the Latin *trepateiare*, meaning to torture with a nasty instrument. And the Greek word for labour, *ponos*, signified pain and effort, and has the same root to the word for poverty, *penia*.

With that in mind, reflect again on the twentieth century, when "labour" was put on a pedestal. The word had both a unifying and a divisive effect. Historically, it bound together a seemingly growing swathe of society opposed to the wealthy – labour versus capital. Labour was both an activity and a body of people, essentially made up of men. This romanticised image was linked to the notion of the working class, a term of affection for many people, a badge of pride for progressive intellectuals, populists, social democratic politicians and Marxist parties and movements. But romanticized labour was corrosive of a vision of a good society based on real freedom, autonomy, creativity, work, self-respect, dignity and societal health.

Labouring has always been associated with onerous activity. Economists have recognised that, referring to disutility of effort involved in labour. Perversely, social democrats have extolled the desirability of increasing the number of adults in labour – "We demand Full Employment!" – and have pushed for shorter working weeks and days, i.e., less labour. The second demand recognises that labour is not desirable *per se*, the first signally fails to do so and weakens resistance to the argument that, within reason, whatever is required to achieve Full Employment is justified, including erosion of rights at work, less economic security and acceptance that "bosses" could organise production as they see fit to maximise the number of "jobs", as long as they kept within modestly defined bounds of decency.

By contrast with labour, work may be defined as activity combining creative, conceptual and analytical thinking and use of manual aptitudes – the *vita activa* of human existence. There are respectable reasons for not placing either work or labour as the primary human activity, and for reserving primacy for reflection or contemplation.[1] Yet contemplation is part of great work, implicit in creativity. It gives a balance to the functions of work, strengthening and developing human personality, as well as fulfilling more immediate needs.

Work involves an individual element and a social element, an interaction with objects – raw materials, tools, 'inputs', etc. – and an interaction with people and institutions. The degree of creativity in work may be small or at a level of "genius". Work may or may not produce "goods" or "services", or objects of "use value", although one could define it as "productive work" if the intention were to produce such an outcome. Each of the words in inverted commas raise important semantic and philosophical issues.

The notion of work encompasses four meanings. Work is an activity, a series of linked actions. It is also a conscious use of effort, mental and physical, to achieve some typically predetermined objective. A "piece of work" is also the outcome of some activity, that is, it is an inactive object. And we also refer to an artistic achievement as a "great work". It is this multiple use that makes it hard to use, but which shows its richness and goal orientation.

4 Employment

What of the notion of employment? In the twentieth century this word became a loose cannon, along with its much used opposite "unemployment". When did employment become so precious? In the nineteenth century, to be "in employment" was a term, if not of abuse, at least of regret. It was a term showing that one belonged to a dependent status. Employment is a profoundly class-based term. It became important as the middle class became a large part of the population. In a feudal system or in any peasant-based society, the term is almost meaningless. In the early phases of industrialisation, the working class had labour, only wanting employment when having nothing else to which to turn. Only the "labour aristocracy" had occupation, a sense of career. The *bourgeoisie* had "capital", the *petite bourgeoisie* had their shops and their trades.

As industrialisation and the social and detailed division of labour progressed, notably with more service jobs, the notion of employment became more prominent. It was quintessentially a twentieth-century notion. Although population censuses had been conducted for several centuries, it was only in the 1930s that attempts were made to conceptualise and measure the level of employment, and with it the unemployment rate. This means society has only felt the need to know about employment for about two-thirds of a century. The point is not trivial, because employment became a defining "need" of the century of the labouring man. Industrial capitalism sucked in labour, and became organised in ways that put a premium on labour stability. For the working class, labour evolved into employment. For a minority it had long done so, but early in the twentieth century the probability of prolonged employment grew.

Employment is also used with several meanings. For many analysts, it only covers activity entailing the expectation of a wage for tasks performed. This is coupled with use of such terms as "self-employment" or "own-account work", defined as work for profit, income or family gain. Debates over what should count as employment have raged for over a hundred years. Alfred Marshall's celebrated point that if he hired a woman as a domestic servant national income would increase, whereas if he married her it would go down, is only one of several quandaries that have bedevilled the term. In the end, statistical practices have been based largely on convention and concern over "unemployment", as discussed later.

Is employment a "basic need"? It would surely not be in a society of absolute abundance, or in one in which material needs were modest, *or* in one where wage labour was unimportant. Surely employment *qua* labour cannot be construed as a basic human need. Maximising employment as "Full Employment" may have an instrumental rationale, but most economists presume that maximising employment is desirable in its own right. This is at best unproven, at worst a source of injustice.

A peculiarity of employment is that it covers all forms of labour but not all forms of work. It strangely excludes certain types of work that contribute to human welfare and development, whereas it includes some activities that are unproductive or that do not contribute significantly to either. Most analysts recognise this, then continue with their analyses as if it did not matter. A way of interpreting this schizophrenia is that they feel that trying to solve the ambiguity would be too complex. Consider an example. If you do voluntary work caring for the elderly in your community, that does not count as employment. If I offer to pay you a commission to sell clothes to the elderly and you fail to sell anything, you are likely to be counted as employed. This does not make much sense.

Popular defences of the desirability of employment cite some of the following:

1 Employment is a form of social participation.
2 Employment contributes to social integration.
3 Employment enables individuals to be integrated into society, and is increasingly important because other traditional institutions, such as the church and family, are being eroded as social institutions.
4 Employment is economically necessary to sustain the welfare state.[2]

It is not clear that employment is the best way to achieve social participation or social integration. It is not difficult to imagine types of employment that would reduce an individual's prospect of desirable social participation or integration. As for economic necessity, this cannot apply if governments choose to operate with high unemployment, or if the employment generates little or no output, or if the output is so polluting that the social cost exceeds the benefits. And why should employment be so much more desirable than other forms of work, such as domestic work, childcare or community work done on a voluntary or personal basis?

It is worth reflecting on use of the terms work, labour and employment in international statements and conventions. In the passage from the UN Declaration of Human Rights cited in the next section, one notices that the right to work slips into language of "employment" and "unemployment". All the key words raise questions about definition and realism. Consider too Article 6 of the *International Covenant on Economic, Social and Cultural Rights*, the first Article dealing with specific rights:

1. The States Parties to the present Covenant recognize the right to work, which includes the right of everyone to the opportunity to gain his living by work which he freely chooses or accepts, and will take appropriate steps to safeguard this right.

2. The steps to be taken by a State Party to the present Covenant to achieve the full realisation of this right shall include technical and vocational guidance and training programmes, policies and techniques to achieve steady economic, social and cultural development and full and productive employment under conditions safeguarding fundamental political and economic freedoms to the individual."

The ILO's Constitution states that one of the Organisation's purposes is to promote policies to achieve

(a) full employment and the raising of standards of living;

(b) the employment of workers in the occupations in which they can have the satisfaction of giving the fullest measure of their skill and attainments and make their greatest contribution to the common well-being;

(c) the provision, as a means to the attainment of this end and under adequate guarantees for all concerned, of facilities for training and the transfer of labour, including migration for employment and settlement;

These worthy sentiments reflect the mood of an era when labour market trade-offs were not fully understood. It seems from this and related documents that "the right to work" is interpreted as "opportunities for employment", or "productive employment". The right could be interpreted to mean there must be both opportunities and no barriers to obtaining them. This seems the essence of the ILO's Employment Policy Convention No. 122 of 1964, which defined the objectives of active policy:

The said policy shall aim at ensuring that –

(a) there is work for all who are available for and seeking work;

(b) such work is as productive as possible;

(c) there is freedom of choice of employment.

It is significant that this Convention came into existence at the height of faith in "Full Employment", Keynesian economics and the "welfare state". It states that countries ratifying it should pursue an "active policy" to achieve "full, productive and freely chosen employment". All the words in inverted commas can be interpreted with some latitude, without doing injustice to the stated objectives. This does not mean one should reject the Convention's heuristic value, since it may be regarded as setting monitoring standards for evaluations. But one must admit that the Convention is hard to apply or define consistently. In the 1960s, a European country operating with 8 per cent unemployment would have been seen as failing to satisfy the *Convention;* in the new century, such a judgment would be less likely, which would not be a matter of cynicism or "real politics". In any case, one should be cautious about making the maximisation of employment the overriding objective.

5 Jobs

Like labour and employment, "jobs" are not compatible with the positive idea of work. If one focuses on "more jobs" or on valuing the number of jobs as some desirable social goal, the same distorting prism as is involved with labour comes to bear on our thinking, debates and policy formulation. The etymological roots of the word "job" give the game away. A job was long known as a limited and limiting set of activities, of limited duration with limited development or application of technical skills. "Jobbing" has connotations of casual labour. One still speaks in English of "doing odd jobs", highlighting the instrumentality of the tasks and the lack of a long-term. "Job work" was traditionally a term denoting labour of a low-level type. If you think we should maximise the number of jobs in society, you implicitly condemn us to be a society of jobholders.

You may protest that this is not so, but if you idealise labour and jobs you set up a mind set: We must do what is necessary to maximise the number of jobs and the available amount of labour, and must ensure that those capable of doing and needing to do labour are in jobs. This accentuates the undervaluing of other forms of activity or work that human beings have undertaken throughout history. Work that does not have exchange value is disregarded. Work that has use value but not exchange value is given lower status, less protection and lower income, if given any at all.

Coupled with the twentieth-century distortion of labour, there was an idealisation of "jobs". Most people in most societies have been obliged to labour in narrow jobs that give them little scope for imagination or development of their competencies. Jobs are always dead end. What we need to do is rescue the idea of occupation, where this means development and refinement of competencies in a "career" of working. A job is what one does, an occupation is what one has become or is becoming.

6 The Right to Work

> Everyone has the right to work, to free choice of employment, to just and favourable conditions of work and to protection against unemployment.
> (United Nations Declaration on Human Rights)

The problematic character of that resounding acclamation of 1948 is such that at the outset of the twenty-first century it would not be put forward. A great theme throughout history has been the place of work in the life of a citizen. Alongside debates on what constitutes work, and what types of work are appropriate, has been a rhetorical discourse on the right to work. It has been a source of ambiguity and political nervousness.

The term is traced to Charles Fourier in the early nineteenth century, derived from the French Declaration of the Rights of Man and the Citizen of 1789. Fourier fumed that "politics extol the rights of man and do not guarantee the prime and only useful right, the right to work". It took De Tocqueville to see the implications of granting such a right, and it is worth quoting what he wrote since he captured themes that have echoed through-out the succeeding century and a half:

> To grant every man in particular the general, absolute and incontrovertible right to work necessarily leads to one of the following consequences: Either the State will undertake to give to all workers applying to it the employment they lack, and will then gradually be drawn into industry, to become the industrial entrepreneur that is omnipresent, the only one that cannot refuse work and the one that will normally have to dictate the least task; it will inevitably be led to become the principal, and soon, as it were, the sole industrial entrepreneur. . . . Now that is communism.
>
> If, on the contrary, the State wishes . . . to provide employment to all the workers who seek it, not from its own hands and by its own resources, but to see to it that they always find work with private employers, it will inevitably be led to try to regulate industry. . . . It will have to ensure that there is no unemployment, which means that it will have to see that workers are so distributed that they do not compete with each other, that it will have to regulate wages, slow down production at one time and speed it up at another, in a word, that it will have to become the great and only organiser of labour. . . . What do we see? Socialism.[3]

This concern about its implications has bedevilled the debate ever since. But there has also been philosophical and political dispute whether the "right to work" *is* a right. Thus, at the height of the French debate in the mid-nineteenth century, a scarcely noticed Karl Marx was writing dismissively that under capitalism the right to work was "an absurdity, a miserable pious wish".[4]

There has always been a paternalistic element in the promotion of the right to employment or work. It figured in the Speenhamland system in England (1785–1834), in the Declaration of the Rights of Man, in the Prussian Civil Code of 1794, and in successive episodes during the nine-teenth and twentieth centuries. The state's obligation to create labour for its poor has been a continuing theme, derived from a mix of political con-science, paternalism, fear and desire for control. Putting the poor in labour, usually for as little as the state could pay as possible, has been a way of achieving several social and economic objectives. It has been a way of disciplining the poor, as well as others whose wayward behaviour might lead them to fall into similar circumstances. The right to labour reached one of its cruellest nadirs in the late nineteenth century when it was used to justify the onerous conditions of the workhouse in Britain, when only the most desper-ate and destitute accepted the labour offered by the state. In the twentieth century, communist and fascist states found ways of transforming the right to work into an obligation to labour.

There has been a more benign side of this too. Liberals have consistently presented the right to employment as a human right with liberating properties. A powerful influence has been the Roman Catholic Church, the leadership of which has dealt with it in several encyclicals, each of which coincided with socio-political crises. The famous *Rerum Novarum* (referred to as *The Condition of Labour*) was written in 1891 when Europe was faced by an economic crisis and a growing socialist challenge. The Pope, Leo XIII, was a progressive paternalist, cautiously supporting workers' rights. This has continued in his successors. Thus, Pope Pius XII claimed in 1941, in the midst of the Second World War, that labour was a right and a duty of every human being. In 1963, Pope John XXIII asserted that employment was a natural right in his *Pacem in Terris*, and in 1981 Pope John Paul II issued the *Laborem Exercens* (Performing Work) encyclical reiterating the right. His document ten years later, *Centesimus Annus* (The Hundredth Year), issued to celebrate the centenary of *Rerum Novarum,* was more circumspect. It supported labour market policies, but undercut the right to work by concluding that "the state could not directly ensure the right to work of all its citizens unless it controlled every aspect of economic life and restricted the free initiative of individuals."[5]

Besides the mix of morality and paternalism epitomised by Catholic agonising, the political demand for the right to work was strengthened by the Depression, and by the Keynesian revolution, a message of which seemed to be that the state could ensure that everybody who wanted a job could have one. The Second World War boosted this perspective; returning combatants did not want to go back to the dole queue.

Since then, difficulties of giving substance to the right to work have shaped international positions. The right was asserted in the UN's Universal Declaration of Human Rights of 1948, the Organisation of American States' Declaration of Rights and Duties of Man of 1948, the Council of Europe's European Social Charter of 1961, the International Covenant on Economic, Social and Cultural Rights of 1966, and the Organisation of African Unity's African (Banjul) Charter on Human and People's Rights of 1981. The ILO's *Employment Convention* No. 122, which, although not asserting the right to work, was in the same tradition. As the 1983 International Labour Conference's Employment Committee stated,

> "The promotion of full, productive and freely chosen employment provided for in the Employment Policy Convention and Recommendation, 1964, should be regarded as the means of achieving in practice the realisation of the right to work."[6]

In spite of the Declaration of Human Rights and its successors, few industrialised countries have entrenched the right to work in their constitutions, exceptions being Norway, Portugal and Spain.[7] Where it has been asserted it has been matched by an Article asserting the duty to work as well. The regimes most forceful in promoting the right to employment were the communist bloc, which took state paternalism to its extreme. Constitutions of communist states guaranteed the right to employment, and their policies amounted to the view that if citizens did not labour they were "parasitic" (a widely used term), since the status of unemployment was abolished. Some other states plunged in this direction.

There have been several intellectual defences of the right to work – the natural rights perspective, the legal positivist case, and the human development right perspective. The natural rights case has been most associated with Roman Catholicism, although some philosophers have also made a defence along those lines.[8] Siegel concluded that the natural rights case is strong because of the "identity" and "reputation" of its supporters.[9] This is scarcely adequate. The legal positivists' case rests on the existence of a body of international covenants and Declarations, to which lawyers can refer. What these amount to is hard to determine, but the direction seems to be towards a right to fair and equal treatment with respect to employment, to equal protection and non-discrimination, rather than a right to employment *per se*. They have dealt mostly with issues of security. In any case, the legal positivists have had little chance to draw on national legislation, since few countries have legalised anything like a right to employment.

This leaves the development rights' theorists, who have many issues to resolve before they make a strong case. It is here where the slippage between work, labour, job and employment has been crucial. Some philosophers claim there is a "human right to self-respect".[10] But while absence of work may undermine self-respect, it is another matter to deduce that this means everybody should have the right to a job. One supporter of the right to work drew on Rawls' *Theory of Justice*, which emphasised self-respect and minimal standards while giving priority on liberty, and took the argument to its logical conclusion:

> The justification for a universal right to employment would lie, in this view, in the fact that because of class interests and various group prejudices any non-universal distribution of employment opportunities will be unfair to the disadvantaged classes and minorities. Hence the only fair distribution available is one that guarantees each person a job.[11]

One would have to go further, since not every job is equally attractive or "fair". Indeed the word "available" merely highlights that in reality no such option arises. What type of "job" would be "guaranteed", and with what income? And what if a person refused the kind guarantee?

Suppose full-time jobs were scarce, that they have value for those holding or wanting them, and that everybody had an equal right to a job. Then, suppose you work 60 hours a week baking and selling bread, and as a result I cannot sell any. One option would be to insist that you work only 30 hours a week, to enable me to do the same. This option, widely canvassed in one form or another, prompts unease, for economic reasons but mainly because it interferes with liberty.

Another option is to suggest that full-time jobs should be taxed to provide compensation to those who do not have them, as a matter of social justice.[12] To this a libertarian might retort that justice does not require that, since everyone is free to compete for the scarce jobs. But this is not true, since people have different endowments. Another retort is that, as long as market rigidities were removed, imbalance would be corrected by declines in the wage until the market cleared. But this may be prevented by a wage floor, defining "subsistence" or "efficiency". If the market cannot clear or if the government is compelled to operate with high unemployment, then a job scarcity tax has more appeal. However, taxing jobs as a distributive device in response to initial injustice would be counter-productive if a tax merely led to a further cut in the supply of scarce asset (jobs), especially if it offended the Difference Principle by hitting the worst-off. To avoid this pitfall, and the consequences, one could consider compensating those without the scarce asset.

This argument may seem esoteric. For our purposes, suffice it to assert that those who feel there is a right to work should have an ethically acceptable and feasible response to the argument, *if* they equate jobs with work.

A more basic dilemma arises from the difficulty of defining the right to work. Do I, as someone ignorant of the skills, have the same right to be a surgeon as someone who has passed exams in surgery? This would offend common sense. Do I have the same right to work in IBM as someone already employed there? What we mean, minimally, is that everybody should have an equal opportunity to learn the skills required.

Another problem arises from that fact that for most of the twentieth century the right was seen as a state-guaranteed right to employment, implying an *obligation* that could not be binding because from an individual's viewpoint, it could not be enforceable. In what way, then, is it a right?

Because of these difficulties, it has become common to define the right to work in indirect terms, i.e., that there should be no barriers, legal or institutional, blocking people from applying for and obtaining paid forms of employment, as there were in the past.[13] But this reduces it to sophistry.

In his classic definition of civil rights, T.H. Marshall stated that "in the economic field the basic civil right is the right to work", but he qualified this by stating that it entails "the right to follow the occupation of one's own choice in the place of one's choice, subject only to the legitimate demands for preliminary technical training."[14] He too saw the right to work as derived from the seventeenth century when guilds, local regulations and apprenticeship systems restricted access to certain occupations. He then argued there was an *obligation* to work, a classic slip into labourism.

This sense of the right to work is a negative one. Some thinkers have gone further, claiming there is no such right at all. For Ralf Dahrendorf, it cannot exist because "no judge can force employers to hire unemployed people".[15] More than that, there surely cannot be a right to do something unless there is a corresponding right not to do it. As he argued,

> In terms of liberty, it is more important to establish a right not to work, so that governments cannot force people into a dependency [from] which they want to escape.[16]

Dahrendorf was concerned with citizenship rights, and he differentiated between these, which are unconditional, and matters belonging to private contracts:

> Citizenship is a social contract, generally valid for all members; work is a private
> contract . . . when the general rights of citizenship are made dependent on
> people entering into private relations of employment, these lose their private and
> fundamentally voluntary character.[17]

He argued that this became a form of "forced labour". He followed
Marshall in believing that citizenship does entail "general obligations". To be
a good citizen may mean providing "community service". This raises ethical
problems, which are left aside for the moment. One may also reflect, in
passing, that most commentators have asserted the right to work without
making any attempt to define what they mean or to justify the assertion.

One could retreat, accepting it as the negative right, in the sense that
social and economic policy cannot be justifiable if it *deliberately restricts any
individual's opportunity to choose work relative to others' opportunity*. This is stated
in this manner to preclude the situation in which a government operates a
macro-economic policy that knowingly raises unemployment. The implications are profound for evaluating recent social and labour market policies.

The right to work should be analogous to other "rights", if it is a right.
Consider the right to vote in a democracy. To most people, it means that
not only do you have a right to vote for whom you wish but that if you do
not like the available options, you can exercise the right not to vote.
Similarly, it is a funny sort of right if one had to vote or if there were only
one candidate, especially if his dastardly deeds were well known. If one
were to apply this reasoning consistently to liberty, there must be a
meaningful choice. A right to do something can only exist if there is the
right not to do it. Oddly enough, while politicians and analysts speak much
about the right to work, they are loath to admit the right not to work, and
much has been done to emphasise the obligation to labour, notably in
social security systems. Indeed, whereas in modern societies there is a right
to vote and not an obligation, with work there is no practical right, but
there is an obligation to labour. This asymmetry should cause more unease
than it appears to do.

As strange is the obligation to take jobs when there is unemployment,
i.e., when under the "musical chairs' principle" x per cent of people must
fail. An obligation that cannot be met by everybody, even if they wished to
satisfy it, is manifestly unjust. Some advocates of the right to work have
argued pragmatically that there should be an obligation to labour because
that would oblige governments to be concerned to promote employment.
But this could easily lead them to care less about income security, which is
scarcely desirable.

Another difficulty is that most jobs involve labour where a private "bargain"
is made between people in unequal power relations. To put it in basics: What
sort of right is it to be able to doff your cap and say, "Sir"? No assessment of
protective regulations can overcome such situations, although they may
ameliorate them.

The failure to differentiate between labour and work has been matched by
a failure to differentiate them in statements about the right to work. What is

so laudable in creating circumstances in which a man will work in a sewage plant for twenty years or risk life and limb crawling along a rock face? Why should we wish to maximise labour? Surely, a vision of humanity has been escape from labour. This has had many advocates, including Paul Lafargue, Marx's son-in-law, whose *The Right to Laziness* was kept out of debates within the labour movement because of its emphasis on liberty. Bertrand Russell's *In Praise of Idleness* and Ivan Illich's *The Right to Useful Unemployment* and other writings were also in that tradition.

Then, of course, we have the alleged link between the right to work and social inclusion or integration. Consider the following confident statement, from a respected social scientist, echoing many comparable statements:

> It is by having paid work (more particularly, work for a wage) that we belong to the public sphere, acquiring a social existence and a social identity (that is, a "profession") and are part of a network of relations and exchanges in which we are measured against other people and are granted certain rights over them in exchange for the duties we have towards them.[18]

If this were true, it would imply that someone who is "self-employed" or doing voluntary or domestic work is less in the "social sphere" and has a diminished existence and identity compared with a wage labourer in a factory or on a construction site. It would imply that everybody paid a wage had a "profession", and that a woman working as a maid acquires rights over other people.

These are not minor points. Most people in employment, one dares to suggest, would be inclined to think they would be able to "belong to the public sphere" more effectively outside their job. Imagine the woman hunched over the lathe, the man chiselling away at the rock face deep underground, and wonder at the idealisation of employment. This is not the same as saying that work could not enrich one's existence or be a means of defining oneself. But idealising wage labour is dubious because it leads to a distorted policy perspective.

Now consider the claim that there is an obligation to work, or a duty to do so. Leaving aside views associated with Catholicism, the main arguments can be considered by drawing on the "working perspectives" programme of the Netherlands Scientific Council for Government Policy. There are four contentions:

> (i) Paid employment enables people to enter social networks and thereby contribute to the integration of society. If people are not in jobs, other institutions would be required to generate social integration. Since other institutions for achieving social integration have been declining (family, church, etc.), employment is increasingly important for social integration.

This prompts some questions. Is integration actually desirable or meaningful? Is it feasible through employment? If certain institutions are becoming less capable of integrating people into society, does it follow that jobs should be held responsible for fulfilling this function? Does it mean that employment would be better than other alternatives for "social integration"? If those institutions are failing, does that mean there should be a duty to join churches or form families, at pain of condemnation or sanctions if one did not?

These questions have never been answered satisfactorily. The integration imperative looks suspiciously like a justification for control. As Dahrendorf put it,

> Worried neo-conservatives join forces with bewildered socialists in extolling the virtues of hard work when neither have enough employment to offer to all. They are really talking about social and political control, for which no other mechanism than the discipline of employment has been found.[19]

Although this is a polemical way of posing the issue, the unresolved issues undermine the claim that desire for social integration implies a duty to take paid jobs.

> (ii) High labour force participation is necessary as the economic condition for a sustainable welfare state. Without that, society would not be able to afford the social rights offered by the welfare state.

Even if one accepted that a high participation rate were desirable, there is no reason for regarding that as justification for imposing an obligation on individuals to raise it. And if there were high unemployment, raising the participation rate might raise unemployment or be unnecessary unless it boosted economic growth and raised employment. But in any case the premise is unproven, since there are means of affording a "sustainable welfare state", including measures to raise the labour force participation of the idle wealthy.

> (iii) An individual has an obligation to work to match the state's obligation to provide conditions for such work, through training facilities, childcare, etc.

It is not clear what the individual's obligation means, or why the state has such an obligation. One may suppose that it is because it should enhance rights. But if so, it would be to promote equal opportunities, and there is no justification for converting opportunities into obligations. Moreover, if the state has such an obligation, it is far from clear that it is honoured.

> (iv) An individual has the duty to take employment because of what Marshall stated was "the general obligation to live the life of a good citizen, giving such service as one can to promote the welfare of the community."[20]

This is related to the first contention. It prompts the same questions. It can also be criticised for assuming that wage employment is the only means of promoting welfare. Community service and forms of unpaid work may do that just as well, while there can be no presumption that all wage employment does promote social welfare.

The issue of obligation to work was discussed in assessing the powerful trend to *workfare*. The conclusion is that neither the right nor the obligation to work are easily demonstrated, and that in practice proponents of the right to work have actually had in mind the right to labour, and implicitly or explicitly the obligation to labour. For real freedom, the emphasis should be on how to enable people to escape from labourism, and on how to be able to work.

7 The Pursuit of Occupational Security

I am a journeyman. I try to carve it a little better each night.
(Sir John Gielgud, actor)

The character of men depends more on their occupation than on teaching we can give them.
(John Ruskin, 1880)

So work should be more clearly juxtaposed with labour, jobs and employment. In the positive idea of work, we think of the link between imagination and action, creativity in the mind and in the hands. It is the combination of conception, conceiving product and process – from the timid fumblings of childhood to the intellectual force of an Einstein or a Leonardo da Vinci, and through the humdrum musings of most of us and the gentle reflections of elderly sages – and the execution of effort toward predetermined ends. It entails pride in the process, a satisfaction in the attainment, and acknowledgement from one's closest and dearest.

We define ourselves by our occupation, a word that has a double sense in the English language – meaning taking possession of a piece of territory (the earlier meaning of the word) and also a set of related activities learned or refined through a career, meaning the development of skills, competencies and capacities through learning, the application of effort and the experience of work. The set of tasks may be small, the learning career may be short or long. Yet an occupation has always implied a niche in the production process. Occupations cannot exist outside society, but by having occupation one belongs to society. By contrast, a jobholder is a consumer who obtains income needed to continue to consume. Someone with a sense of occupation intuitively understands the craft ethic, not the instrumentality ethic of labour.

A "job" is a humbler word, conveying a set of tasks that might or might not be combined into an occupation. Often, it has had a pejorative meaning attached to it, implying a lack of permanency, a lack of accumulated wisdom and skill. Usually, it conveys a task or short period of employment. "Job work" is another term for "piece work". A job is what one does, an occupation is what one is. Unlike a job, an occupation conveys impressions of status as well as complexity of activity. As Raymond Williams noted,

Career now implies continuity if not necessarily promotion or advancement, yet the distinction between a career and a job only partly depends on this and is associated also with class distinctions between different kinds of work.[21]

One may still think of an occupation as a calling. The term stems from a social division of labour in which the detailed division of labour was relatively undeveloped, when apprentices were introduced to the mystery of the craft. In intention at least, occupation refers to the positive sense of work, as creative activity, the combination of intellectual and manual activities – conception and execution – in the context of progressive refinement of individual competencies.

In considering the distinction between occupation and job, note that there is no statistical representation of the occupational distribution of the population in any country. Statistics giving the "occupational structure" actually give the "job distribution" of employment. Thus, a person who perceives his occupation as a gardener who is currently working as a postman is classified as a postman. Someone may have a doctorate in economics, but if working as a secretary is counted under "secretarial". Suppose doctors were paid low wages, as a result of which many took up higher-paying labouring jobs. Vacancy rates might suggest there is a "shortage" of doctors and – if unemployment were high – "structural unemployment". But all they show is that there are vacancies, which may be due to doctors preferring other jobs or an insufficient number of doctors. We may know something about the distribution of jobs, but not about the occupational capacities of the population.

In distinguishing between occupation and jobs, one can hypothesise that the detailed division of labour has undermined the basis of occupation over a wide range of employment, and created conditions in which a large proportion of people are in jobs. Usually when a new occupation is created it represents an extension of the detailed division of labour. In antiquity, a person could be a carpenter and farmer, a blacksmith and fisherman. Such occupational multiplicity is still common in agrarian and industrialising economies. Using conventional statistics to allocate a person to one "occupation" is an artificial representation of the division of labour, and reality.

With industrialisation, occupations in the early sense of craft have been chipped away, resulting in a greater focus on hierarchy in forms of employment. In the refinement of classification systems, this has been strengthened, and was illustrated by the British *Classification of Occupations and Directory of Occupational Titles*:

> The broad structure of the classification is based on the organisational pattern of many large manufacturing companies with top or general management at the beginning, followed by professional and related specialist occupations *supporting top management* and frequently found in headquarters offices, and then by technical, scientific and other specialist occupations engaged in background work. These are followed by line management and the production and service occupations *under their control*.[22]

The language indicates the priority given to elements of hierarchy and control, and the implied structure contrasts with the more horizontal patterning of occupations that prevailed when the detailed division of labour was less extended.

Here is not the place to discuss occupational classifications. Nevertheless, it is instructive to dwell on features of the International Standard Classification of Occupations (ISCO). As designed in 1958, and as revised in 1968 and 1988, a difficulty is that ISCO was intended to fit several uses, the main ones being:

1 a basis for the design of occupational job-placement services;
2 a guide to vocational training curricula, and for vocational guidance;
3 a model to promote the international comparability of labour statistics;
4 a basis for identifying socio-economic groups;
5 a basis for "manpower planning" (*sic*);
6 a basis for monitoring available "skills";
7 a source of analytical categories for examining the determinants of many behavioural and cultural phenomena;
8 for use in collective bargaining.

These multiple uses make the task of classification extremely messy and hazy. The original objective was a classification based on "type of work performed". But this is vague. It is scarcely surprising that classifications blossomed into awesomely complicated exercises. The US *Dictionary of Occupational Titles* identified over 20,000 "occupations" by the late 1970s; the Canadian *Classification and Dictionary of Occupations* had over 6,000 titles. Changes in the US Current Population Survey in the 1980s enlarged the number of categories, indicating the growing detailed division of labour. The "professional and technical" grouping was split into two, as were "administrators", with "administrative support" being downgraded to join "clerical".

Such disaggregation has continued. Yet most labour market, economic and sociological analyses have utilised aggregates of eight or nine categories, and at the highest level of aggregation ISCO has been criticised for being too heterogeneous for analysis and insufficiently differentiated in terms of "skill".

While hierarchy has been a prominent feature of classifications, other criteria have included kind of main activity, type of materials used, equipment used, services rendered, level of authority, skill, employment status and qualifications. A French schema used skill, authority level, employment status and socio-economic status. Most systems have used those criteria. But a common view is that occupations should be mainly classified according to the amount of "skill" involved. This underlay the revision of ISCO in 1988, by which "occupations are identified, defined and grouped mainly on the basis of the similarity of skills required to fulfil the jobs' tasks and duties". The trouble is that skill is one of the vaguest work notions of all.

So we have a situation in which we want to revive the sense of occupation and yet have statistics and classifications that do not serve our needs. The sphere of work is in a state of upheaval. A small minority is experiencing a liberating set of possibilities, while a vast majority seem to be trapped in an insecure existence of labour and jobholding. Any vision of a good society must surely change this. How many people are in forms of work that allow them to develop as creative, secure persons? In a flexible system, the idea of occupation should entail disciplined diversity of activity. This must be self-discipline, which can only evolve when controls over the person are removed, when there is real freedom to make choices.

The twenty-first century should bring a focus on the right to occupation, giving the ability to everybody to bundle competencies in ways that suit their individual preferences and capabilities. To achieve this, new institutions will be required, and new forms of social protection that facilitate personal flexibility rather than impose arbitrary labourist obligations – against the tendency of the current generation of policymakers to assert that "only if you take a job that we will decide will you be entitled to state benefits". Means-testing deters this type of flexibility, as does any form of conditional selectivity in benefit systems.

For instance, you may earn $100 a week every month, while a selective state benefit could follow the rule that a transfer payment could be paid only if a person's income fell below $80. I may follow a flexible work schedule that involves me in earning $60 in one month and $140 in another. Ignoring the other problems with selective schemes – unemployment traps, poverty traps, savings traps, moral hazards, adverse selection, etc. – a selective scheme of social support based on short-term income-testing is more inequitable in societies based on flexible work. Yet we want this flexibilisation because it is part of the right to occupation. This is why the pursuit of occupation for all will lead to a revival of universal income support schemes, pointing towards the provision of a basic citizenship income.

For citizens in a work-based society, a source of distributive justice is the opportunity to pursue occupation. This involves the positive senses of skill and creativity, activity and self-control – the pride of craft. Occupation is never a finished process. One bundles competencies and "functionings", learning, refining and extending the self through work, always allowing for leisure and contemplation. Since occupation is necessarily risk-taking activity, it accepts that some insecurity is tolerable, but is premised on basic security in the same way that Rawls and others have regarded fair opportunity as a necessary condition for distributive justice.

Occupational security requires work complexity, sufficient freedom from supervision to realise responsibility, occupational discipline, and some freedom from routine, to permit creativity. It has been accepted since Durkheim's great work that "activity becomes richer and more intense as it becomes more specialised".[23] But we also understand that a specialist is not the same as someone who has to perform the same narrow set of tasks day after day, year after year, even it is for several employers. In this, psychologists and others have shown how important self-direction and self-control are to human personality. As a group studying the process over many years concluded, "The experience of occupational self direction has a profound effect on people's values, orientation, and cognitive functioning".[24]

Freedom in work is not something paternalists should be allowed to neglect. It is part of occupational security. It would also create more healthy communities. Those who can exercise self-control and self-direction in their occupation value these traits in other realms of life.[25] They are less likely to exhibit traits termed the "authoritarian personality", so chillingly associated with the mid-century madness of fascism. All forms of control undermine the sense of responsibility, and this applies to paternalism of any sort as well as to cruder forms.

Durkheim thought that modern life would depend on occupation, seeing the nation state and organisations as too large and distant to provide individuals with a sense of security and meaning. He rightly condemned dilettantism and spoke up for occupational depth. But we have learned that the technical division of labour can turn the specialist into the specialised. To prevent dilettantism or a life of flexiworking or detailed labour, individuals must have self-control and access to good opportunity. They must, *in extremis*, be able to refuse oppressive, exploitative, dehumanising labour. This requires both income security and representation security. History shows that without an association to represent it, an occupation withers under the pressures of other control systems. But it also requires the individual to have the freedom to opt out of collective control. Only if individuals have the "Drop dead!" option will institutions remain representative, and only then will state and commercial bodies be constrained from opportunistic or paternalistic control behaviour.

Occupational security requires standards, regulation and forms of income protection appropriate to the occupation in question. Most types of work have scope for opportunism in terms of performance, and most have scope for skill broadening or dilution. Those in an occupation would wish to control job content and the mobility between jobs. Individualistic opportunism could harm those practising the work; there are externalities. So, security must include preservation of standards, while allowing for diversity. It comes from facilitating creativity and ingenuity, while limiting fraudulent gimmickry, which could undermine the occupation's reputation, credibility and sustainability. As a worker, the individual needs the collective, and the collective needs the individuality that establishes the occupation's legitimacy. This is why *voice regulation* of occupation, through associations or other representative bodies, should complement statutory regulation (licensing, standard-setting, etc.).

Occupational security is not the same as professionalism, which is a mechanism of privilege and control by exclusion. Professionalism does possess characteristics that should be part of occupational security, but it also detaches, in that its ideology is that only members of the profession possess the specialised knowledge to give it legitimacy, status and control. Unless occupations are open and subject to social regulation, they will be opportunistic and operate to command more than a fair share of society's income. This has surely been the case with lawyers, surgeons, accountants and other professions. In this respect, it is noteworthy that many economists have criticised unions for allegedly protecting "insiders" at the expense of unemployed "outsiders", but have been silent about middle-class professions that have jealously guarded the mysteries of their profession and the income accruing to them, notably by restrictive practices over recruitment, licensing, qualifications, and so on.

Professionalism is a feature of fragmentation. The sense of occupational security that one wishes to promote is one of societal integration, consistent with what Durkheim seems to have had in mind. De-skilling and occupational erosion through job insecurity have been features of Taylorism, bureaucratic enterprises and much of what is covered by external and functional flexibility. Professionalism, with its exclusive associations, symbols and presumed authority over clients, has been a defence against administrative control and a mechanism for economic advantage and rent-seeking. By contrast, occupational security must apply to the lowliest as much as to those with mighty qualifications and the taboos of history behind their names.

With flexible production systems, the scope for occupational security will be enhanced. That does not mean it will be realised. That will depend on the emergence of appropriate forms of collective voice representation, coupled with individual opportunity. For that, basic income security and representation security will be essential – the real basis for reciprocity and societal solidarity. The representation will have to permeate the governance structures of occupations as well as companies and policy institutions. Recently, a great deal of attention has been given to corporate governance and the characteristics of good firms. Remarkably little has been given to occupational governance. This will require more flexible forms of voice regulation than existed in the twentieth century.

Occupational security could evolve only if there were mechanisms to reduce hierarchical administrative and managerial control and to prevent opportunism and rent-seeking inherent in occupational control in professions. There are examples of experimental structures that may point the way forward. Probably none have been unqualified successes, and may require state intervention to overcome institutional weaknesses. The essence of the initiatives is that members – or in the popular jargon, stakeholders – construct an organisation in which complementary groups *all* have a voice in the governance and structuring of the organisation, where intra-preneurship is encouraged, and where costs and benefits are shared. In this mould have been health collectives, community service collectives, non-governmental charity organisations and producer co-operatives. In these, there is some mutual control, to limit opportunism and to enable different groups to have access to information possessed by others in the firm, so as to give members the opportunity to rotate work tasks, if feasible or desired, and to share in control over the unit's work and development.

Lack of hierarchical control does create problems. Some observers have called them organised anarchy.[26] There is ambiguity over objectives, unstable membership, time-consuming decision-making, fuzzy evaluation and monitoring, and so on. The question is whether these failings are inevitable, or whether the processes can be adapted to the flexible work and production patterns that are emerging.

The good news is that there have been cases of successful democratic communities, where a sense of occupation and self-control have been encouraged in an atmosphere of security. They have tended to be in niches and to be service-oriented. They have included law clinics, alternative schools, food co-operatives and community health centres. They are apparently difficult to maintain, and are subject to external pressures, such as bureaucratic requirements from state authorities and donor demands and obligations.[27] They are also subject to internal pressure to become more hierarchical. What seems essential for success is that the occupational basis of the organisation's existence must be preserved and enhanced.[28] Those who are skilful and occupationally good must be allowed to do what they are skilful and good at doing. "De-professionalisation" must not be allowed to breed dilettantism or anti-intellectualism. Unless occupational skill is preserved and valued, the viability of the democratic enterprise will be undermined.

Occupational security will also require support for a more flexible lifetime system of career learning – not a whirl of short-term jobs and modules of employable skill, as captured by the image of the flexiworker, but a sense of progression, improving technical skill, status and craft control. One novel idea, to be applauded, is a "university of the community", by which people could be apprenticed to a registered non-profit organisation, receiving a diploma at the end of a period of community work, which would licence them to do similar work elsewhere.[29]

Occupational security is not a prescription for privilege for an elite or one applicable only to the educated or to those belonging to well-established professions. We all have occupations in ourselves. It is the bundle of enthusiasms, competencies and functionings that we develop. We will never have total freedom and opportunity to develop and apply those bundles. Yet we must judge policies and institutions by whether or not they move in that direction. The goal should be to enable as many people as possible to pursue their sense of occupation with security, and to enable them to benefit themselves and their communities without doing harm to others.

8 Interest versus Passion?

The idea of occupation should stimulate thoughts of both interest and passion. The medieval striving for glory, or honour, was the calling that motivated numerous individuals in numerous communities in the Middle Ages. The act of striving and the commitment to it marked an individual's virtue and dignity. This is more than decency, and stands opposed to decency. Decency is to accept one's lot with forbearance, if not resignation, at least quietly. It is not to challenge; it is to accept. Dignity and honour lie in the striving, for change in oneself and one's surroundings.

As individuals, and as members of groups with which we identify, we have interests. Albert Hirschman wrote an intriguing essay on the evolution of the idea of interest, in which he contrasted interests with passions, seeing the free rein to passion as leading to a calamitous state of affairs.[30] The notion of interest has usually implied economic interest, or the desire for material advantage. One could say that passion motivates interest calculation, passion appealing to risk-taking, interest to prudence and to efficient behaviour. One can easily denigrate passion as "a destructive force" and praise interest as "a calm desire" as "one that acts with calculation and rationality", as in "the calm desire for wealth".[31] From there it is a short step to making interest and money-making almost synonymous, and treating activity that does not contribute to those outcomes as secondary.

A difficulty with the notion of interest, not confronted by Hirschman, is that there is the interest of atavism – preserving or defending what you are, combating the fear of losing by guarding what you have – and the interest in becoming, combating the fear of not winning, by risk-taking that stops short of opportunism and that avoids the contradictory dangers of exploitation and self-exploitation.

It is the interest in becoming that must be strengthened in global capitalism.[32] The jobholder society, consisting of a large and growing number of flexiworkers flitting between jobs, retraining and other roles, is one in which the defence of interests is likely to be predominantly atavistic. A fear articulated by Adam Smith and others in the eighteenth century was that the division of labour would leave a mass of workers performing a few simple operations in a sedentary, unchallenging existence, while the life of commerce "sinks the courage of mankind" and makes "the mind of men contracted and rendered incapable of elevation". Smith's worry about "the commercial spirit" has come to us through the ensuing centuries. Under its influence, "Education is despised, or at least neglected, and the heroic spirit is almost utterly extinguished. To remedy these defects would be an object worthy of serious attention."[33] We suffer today from this neglect, and the labourists and paternalists give it scant respect.

Since the eighteenth century, and in a frenzied manner in the latter part of the twentieth, conspicuous consumption, or the endless pursuit of goods and money, has trickled down the income spectrum. In doing so, it has corroded the distinction between work and labour, by making instrumentality of labour so essential for participation in consumerist society. But ironically (and hopefully) it is running against a tendency of global capitalism, which is that the income from labour is a diminishing part of social income for those with income security.

There was always a tension between the primary motivations for labour (material "needs" and money) and the motivations for work (honour, vanity, family reciprocity, satisfaction, dignity, recognition). If the pursuit of money, and the goods that come with it, is the overwhelming motivation, then family, friendships and community become burdening costs.

There is a further puzzle, in that "happiness" seems separate from "satisfaction". Psychological surveys suggest that workers with greater work satisfaction are no more likely to be happy than others.[34] The notion of the "happy worker", so beloved by party functionaries and management consultants, actually conjures up a mixed image, and part of that is the frightening image of subjugation.

9 The ILO's "Decent Work" Programme

With this in the background, let me make a link with the ILO's new orientation to promote "decent work" – or, a preferable term, "dignified work".[35] Figure 10.2 is an attempt to portray stylised tendencies. It starts at the centre, with the notion of labour. Labour is hard and should not be romanticised. Its primary function is to produce marketable output or services (exchange value), and thus those who control labour usually want to take advantage of others, and often will oppress and exploit those performing labour. Those performing labour want to shirk and avoid it as much as they can. Controls have to be considerable.

Labour is associated with the proliferation of "jobs" and the "jobholder society" so memorably deplored in Hannah Arendt's *The Human Condition*. Jobs are limiting, instrumental. The performance of labour has a disutility, captured in the standard economic textbooks. Labour is also a matter of demand and supply, so that employers and workers exit from their relationship if demand or wages fall. Finally, of the three forms of regulation (statutory, voice and market (fiscal)), it is statutory regulations that tend to be given the primary role, although market regulation may also be strong.

At the right hand side is employment, which might be called stable labour. The standard model of employment involves an implicit social contract in

Figure 10.2. From labour to work

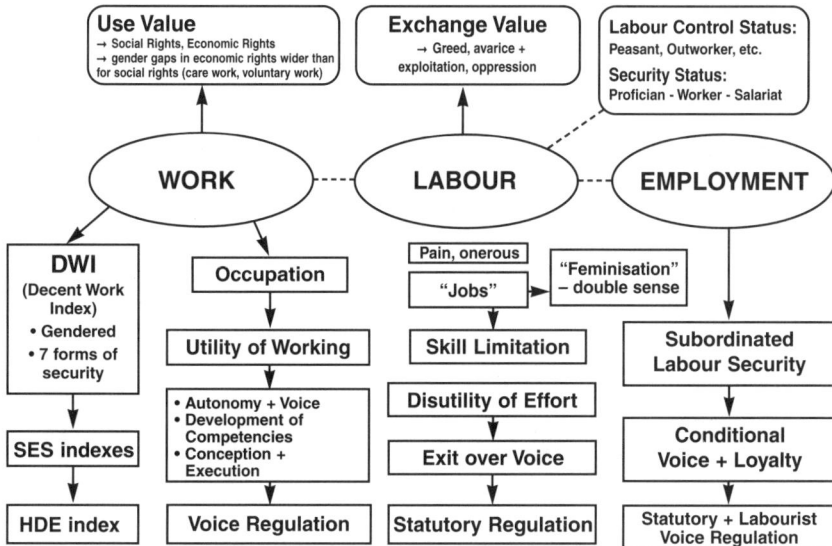

which workers and employees receive labour security in return for accepting controls over them, a disciplined, subordinated role in the production process. Employment relationships emphasise notions of loyalty to a firm and to the employer, in which a Voice role has carefully prescribed limits.

Both labour and employment are associated with a complex set of labour statuses, and are also associated with what might be called class. This is not quite appropriate for the evolving global process of socio-economic stratific-ation. But thinking along this line, one might have control status (the number of status groups depending on the type of society, etc.) and security status (our seven strata: elite, proficians, salariat, core, flexiworkers, unemployed, detached).

The idea of work captures the positive sense or productive and creative activity, in which the conception and execution aspects are combined (in Braverman's imagery) and, more importantly still, in which there is room and respect for inaction and contemplation. When we think of work in positive terms, we think of the utility of working, in which the pressures come from within ourselves, in which we feel in control, so that we give proper place to the vital activity of stillness, of contemplation. Labour and employment do not leave space for this stillness. The economic imperative rules. Modern technologies, and every technological revolution, result in a greater intensity of labour for millions of people. Stress, burn-out, loss of control over time are what characterise labour. In thinking of what constitutes dignified work, we must give priority to enhancement of self-control, which consists of growing autonomy and the support of strong collective and individual voice, allowing real freedom over what to do and not to do, and when to do it. This leads us back to the complex idea of occupation, in which we develop our competencies in ways that we choose through working.

If we focus on what work can provide and what labour cannot, we may have a richer view of distributive justice in which the negation of controls will be given more systematic attention. This leads to other tensions implicit in the diagram. A focus on maximising jobs and "restoring Full Employment" would lead inexorably to pressure on people to accept subordinated flexibility – with calls on workers to make concessions in order to help to create more jobs. A focus on work leads in the direction of thinking about liberating flexibility – a desire to be informal in the sense that increasingly we should be able to choose how to allocate time. A focus on work also leads back to the values of universalism and social solidarity, and away from the use of social protection as regulatory policy and labour-based selective entitlements.

The gender implications of the shift from labour to work are substantial. Labour and jobs encourage feminisation in the double sense that more women are in more jobs in part because a growing proportion of total job opportunities are of the type traditionally taken by women, that is, casual, informal, insecure and careerless. If we reflect on work we know that many forms that are not labour are done mainly by women and deserve to be compensated and given Voice if we are serious about promoting a strategy for dignified work. Work has use value, and it is a sign of progress that the social rights of those doing non-labour work are becoming more topical in many parts of the world.

As full-time wage labour has shrunk, it has become increasingly anomalous that work that is not labour should be disregarded. The work of caring for others is one type of work that is being legitimised, in part because governments have been wishing to privatise social services and reduce the state's direct responsibility for caring for ageing populations, in part because larger proportions of the voting population are in need of care, in part because it is no longer seen as work done by and for working-class people. Similarly, voluntary work is booming, both at the individual level and in the institutional phenomenon of the era, NGOs. For politicians this has been convenient because it fills a gap left by shrinking state provision. We will come back to the contradictory character of all this. The point here is that more people are visibly doing this work, so that ignoring it in statistics and in fiscal, social and regulatory policymaking is evidently peculiar.

At the same time, flexiworkers – those doing all sorts of work on a non-regular basis – are needed partly because they provide firms with lower-cost labour and partly because firms are facing more economic insecurity themselves. But the danger that their incomes and security would be inadequate to ensure that they will continue to provide an efficient, reliable labour supply means that governments will want to facilitate such flexiworking by various fiscal and regulatory means, enabling more people more easily to move in and out of employment, retraining, own-account activities, and so on. All this means that the notion of labour is giving way to a potentially richer concept of work. The vision for the twenty-first century is that we will shift away from the distorted view of work associated with both the labour theory of value and neo-classical economics, with trade unionism and much else.

In the twentieth century, it was common to say of someone that "she does not work" when what was meant was that she did not "go out to labour" for a wage. This was linked to the distortion that made labour the ideal, while domestic work was something left to women. Suppose 20 per cent of the adult population were working caring for the other 80 per cent and for children, and that the remainder did none of that work at all. Because of twentieth-century norms, the image of married women doing housework comes to mind, a typical sexist image. However, if we moved to a situation in which all of us were spending 20 per cent of our time caring for others, most of us would and should regard that as a fair and potentially attractive way of living. Indeed, to specialise in doing the same type of labour day after day, year after year is surely not attractive – although most people have been obliged to do precisely that.

10 Citizenship Work

Two work trends are subversively eroding the labourist bias of the twentieth century – the legitimation of care and the spread of voluntary work. These two forms of work are eroding the legitimacy of distinctions between labour and work, to the dismay of mostly male representatives of labouring man. Governments are recognising this by introducing payments for activities hitherto regarded as work but not labour.

Care work became topical towards the end of the century of labouring man. In the early years of the century, there had been a struggle to enable women to undertake caring work, through "breadwinner" or family wages, pensions for widows and single mothers, maternity leave and protection for women. That care regime made women dependent on husbands. If initial reforms mainly meant some selective "liberation" from labour, by mid century there was a two-track system, with family compensation, benefits paid to husbands and a professional care system, as part of the "service state". Care was an integral part of socio-economic security, in different ways in different welfare states. Then, in the era of market regulation, entitlement to care was cut, leading to more reliance on social assistance for single mothers, maternity leave and residential and home care for the elderly.[36] But by the end of the century new forms of care were being legitimised, through parental leave and subsidised privatised care.

So far, citizenship rights have omitted the need for care and the need to give care. Because it was domestic work, it was not recognised socially or economically. As more women have become regular labour force participants, loss of citizenship status while caring and being out of the labour force has become more transparently peculiar. To overcome gender bias in systems of social protection, care must become a dimension of citizenship with rights equal to those received from employment.

Libertarians support the marketisation of care because purchased services widen individual choice and encourage efficient delivery. Others welcome the trends because they see them as empowering. One middle way is vouchers, which are attractive to governments as a means of formalising the grey labour market, thereby raising tax revenue, but which retain a paternalistic danger. One imagines a future in which each citizen has a voucher card, with so many points for care, so many for education, so many for basic health, so many for training, and so on.

Feminists see care as leading in two directions, towards what Nancy Fraser has called the Universal Breadwinner model, where state services are provided for day care for children so that women can go to jobs, or towards a Caregiver Parity model, legitimising and rewarding informal care work through caregiver allowances. One might say that the first is the labour line, the second the work line.

One strength of an approach that brings care work into the market economy, through allowances and so on, is that it boosts small-scale local activities and organisations, including charities and other voluntary NGOs, strengthening community and trust.[37] The "new volunteering" can be a means of social integration of both carers and recipients of care. The danger of most approaches taken so far is that they give insufficient attention to the issue of control. Three classic failings of labour must be overcome. The caregiver model could lead to carers being confined to private care roles, isolated from the public sphere. Ruth Lister, in a brilliant flash, captured the problem by describing it as "the modern variant of Wollstonecraft's dilemma".[38]

If commodifying care merely strengthened the sexual division of labour, with women doing most of the care, it would be a form of inequality. The loneliness of the long-distance caregiver is an image of female dependency associated with social hierarchies of the worst kind. An individualised system could also lead to the Taylorisation of care, with individuals having to obtain licences to perform care of certain types, and restrictions based on demarcation and procedural rules. This would prevent occupational security, and induce moral hazards. And it could intensify self-exploitation, in the Chayanovian sense, whereby the carer gives more time and effort than justified by the allowance because the "gift" relationship dominates the "market" relationship. Or it could intensify exploitation through the care recipient taking advantage of the other's labour. These dangers suggest that the care market could remain sexually and ethnically segregating.

The way to avoid these dangers must be through a mix of citizenship rights and strong voice regulation. Unless there are associations to give collective voice to carers and to care recipients, the goal of balanced reciprocity could not be obtained. Intermediary associations have been springing up all over the world to fill these representation spaces, and are an exciting development. But they must give representation and other forms of security, notably work security. The dangers of stress and burn-out are extreme in care work.

There are three types of care relationship.[39] There are personal services given by a dependent person to someone in a position of financial, social or labour control. There is caregiving work given to those who are frail or otherwise dependent on help. And there is spontaneous care, where each person is equal in the eyes of the other and in their own eyes, and where there is balanced reciprocity. It is this that should be sought through policies and institutions.

In this regard, the notion of dependence has been pernicious. Only a fool believes in full independence. In society, individuals are interdependent. The attack on "dependency" has been a cry of the privileged throughout history. For the future, we need institutions that enhance self-control in a context of mutual dependency, which some call fraternity and others conviviality. The atomisation of consumer-based individualism is a patho-logical prescription, creating a wild west independence. When politicians and libertarians criticise "dependency", they should be reminded that they too are dependent – we all are. We cannot work and develop occupation without others' support, and we cannot predict what support they might give, how indirect that might be, or even when we will need it. Recognition of these eternal verities is what defines the human community we call society. This is why the right to live as a human being with dignity – the right to self-respect – overrides the paternalistic reciprocity principle. What right or superior quality do I possess that I should deny you basic security in which to pursue your sense of occupation? This question should be addressed to paternalists and labourists everywhere.

The ways policymakers treat labour market services and care work will
determine the character of society and work in the future. The issue of care
raises one of the great dilemmas of the movement from a labour-based
society to a work-based society. How can it be compensated in a way
that does not merely provide income security while confining women, in
most cases, to a lower-status, socially-excluding role? This is Ruth Lister's
Wollstonecraft dilemma.

Part of this dilemma is how to pay for care. If payment were indirect,
through tax credits or family-based benefits, it would be gender-segregating,
and so not give citizenship rights, since it would be a family-unit entitlement,
not an individual right. If care were provided directly by the state, paternalism and bureaucratic control of access, cost, inclusion and so on would
come into play, with discretionary judgments all over the place. If a payment
were given to the caregiver, that would strengthen individual rights, but
could produce moral hazards and monitoring problems. For instance, the
carer could make the recipient dependent on the need for care, or not
provide the care for which compensation is paid. The recipient would be
unlikely to be in a position to "voice regulate". Or if a payment were made to
the care recipient, analogous problems would arise. Often the person would
not know what is required or even provided, perhaps being young, elderly or
frail. So, each of the options – paying the carer, paying the cared-for, family-
based benefits or tax credits, and direct public or private provision – raise
distinct problems.

The trend towards cash payments represents a reduction in bureaucratic
control and promotes "welfare citizenship", by giving contractual rights
(contractual justice) rather than merely procedural rights. Payment for care,
although commodification, represents legitimation of work that is not labour.
The payment allows more self-control in principle and reduces the drawbacks of the paternalism of social workers and professionals. It also erodes
the distinction between the gift and the market economy. The trouble is that
individuals are not equal in their bargaining position, or with respect to the
information needed to make optimal decisions.

It is powerfully subversive that care work has emerged from the shadows
into the public domain, not only by having a public face but also by being
legitimised socially in a context of a labourist welfare state under strain.[40]
Caring for a disabled relative, a sick child or an infirm elderly person is
scarcely less valuable than pouring the tea for the boss or standing on a
production line *à la* Charlie Chaplin. Neo-classical economics taught to
undergraduates, orthodox labour statistics, welfare state designers fuelled by
their zeal for labour and generations of politicians all ruled otherwise. Only
late in the twentieth century, as a result of two forces that made uneasy bed-
fellows – a desire by mainstream politicians and orthodox economists to cut
back on the welfare state, and pressure from feminists to recognise such work
– did care work start to become legitimised.

For instance, it is more widely recognised that care work should be
covered by social protection policy. Perhaps the most subversive development
was the introduction of care insurance in Germany, the first new form of

social insurance for many decades. But still the work of caring has not been adequately recognised as part of a total person as a working being. That will happen only when the social division of labour is profoundly changed.

All of us fortunate enough to have good health and the capacity to do so could probably benefit from spending part of our time working in caring for others, just as one day – any day – we will need to rely on the care given to us. Yet labour force statistics and national income calculations ignore such work, except when it is paid labour. In most cases, making it into paid labour is likely to make it less valuable and less valued by the giver of care because it involves a reduction in the gift relationship.

A fundamental question is whether the commodification of care can defy the Wollstonecraft dilemma, the difficulty of reconciling the desire to see the activity move into the public sphere (potentially involving commodification) while avoiding the prospect of women remaining predominantly in low-status activity.

At the outset of the twenty-first century, there is an approaching unity of purpose among policymakers, feminists and egalitarians about the need to legitimise care work. There is a pragmatic, even cynical element in this. Politicians may see carers as reducing the need for social services and state transfers, with "private", personal and low-cost suppliers replacing "public" support. Nevertheless, there is a growing demand for such work to be recognised and compensated properly. There is no prospect of gender equality until all forms of work are treated equally in social policy. A key question is whether the compensation system that emerges will lead in a paternalistic direction or to greater self-control. It must do the latter.

Voluntary work is no less subversive of the labourist society. It is as essential to every society as paid labour, further invalidating economistic distinctions between work and labour. Apparently, more than one in every three American adults does about five hours a week of voluntary service. But the restructuring of social income has given such work a greater role in most societies. The erosion of extended families and communal reciprocities in developing countries, and the rollback of universal state transfers and services in industrialised and "transition" countries are leaving gaps in the lives of millions of people. This is not necessarily bad or good. But it is one source of the growth of voluntary work. Another has been the unchecked social externalities of global capitalism, which have left communities more polluted or vulnerable in some way or another. The voluntary work explosion also owes something to the spread of higher levels of education (despite the best attempts to turn it into extended job preparation, or schooling), as well as the ageing of societies and the failure of labourist institutions to appeal to the new generation of potential egalitarians.

Angry youth and irritated wrinklies find common ground. Voluntary work has emerged as a global force, almost as a spontaneous protest against individualisation and against the paternalism that has been trying to cement new social norms as "best practice" lifestyles. Youth have provided the energy, have shared the leadership and have added voluntary work to their occupational biographies. Such work, be it to provide "social service", to protect the environment or to combat crime, or whatever, provide the avenue to co-operative individualism.

It is promoting a new sense of occupation, by allowing individuals to bundle informal competencies and aspirations with the pursuit of a sense of craft, the essence of occupation. Yet however one interprets the role of voluntary work, it requires the same combination of securities as other forms of work. There must be basic income security and voice representation, to avoid the dangers of self-exploitation and oppression. The voluntary worker – just like the altruistic social worker of the welfare state – can easily be reduced to a whimpering loser, defeated by a surfeit of enthusiasm and that self-destructive willingness to push beyond tolerable endurance. No healthy society should accept that. That is why Voice associations are required even within communities of voluntary work, to check self-exploitation as well as hierarchy, and to create healthy space for themselves. Nor must it be a means by which the affluent and powerful live more comfortably, because others' voluntary work just about maintains an environment of sustainable insecurities.

Only if voluntary work has collective representation will those involved in it be able to challenge the sources of their own insecurity, and perhaps help to reduce the need for their voluntary work. This brings us to the danger that, as with care work, volunteering can become self-perpetuating simply because those doing it want to continue to be wanted. There is a need for a mechanism to prevent this, or at least to pose the question. Looking in the proverbial mirror is a part of any good mechanism of representation, and is one of several reasons for believing that collective Voice security is as important for voluntary work as for any other type of work.

Volunteering and civil society organisations are perhaps the most dynamic part of social participation. While much of the noise may be little more than that, recognising that much of the activity is real work is subversive against claims of old-style labourism, because we need to measure it, ensure that those involved have basic security and ensure that the vulnerable drawn to a cause are enabled to retain their sense of self-control and pursue their sense of occupation along with everybody else.

11 Acquiring Control of Time

For a great many people, an industrial revolution brings an intensification of labour. The Industrial Revolution of the eighteenth century swept away many of the more leisurely ways of rural life, with their numerous holidays and more reflective pace and the styles that went with it.

As the new millennium began, a new industrial revolution was sweeping away the seams of industrial life, removing the zones of time and space. The 24–hour-day means that all hours are available for labour and work, and every day is a working day, the holidays of one place are the open days for labour in others. Transactions, emails, credit cards and teleconferencing brook no time-zone limits. If the culture of the seasons was swept away by the eighteenth-century Industrial Revolution, the culture of the working day is being swept away by the present economic and social revolution. With it is a threat to the sense of balanced control over time for groups that could have expected to be relatively privileged.

Recall the discussion of work insecurity. To add urgency, reflect on the fact that in the second half of the twentieth century, the rate of depression among young people rose sharply. One in four British adults now suffers from a chronic lack of sleep; one in every five schoolchildren have psychological problems; private mental health insurance claims rose by one-third between 1987 and 2000. The World Health Organisation predicts that by 2010 depression will have become the second most common disease in the industrialised world.

These are not the statistics of a healthy society. They are the statistics of a society under stress and with a need to slow down. If the pressure to consume and to increase one's money income crowds out the simple act of reflective stillness, and induces the sort of feverish job addiction highlighted earlier, we could see the globalisation of *karoshi*, through burn-out, depression and self-destructive consumerism.

We need to slow down. This is not just a call for slower growth, although the growth fanatics should be confronted. It is a call for collective self-regulation. It is recognition that merit or worth is not necessarily revealed in market behaviour or success. One of the great insecurities of the early part of the twenty-first century is what might be called time insecurity, reflecting the pressures to undertake an excessive number and range of activities. It goes with the faith in flexibility and adaptability, and beyond those, on the focus on individualistic behaviour. An unappreciated aspect of collective organis-ations and institutions, and voice regulation, is that they provide mechanisms to limit the rush and hold back the pressures that contribute to people's loss of control over time.

The strategy outlined in the last two chapters offers hope in this respect. Basic income security – assurance against penury – coupled with a diversific-ation of income through social sharing of the surplus gained from techno-logical advances would reduce the income insecurity that has driven the feverish labour that is the source of our social sickness and loss of control over time. And more diversified voice representation would remind us that disempowerment is civilising and liberating, not in the sense of turning one's cheek, but in the sense of preventing the powerful from converting our representation into a means of social control, which so many nominally progressive institutions have become in the past.

12 Concluding points

The twentieth-century development models made labour and jobs the yard-stick of social and economic policy, at the expense of work and occupation. Among the consequences was that certain types of work were systematically ignored, taken for granted or simply undervalued by policymakers and mainstream social scientists. They became zones of chronic insecurity and low status.

We need to shift decisively away from a focus on labour, and on labour security *per se*, and focus on how to strengthen occupational security. Of the seven forms of labour security, those given primacy during the twentieth century, namely labour market and employment security, are potentially dispensable, as they are mainly instrumental, cannot be offered equally or fairly in a globalising economy and could be attained only at the cost of sacrifice of more valuable forms of security. Labour market security cannot be envisaged with foreseeable economic policies, in which a NAIRU is either seen as necessary, so that governments deliberately maintain a pool of unemployed, or is lowered by means that impinge on the liberty and security of vulnerable groups. As for employment security, it is a privilege for a minority. Even in the dynamic US economy, the average life of Fortune 500 companies (the leading firms) is only forty years, so employment security for most workers entering firms is scarcely realistic. At best, only a minority could have strong employment security.

This does not mean labour market and employment security are undesirable. The claim rather is that they should not be given priority. To make progress, we must escape from the labourist bias. Only a romantic utopian would imagine the "end of labour". Yet labour is a means to an end, not an end in itself. Maximising the number of people in labour is a fetish. It can be done, at a cost, in terms of lower wages, less social protection, more stress, social illnesses and inequality. We need freedom from labour, so that we can pursue work in conditions where multiple forms of activity are valued as preserving community and fraternity. It is no coincidence that the most thriving work is taking place outside the labour relationship, in voluntary service and community work, in which people are organised around their enthusiasms.

Much of this is work, not labour. The labour fetish has resulted in its denigration or undervaluation. Societal health in the future will depend on how community work blends with other forms of activity. Much of it will remain non-contractual, with little or no pay. Its spread and extraordinary dynamism testify to the fact that it is not just the prospect of a wage that makes a person work. But it will flourish only if it becomes part of the mainstream of society. Pushing people into full-time wage labour, or taking away entitlements if they do not seek or remain in it, is not the way to legitimise this work or to encourage flexibility of working that new technologies and work arrangements make possible. It will do that only if the state adopts a passively supportive relationship to such activity.

Labour should not be idealised for many reasons, among which are that for a growing number of people, the returns to labour are uncertain, and for many obtaining income security through the labour market is not possible, because the wage and jobs available are inadequate. Increasingly, the main means of ensuring decent income security is to participate in the capital market. Yet everywhere the capital market participation rate (CMPR) is well below the labour force participation rate (LFPR). Social progress in the future may be measured by both rates, with more emphasis given to the CMPR.

The labourist prejudice that the difference in income security between those inside and those outside jobs should be large should be rejected. There should be no presumption of any sort. This prejudice has been asymmetrically applied, not used to justify taking away from the rich who do not labour but used to justify reducing the income security of the poor. There may be reasons for narrowing the income differences between those in jobs and those outside them, but there should be no presumption that a large differential is desirable.

In his analysis of citizenship, T.H. Marshall claimed that civil rights emerged in the eighteenth century, political rights in the nineteenth, and social rights in the twentieth. Perhaps economic rights will emerge as the norm of decency in the twenty-first century. If those are to include the right to work, it must be something else than the duty to labour, by allowing for the right *not* to work. And the right to work must mean a right to choose what one perceives as rational activity, for only that can be the basis of citizenship and occupational security. Jobs for their own sake are not consistent with this sense of rationality. And the right to a job that is chosen for you by somebody else against your wishes, however well meaning that person may be, is no right at all.

The failure of the century of the labouring man was epitomised by the desire of reformers to find ways of maximising jobs and pushing more people into them. The conventional wisdom is that people need jobs, because that is good for them, and those who do not want jobs must be induced to want and accept them, because that leads to "social inclusion". This modern paternalism is found everywhere. However, while work is valuable if it contributes to human creativity and development, there is no reason to suppose that maximising labour is the best means of facilitating the optimum amount or quality of work in society. Much of the most creative and useful work could not be easily or sensibly turned into jobs. This is well known, yet an extraordinary number of people find it impossible to adhere to that insight. They seek ways of multiplying the number of jobs and the pressure on the poor to slip into them. Jeremy Rifkin and others are wrong when they refer to the end of jobs. There are more of them than ever.

Work in occupation is a privilege, labour in a job is not. Labour can be a constraint on work, restricting the development, application and refinement of skills through a career. Habituation to labour of low complexity erodes intellectual flexibility and the capacity for self-direction and high-productivity work.[41] Labour gives little scope for creative and regenerative contemplation. So-called workaholism should be called labouraholism, were it not such an ugly word. Addiction to job, and the stress it brings stem from turning work into labour. Although a sickness of middle-income and higher-income groups, this extends to the lower reaches of the labour market. Workfare and the paternalistic decision that almost everybody should labour restrict the flexibility and creativity of those driven into labouring or fearful of being driven into it. To borrow from Beveridge's aphorism, if people are driven by fear, insecurity and coercion, they will respond like cattle.

If labour should not be idealised, paternalistic control over those on the margins of the labour market should be regarded as a source of insecurity and a threat to liberty. Work is valuable, as well as essential for production and income generation. The issue is what sort of work and what sort of security should be promoted in place of paternalism and the jobholder society.

With the emerging patterns of work activity and institutions of civil society, the need to dethrone labour will become urgent. Consider this set of forecasts:

> The era of lifelong company jobs with regular promotions and annual wage increases is over. It is your responsibility to manage your own lifetime career. But you won't have a lifetime career. No one can manage his or her own career without a road map, and economic road maps cannot be drawn unless there are career ladders across companies. And they simply don't exist. In Europe, the Middle Ages saw vast numbers of masterless labourers wandering back and forth across the countryside. Walled cities and towns were the answer. The Japanese talk about the chaos of having samurai without masters. Our future is the masterless American labourer, wandering from employer to employer, unable to build a career.[42]

These predictions may seem realistic, but they presume one needs "masters" and are suffused with a deterministic pessimism. A tendency towards "careerlessness" may exist, although a career has always been the privilege of an elite. There never was an era of "lifelong jobs" for most people anywhere. But the fatalism that careerlessness is the future is unjustified. The challenge is to find the means of ensuring that a growing proportion of the population have the opportunity, capacity and desire to build an occupation, without needing or wanting "masters". Rather than "the end of career", we could be seeing it blossoming into "the beginning of career", for many more people as they escape from employment security.

Besides real freedom, we must restore the status of leisure and contemplative activity. Several aphorisms of Bertrand Russell have been cited earlier, and we may reflect on two more in this context:

> The idea that the poor should have leisure has always been shocking to the rich.

> The wise use of leisure . . . is a product of civilisation and education. A man who has worked long hours all his life will be bored if he becomes suddenly idle.[43]

While agreeing with these sentiments, they prompt another that would not have occurred to Russell's generation to the same extent as it should now. This is that over-labour is ecologically unbalanced and unsustainable. Energy and time are consumed intensively leaving little attention to reproductive pursuits, whether personal, social or ecological. Intensified pursuit of individual gain leaves no space for attention to the finer points of nature, which include what Russell called idleness and Arendt and Aristotle called contemplation. With existing institutions, a powerful coalition of interests favours economic growth. Although each generation of economists has produced its sages who deplore the unbridled pursuit of growth, unless the distribution of income, economic power and security are addressed, those voices will continue to be heard with little more than a benevolent smile.

The Good Society of the twenty-first century will be based on the right of occupation, or occupational security, where increasing numbers of people will be able to combine competencies to create their own occupation, with varying work statuses, and moving in and out of economic activity. In one sense, this will be an extension of individuality, with a growth in the realm of autonomy. In another, the individuality will only flourish if there is a sense of collective security, a sense of community to which the individual belongs. There is a danger that without a collective anchor, individual flexibility could mean for many a careerless sort of nomadic existence, as suggested by the fragmentation that characterised the era of market regulation. Individual security without collective security is inconceivable. The character and strength of representative organisations and the networking that they facilitate will be crucial to both personal security and the development of the right to occupation.

The latter requires fresh thinking about the institutional structures to make it feasible and desirable. Traditional notions of household, firm, state and class are not appropriate. We must recreate the imagined community and a sense of socio-economic solidarity. What is needed is a structure of firms, associations and public agencies that generate and thrive on communal individualism. For this, we must be sceptical about all forms of control, except self-control. Control does not engender loyalty; it obtains obedience, for a while and at a cost. Use of controls reflects a lack of trust and loyalty. If loyalty is important, between workers and managers, between citizens, and between those who do wage labour and those who do other forms of work, then promoting self-control is essential.

This can only come from ceding control over others and from providing all with basic security and good opportunity. Provide assistance, community and services, not controls. Overcoming the oppressive controls exercised by village elders, powerful landlords, commercial middlemen and sundry others is the beginning of freedom. But so too is overcoming administrative controls exercised in hierarchical firms and paternalistic controls exercised by bureaucrats who push workfare from the safety of their middle-class affluence and detachment from the regulatory process applied to the losers of flexible labour markets.

Occupational security will grow when social, economic and institutional policies create an environment in which more and more people are able to pursue their own sense of occupation. Mechanisms to de-link income security from labour will help. With flexible, fragmenting labour markets social protection must move away from labour-conditional policies if distributive justice is to be achieved. The floor constraint requires a citizenship allowance, de-linked from performance of labour, while capital sharing will be required to satisfy both the Difference and Paternalism Test Principles.

This should not be approached in terms of the old ideological split, although the privileged have always opposed diminution of privilege and find it emotionally wrenching to assume a position of the veil of ignorance.

The legitimation of all forms of work requires Voice regulation and representation for all interests, all forms of work. Recalling the Polanyian framework, we may say that the new economy requires new forms of voice regulation to re-embed it in society, alongside new forms of social protection and new mechanisms of redistribution. In this spirit, we need something like citizenship or community associations rather than traditional trade unions, but based on many attributes of unions. If civil society stays outside the production and distribution system, gross inequalities and insecurities will persist.

Besides democratic citizenship associations, citizenship income and communal profit sharing could redress the fragmentation associated with flexible labour markets and globalisation. Economic democracy within firms is essential if political and social democracy outside them is to be meaningful and sustainable. An era of democratic regulation favouring distributive justice may seem a distant prospect, yet critics must stop looking back in anger and despair. We must stop being traumatised by the era of market regulation. Every such era has bred a new set of progressive possibilities. Nemesis is not far when the era's victors think we are at the end of history. The forward march is usually resumed when the losers remember their history and find their voice.

Paternalistic control must be overcome as part of an agenda for occupational security. In doing so, how can a balance be achieved between freedom as autonomy and freedom as responsibility? The anti-paternalist believes in freedom from controls and freedom to be able to make rational choices – "the wish to be self-directed and not to be directed by others".[44] But freedom is not unbridled individualism. Any individual needs some constraints – boundaries or pressures to direct him or her away from pure egotism. The desirable constraint is some form of collective that limits opportunism while facilitating the freedom to develop. This is the Voice security that we should be seeking.

The trouble is that any collective by itself will become oppressive unless checked by some other form of collective. Thus, the family will be oppressive unless its members can draw strength from belonging to a wider community; the union will be oppressive unless civic associations can give strength to individuals; the civil society organisation will become oppressive and opportunistic unless its members can identify with a balancing group, and so on. We need a set of collectives. As noted earlier, G.D.H. Cole put it well in 1920, at a time of ferment as trade unions and co-operatives struggled for identity, "A person requires as many forms of representation as he has distinct organisable interests or points of view." In short, freedom requires a system of collective or co-operative individualism in order to restrain moral and immoral hazards.

This should lead us to consider more current populist imagery. The notion of "empowerment" should be disquieting. We should feel uneasy about the language of battle. Of course, social relations are about adversarial bargaining and "struggle". It is intellectually reprehensible to talk or write as if there were no conflicts of interest; this leads to flabby thinking by bureaucratic minds unwilling to take intellectual risks. However, a danger of the current discourse around "development as freedom" is that it depicts freedom as competitive individualism, consumerism, possession, aggrandise-ment, maximisation of short-term profits and individual advantage. It fosters a Hobbesian mentality, which turns all social relations into "winners" and "losers". This freedom to be endlessly at war with our fellow beings, with nature and ourselves, is driving us into a frenzy of "competitiveness", egotism, stress, "labouraholism", "presenteeism", karoshi and other social sicknesses.

Of course we need production, which requires incentives. However, we must reflect more. We need a softer tone, a less abrasive way of living, in which self-control does not mean merely freedom to compete opportunis-tically and frenetically with others more "equally". The stress that is the modern illness of the labour ethic will not be addressed by this route. We must reject the language of empowerment. It is dis-empowerment that is required; it is the negation of those controls, in order to liberate our enthusiasms, our creativity, and most of all, our capacity for contemplation and reflection. That is real security. The greatest freedom of all is to be still. Dignified work can only evolve if ordinary people have the capacity to say "No". This is a disturbing message for those who want to see the extension of markets to every crevice of human existence and who see the multiplication of jobs as the answer to the human condition. Dignified work needs basic security, or real freedom is denied. The ultimate paradox is that it requires the freedom to do no work at all. Dignified work can only exist when it is done for intrinsic reasons, not because a landlord, a boss or the state says it shall be so.

Notes

Prologue: Security versus Control

1 For a review of studies in this tradition, see Rosamund Stock, "Socio-economic security and the creation of citizenship", paper prepared for the ILO's Socio-Economic Security Programme, Geneva, August 2000.

1 Recalling the Century of Labouring Man

1 The ILO was established in 1919, in the wake of the Bolshevik Revolution and the Great War that had butchered the heart of the European working class. The message to civil servants, politicians and reformers everywhere seemed clear: better to induce governments and elites everywhere to improve working conditions than to see the working-class successors become radical in asserting the rights of labour.

2 For an attempt to differentiate between the variants of "Keynesianisms", including Austro-Keynesianism, see G. Standing, "Structural adjustment and labour market policies: Towards social adjustment?", in G. Standing and V. Tokman (eds), *Towards Social Adjustment* (Geneva, ILO, 1991), pp. 5–52.

3 A source of income not highlighted in this decomposition is income from the sale of goods and services. These are included in W, and effectively in the flexible part of W.

4 K. Polanyi, *The Great Transformation: Origins of Our Time* (New York, Rinehart, 1944).

2 The Era of Market Regulation

1 A variant of the behavioural explanation for the persistence of unemployment in a capitalist economy was that it was necessary as a disciplinary device, checking workers from shirking and unions from making strong redistributive demands.

2 J. Bhagwati, "External sector and income distribution", in V. Tanzi and Ke-Young Chu (eds), *Income Distribution and High Quality Growth* (Cambridge, Mass., MIT Press, 1998), p. 278.

3 J. Burke and G. Epstein, "Threat effects and the internationalisation of production", paper presented at Workshop on Globalisation, Income Distribution and Structural Change, Chennai, 14–17 December 2000.

4 S. Anderson and J. Cavanagh, *Top 200: The Rise of Corporate Global Power* (Washington, DC, Institute for Policy Studies, 2000).

5 Each revolution in communications has brought a shift of social and class-based power. The movable-type printing press in the sixteenth century decisively reduced the power of the Church, which had controlled information through scribbling monks. Thereafter, pamphlets and books facilitated the spread of bourgeois ideas and ideals. The new information technology of the late twentieth century has had the effect of decentralising information and has made it harder to regulate economic exchange. It has also contributed to economic turbulence and has generated new inequalities, insecurities and social fragmentation.

6 R. S. Avi-Yonah, "Globalisation, tax competition and the fiscal crisis of the welfare state", *Harvard Law Review*, No. 113, May 2000.

7 Anderson and Cavanagh, 2000, op. cit.

8 For a discussion, see G. Standing, "The babble of euphemisms: Social protection in 'transformed' labour markets", in A. Rainnie, A. Smith and A. Swain (eds), *Work, Employment and Transition: Restructuring Livelihoods in Post-Communism* (London, Routledge, 2001).

9 The issues covered in this section were dealt with at length elsewhere. G. Standing, *Global Labour Flexibility: Seeking Distributive Justice* (Basingstoke, Macmillan, 1999).

10 G. Standing, "Global feminisation through flexible labour", *World Development*, Vol. 17, No. 7, 1989, pp. 1077–95; idem, "Global feminisation through flexible labour: A theme revisited", *World Development*, Vol. 27, No. 3, 1999, pp. 583-602.

11 J. Alber and G. Standing, "Social dumping: Catch-up or convergence?", introduction to Special Issue of *Journal of European Social Policy*, Vol. 10, No. 2, March 2000, pp. 99–119.

3 The Spread of Labour Insecurity

1 G. Standing and L. Szoldos, "Worker insecurities in Ukrainian industry: The 1999 ULFS" (Geneva, Socio-Economic Security Programme Paper, May 2000).

2 See, for instance, the leader in *The Financial Times* on 17 July 2000, entitled "Europe goes back to work". There was no recognition of the substitution of labour force work for other types of work when the labour force participation rises. This reflects the labourist bias that permeates public debate.

3 The classic analysis is that by Braverman, which spawned a rich literature on the labour process in the 1980s. H. Braverman, *Labour and Monopoly Capital: The Degradation of Work in the Twentieth Century* (New York, Monthly Review Press, 1974).

4 The term, so much part of the language of the era, should still prompt recall of Marx's quip that capital is not a thing, but a relationship.

5 World Health Organisation, *Health for All* (Geneva, WHO, 1996).

6 U.S. General Accounting Office, *Workers at Risk: Increased Numbers in Contingent Employment Lack Insurance, Other Benefits*, Report to the Chairman, Subcommittee on Employment and Housing, Committee on Government Operations, House of Representatives (Washington, DC, US Government Printing Office, March 1991), Appendix III, p. 22.

7 See, for instance, A. Soares, "The hard life of the unskilled workers in new technologies: Data-entry clerks in Brazil", in H.J. Bullinger (ed.), *Human Aspects of Computing* (Amsterdam, Elsevier Science Publishers, 1991); U. Huws, "Teleworking, An overview of the research" (London, report prepared for the British Government, 1996), p.105.

8 Huws, 1996, op. cit., pp. 14, 49.

9 N. MacErlean, "Workers unite – with your bosses", *The Observer*, 5 April 1998, "Work", p. 1.

10 AFL-CIO, *Workers' Compensation and Unemployment Insurance under State Laws* (Washington, DC, AFL-CIO, Publication 36, 1989).

11 M. Linder and I. Nygaard, *Void Where Prohibited: Rest Breaks and the Right to Urinate on Company Time* (Cornell, ILR Press, 1998).

12 R.M. Kantor, *When Giants Learn to Dance* (New York, Simon and Schuster, 1989), p. 268.

13 J. Schor, *The Overworked American* (New York, Basic Books, 1991).

14 Princeton Research Associates, 1997, op. cit.

15 The Industrial Society, *Promoting Well Being* (London, Managing Best Practice, No. 76, 2000).

16 C.L. Cooper, P. Liukkanen and S. Cartwright, *Stress Prevention in the Workplace: Assessing the Costs and Benefits to Organisations* (Dublin, European Foundation for the Improvement of Living and Working Conditions, 1996).

17 "Le fin de l'absentéisme", *L'Hebdo*, 8–19 February 1998, pp. 10–17.

18 Committee for Economic Development, *American Workers and Economic Change* (New York, 1996).

19 "Trade unions come in from the cold", *The Observer*, 8 June 1997.

20 The main findings were published in *The Lancet* (London), July 1997.

21 G. Standing, "Societal impoverishment: The challenge for Russian social policy", *Journal of European Social Policy*, Vol. 8, No. 1, February 1998, pp. 23-42.

22 A.R. Hochschild, *The Time Bound* (New York, Metropolitan Books, H. Holt and Co., 1997).

23 H. Phelps-Brown, "The counter-revolution of our time", *Industrial Relations*, Vol. 29, No. 1, Winter 1990, pp. 1–14.

24 For more extended analysis, see G. Standing, "Labour market governance in Eastern Europe", *European Journal of Industrial Relations*, Vol. 3, No. 2, July 1997, pp. 133–59.

25 G.Standing, *Russian Unemployment and Enterprise Restructuring: Reviving Dead Souls* (Basingstoke, Macmillan, 1996), ch. 9.

26 K. Tapiola, "Trade union development in the CEECs", *Transfer*, Vol. 1, No. 3, 1995, pp. 360–77.

27 A. Gorz, *Farewell to the Working Class* (London, Pluto Press, 1982).

28 For a critique of the statistics, see G.Standing, "Voice representation security", paper presented at Conference on Quality of Employment Statistics, organized by the UN Economic Commission for Europe, EUROSTAT and the ILO Bureau of Statistics, 2–5 May 2000.

29 AFL-CIO, *The Changing Situation of Workers and Their Unions: A Report by the AFL-CIO Committee on the Evolution of Work* (Washington, DC, AFL-CIO, February 1985), p. 4.

30 H. Streefkerk, *Industrial Transition in Rural India: Artisans, traders and tribals in South Gujarat* (Bombay, Popular Prakashan, 1985), p.243.
31 W. Brown, S. Deakin and P. Ryan, "The effect of British industrial relations legislation 1979–97", *National Institute Economic Review*, July 1997.
32 J. Weeks, "Economic integration in Latin America: Impact on labour" (Geneva, ILO, 1998, mimeo).
33 P. Leisink and L. Beukema, "Participation and autonomy at work: A segmented privilege", in Coenen and Leisink, 1993, op. cit., p. 165.
34 D. Gallie, M. White, Y. Chang and M. Tomlinson, *Restructuring the Employment Relationship* (Oxford, Oxford University Press, 1998).
35 EPOC Research Group, *Direct Employee Participation in Europe* (Dublin, Foundation for the Improvement of Living and Working Conditions, 1997).
36 P. Berg, E. Applebaum, T. Bailey and A. Kalleberg, "Performance effects of modular production in the apparel industry", *Industrial Relations*, Vol. 35, No. 3, July 1996, pp. 356–73.
37 R. Sennett, *The Corrosion of Character: The Personal Consequences of Work in the New Capitalism* (New York and London, W. Norton, 1998), p. 16.

4 The Crunch of Income Insecurity

1 OECD, *Income Distribution and Poverty in Selected Countries* (Paris, OECD, 1997), Annex 1.
2 G.A. Cornia, "Liberalisation, globalisation and income distribution", *WIDER Working Paper No. 157* (Helsinki, UNU/WIDER, 1999).
3 We should note the recent revision in "occupational classes" for UK statistics. This is undoubtedly an improvement, although it does not cover the issues raised in this analysis. Elsewhere, a classification based on forms of control is proposed.
4 *The Observer*, 16 July 2000.
5 A.B. Atkinson, "The changing distribution of income: Evidence and explanations", *German Economic Review*, Vol. 1, 2000; A. Singh and R. Dhumale, "Globalisation, technology and income inequality: A critical analysis", paper presented at conference on globalisation, Chennai, 14–17 December 2000.
6 J. Micklethwait and A. Wooldridge, *A Future Perfect: The Challenge and Hidden Promise of Globalisation* (New York, Crown Business Books, and London, Heinemann, 2000).
7 P. Iyer, *The Global Soul: Jet Lag, Shopping Malls and the Search for Home* (London, Bloomsbury, 2000).
8 D. Brooks, *Bobos in Paradise: The New Upper Class and How They Got There* (New York, Simon and Schuster, 2000).
9 See, for instance, L. Gratton, *Living Strategy: Putting People at the Heart of Corporate Purpose* (New York, Prentice Hall, 2000).
10 G. Standing and D. Vaughan-Whitehead (eds), *From Protection to Destitution? The Minimum Wage in Central and Eastern Europe* (Budapest, European University Press, 1995).
11 S. Nickell, "A picture of the job insecurity of British men" (London, London School of Economics, Centre for Economic Performance, December 1999).

12 R. Dickens, "Wage mobility in Great Britain", *Employment Audit*, Spring 1997.

13 G.J. Borjas and V.A. Ramey, "Foreign competition, market power and wage inequality: Theory and evidence" (Cambridge, Mass., National Bureau of Economic Research, Working Paper No. 4556, 1993); A. Wood, *North–South Trade, Employment and Inequality: Changing Fortunes in a Skill-Driven World* (Oxford, Clarendon Press, 1994); R.Z. Lawrence, "Trade and wages. The past and the future", paper presented to Centre for Social Theory and Comparative History, University of California at Los Angeles, 22 April 1996.

14 P. Osterman, "Work/family relationships and the employment relationship", *Administrative Science Quarterly*, Vol. 40, December 1995, pp. 681–700.

15 R. Freeman and J. Medoff, *What do Unions Do?* (New York, Basic Books, 1984); for industrialising countries, see G. Standing, "Do unions accelerate or impede structural adjustment?", *Cambridge Journal of Economics*, Vol. 16, No. 3, 1992, pp. 327–54.

16 OECD, *Employment Outlook* (Paris, OECD, 1997), p. 129.

17 G. Esping-Andersen, *The Three Worlds of Welfare Capitalism* (Cambridge, Polity Press, 1990).

18 B. Hobson, "No exit, no voice: A comparative analysis of women's dependency and the welfare state", *Acta Sociologica*, Vol. 33, No. 3, 1990, pp. 235–50.

19 I. Gough, J. Bradshaw, J. Ditch, T. Earley and P. Whiteford, "Social assistance in the OECD countries", *Journal of European Social Policy*, Vol. 7, No. 1, February 1997, p. 24, Table 2; T. Salonen, *Margins of Welfare: A Study of Modern Functions of Social Assistance* (Lund, Hallestrad Press, 1993).

20 C. Murray, *Losing Ground: American Social Policy 1950–1980* (New York, Basic Books, 1984), pp. 212–16.

21 R. Goodin and J. LeGrand (eds), *Not Only the Poor: The Middle Classes and the Welfare State* (London, Allen and Unwin, 1987); and LeGrand, cited in *The Economist*, 20 September 1997, p. 25.

22 M. Lipsky, *Street-level Bureaucracy: Dilemmas of the Individual in Public Services* (New York, Basic Books, 1980).

23 J. Bradshaw et al., *The Employment of Lone Parents: A Comparison of Policy in 20 Countries* (York, Family Policy Studies Centre, 1996).

24 W. van Oorschot, "Non take-up of social security benefits in Europe", *Journal of European Social Policy*, Vol. 1, No. 1, 1991, pp. 15–30; A.B.Atkinson and J.Hills, "Social security in developed countries: Are there lessons for developing countries?", in E. Ahmad, J. Drize, J. Hills and A. Sen (eds), *Social Security in Developing Countries* (Oxford, Clarendon Press, 1991), p. 89; R. Goodman and I. Peng, "The east Asian welfare states", in G. Esping-Andersen (ed.), *Welfare States in Transition* (London, Sage, 1996), pp. 192–224.

25 G. Standing, "The folly of social safety nets: Why a basic income is needed in eastern Europe", *Social Policy*, 1998.

26 Atkinson and Hills, 1991, op. cit., p. 89.

27 Gough et al., 1997, p. 32.

28 For a set of international studies, see the Special Issue of the *Journal of European Social Policy*, March 2000.

5 Ageing: Time Bomb or the Spark of Good Society?

1 United Nations Population Division, *World Population Prospects, the 1998 Revision* (New York, UN Publication, !998), Table A29.

2 Cited in the *Financial Times*, 2 July 1999, p. 9.

3 OECD, *Ageing in OECD Countries: A Critical Policy Challenge* (Paris, OECD, 1997), p. 17.

4 As of early 2000, social security recipients in the USA aged 62 to 65 lost $1 for every $2 earned above $10,080, those aged 65 to 69 lost $1 for every $3 earned beyond a maximum of $17,000. Those aged 70 or above did not lose anything if they gained earned income. This was changed in 2000, so that those aged 65–69 could earn as much as they wished without losing social security benefits.

5 B. Jupp, "Reasonable force: The place of compulsion in securing adequate pensions" (London, Demos, February 1998).

6 E. Overbye, "Mainstream pattern, deviant cases: The New Zealand and Danish pension systems in an international context", *Journal of European Social Policy*, Vol. 7, No. 2, 1997, pp. 101–17.

7 P.R. Orszag and J. Stiglitz, "Rethinking pension reform: Ten myths about social security systems", paper presented to Conference on "New ideas about old age security", Washington, DC, The World Bank, 14–15 September 1999.

8 S.K. Chand and A. Jaeger, "Aging populations and public pension schemes" (Washington, DC, IMF Occasional Paper 147, December 1996).

9 For good reviews, see L. Thompson, *Older and Wiser: The Economics of Public Pensions* (Washington, DC, The Urban Institute Press, 1998); D.M. Nuti, "Alternative pension systems: Generalities and reform issues in transition economies" (London, London Business School, April 1998). Eastern European countries were pushed into private funded schemes prematurely before sound financial markets, regulatory systems and economic stability were assured, or likely. The Kazakhstan reform was particularly irresponsible, and in Poland the teething pains were predictable.

10 J. Eatwell, "The anatomy of the pensions 'crisis'," in United Nations Economic Commission for Europe, *Economic Survey of Europe* 1999, No. 3 (Geneva, UNECE, 1999), pp. 57–61. For eastern Europe, see Standing, 1997, op. cit.

11 E. James, "Public pension plans in international perspective: Problems, reforms and research ideas", in S. Valdes-Prieto (ed.), *The Economics of Pensions: Principles, Policies and International Experience* (Cambridge, Cambridge University Press, 1997).

6 End of Unemployment Benefits?

1 ILO, *Into the Twenty-First Century: The Development of Social Security* (Geneva, ILO, 1984), p. 3.

2 Where there are social funds or micro-insurance schemes, they could have elements of private insurance, community transfers and means-tested benefits.

3 We consider later the wider notion of employment insurance benefits, designed to give protection against fluctuations in income whether the person is employed or not.

4 Defining the political lines need not concern us here. The point is that particular political groups are likely to favour different combinations of policies for reasons that do not relate just to efficiency or effectiveness in providing income security.

5 This is precisely what happens, according to surveys of attitudes and behaviour. For a nice study, see K. Rowlingson, *A balancing act: surviving the risk society* (Derby, University of Derby, 1999).

6 J. Rubery and D. Grimshaw, "Workforce heterogeneity and unemployment benefits: The need for policy reassessment in the European Union", *Journal of European Social Policy*, Vol. 7, No. 4, November 1997, pp. 291–315.

7 In Ukraine in 1999–2000, about one in five industrial workers was on unpaid leave or expected to turn up to their jobs without receiving wages. G. Standing and L. Szoldos, "Worker insecurities in Ukraine" (Geneva, ILO, May 2000). We have also found such practices to be extensive in Russia and other eastern European countries.

8 A.B. Atkinson and J. Micklewright, *Turning the screw: Benefits for the unemployed 1979–88* (London, Economic and Social Research Council Research Report, 1988).

9 I. Shapiro and M. Nichols, *Unemployed and Uninsured* (Washington, DC, Centre on Budget and Policy Priorities, 1991).

10 W. Corson and W. Nicholson, "Unemployment insurance, income maintenance and re-employment trade-offs in a competitive world economy", *The Secretary's Seminars on Unemployment Insurance* (Washington, DC, US Department of Labor, Occasional Paper 89–1, 1989).

11 See the series of reports, OECD, *Benefit Systems and Work Incentives* (Paris, OECD, various dates).

12 A.B. Atkinson and J. Micklewright, "Unemployment compensation and labour market transitions: A critical review", *Journal of Economic Literature*, Vol. XXIX, No. 4, December 1991, pp. 1679–1727.

13 J. Martin, "Measures of replacement rates for the purpose of international comparisons: A note", *OECD Economic Studies*, No. 26/1, 1996, p. 106.

14 See, for instance, S. Scarpetta, "Assessing the role of labour market policies and institutional settings on unemployment: A cross-country study", *OECD Economic Studies*, No. 26, 1996/1, p. 63. Scarpetta used an average of statutory replacement rates for different durations of unemployment, family situations and earnings. This ignores the probability of entitlement. Some countries may have a high probability of entitlement and a low replacement rate, others a low probability of entitlement and a low replacement rate; in some the unemployed may be concentrated in groups with high replacement rates, in others in groups with low replacement rates, and so on.

15 The justification is that the probability of being passively unemployed should be inversely related to probability of entitlement to benefits. The index could omit this probability of claiming ratio.

16 M.Lipsky, *Street-level Bureaucracy: Dilemmas of the Individual in Public Services* (New York, Basic Books, 1980).

17 Robert Reich, the former US Secretary of Labour, has used the term wage insurance, and seems to mean something different from what advocates of employment insurance have in mind. For Reich, wage insurance would make up

part of the difference between the income received in the lost job and the income received from a new job, on the grounds that workers who lose jobs are usually only able to obtain others paying lower wages.

18 See, in particular, G. Schmid, "Transitional labour markets: A new European employment strategy", in B. Marin, D. Meulders, D.J. Snower (eds.), *Innovative Employment Initiatives* (Aldershot, Ashgate, 2000), pp. 223-54; G. Schmid, "Mutually supportive social protection and employment policies", paper presented at the Conference on Social Protection as a Productive Factor, organised by the European Union under the Portuguese Presidency, Porto, 13–15 April 2000.

19 G. Schmid and B. Reissert, "Unemployment compensation and labour market transitions", in G. Schmid, J. O'Reilly and K. Schomann (eds), *International Handbook of Labour Market Policy and Evaluation* (Cheltenham, Edward Elgar, 1996), pp. 246–7.

7 The Paternalistic Consensus

1 A. Gutmann and D. Thompson, *Democracy and Disagreement* (Cambridge, Mass., Harvard University Press, 1996).

2 Speech to Global Ethics Foundation, Tübingen University, 30 June 2000 (cited in The Guardian, July 1, 2000, p. 5).

3 Cited in the *Observer*, 25 June 2000, p. 17.

4 Cited in the *Economist*, D4 ecember 1999, p. 62.

8 The Road to Workfare: Route to Integration or Threat to Occupation?

1 This is also how others have defined it. I. Lodemel and H. Trickey, *An Offer You Can't Refuse: Workfare in International Perspective* (Bristol, Polity Press, 2000).

2 For a critique, see T. Corbett, J. Deloya, W. Manning, L. Uhr, "Learnfare: The Wisconsin experience", *Focus* (University of Wisconsin-Madison, Institute for Research on Poverty), Vol. 12, No. 2, Fall-Winter, 1989, pp. 1–10.

3 N. Kiddall, "Workfare tendencies in Scandinavia" (Geneva, ILO, 2000).

4 A. Gorz,"L'allocation universelle: version de droite et version de gauche", *Revue nouvelle* (Brussels), No. 81, 1985, pp. 419–28. Subsequently, he changed his view.

5 D. Marquand, "Moralists and hedonists", in D. Marquand and A. Seldon (eds), *The Ideas that Shaped Post-War Britain* (London, Fontana, 1996), p. 21.

6 Cited in L. Kerr and H. Savelsberg, "Unemployment and civic responsibility in Australia: Towards a new social contract", *Critical Social Policy*, Vol. 19, No. 2, May 1999, p. 248.

7 For a defence of "fair workfare", see A. Gutmann and D. Thompson, *Democracy and Disagreement* (Cambridge, Mass., Harvard University Press, 1996), pp. 291–4.

8 C. Murray, *Losing Ground: American Social Policy 1950–80* (New York, Basic Books, 1984), pp. 231–4.

9 Gutmann and Thompson, 1996, op. cit., p. 290.

10 L.M. Mead, *Beyond Entitlement: The Social Obligations of Citizenship* (New York, Free Press, 1986), p. 7.

11 M.B. Katz, *The Undeserving Poor: From the War on Poverty to the War on Welfare* (New York, Pantheon Books, 1989), p. 164.

12 Gutmann and Thompson, 1996, op. cit., p. 293.

13 L. Mead, *The New Politics of Poverty: The Non-working Poor in America* (New York, Basic Books, 1992), p. 168.

14 B. Friedman et al., *An Evaluation of the Massachusetts Work Experience Program* (Washington, DC, US Department of Health and Human Services, 1981), p. 157.

15 N. Delruelle-Vosswinkel, "The socio-cultural factors of new poverty", paper presented at Seminar on New Poverty in the European Community, Université Libre de Bruxelles, 28–29 April 1988, p. 5.

16 A. de Tocqueville, "Memoir on pauperism", in S. Drescher (ed.), *Tocqueville and Beaumont on Social Reform* (New York, Harper and Row, 1968), p. 15.

17 R. Spalter-Roth, B. Burr, H. Hartmann and L.B. Shaw, *Welfare that Works: The Working Lives of AFDC Recipients* (Washington, DC, Institute for Women's Policy Research, 1995).

18 R. Layard and S. Prais, "Employment training: Time to think about compulsion", *Financial Times*, 15 March 1990, p. 15.

19 M. Tanner, S. Moore and D. Hartman, "The work vs welfare trade-off: An analysis of the total level of welfare benefits by State", *Policy Analysis* (Washington, DC, Cato Institute), No. 240, 19 September 1995.

20 K. Olson and L. Pavetti, "Personal and family challenges to the successful transition from welfare to work" (Washington, DC, The Urban Institute, May 1996).

21 R.A. Maynard, "Subsidised employment and non-labor market alternatives for welfare recipients", in D.S. Nightingale and R.H. Haveman (eds), *The Work Alternative: Welfare Reform and the Realities of the Job Market* (Washington, DC, Urban Institute Press, 1995), pp. 109–36.

22 N. Zill, K. Moore and T. Stief, *Welfare Mothers as Potential Employees: A Statistical Profile based on National Survey Data* (Washington, DC, Child Trends, 1991), p. 116.

23 H.B. Presser and A.G. Cox, "The work schedules of low-educated American women and welfare reform", *Monthly Labor Review*, April 1997, pp. 25–33.

24 M.J. Williams, "Is workfare the answer?", *Fortune Magazine* (New York), 27 October 1986, p. 80.

25 Mead, 1986, op. cit., p. 65.

26 B. Casey, "Back to the poor law? The emergence of 'workfare' in Britain, Germany and the USA", *Policy Studies*, Vol. 7, No. 1, July 1986, pp. 52–64.

27 Council for Economic Advisers, "Explaining the decline in welfare receipt, 1993-1996" (Washington, DC, US Government Printing Office, Technical Report, 1997).

28 M. Diller, *The Revolution in Welfare Administration: Rules vs.Discretion – Round II* (Fordham University School of Law, 2000, mimeo.).

29 *Financial Times*, 8 November 1996.

30 Manpower Demonstration Research Corporation, *Workfare: The impact of the Reagan program on employment and training* (New York, MDRC, 1983).

31 D. Friedlander, B. Goldman, J. Gueron, D. Long, "Initial findings from the demonstration of state work/welfare initiatives", *American Economic Review*, Vol. 76, No. 2, May 1986, pp. 224–9; D. Friedlander and J. Gueron, *Are High-Cost Services Less*

Effective than Low-Cost Services? (New York, Manpower Demonstration Research Corporation, 1990).

32 G.T. Burtless, "Welfare recipients' job skills and employment prospects", *Welfare to Work*, Vol. 7, No. 1, Spring 1997, pp. 39–51.

33 J. Riccio, D.Friedlander and S. Freedman, *GAIN: Benefits, costs and three-year impacts of a welfare-to-work program* (New York, Manpower Demonstration Research Corporation, September 1994). Similar figures were found for other schemes in New Jersey. Hershey and Pavetti, 1997, op. cit., p. 77.

34 J. Bernstein, "Welfare reform and the low-wage labour market: Employment, wages and wage policies" (Washington, DC, Economic Policy Institute, November 1997).

35 A.M. Hershey and L.A. Pavetti, "Turning job finders into job keepers", *Welfare to Work*, Vol. 7, No. 1, Spring 1997, pp. 74–86.

36 K.J. Edin, "The myths of dependence and self-sufficiency: Women, welfare and low-wage work", *Focus*, Fall/Winter 1995, Vol. 17, No. 2, pp. 1–9.

37 G.J. Duncan, K.M. Harris and J. Boisjoy, "Time limits and welfare reform: New estimates of the number and characteristics of affected families" (Northwestern University, 1997, mimeo.), p. 10.

38 M. Waller, "Welfare-to-work and child care: A survey of the ten big States" (Washington, DC, Progressive Policy Institute, July 1997).

39 The Employment Centre, *Would workfare work?* (Buckingham, University of Buckingham, 1987).

40 *The Guardian*, 23 June 1990, p. 3.

41 *The Nation*, 2 June 1997, p. 13.

42 D. Patino, "Finding work for the poor in Arizona", *Public Welfare*, Vol. 44, No. 1, 1986, pp. 16–17.

43 J.C. Taylor, *Learning at Work in a Work-Based Welfare System: Opportunities and Obstacles* (Boston, Mass., Jobs for the Future, April 1997).

44 G. Standing, "The road to workfare: Alternative to welfare or threat to occupation?", *International Labour Review*, Vol. 129, No. 6, 1990, pp. 677–91.

9 Basic Security as Reviving Equality

1 A. Sen, "Equality of what?", in S. McMurrin (ed.), *The Tanner Lectures on Human Values* (Salt Lake City, University of Utah Press, 1980), Vol. 1.

2 A. Sen, "Capability and well-being", in M. Nussbaum and A. Sen (eds), *The Quality of Life* (Oxford, Clarendon Press, 1993).

3 J. Roemer, *Theories of Distributive Justice* (Cambridge, Mass., Harvard University Press, 1996), p. 193. Sen's work has underpinned the UNDP's *Human Development Report* and its Human Development Index.

4 R. Dworkin, "What is equality? Part I: Equality of welfare", *Philosophy and Public Affairs*, Vol. 10, 1981, pp. 185–246; "What is equality? Part 2: Equality of resources", *Philosophy and Public Affairs*, Vol. 10, 1981, pp. 283–345.

5 R. Dworkin, *Sovereign Virtue: The Theory and Practice of Equality* (Cambridge, Mass., Harvard University Press, 2000).

6 G.A. Cohen, "Incentives, inequality, and community", in G.B.Peterson (ed.), *The*

Tanner Lectures on Human Values (Salt Lake City, University of Utah Press, 1992), Vol. 13.

7 R. Nozick, *Anarchy, State and Utopia* (New York, Basic Books, 1974), ch. 7.

8 G.A. Cohen, *Self-Ownership, Freedom and Equality* (Cambridge, Cambridge University Press and Editions de la Maison des Sciences de l'Homme, 1995), p. 12.

9 F. Fukuyama, *The End of Order* (London, The Social Market Foundation, September 1997).

10 B. Russell, "Work and pay", in *Roads to Freedom* (London, Unwin Books, 1966 (first published in 1918), p.81.

11 In 1986, a group formed the Basic Income European Network (BIEN), with academics and policy specialists from across Europe. It now has membership from across the world. BIEN has produced a quarterly Newsletter summarising research, publications, meetings and relevant policy reforms. In its Berlin Congress held in October 2000, it was proposed that it should be renamed the Basic Income Earth Network to reflect the growing support in other parts of the world.

12 For a liberal rationale, see S. Brittan and S. Webb, *Beyond the Welfare State: An Examination of Basic Incomes in a Market Economy* (Aberdeen, Aberdeen University Press, 1990).

13 A. Hirschman, *The Rhetoric of Reaction: Perversity, Futility, Jeopardy* (Cambridge, Mass., Harvard University Press, 1991).

14 N. Frohlich and J.A. Oppenheimer, *Choosing Justice: An Experimental Approach to Ethical Theory* (Berkeley, University of California Press, 1992).

15 Lack of support for the Difference Principle in the Frohlick-Oppenheimer study could be explained by this and the fact that participants were asked to select *one* fundamental principle of justice.

16 See, for instance, S. White, "Liberal equality, exploitation and the case for an unconditional basic income", *Political Studies*, Vol. XLV, 1997, pp. 312–26.

17 Gutmann and Thompson, 1996, op. cit., p. 279.

18 The UNDP's *Human Development Report 1995* guesstimated that globally women's housework was worth $17 billion. In the UK, the Office for National Statistics estimated that in 1997 housework would have cost the equivalent of $550 billion had it been paid at market wages, nearly as much as the workforce received from wage labour. Women did about 60 per cent of the unpaid work.

19 Gutmann and Thompson, 1996, op. cit., pp. 279–80.

20 How could one mention reciprocity without tongue in cheek when vast subsidies are given to corporations and affluent individuals to attract them to the country, and when taxes are being cut on higher-income groups and on capital on grounds of expediency, i.e., that if taxed more than the international norm they would move abroad?

21 Ibid, p. 280. The Malibu surfer image was originally developed by John Rawls.

22 R. Goodin, *Protecting the Vulnerable: A Re-Analysis of Our Social Responsibilities* (Chicago, Chicago University Press, 1985).

23 R. Goodin, *Reasons for Welfare* (Princeton, Princeton University Press, 1988), p. 183.

24 See, for instance, H. Parker, *Instead of the Dole* (London, Routledge, 1989).

25 P. van Parijs, *Real Freedom for All: What (if anything) Can Justify Capitalism?* (Oxford, Clarendon Press, 1995). He tried to justify a funding approach compatible with

libertarianism. P. Van Parijs, "Reciprocity and the justification of an unconditional basic income: Reply to Stuart White", *Political Studies*, Vol. XVI, 1997, pp. 327–30.

26 C.M.A. Clark and J. Healy, *Pathways to a Basic Income* (Dublin, Report for the Justice Commission of the Conference of Religious of Ireland (CORI), April 1997); S. Ward, "A basic income system for Ireland", in CORI, *Towards an Adequate Income for All* (Dublin, CORI, 1994); F. O'Toole, "The costings of a basic income scheme", in CORI, *An Adequate Income Guarantee for All: Desirability, Viability and Impact* (Dublin, CORI, 1995).

27 G. FitzGerald, "Basic income system has merit for Ireland", *Irish Times*, 12 April 1997.

28 M. Desai, "A basic income proposal" (London, London School of Economics, June 1997, mimeo.).

29 J. Meade, *Full Employment is Possible* (London, Institute for Fiscal Studies, 1994).

30 H. Adriaansens and W. Dercksen, "Labour force participation, citizenship and a sustainable welfare state in the Netherlands", in Coenen and Leisink, 1993, op. cit., p. 201.

31 B. Hedges, "Work in a changing climate", *British Social Attitudes* (London, Social and Community Planning Research, 11th Report, 1994).

32 This was also the position of Andre Gorz. A. Gorz, "On the difference between society and community, and why basic income cannot by itself confer full membership of either", in P. Van Parijs (ed.), *Arguing for Basic Income* (London, Verso, 1992), pp. 178–84. He has since been converted to an unconditional basic income. A.Gorz, *Miseres du present, richesse du possible* (Paris, Galilee, 1997).

33 G. Rehn, "Towards a society of free choice", in J.J. Wiatr and R. Rose (eds), *Comparing Public Policies* (Wroclaw, Ossolineum, 1977), pp. 121–57.

34 C. Mackin, "Employee ownership and industrial relations", *Perspectives on Work*, Vol. 1, No. 1, 1997, p. 67.

35 M. Blair, D. Kruse and J. Blasi, "Is employee ownership an unstable form? Or a stabilising force?" (Washington, DC, Brookings Institution, mimeo., 1998).

36 J. Blasi, M. Conte and D. Kruse, "Employee ownership and corporate performance among public corporations", *Industrial and Labor Relations Review*, Vol. 50, No. 1, October 1996, pp. 60–79.

37 H.A. Henzler, "The new era of Eurocapitalism", *Harvard Business Review*, July–August, 1992, pp. 57–63; D.I. Levine and L. D'Andrea Tyson, "Participation, productivity and the firm's environment", in A. Blinder (ed.), *Paying for Productivity* (Washington, DC, Brookings Institution, 1990).

38 M. Blair, *Ownership and Control: Rethinking Corporate Governance for the Twenty-First Century* (Washington, DC, The Brookings Institution, 1995).

39 D. Levine, *Re-Inventing the Workplace* (Washington, DC, The Brookings Institution, 1995).

40 Thus, profit-sharing pay in Volvo helped undermine the Swedish model, eroding the solidaristic wage system that was a vital part of its redistributive strategy. G. Standing, *Unemployment and Labour Market Flexibility* (Geneva, ILO, 1988), ch. 6.

41 For a proposal for the USA, see B. Ackerman and A. Alstott, *The Shareholder Society* (New Haven, Yale University Press, 1999); for the UK, see, *inter alia*, G. Kelly and

R.Lissauer, *Ownership for All* (London, Institute for Public Policy Research, 2000); D. Nissan and J. Le Grand, *A Capital Idea* (London, Fabian Society, 2000).

42 Netscape, cited in Handy, 1998, op. cit., pp. 149–50.

43 R.H. Waterman, *The Frontiers of Excellence: Learning from Companies that Put People First* (London, Nicholas Brealey Publishing, 1994). In the USA, this was published under the title *What America Does Right* (New York, Norton, 1994).

44 M. Friedman, *New York Times Magazine*, 13 September 1970, pp. 32–3. See also, M. Friedman, *Capitalism and Freedom* (Chicago, University of Chicago Press, 1962).

45 Price Waterhouse, *In Search of Shareholder Value* (London, Pitman, 1997).

46 A.D. Chandler, "Organisational capabilities and industrial restructuring: A historical analysis", *Journal of Comparative Economics*, Vol. 17, No. 2, 1993, p. 310.

47 T.A. Kochan and P. Osterman, *The Mutual Gains Enterprise: Forging a Winning Partnership among Labor, Management and Government* (Boston, Mass., Harvard Business School Press, 1994).

48 J. Pfeffer, *Competitive Advantage Through People* (Cambridge, Mass., Harvard Business School Press, 1994). The danger of paternalism was not recognised by Pfeffer or Waterman. Our model is potentially more robust, through emphasising voice regulation.

49 The Centre for Tomorrow's Company, *The Inclusive Approach and Business Success: The Research Evidence* (London, CTC, 1998).

50 S. Smith, "Political behaviour as an economic externality: Econometric evidence on the spillover of participation in US firms to participation in community affairs", *Advances in the Economic Analysis of Participatory and Labour-managed Firms*, No. 1, 1985, pp. 123-36.

51 H. Bahrani and S. Evans, "Flexible re-cycling and high-technology entrepreneurship", *California Management Review*, June 1995.

52 "Career opportunities", *The Economist*, 8 July 1995, p. 69. The book was J.C. Collins and J.I. Portas, *Built to Last – Successful Habits of Visionary Companies* (New York, Century, 1995).

53 S.M. Jacoby, "Current prospects for employee representation in the U.S.: Old wine in new bottles?", *Journal of Labor Research*, Vol. XVL, No. 3, Summer 1995, p. 388.

54 C. Heckscher, *The New Unionism: Employee Involvement in the Changing Corporation* (New York, Basic Books, 1988); D. Lewin and R. Peterson, *The Modern Grievance Procedure in the United States* (New York, Quorum Books, 1988).

55 B. Anderson, *Imagined Communities: Reflections on the Origin and Spread of Nationalism* (London, Verso, 1983). Anderson was concerned with the emergence of "national community" from "religious community" and the "dynastic realm". The challenge now is to create a democratic, pluralistic and sustainable alternative in a context of globalisation. Robert Putman is widely quoted for the notion of "social capital", which seems to mean a network of institutions embedding economic actions in society. R. Putman, *Making Democracy Work* (Princeton, Princeton University Press, 1993). The term is unfortunate, since it is not capital. It may refer to institutions modifying capital control over citizens.

56 M. Olsen, "Big bills left on the sidewalk: Why some nations are rich and others poor", *Journal of Economic Perspectives*, Spring 1996.

57 R. Freeman and J. Rogers, "Worker representation and participation in the US" (Princeton, Princeton Survey Research Associates, 1995).

58 L.M. Salamon, "The rise of the nonprofit sector", *Foreign Affairs*, Vol. 73, No. 4, July–August 1994, pp. 2–16.

59 A community for organisational and distributional purposes may be defined as an association of persons having compatible interests, perhaps regional, or a group facing a similar set of insecurities.

60 S. Early and L. Cohen, "Jobs With Justice: Mobilising Labor-Community Coalitions", *Working USA*, November-December 1997, pp. 49–57.

61 P. Waterman, "Social movement unionism: A new model for a new world order", *Review*, Vol. 16, No. 3, Summer 1993, pp. 245–78; C.C.Heckscher, *The New Unionism: Employee Involvement in the Changing Corporation* (Ithaca, New York, ILR Press, 1996; first edition, 1988).

62 G.D.H. Cole, *Guild Socialism Restated* (London, Leonard Parsons, 1920), p. 95.

63 J. Tasini, *The Edifice Complex: Rebuilding the American Labour Movement to Face the Global Economy* (New York, Labour Research Association, 1995).

64 T. Besley, "Political economy of alleviating poverty. Theory and institutions", in *Annual World Bank Conference on Development Economics 1996* (Washington DC, World Bank, 1997), pp. 117–34.

10 Reviving Work and Occupation

1 H. Arendt, *The Human Condition* (Chicago, University of Chicago Press, 1957).

2 See, for a discussion, P. Leisink and H. Coenen (eds), *Work and Citizenship in the New Europe* (Aldershot, Edward Elgar, 1993), pp. 14–15.

3 *Discours de M. de Tocqueville sur le droit au travail* (Paris, Librairie L. Curmer, 1848), pp. 7–9;

4 K. Marx, *The Class Struggles in France, 1848–50* (Moscow, Progress Publishers, 1972)

5 Pope John Paul II, *Centesimus Annus* (Rome, The Vatican, 2 May1991), p. 19.

6 International Labour Conference, 69th Session, "Resolution concerning employment", adopted 21 June 1983, *Record of Proceedings* (Geneva, ILO, 1983), pp. lxxxii-iv.

7 J. Mayer, "The concept of the right to work in international standards and the legislation of ILO member States", *International Labour Review*, Vol. 124, No. 2, March–April 1985, pp. 225–42.

8 J.W. Nickel, "Is there a human right to employment?", *Philosophical Forum*, No. 10, 1978–9, p. 158.

9 R.L. Siegel, *Employment and Human Rights: The International Dimension* (Philadelphia, University of Pennsylvania Press, 1994).

10 C. Bay, "Self-respect as a human right: Thoughts on the dialectics of wants and needs in the struggle for human community", *Human Rights Quarterly*, Vol. 4, No. 1, Winter 1982, pp. 53–75.

11 Nickel, 1979, op. cit., p. 161.

12 van Parijs, 1995, op. cit.

13 D. Held, "Between state and civil society; Citizenship", in G. Andrews (ed.), *Citizenship* (London, Lawrence and Wishart, 1991), p. 21.

14 T.H. Marshall, *Class, Citizenship and Social Development* (Westwood, Connecticut, Greenwood Press, 1973), p. 75. Marshall first gave his well-known lectures on rights in 1949.

15 R. Dahrendorf, *The Modern Social Conflict: An Essay on the Politics of Liberty* (New York, Weidenfeld and Nicolson, 1988), p. 148.

16 Ibid. Similar points were argued by the present writer in a paper prepared for Bruno Kreisky's Commission on European Employment in 1986, in which Dahrendorf and I had "minority" views, in that the majority favoured a Keynesian approach. The Kreisky Commission, *A Programme for Full Employment in the 1990s* (Oxford, Pergamon Press, 1989).

17 Dahrendorf, 1988, op. cit., p. 33.

18 Gorz, 1989, op. cit., p. 13.

19 Dahrendorf, 1988, op. cit., p. 144.

20 Marshall, 1973, op. cit.

21 R. Williams, *Keywords* (London, Basic Books, 1976), p. 45.

22 *Classification of Occupations and Directory of Occupational Titles* (London, Her Majesty's Stationery Office, 1972), Vol. 1. Emphasis added.

23 E. Durkheim, *The Division of Labour in Society* (New York, The Free Press, 1964 edition), p. 404.

24 M.L. Kohn, A. Naoi, C. Schoenbach, C. Schooler and K. Slomoczynski, "Position in the class structure and psychological functioning in the United States, Japan and Poland", *American Journal of Sociology*, Vol. 95, No. 4, January 1990, p. 967.

25 M. Kohn and C. Schooler, *Work and Personality: An Inquiry into the Impact of Social Stratification* (Norwood, Ablex Publishing Corporation, 1983), p. 142.

26 J. March and J. Olsen, *Ambiguity and Choice in Organisations* (Bergen, Germany, Universitetsforlaget, 1976).

27 J. Rothschild and A.A. Whitt, *The Co-operative Workplace: Potentials and Dilemmas of Organisational Democracy and Participation* (Cambridge, Cambridge University Press, 1986).

28 R. Jackall and H.M. Levin (eds), *Worker Co-operatives in America* (Berkeley, University of California Press, 1984), p. 99.

29 C. Handy, *The Hungry Spirit* (New York, Broadway Books, 1998), p. 217.

30 A. Hirschman, *The Passions and the Interests: Political Arguments for Capitalism before Its Triumph* (Princeton, Princeton University Press, 1977), p. 9.

31 Ibid, p. 65.

32 There is a respectable view that the fear of losing leads to support of tyranny and to acquisitiveness. Does globalisation, with its scramble for economic interest, lead to opportunisitic support for the competitive strong over the dignified, deliberative ways of craft?

33 A. Smith, *Lectures on Justice, Police, Revenue and Arms*, edited by E. Cannan (Oxford, Clarendon Press, 1896), p. 259.

34 K. Rowlingson , "Future tense – Are growing occupations more stressed-out and depressive?" (Bath, University of Bath, 2000, mimeo.).

35 Director General's "Transition team" of advisers, what follows should not be attributed to the ILO. Although I was involved in formulating the strategy, as a member of the ILO's newly elected Director General's "transition team" of advisers, what follows should not be attributed to the ILO.

36 A. Jamieson (ed.), *Home Care for Older People in Europe: A Comparison of Policies and Practices* (Oxford, Oxford University Press, 1991).

37 A. Evers, "Payments for care: A small but significant part of a wider debate", in A. Evers, M. Pijl and C. Ungerson (eds), *Payments for Care: A Comparative Overview* (Aldershot, Avebury, 1994), pp. 27–8.

38 R. Lister, "Dilemmas in engendering citizenship", paper presented at Crossing Borders Conference, University of Stockholm, May 1994, p. 19.

39 K. Waerness, "Caring as women's work in the welfare state", in H. Holter (ed.), *Patriarchy in a Welfare Society* (Oslo, Universitetsforlaget, 1984), pp. 67–87.

40 On this, see the papers by Mary Daly, Nancy Folbre, Jane Lewis, Trudie Knijn and others in M. Daly and G. Standing (eds) *Finding Care Work Security: A 21st Century Challenge* (Geneva, ILO, 2001).

41 M.L. Kohn and C. Schooler, "The effects of the substantive complexity of the job on intellectual flexibility: A longitudinal perspective", *American Journal of Sociology*, Vol. 84, 1978, pp. 24–52.

42 Lester Thurow, *New York Times*, 3 September 1997.

43 B. Russell, *In Praise of Idleness* (London, Unwin Books, 1935), pp. 14, 15.

44 I. Berlin, *Four Essays on Liberty* (Oxford, Oxford University Press, 1969), p. 131.

Index

Hungary 120, 131, 242
Huws, U. 280n7, 280n8

idleness 128, 138, 146, 218, 253, 274, 293n43
ignorance, veil of 180, 206, 276
Illich, Ivan 253
ILO (International Labour Organisation) 8, 13, 60, 65, 82, 122,164, 246, 249, 263; Philadelphia Conference (1944) 8
IMF (International Monetary Fund) 21, 26, 27, 28, 35, 82, 89, 111, 151, 159, 160
income security/insecurity 10, 59, 70–110, 111, 121, 122, 124–30, 132, 133, 135, 137, 143, 146, 147, 150, 151, 154, 156, 157, 158, 169, 189, 194, 201, 203, 204, 205, 208, 210, 212–216, 222, 226, 227, 230, 232, 237, 238, 252, 259, 260, 262, 268, 270, 271–75, 284
Income Support (UK) 27, 32, 99, 125, 126, 128, 176, 178, 179, 193, 209, 211, 212, 258
India 67, 208, 233
individual security2, 86, 275
individualism x, 5, 69, 201, 267, 270, 275, 276, 277
industrialisation 13, 63, 72, 79, 105, 137, 244, 256
inefficiency, in bureaucracies 98
inflation 11, 17, 19, 20, 21, 27, 82, 85, 89, 130, 135, 165, 192
informalisation/informal sector 33, 34, 37, 71, 72, 87, 105, 141, 156, 186–7, 217
information technology 47, 279n5 (Ch. 2)
insecurity, as anxiety 1, 2, 4, 5, 6, 51, 54, 56, 72, 73, 78, 162, 194
insurance 15, 17, 20, 29, 32, 48, 51, 54, 71, 73, 78, 79, 84, 87, 88, 89, 90, 94, 98, 99, 100, 103, 105, 110,
114, 125, 126, 127, 128, 129, 130, 131, 132, 133, 134–37, 139, 142, 143, 144, 147, 148, 152, 153, 154–57, 175, 194, 208, 211, 212, 213, 217, 219, 223, 235, 268, 269, 271, 283n3 (Ch. 6), 284n17
International Covenant on Economic, Social and Cultural Rights 245, 249, 250
International Standard Classification of Occupations 257
international trade 13, 25, 35, 165, 230
intra-preneurship 260
Ireland 30, 52, 53, 90, 114, 116, 119, 120, 121, 239, 150, 211
Italy 40, 42, 52, 53, 61, 114, 116, 119, 120, 121, 148, 149, 150, 151, 177
Iyer, P. 281n7

Jamieson, Annie 292n36
Japan 23, 24, 54, 55, 63, 78, 82, 98, 113, 114, 118, 149, 150, 231, 232, 274
job creation 100
job insecurity 46, 79, 260
job security 10, 11, 12, 46, 108, 234
job structure flexibility 33
Jobs with Justice movement (US) 233
Jobseekers' Allowance 100, 146, 151, 212
John Paul II, Pope, *Laborem Exercens* 249
John XXIII, Pope, and right to work 249
Justice, theories of 2, 12, 22 (*see also* distributive justice)

Kalleberg, A. 281n36
Kantor, R.M. 280n12
karoshi 54, 56, 78, 271, 277
Keynes, John Maynard 4, 19
Keynesian economics 8, 11, 21, 31, 37, 125, 130, 131, 167, 230, 239,